Naturalizing Mexican Immigrants

Naturalizing Mexican Immigrants: A Texas History

BY MARTHA MENCHACA

University of Texas Press   *Austin*

Requests for permission to reproduce material from this work should be sent to:
  Permissions
  University of Texas Press
  P.O. Box 7819
  Austin, TX 78713-7819
  www.utexas.edu/utpress/about/bpermission.html

♾ The paper used in this book meets the minimum requirements of ANSI/NISO
Z39.48-1992 (R1997) (Permanence of Paper).

Library of Congress Cataloging-in-Publication Data
Menchaca, Martha.
  Naturalizing Mexican immigrants : a Texas history / by Martha Menchaca.
— 1st ed.
    p.   cm.
  Includes bibliographical references and index.
  ISBN 978-0-292-72557-7 (cloth : alk. paper) — ISBN 978-0-292-72644-4 (pbk. :
alk. paper)
  1. Mexican Americans—Government policy—Texas—History. 2. Mexican
Americans—Legal status, laws, etc.—Texas—History. 3. Immigrants—Texas—
History. 4. Naturalization—Texas—History. 5. Citizenship—Texas—History.
6. United States—Emigration and immigration—History. 7. Mexico—
Emigration and immigration—History. 8. Texas—Ethnic relations. 9. Texas—
Politics and government. 10. Naturalization records—Texas. I. Title.
  F395.M5M46 2011
  323.6′2—dc22
                                                                    2010049957

This book is dedicated to my mother, Maria Isabel Esparza de Menchaca, who ever since I was a child taught me the value of voting and being a responsible citizen.

Contents

Illustrations

Tables

Map

Figures

Acknowledgments

This book would not have been possible without the contributions of a number of individuals. I gratefully thank Theresa J. May, Assistant Director and Editor-in-Chief at the University of Texas Press, for her support throughout this project. I also offer my gratitude to Dr. James Diego Vigil and Dr. Victor Ortiz, the two external reviewers, who provided a number of excellent suggestions for improving the manuscript. Appreciation is also extended to my husband, Dr. Richard R. Valencia, whose research on schooling theory helped me conceptualize how poor people struggle to improve their lives. I also want to thank Dr. Luis Plascencia, who through our conversations over the years clarified for me how immigration policy is negotiated in the United States.

I thank The University of Texas at Austin for a Faculty Research grant to dedicate my full attention to researching the citizenship history of the Mexican immigrant in Texas. I also thank Dr. José Limón, Director of the Center for Mexican American Studies, for the research grants I received to visit archives.

Finally, I thank my wonderful twin sons, Juan and Carlos Valencia, who often accompanied me to the archives and whose conversations about Texas history inspired me to complete this book. They are the best sons a mother can have and without a doubt are on the path to becoming American historians.

Introduction

The aim of this book is to examine the naturalization history of Mexican immigrants in Texas. A large body of literature exists on Mexican immigration, yet the study of their incorporation as U.S. citizens has been largely neglected. I seek to understand how Mexican immigrants became incorporated as citizens of the United States and to explore their exodus from one country and entry to another. My work is strategically situated in Texas because of methodological and historical constraints. To conduct a historical analysis of the Mexican's naturalization process it was necessary to focus on one state because most naturalization records prior to 1906 are not centralized. Rather, they are located in county, state, or federal regional archives. In the case of Mexican immigrants, the records are scattered throughout the United States, and I am the first scholar to examine a statewide database. Focusing on Texas was also necessary because during the nineteenth century Texas federal courts resolved the philosophical debates over denying or granting all Mexicans the right to naturalize. Therefore, to unravel how these events unfolded it is imperative that I examine the political action of the Tejanos since they were actively engaged in their struggle for inclusion. Although my study is centered on Texas, it provides an overview of how U.S. naturalization laws impacted Mexican immigrants in the United States. In the concluding chapter I also offer a nationwide analysis of the contemporary obstacles Mexican immigrants face in their pursuit of membership in the U.S. polity. A shift to a nationwide analysis was necessary because Mexican immigrants are now no longer concentrated in Texas, as they were in the past. In the nineteenth and early twentieth century approximately one-half to two-thirds of the Mexican immigrant population of the United States resided in Texas (U.S. Census 1922a: 302–303). By the year 2000, Mexican Tejanos continued to constitute a large percentage of the Mexican immigrant population, numbering 21 percent of the total. The rest are scattered throughout the United States, with 43 percent residing in California (U.S. Census 2003: 7).

Theoretical and current concerns on citizenship formation inspired me to write this book and to take a historical approach in doing so. Following in the anthropological tradition of Michel-Rolph Trouillot (1995), I concur that history is central to understanding and theorizing how the present is shaped by the past. By employing Trouillot's historical approach I will revisit many national immigration events. I will, however, reexamine them from a critical perspective and explore how international relations between Mexico and the United States influenced the closure and opening of opportunity structures given to Mexicans to become U.S. citizens. Furthermore, in unfolding my narrative I will emplot events that have been ignored or treated as insignificant. I agree with Trouillot that when staging a historical narrative the selection of events influences how one views the actors. By taking this approach, I hope to portray the significant roles ordinary Mexican immigrants played in shaping their political destiny. My intent is to illustrate that Mexicans, notwithstanding the fact that most were from the laboring classes, were people with dignity who were aware that choosing one's citizenship was a political act. My anthropological gaze into this process also follows in the historical tradition of Eric Wolf (1982) and Sidney Mintz (1985), who for generations have influenced anthropologists to historicize the past by examining the political and economic bases of the societies under study. Throughout my book I unravel the Mexican immigrants' citizenship incorporation in the United States by exploring the political and economic conditions that forced them to leave their homes. Likewise, I critically examine their reception in Texas by looking at national and state events as well as the racial ideologies of the period, which often made it very difficult for them to be accepted as U.S. citizens.

This project is also highly motivated by personal concerns over U.S.-Mexico relations. As a U.S. citizen of Mexican descent, I am highly concerned with the ongoing portrayal of Mexicans in the news media as parasitic people who invade this nation, take its resources, and feel no moral obligation to give anything in return because allegedly their political allegiance is to Mexico and not to the United States. Television programs like *The O'Reilly Factor* and, in recent years, *Lou Dobbs Tonight* and his series "Broken Borders" and the commentator Glenn Beck regularly depict Mexicans in this untruthful way. Although programs like *The O'Reilly Factor* openly state that their critique of Mexicans is limited to "illegals," this disclaimer does not dispel the harmful portrayal of all people of Mexican descent as newcomers and as disloyal people. Moreover, when Bill O'Reilly, the anchor and host of *The O'Reilly Factor*, gives airtime to Mexican Americans who disagree with his position on immigration, the facade of fairness becomes a transparent mockery when O'Reilly's closing comments mark them as leftists and dismiss their arguments as misinformed distortions. Generally, only Mexican American guests who agree with O'Reilly are portrayed as balanced and reasonable. Interestingly, they are also praised for their patriotism and bravery in speaking out against "broken borders." In essence, programs like this place Mexican Americans in an iron cage. They must either openly endorse a conservative political agenda against undocumented workers or suffer the consequences and risk being considered part of the problem. *The O'Reilly Factor*, however, is not the program that depicts Mexican immigrants in the most unfavorable light. Unlike O'Reilly, who at least attempts to be balanced and open to debate, the radio and former television news anchor Lou Dobbs visibly crusades against the social ills immigrants allegedly introduce to the United States (Hutchinson 2009). Resembling O'Reilly in his statements that his critique is directed only at illegal aliens, Dobbs's transparent disclaimer is an obvious mockery, as he allows his guests to express inflammatory and misleading information. Especially hurtful are the letters Dobbs reads on the air, thereby creating a legitimate space where his viewers can insult people of Mexican descent. By reading these letters, Dobbs strategically is able to disassociate himself from the vicious comments while simultaneously giving airtime to misleading anti-immigration propaganda. Likewise, Dobbs's negative comments about Mexican American civil rights organizations totally destroy his claim of impartiality. His frequent portrayal of the National Association of Latino Elected Officials, the National Association of La Raza, the League of United Latin American Citizens, the U.S. Hispanic Chamber of Commerce, and on occasion the Latino Congressional Caucus as radical advocates of open borders serves to create the image of Mexican Americans as unpatriotic leftists. If these civil rights organizations are portrayed as un-American and their leadership as villains who promote the illegal invasion of America, how are other Mexican Americans to be viewed if the highly educated officials of these organizations are assumed to be unpatriotic? Are we to assume that Dobbs's critique does not apply to most people of Mexican descent?

Dobbs's hurtful commentaries are presently limited to his nationally syndicated radio show (*Lou Dobbs, Mr. Independent*), following the cancellation of his "Broken Borders" television series, but he has promised to remain in the public arena and be an advocate against illegal immigration. He is also considering running for the U.S. Senate (Shea 2009). Dobbs was released from his CNN contract after he crossed the line on several occasions. CNN management became alarmed when Hispanic organizations and progressive groups such as the Southern Poverty Law Center demanded that Dobbs be fired for untruthfully claiming that undocumented immigrants from Latin America were introducing leprosy into the United States. Dobbs was not fired at this point, but he was asked to apologize (Folkenflik 2009). CNN was finally pressured into asking Dobbs to tone down his advocacy against immigrants or leave CNN if he continued to be a crusader for the birther movement (Folkenflik 2009; Stelter and Carter 2009). Dobbs's critics alleged that his television program gave legitimacy to birther movement groups, who claimed that many people, including the first African American president, Barack Obama, were not American citizens. This position reflected badly on CNN, and management was eventually pressured to amicably release Dobbs from his contract.

Another reason I chose to write a book about the naturalization history of Mexican immigrants was my desire to address what I perceived to be academic misconceptions expressed by visiting Mexican scholars and government dignitaries who have given presentations at the University of Texas at Austin, where I am a professor of anthropology. Throughout my career, I have been fortunate to attend numerous conferences at the university in which Mexican academics and government representatives are invited to speak on U.S.-Mexico relations. In general, the presentations of the visitors have been informative and at times spectacular. For example, one year we were honored by the visit of President Carlos Salinas de Gortari of Mexico, who spoke warmly about Texas-Mexico relations and encouraged further trade and international *convivencia* (cordial coexistence). Over the years, however, I have observed a common problem in the commentaries of most visitors, namely, their reluctance to address the political factors that lead Mexican people to relocate to the United States. That is, the exodus of Mexican immigrants has been mainly approached from a structural perspective and represented as a mechanical labor process that acts as a safety valve to stabilize the Mexican economy. The Mexican immigrant is portrayed as a mere machine without needs and desires. The visitors are generally interested in discussing issues dealing with commerce, finance, the effects of remittances on sending areas, and other practical issues such as increasing the number of academic exchange scholars from Mexico to the United States. In essence, if Mexican immigration is discussed at all it is reduced to concerns about how immigration impacts the Mexican economy. Mexican workers are depicted as valuable foreign exchange commodities that produce income for the state. The needs, desires, and political longing of the migrants, however, are not issues meriting serious discussion. Furthermore, when members of the audience raise questions about the lives of the migrants, in most cases I have observed the visitors respond politely and intelligently yet generally suggest that the issue is not relevant to their talk. One of the few occasions on which I observed the Mexican scholars and government representatives partly move away from this format was at a conference I attended in the spring of 2008. The subject of the conference was Mexico-U.S. migration and development. I observed that the usual unengaged treatment and structural representation of the Mexican laborer were reproduced by most speakers, yet at the conclusion of the conference, when the keynote speaker asked the audience for comments, a critical dialogue erupted. Many questions were raised about the poverty and the other problems Mexicans experience in the United States.

The aim of the conference was to bring together international scholars and policy makers to exchange ideas on the intersection of migration, rural development, and social policy. The guest speakers addressed matters of migration and trade and how they impact the economies and development of rural communities in Mexico and the United States. The presentations provided valuable information on trade, remittances, and current statistical data on the projected number of undocumented people living in the United States. Overall, the conference was exceptionally well organized and enlightening as the interaction between the audience and the speakers generated new insights and dialogue over how the economies of the Mexican countryside can be improved.

I was glad to learn that at the closing ceremony the keynote speaker planned to address current U.S. immigration reform policies and focus on agricultural laborers. I attended the speech in the hope of learning how the Mexican government interpreted the recently failed U.S. congressional efforts to reform immigration policy (I address this issue in the concluding chapter). Specifically, I wanted to learn about Mexico's reaction to the U.S. Congress's refusal to extend amnesty to undocumented workers. Once again, the presentation was very informative. But it was disappointing. Besides the most recent statistical data on the number of agricultural workers who enter the United States on work permits and the amount of remittances sent to Mexico, the only comments on U.S. immigration policy centered on the Mexican government's disappointment that a new agricultural guest worker program was not agreed upon by the Congress.

It was not until the question and answer period that the topic of amnesty for undocumented workers was addressed. It was the audience who raised the issue, however, not the keynote speaker, who had ignored the topic altogether. Our guest responded that the Mexican government was extremely disappointed, but it had not expected an amnesty resolution to pass Congress, as a large sector of the American public was outspokenly against it. He added that perhaps the congressional resolution was the best plan of action after all, as Mexican immigrants should remain Mexican citizens. He believed that Mexicans should be able to work in the United States under some labor agreement but eventually return home. Most attendees felt satisfied with the response, but some, including myself, wanted to continue the dialogue. We asked what effect a guest worker agreement would have on the ability of undocumented farmworkers to adjust their status to permanent legal residency. I said, "A guest worker program will ensure that the U.S. agricultural industry has a cheap source of labor. As well, that Mexico will benefit from the remittances, but it will not give laborers the choice to become free agents in determining their destiny. Only policies that allow people to adjust their status to permanent legal residency gives Mexicans the ability to shape their future and choose the country of their political allegiance." Many people agreed with my statement, and they followed with critical questions on Mexico's failure to legislate a fair living wage. The keynote speaker, in posturing tones, responded to all the questions on the agricultural workers' right to choose their political sovereignty. Some of his answers were rather hostile, however, and seemed to be responding to impudent questions. He iterated his position that it is in the best interests of Mexico and the United States for the migrants to return home. He also believed that most Mexican migrants did not want to become U.S. citizens, so the fact that they could not obtain legal residency was not a problem. In reflecting on the dialogue that took place during the closing ceremony, I partly concur with the keynote speaker's remarks. It is true that a circular migration guest worker program benefits both countries. Mexico's economy benefits by the remittances it receives, and a guest worker program reduces unemployment in Mexico. Likewise, the U.S. agribusiness industry acquires cheap labor, and the federal and state governments are absolved of their responsibilities toward labor. For example, the U.S. government does not have to extend unemployment insurance to agricultural workers during the off-harvest season or provide them with medical services for health problems related to occupation that often arise in old age. Economically, both countries benefit, and the U.S. government does not have to be responsible for the reproduction of its agricultural labor force. This arrangement obviously works well for the governments, but I ask, what benefits do the agricultural laborers derive from it? Are they rewarded sufficiently for the service they provide the United States, given that these types of workers perform job functions few Americans want to do? Shouldn't they have the right to choose where they live in exchange for their labor? Obviously, the latter question is rhetorical, as it is a fact that the U.S. federal government makes all immigration decisions, and its current answer to that question is a resounding no. In the 2005–2006 congressional deliberations on immigration, when House Resolution 4437 was debated, the majority in Congress clearly articulated their stance against giving these types of laborers the opportunity to obtain legal residency and start on the path toward citizenship. This position, however, may change in the future, and the Congress installed in 2009 may recognize the value of this occupation. During various periods in the past, the U.S. government has indeed valued this occupation and granted agricultural workers legal residency, thus giving them the opportunity to pursue U.S. citizenship.

In conducting my research, I have found that Mexican agricultural workers as well as other types of Mexican immigrants are very concerned about their political destiny. I strongly disagree with the perspective that Mexican immigrants do not want to become U.S. citizens. The Mexican immigrant's naturalization history is exactly a history of a people's struggle to gain political representation. They are people who live their lives in a proactive manner and search for a government that is willing to protect them and provide them with more than the bare essentials of life. I concur with Giorgio Agamben (2000) that people pursue a life of happiness and are not satisfied to live a "naked life"—meaning that they aspire to enjoy resources beyond the basic needs required for biological existence. Mexicans who choose to naturalize are political agents who refuse to be reduced to what Agamben calls "bare life." As working people they search for labor markets that enable them to sell their labor to the highest bidder, and in turn they convert their wages into commodities that allow them to live beyond the existence of "bare life." To escape such an existence, immigrants must emancipate themselves from their sovereign nation and find a way to become voting members of a new country. However, as Agamben argues in regard to the poor, it is difficult to acquire membership in a new polity because it is restricted by the rules of the groups in power. Although I agree with Agamben, my view is not as bleak as his. History has taught me that all societies undergo attitudinal changes in majority group opinion, and hence I choose to support the view of Pierre Bourdieu (1992), who asserts that every generation determines its own ideological outlooks. Agamben, however, is correct that attitudinal positions toward immigrants are highly dependent upon the health and prosperity of the host economy. Wealthy countries, which are most often the sites the poor wish to migrate to, do not want to economically absorb the world's poor. It is insufficient for the immigrant to act as a free agent because the country they try to enter will determine whether they can be emancipated from their sovereign nation. I concur that entry for the poor is very difficult, and, as Aihwa Ong (2007) argues, unlike the wealthy migrants who are global citizens and not bound by borders, the poor do not have the ability to enter and exit the country they wish to visit. Today, the poor must enter with work permits, and if they do not qualify for temporary legal entry they move illegally across borders.

In the United States, immigration policy toward the poor has varied and in most periods has been quite liberal. This was the case, for example, in the nineteenth century, when the country was expanding its frontiers west of the Mississippi and southwest toward the Rio Grande. Since the mid-1960s, however, while U.S. immigration policy toward the professional and wealthy classes has remained very liberal, its policy toward the poor has become highly restrictive. This institutional position, in turn, has determined who can become a U.S. citizen, as in most cases legal entry is necessary to qualify for citizenship.

It is a fact that the majority of Mexican immigrants have come from the laboring classes. But over the years the border crossers have differed economically and socially. Moreover, for various reasons the majority have chosen to live in the U.S. Southwest, that is, in the border region that was acquired from Mexico following the Mexican-American War of 1846–1848. Like Ernesto Galarza (1964), I believe that the large-scale pattern of Mexican migration to the United States commenced with the dictatorial presidency of Porfirio Díaz in the 1870s, not following the Mexican-American War. In the late nineteenth century, Díaz's economic development plan ravaged the nation's resources and dismantled workers' protective labor laws. The idea was to stimulate Mexican capitalism by creating a social space in which U.S. and European investors could find a docile and cheap source of labor (Gilly 1994). An economic dependency structure was established, one which Mexicans did reform, but which they have been unable to completely dismantle or detach themselves from. Over the years, many Mexicans who opposed their country's treatment of labor or have been discontented with the outcome of their nation's governance have chosen to seek a better life by migrating to the United States.

Thus my narrative, besides being a historical recovery project, aims to deal with current issues. I hope to use this account to illustrate that historically Mexican immigrants have chosen to emancipate themselves from the governance of Mexico because they are free agents who recognize that a state must generate opportunities for its citizens to pursue a better life. Political allegiance to a nation is shaped by nativity, but also by a rational calculation that a state must protect and provide for its citizens. Mexican immigrants have shown their political allegiance to the United States in abiding by the laws of the country, working productively, and fulfilling all of the obligations and responsibilities a state demands of a citizen.

Related to the above is my intent to illustrate theoretically how political ideologies facilitate or hinder an immigrant's entry and membership within a new polity. Central to the shaping of my understanding of how ideology and social movements influence governmental policy is Michael Omi's and Howard Winant's (1994) concept of racial formation, which proposes that in the United States generational shifts in dominant group ideologies are highly influenced by social movements that reconfigure majority groups' opinions of minority populations. Attitudinal shifts in turn effect changes in daily life, intergroup interaction, and ultimately governmental policies. These attitudinal shifts, however, as I will illustrate, can have adverse or supportive impacts upon immigrants. Social movements differ across time and are not necessarily prompted by humanist ideals.

Also related to generational shifts is how dominant group attitudes in the United States have been shaped by international politics between Mexico and the United States, particularly in such matters as race and immigration policy. I do not argue that international policy determines when liberal or conservative immigration or naturalization policies are instated in the United States. Rather, I assert that history opens a window onto understanding how international policy influences the attitudes of dominant groups when it comes to offering or withholding opportunities for Mexicans to become permanent legal residents and eventually be invited to apply for U.S. citizenship. Examining international policy also allows me to explore why the economy of Mexico has historically been dependent on U.S. capitalism and how this economic relationship has stimulated Mexican emigration to the United States.

Organization of the Book

My book is divided into four major periods and concludes with a chapter focusing on naturalization history from the 1940s to the present. The historical periods include (a) the aftermath of the U.S.-Mexico War of 1846–1848, (b) the U.S. Civil War and Reconstruction, (c) the Populist movement of the 1890s, (d) the aftermath of the Mexican Revolution, and (e) the end of the bracero program to the present. As I articulate this history, I offer an analysis of the naturalization process Mexicans underwent and examine the success of their applications in numerical terms. I pay extensive attention to events occurring between 1848 and 1924 because many policies involving race, class, and language were instituted at this time and thus determined naturalization policy until the early 1960s.

In the first chapter I examine the U.S. citizenship laws that affected the Mexican population after the Mexican-American War. I focus on the naturalization laws of the period and examine why naturalization was restricted to white immigrants (Nat. Act 1790). This chapter deals with the developments leading up to the outbreak of the U.S. Civil War and examines the liberalization of naturalization law with respect to racial ideology. After the U.S. Civil War ended President Abraham Lincoln and President Benito Juárez of Mexico initiated a period of stable and friendly relations, a period which came to benefit the Mexican population of the United States. Mexico and the United States brought closure to the bad sentiments caused by the Mexican-American War and began a new era in which diplomacy was employed to regulate trade and bring order to the movement of people across the border. As part of these friendly relations the first naturalization law specific to Mexicans was passed in 1868. The Naturalization Treaty of 1868 became the legal foundation of the philosophical principle that Mexicans should be extended citizenship on the basis of nation rather than of race. The white only naturalization prerequisite thus did not apply to Mexicans.

Chapter 2 focuses on the first Mexican immigrants to obtain citizenship in Texas. As I narrate this history, I examine the events that led to a surge in Mexicans' naturalization applications from 1862 to 1870. At this time Mexican immigrants were naturalized at an astonishing rate, and nearly everyone who applied was given citizenship. I associate these events with Civil War politics in South Texas and with "good neighbor policies" between Mexico and the United States following Reconstruction. As part of this analysis I discuss why it was politically expedient for the Texas Legislature to allow Mexican immigrants to vote even if they had not finalized their naturalization papers. I also begin here my argument that voting is the main reason Mexicans have chosen to naturalize, an analysis I develop throughout the book.

This chapter closes with an analysis of President Porfirio Díaz's administration. I examine political transitions in Mexico, particularly the country's transformation into a political dictatorship that became oppressive and stimulated immigration to the United States. During this period U.S. businessmen gained political power in Mexico through their investments. As

I will illustrate, the capitalist development of Mexico during the Porfirian dictatorship became the impetus for the growth of large-scale Mexican immigration. As the Mexican capitalist economy changed, the working conditions of the laboring classes worsened, and many sought to emancipate themselves from the governance of Mexico by seeking refuge in the United States.

Chapter 3 examines how politics in Texas during the late 1880s to early 1900s affected the experiences of Mexican immigrants. The political and economic problems that developed in Mexico during President Diaz's administration caused a surge in Mexican emigration, and although the U.S. federal government favored open borders, I illustrate that in Texas many people resented the ongoing immigration of Mexicans into their state. Texans welcomed commerce with Mexico, but not the immigrants who arrived as part of the negotiations between both countries. The resulting growth of anti-Mexican social movements culminated in several legal battles to exclude Mexican immigrants and Mexican Americans from U.S. citizenship (i.e., *In re Rodriguez 1897*). The period is illustrative of Agamben's thesis that immigrants can change their national affiliation only when members of the host country permit them to do so.

In chapter 4, I demonstrate that after 1898 very few Mexicans applied for U.S. citizenship. I associate this decline with the outbreak of the Spanish-American War and the emergence of a nativistic ideology among Americans that negatively affected their treatment of Mexicans following the war. I also associate the decline in Mexican naturalization application rates to voting law reforms in Texas. Within a few years of the Spanish-American War, poll taxes were required of voters in Texas. I argue that poll taxes impacted many Texans but led particularly to the disenfranchisement of a larger percentage of voters of Mexican and African descent. For Mexican immigrants, whose primary reason to naturalize was to gain the ability to vote, the institution of poll taxes made voting expensive and unaffordable. They not only had to pay expensive fees to naturalize, but now they had to pay poll taxes.

In chapter 5 I focus on the end of the Porfirian dictatorship and the mass migration triggered by the Mexican Revolution. Here I examine how changes in federal naturalization law and Texas voting laws made it very difficult for Mexican immigrants to naturalize and to vote. This period coincides with political changes in Mexico. After the Mexican Revolution, when President Díaz was forced to resign and the new government passed foreign investment policies to protect Mexican resources, the U.S. government was displeased and no longer treated Mexico as a friendly neighbor.

What ensued were the passage of hostile policies toward Mexico and the ill treatment of Mexican immigrants.

In Texas an anti-immigrant social movement spearheaded by white suffragists expressed this hostility. Upper-class white women used the national resentment harbored by many Americans against Mexico to initiate a social movement to end immigrant voting in Texas. The chapter includes an overview of the naturalization history specific to Mexican women, as this is the era when women, including those who had naturalized, were given the right to vote. Although the main discussion of this chapter ends in 1924, I survey the main immigration and naturalization events that followed in the 1930s and delve into their impact on Mexicans. I offer only a general view of this decade because the main reforms in naturalization law affecting Mexicans are covered in the succeeding chapter in relation to the bracero generation.

Chapter 6 deals with contemporary issues and draws parallelisms with the past. My analysis of Mexican naturalization patterns focuses on congressional policy and its general impact on the Mexican and Mexican-American population. My account is not solely about Texas, given that the bracero program (1942–1964) transformed Mexican immigration, and by the 1960s very large numbers of Mexican immigrants were residing in every part of the country. My main argument in this chapter is that since 1965 immigration reforms have made it very difficult for working-class people to qualify for legal entry, and this has affected who can become a U.S. citizen. I conclude my analysis by interrogating the Mexican government's response to current congressional immigration reform proposals and exploring the mean-spirited birther movement in Texas and the United States. This social movement advocates the redefinition of citizenship under the Fourteenth Amendment and proposes denying U.S. citizenship to children born in the United States of parents who are undocumented aliens or temporary legal residents. Under this proposal people who lose their citizenship could regain it only by applying for naturalization.

Location of Study and Primary Sources

In reconstructing the naturalization history of Mexican immigrants in Texas I reviewed naturalization records from the Lorenzo de Zavala State Library and Archives in Austin and from the National Archives Southwest Region at Fort Worth (see appendix 1). These records include the naturalization declarations from 1836 to 1939, minutes for district and county civil court naturalization cases, and the naturalization indexes of people naturalized in county, district, state, and federal courts. My aim was to identify how many Mexicans had applied for U.S. citizenship and the location where the applications were filed as well as to determine the percentage of the applicants granted citizenship.

Of particular importance were the naturalization declarations, as these records allowed me to determine the periods of high and low naturalization application rates for Mexicans on a county basis. This information also allowed me to situate the naturalization application flows within a historical timeline and determine where the Mexican immigrants lived in Texas.

Additional primary sources include the Matías Romero Archives, records of the Texas federal courts, election registrars, Jane Y. McCallum Archives, alien entry rolls, Immigration and Naturalization Bureau correspondence, and immigration and naturalization statistics compiled by the U.S. Immigration and Naturalization Service and the Department of Homeland Security. To fully understand the significance of these records, I also studied the evolution of the Texas judicial system and voting laws. This enabled my understanding of who was in control of granting or denying citizenship to immigrants and my further comprehending of Texas politics from the county to the state level. I have also reviewed nineteenth- and early twentieth-century newspapers concerning the Populist movement, legislative debates over immigration and naturalization, the Civil War, and the Texas Woman Suffrage Movement. Of great value to my study was the Spanish-language newspaper *El Regidor,* the *San Antonio Express,* and the *Austin American Statesman.* The editorials written by Pablo Cruz in *El Regidor* were especially useful in that his commentaries often discussed philosophical issues on naturalization and provided detailed information of how naturalization and voting laws affected Mexican immigrants. Furthermore, as a means of understanding Texas records and their relation to federal and state policy, I turned to the Texas House and Senate journals, the congressional records, speeches of Texas governors and senators, and to the U.S. Statutes at Large. I found that by placing my key findings of the naturalization data within this policy context I was able to uncover how Mexican immigrants were affected by political events taking place within the U.S. Congress and the Texas State Legislature.

My study is based on Texas. The core area of the book, however, centers on South Texas and Bexar County, given that nearly 90 percent of naturalized Mexicans resided in these two regions. Because the boundaries of Bexar County and South Texas counties changed over time, I indicate in my discussion how demographic shifts produced changes in the political boundaries of the counties. I am well aware that authors disagree on the territorial boundaries of South Texas. The historian Neil Foley (1997) defines South Texas by its land use specialization and draws boundaries between central, east, and south Texas based on the regions' mode of production, while the geographer David Arreola (2002) and the archeologist Tamra Lynn Walter (2007) define South Texas as a cultural region where the Spanish missions and ranches were founded. The folklorist Américo Paredes (1958) and the legal scholars Richard Jones and Albert Kauffman (1994) define South Texas as a region culturally attached to the border and populated mainly by people of Mexican descent. The main reasons for the differences in their assessments of which counties comprise South Texas, as I see it, are, first, that some of the counties along Texas's eastern coast that were originally part of the Spanish Empire and were associated with the mission societies became populated by a large number of African Americans owing to the growth of the slave trade during the period in which Texas was an independent republic (i.e., Refugio, Victoria, and Gonzales counties). After Texas independence the eastern coastal region therefore developed characteristics that set it apart from the rest of the southern region, which was primarily populated by Mexicans. A second reason for the differences in opinion over what constitutes South Texas is that scholars disagree as to the inclusion or exclusion of Val Verde County. Val Verde County, which is located along the border near west Texas, became populated by a large number of Anglo-Americans during the late nineteenth century, and this demographic shift led the county to develop closer ties to west Texas. Thus Val Verde is part of both South and west Texas. In this book I refer to South Texas as a cultural region primarily populated by Mexicans and located near the Mexico-U.S. border. As new counties were organized and carved out of older counties, I identify which ones I propose to include as part of South Texas.

CHAPTER I

From the Making of the U.S.-Mexico Border to the U.S. Civil War

The U.S. Congress passed its first Naturalization Act in 1790 and chose to allow only white immigrants to become naturalized citizens. This racial stipulation was not nullified until the passage of the Nationality and Immigration Act of 1952 (Hull 1985). Prior to removing the racial clause, Congress did allow certain nonwhite immigrant groups to apply for citizenship. Mexican immigrants were the first to be given an exemption from the nation's racial naturalization statute, followed soon by black immigrants. These naturalization reforms were the outcome of the U.S. government's transformation following the U.S. Civil War, when the U.S. Congress began the process of reforming its citizenship laws. In 1868 African Americans born in the United States were made citizens, and within the next two years Mexican and black immigrants were allowed to apply for U.S. citizenship. Black immigrants were given the right as a means of creating a uniform law consistent with the enfranchisement of African Americans. Mexican immigrants, on the other hand, were given the right as a result of treaty negotiations with Mexico. As a result of political alliances forged during the Civil War, Mexico and the United States entered a phase of improved international relations during which they enacted the Naturalization Treaty of 1868, stipulating that in both countries immigrants had the right to naturalize. For Mexican and black immigrants the reforms were a political triumph, but for many Anglo-Americans the changes were devastating and came to be regarded as unjust. The policies enacted for blacks could not be challenged because the laws were clear. Opponents of extending citizenship to Mexican immigrants, however, charged that the Naturalization Treaty was vague and applied to Mexicans only if they were white or black.

Nearly three decades later, opponents of the Naturalization Treaty, pointing to the fact that most Mexicans were of mixed racial ancestry (Indian, white and black), charged that Mexicans with Indian blood were ineligible to apply for naturalization because Indians in the United States could not be made citizens. This interpretation of the treaty awarded those who opposed giving citizenship to Mexican immigrants a recourse for stopping Mexicans from naturalizing.

To reconstitute the events surrounding the Naturalization Treaty and what I consider to be the first phase of the Mexican immigrant's naturalization history, I begin my historical narrative by examining why, in the nineteenth century, Mexicans in the United States held an ambiguous legal position in American society. I briefly examine the Mexican people's racial history during the nineteenth century to illustrate why their mixed racial ancestry became the legal basis to deny Mexican immigrants U.S. citizenship. For those interested in an expansive analysis of the Mexican American's racial heritage I refer you to my book *Recovering History, Constructing Race: The Indian, Black, and White Roots of Mexican Americans* (Menchaca 2001). Here I provide a summary of this racial history, as my intent is to focus on significant events shaping the Mexican immigrants' naturalization experiences.

I begin my account with a discussion of the formation of the U.S.-Mexico border and conclude with remarks on the racial reforms enacted by the U.S. government after the U.S. Civil War. I also begin to unfold the events that led Mexico to gradually become economically dependent on the United States, a relationship that has endured up to the present.

Race and the Making of the U.S.-Mexico Border

The making of the U.S.-Mexico border began with international disputes over where Texas territory began and ended. In 1845 the U.S. government annexed Texas and made it the twenty-eighth state of the Union (Montejano 1987: 82–85). Acting unilaterally and forgoing any consultation with Mexico, the U.S. Congress set the border at the Rio Grande, claiming South Texas and El Paso were part of the annexed territory. Mexico disputed the boundary, holding that the border lay further north on the Nueces River. Mexico agreed that U.S. territory included the former Mexican city of San Antonio as well as surrounding settlements, but not any of the Mexican settlements in South Texas or along the present Texas southwestern border. The U.S. Congress disagreed, and the dispute became so contentious and unresolvable that the United States declared war against Mexico on May 11, 1846 (Menchaca 2001: 216). Fourteen months later the

U.S. military defeated Mexico and began treaty negotiations to claim one-third of its territory.

The end of the Mexican-American War brought closure to a land conflict that had begun ten years earlier. Dispute over Mexican territory dated back to 1836, when Anglo-American immigrants obtained independence from Mexico and carved a new republic out of Texas. When the U.S. government annexed Texas as part of the Union, it immediately set the U.S.-Mexico border and a year later sent a well-equipped military to enforce its dictate. Because Mexico was unable to defend its territory and lost the Mexican-American War, the Congress assumed the power to take possession of any part of Mexico it wished. Upon Mexico's defeat, U.S. congressmen debated which parts of Mexico should be acquired, some proposing that the entire country be occupied, while others favored occupying only Mexico's northern territories, which today include the present U.S. Southwest as well as the Mexican states of Tamaulipas, Nuevo León, Chihuahua, Coahuila, Sonora, and Baja California (Vázquez and Meyer 1985). The less expansionist plan was agreed upon largely because most congressmen conceded that it was best to acquire the least populated territories. In this way the Congress could avoid governance problems since a smaller hostile population would be easier to control. Furthermore, because the U.S. government was aware that Mexico was populated by racially diverse peoples ranging from pure-blooded whites, blacks, and Indians to people with mixed African and Indian blood, reducing the size of the occupied population was strategic. Individuals who were white and unmixed would not pose a problem and most likely could be easily integrated. The rest of the racially mixed peoples, however, would pose legal ambiguities, and it was best to limit their numbers. In the end, the border states of California, New Mexico, and northern Arizona along with the present-day southern Texas region were acquired by the U.S. Congress (El Paso Valley and South Texas). Mexico also lost parts of its northern frontier that include the modern U.S. states of Nevada, Utah, parts of Colorado, and small sections of Oklahoma, Kansas, and Wyoming; these areas contained no Mexican settlements. Southern Arizona became part of the United States in 1854 when Mexico sold this territory under the Gadsden Purchase.[1]

To bring closure to the Mexican-American War, the Treaty of Guadalupe Hidalgo was executed on February 2, 1848, and ratified on May 30, 1848 (Menchaca 2001: 215). The treaty stipulated the political rights of the inhabitants of the ceded territories, set the U.S.-Mexico border, delineated the political responsibilities of each country in stopping Indian insurrections along the border, and finalized several agreements on economic relations.

The most important stipulations affecting the occupied population were the treaty agreements giving these peoples U.S. citizenship and upholding their property rights. No arrangements, however, were negotiated concerning the political status of U.S. immigrants in Mexico, and no attempts were made to determine the political rights of immigrants who entered either territory following the making of the U.S-Mexico border. By not negotiating immigration policy, Mexico averted passage of a runaway extradition clause, an area of contention that the U.S. government was pressuring Mexico to submit to but that Mexico was unwilling to compromise on (Schwartz 1975; Tyler 1972). Ideologically the two countries held radically different views on slavery, Mexico having abolished slavery in 1829 and extended citizenship to all former slaves.

After the Treaty of Guadalupe Hidalgo was executed, the U.S. government began restoring some of the political rights of the conquered population. The population had been under military orders to remain in their towns and villages; all travel was restricted (Article 3, Convenio Militar, in *Derecho Internacional Mexicano*, vol. 1, 1877: 251), but on March 9, 1848, the U.S. Congress lightened the travel restrictions and authorized some Mexicans to move freely throughout the Southwest. Women and children were allowed to travel freely, but males had to obtain a permit and display a special banner as they traveled. The banner signaled that the men were peaceful and unarmed and had surrendered.

Congress also allowed Mexicans who were unwilling to be governed by the United States to resettle in Mexico. The government preferred that the refugees travel in groups but did give families special permits to travel if they were unwilling to join a colony. Special arrangements were made with the Mexican government to oversee their travel and resettlement. The president of Mexico, José Joaquín de Herrera, under the "Federal Decree of August 19, 1848," instructed all governors to issue land grants to any refugee (*Derecho Internacional Mexicano*, vol. 1, 1877: 255–258).[2] The governors were also asked to assist the settlers economically by giving each person a modest sum of money. Each adult was to receive twenty-five pesos, and the parents of children under fourteen were to receive fourteen pesos per child. The money was to be reimbursed by the federal government. Families who did not have the funds to relocate or to pay for travel expenses were to contact the Office of the Secretary of Haciendas to receive monetary assistance. Families could apply for assistance on their own but were advised to form colonies and apply as groups. President Herrera also asked the governors to be prepared to employ Mexicans within their state government, as many of the refugees were government employees who refused to remain in the

United States. Such people would need special compensation because they were not farmers and were accustomed to a higher standard of living. The refugee resettlement proceeded peacefully, but most Mexicans chose to remain in the United States since they had been told their land rights were protected (Engstrand 1992).

A Broken Treaty: The Racialization Process Begins

Within a year of the ratification of the Treaty of Guadalupe, the U.S. government violated its citizenship stipulation and began a process of racialization that ascribed to Mexicans different legal rights on the basis of race. Mexicans who were white were given full legal citizenship, while mestizos, Christianized Indians, and *afromexicanos* (mixed race people of African descent) were accorded inferior legal rights. Prior to the Mexican-American War, Mexico had extended citizenship to all people living in Mexican territory irrespective of race. This process had begun in 1821, when Mexico obtained its independence from Spain. Indians, whites, mestizos, and free blacks were given citizenship upon independence, and enslaved blacks were extended citizenship when slavery was abolished a few years later. Mexico's citizenship rights included the right to vote, run for office, enter any profession, transact business with whomever one chose, marry freely with no racial restrictions, and obtain title to land grants.[3] But when the United States annexed the occupied territory the federal government refused to uphold Mexico's citizenship legislation and imposed its own racial laws on the conquered territories.

To resolve the problem of how the conquered population was to be treated the U.S. Congress gave the new governments of the ceded territories and states the right to decide which Mexicans would be given citizenship. At this time the states and territories had the legal right to determine citizenship eligibility requirements, a power given to them by the U.S. Constitution (U.S. Constitution, art. 4, sec. 2, cited in Hyman and Wiecek, 1982: 517–531).[4] This move had a severe impact on Mexicans because most legislators chose not to give people of color the legal rights enjoyed by white citizens. The legislature in California, dominated by Anglo-Americans, chose to extend citizenship only to white males (California Constitution, 1849, article 2, sec. 1, p. 4; Grodin, Massey, and Cunningham 1993: 3). In New Mexico, the Mexican-controlled legislature extended citizenship to all former citizens of Mexico (First Legislative Assembly 1851: 20; Larson 1968: 18, 33–34, 37, 64, 82). However, in 1853 Congress rescinded this decree and denied Indians and blacks citizenship. This censure also affected Arizona because from 1848 to 1863 Arizona was governed by New Mexico's territorial government. It was not until 1863 that Arizona received independent territorial status and adopted its own citizenship requirements. Once the territory was separated from New Mexico, its first legislative assembly voted to reserve citizenship for white males (*Organic Act of Arizona* 1863, rev. 1864, ch. 24, sec. 6, in Hoyt 1877: 226). In Texas, U.S. citizenship was extended to Mexicans as long as they were not of black descent. Detribalized Christian Indians who paid taxes and had adopted the lifestyle of Mexicans were also given citizenship but with limited rights. They were not allowed to vote, and property could be inherited only if they could prove that they spoke Spanish and that their ancestors had been legally emancipated from the Spanish missions (*McMullen v. Hodge and Others* 1849). In sum, Mexicans entered a new racial order in which their civil rights were limited on account of their blood quantum.

Mexican Mestizos and Tribal Indians

In the first years of American occupation, the governments of the Southwest politically distinguished people of indigenous descent on the basis of their political affiliations. Spanish-speaking mestizos who resided in the main colonial towns were assumed to be Mexican and were therefore exempt from federal Indian policies (Haas 1995; Menchaca 2001). Indians who had never been subdued by the Spanish or Mexican governments were placed on reservations or forcibly driven out of the Southwest. They were politically labeled warlike, and if they refused to surrender they could be killed. By contrast, Indians who were peaceful and lived in villages were visited by an agent of the Bureau of Indian Affairs (BIA) to determine if they should be extended the legal rights of Mexican mestizos. These Indian groups included the Coahuiltecan and Apache communities in Texas; Pueblos in New Mexico; Pima Indians of the Santa Cruz and San Pedro valleys in Arizona; and Chumash, Gabrileño, Luiseño, and groups of Yuma Indians in California. To determine whether a community was Mexican or Indian, BIA agents were sent to investigate if a tribal council governed the residents. Peaceful communities that had retained a tribal government were classified as Indian rather than Mexican (e.g., Tiwa of Ysleta, Pueblo, Chumash). State and territorial governments were then instructed to implement peaceful governance policies and decide if such people were to be allowed to remain in their villages or be dispersed to other places (Dale 1951; Heizer and Almquist 1977). Once the legislatures had made their decisions, many Indian villagers were relocated onto reservations and some were allowed to remain in their village with their property respected (e.g., the Pueblo), but the majority had their lands confiscated and were forced to move. Individuals who were detribalized and lived among Mexicans but were culturally identifiable as Indian were ordered by the federal government to be counted among the peaceful Indian populations (see *People v. Juan Antonio* 1865), and their governance was turned over to the states and territories. The legislatures were given the power to determine if detribalized Indians were to be granted the political rights of Mexican mestizos (see *Suñol v. Hepburn* 1850; *McMullen v. Hodge and Others* 1849).

After the American occupation, Indians who had formerly been colonized by Spain and Mexico had a major advantage in being politically identified as Mexican, regardless of the fact that not all Mexicans had been given citizenship. For example, only Mexicans and Anglo-Americans were allowed to certify their land grants under U.S. law, a significant advantage for Mexicans, as most were not displaced from their homes. Excluding the Pueblo of New Mexico, most Indians living in former Mexican municipalities lost their property to the U.S. government. Mexicans also did not have to fear being placed on reservations or being subject to punitive laws like those passed in some states.

Whereas Indians benefited from being legally classified as Mexican, it was politically dangerous for Mexicans to be considered Indian. Likewise, it was politically dangerous for Mexicans of African descent to publicly acknowledge their African heritage because in Texas, Arizona, and New Mexico they would lose their Mexican land grants and conceivably be subject to legal codes governing African Americans.

Why Some Mexicans Are of African Descent

During Mexico's phase as a Spanish colony the Crown allowed Spaniards to participate in the transatlantic slave trade and to import enslaved Africans to Mexico (Menchaca 2001). At first, slavery was uncommon in Mexico, but by the early 1600s the practice increased, and several thousand slaves arrived in Mexico annually (Aguirre Beltrán 1944: 426; Aguirre Beltrán 1991a: 10). In 1630 the Catholic Church in Mexico successfully lobbied to restrict the slave trade, and the importation of slaves nearly ceased. Nonetheless, approximately 150,000 to 200,000 enslaved Africans are estimated to have entered Mexico during the country's history (Aguirre Beltrán 1944:

431). Because the Catholic Church in Mexico was against slavery it set in motion legal procedures to ensure that the majority of the children of enslaved people were born free. The clergy pressured the government to enforce Spain's Las Siete Partidas laws, which prohibited the enslavement of the children of enslaved black males and Indian women. These children were legally free and were considered to be black Indians. By 1650 Spanish censuses indicate that 85 percent of the African-descended population was free (Meyer, Sherman, and Deeds 2007: 203).

The migration of people of African descent to the Southwest began in 1598, when the first colony was established in New Mexico. They entered as free *afromestizo* people.[5] At first their numbers were few, as most afromestizos were unaccompanied by a family (Hammond and Rey 1953). By the early 1700s, when the large-scale colonization of Texas began, the number of afromestizos increased substantially, most afromestizo families settling primarily in San Antonio, Los Adaes, and La Bahia. Families of African descent joined the northern migration in response to the opening of opportunity structures. The Spanish government, as a means of attracting colonists to settle in the north, an area considered to be extremely hostile and dangerous, chose to relax its legal racial order and give settlers of color special privileges denied to them in the interior of Mexico. To make the area attractive to settlers, people of color, including free afromestizos, were given land grants and allowed to enter professions that in the interior of Mexico were reserved for whites. Afromestizos were given legal rights similar to those of mestizos. In return for the privileges accorded to them, the colonists of color were required to defend their settlements from hostile Indians. Afromestizos, like the Indians and mestizos, however, were prohibited from governing themselves. With few exceptions only unmixed Spaniards were allowed to hold government positions. This practice continued until Mexican independence.

When the United States annexed the Southwest in 1848, many Mexicans of African descent resided in California, but the largest number lived in Texas. Spanish censuses indicate that in 1793, 30 percent of the colonists in Texas were of African descent (Tjarks 1974: 325) while in California around 20 percent were (Cook and Borah 1974: 220; Forbes 1966: 11). Few afromestizos are believed to have settled in Arizona and New Mexico, although the demographic size of the mixed-population in those two territories is uncertain because many local censuses omitted racial categories. Nonetheless, Spanish censuses of New Mexico indicate that afromestizo families lived in seventy-six settlements, the largest concentration being in Santa Fe (Olmstead 1981). Most of these families were of mixed race, some members being identified as black and others as Indian, mestizo, or afromestizo.

Early Examples of Racialization Under the Law

The process of racializing Mexicans in the Southwest resulted in their being placed in different legal categories. Outside of New Mexico, Mexicans of color had limited civil rights. For example, in California and Arizona, Mexicans of color were not eligible to vote, hold public office, or practice law because citizenship was a prerequisite (see Konvitz 1946; Murphy 1970). Serving on juries was also limited by race. In Arizona, Mexicans could serve on juries only if they were white, and in Texas if they were white or mestizo and eligible to vote (*Compiled Laws of Arizona, 1864–1877*, XLVI, sec. 4, p. 403; *Laws of Texas*, 4:234). In California, although a similar restriction was not in effect, the legislature excluded most people of color from acting as witnesses against whites in legal affairs. Indians, blacks, and persons of mixed descent who had one-fourth or more Indian blood or one-half or more negro blood could not testify against whites (California Statutes 1851, title 9, ch. 1, sec. 394, p. 114).

Concerning land rights, the states and territories passed unfair racial laws that treated groups differently on account of their race. The laws either rescinded a group's property titles or prevented them from applying for government homesteads. In California the legislature ruled under the Act of 1851 that Mexican land grants owned by Indians were void, regardless of whether such people held a deed or claimed they were Christianized Mexican Indians (Menchaca 2001: 259–261; *Suñol v. Hepburn* 1850: 254). This law did not apply to whites, mestizos, or afromestizos. The law was specifically designed to nullify the Spanish and Mexican land grants of indigenous communities because they owned the most coveted property in California. A similar law had been passed in Texas following its independence from Mexico. In Arizona, Christian Indians were subject to a similar land displacement pattern: they too were prohibited from submitting their Mexican land grants for confirmation (Mattison 1967: 71–90; Menchaca 2001: 254; Soza 1998, 1994). Further, in 1862, when the federal government began giving homestead grants to people in the Southwest, laws were passed to disqualify most people of color, including Mexicans (Thompson 1878). For example, in California and Arizona a person had to be either a citizen or eligible to naturalize to obtain a homestead grant. The problem with this policy is that only whites qualified for citizenship. In New Mexico, where most Mexicans qualified for U.S. citizenship, the federal government passed special homestead provisions to disqualify them from receiving land. The U.S. Congress decreed that any person who had received a land grant from Mexico or Spain was disqualified (Hibbard 1965: 354; Westphall 1965: 37). The latter policy made ineligible virtually all Mexicans in New Mexico since most had acquired some property through previous laws passed by Spain or Mexico. Similar homestead laws were passed in Texas while it was a republic, the period when the vast majority of its free public lands were distributed. From 1838 to 1841 homestead grants were issued to settlers only if they were white and had settled in Texas after the Texas War of Independence (*Laws of Texas*, 2:35, 90). People who had lived in Texas prior to independence had their land grants confirmed as long as they were neither black nor Indian. Although the racial laws were removed from the homestead acts by the late 1880s, the reforms came too late for Mexicans since few land grant programs were available by then.

Mexican Immigration in the Aftermath of the Mexican-American War

Following the Mexican-American War, the U.S. Census Bureau was uncertain both of the size of the conquered population and of the exact number of Mexicans who had immigrated after the war. The bureau estimated that from 1848 to 1850, 13,317 Mexicans immigrated and were dispersed throughout the southwest region of the United States (U.S. Census 1853: xxxviii). The bureau also offered an estimate of the Mexican population who had resided in the Southwest prior to the war. In 1854 the total number of Mexicans who had been conquered in California, New Mexico, and Arizona was estimated to be around 60,000 (U.S. Census 1854: 39). No estimate was given for Texas, and no explanation was given of how the enumerations were conducted in the other regions. Although there is no U.S. enumeration for the annexed Mexican population of Texas, the Mexican government in the mid-1820s took the last census of this region. The total number of Mexican and Christian Indians (i.e., mission and Christian Indian *ranchería* Indians) was estimated to be around 16,041 (Alonzo 1998: 41; Meyer, Sherman and Deeds 2007: 291; Weber 1982: 4–5).

By the late 1850s the U.S. Census Bureau had developed a better accounting system of the Mexican immigrant population and from then on kept a careful count of their numbers. In 1860 the bureau estimated that in the past ten years the Mexican immigrant population had increased by

106.2 percent, and 45 percent of those (out of 27,466) lived in Texas (U.S. Census 1864: 34; U.S. Census 1922a: 305). Texas had become the preferred place of settlement for the majority of Mexican immigrants. The growth of the immigrant population in Texas was largely due to earlier settlement patterns. After the Mexican-American War many of the ranching families whose property lay on both sides of the U.S.-Mexico border, but whose homes were located in Mexico, chose to relocate and move to South Texas (Galarza 1964; Weber 1982). Likewise, many Mexicans whose extended family lived on the U.S. side of the border chose to reunite with them by moving to South Texas. Those families became the first Mexican immigrants.

Although the bureau kept a detailed count of the Mexican immigrant population over the years, it failed to enumerate the number of people of Mexican descent born in U.S. territory, including the children of the immigrants. People of Mexican descent born in the United States were counted by various statistical methodologies that changed each time a decennial census was taken. Sometimes Mexicans born in the United States, whom I refer to as Mexican American, were counted by race and at other times if one parent was born in Mexico they were counted under a family immigrant stock category.[6] The problem with these enumeration statistical models is that the U.S. Census offered an accurate count only of the Mexican foreign born and occluded the total number of people of Mexican descent living in the United States. Although the numerical size of the total Mexican-origin population cannot be ascertained for some decades, this did not pose a problem in identifying the generational growth of the Mexican immigrant population in the United States because a detailed and consistent enumeration format was maintained in their case.

My point is that the generational growth of the foreign-born population can be outlined and a description of their demographic concentration in Texas reconstituted. This in turn has allowed me to identify the periods during which the Mexican immigrant population increased in great numbers and to explore the events that led to their exodus from Mexico and entry into the United States.

Mexicans in Texas Slave Society

When Mexican immigrants settled in Texas they entered a society that had been transformed by slavery. It was not advisable for any Mexican of African descent to live in Texas unless they were prepared to suffer the consequences. A short discussion of slavery will illustrate that it was very unlikely that the Mexican immigrants who settled in Texas prior to the Civil War were afromexicanos. On the contrary, during this period the migration of people of African descent was to Mexico, not the other way around.

Prior to Mexico's Emancipation Proclamation the Mexican and Spanish censuses indicate that the enslaved black population never exceeded thirty-seven people (*Residents of Texas 1732–1836*). Slavery, rare in Texas before the arrival of the Anglo-American population, increased on a large scale when Texas obtained its independence from Mexico, and by the time Texas was annexed by the U.S. Congress slavery had increased immensely. In 1850, the U.S. Census counted 58,161 enslaved blacks in Texas (U.S. Census 1862: 130). It also counted 397 free blacks. The census noted that the "free colored" category included emancipated slaves and part of the mestizos acquired from Mexico who had more than one-eighth African blood (U.S. Census 1854: 39). The census noted further that the colored mestizo population was much larger, yet they were enumerated under other racial categories according to their mixture.

Placing afromexicanos in a clear legal and social category had been traditionally acknowledged to be a problem by government officials in Texas. These people were considered to be a political nuisance because they had never been slaves, and it was unclear if they should hold the rights of slaves or of Mexicans. Early observations of Anglo-American settlers in Texas indicate that many Mexicans were of African descent, and Anglo-Americans did not know how to deal with them. Stephen Austin, the father of Texas independence, acknowledged this hybridity in letters to his business associates. He warned them about the political rights afromexicanos held in Texas and laid out a plan to deal with this free population. On June 16, 1830, Austin wrote to several heads of colonies whom he was recruiting to settle in Texas that he had developed procedures to ensure free negroes and Mexican mulattos would not live in the Anglo-American colonies (*Austin Papers*, box 2Q410, file 1830). In a letter to Richard Ellis, Austin wrote, "Measures have been taken to exclude free negroes and mulattoes, not indentured servants, so that there is no danger of being crowded with that class which is probably a worse nuisance than slaves." In a second letter, Austin further characterized Mexican Tejanos to be of a mixed black race. On May 4, 1836, he wrote to U.S. Senator L. F. Linn that the impending war between Mexico and the Anglo-American settlers was "a war of barbarism and of despotic principles waged by the mongrel Spanish-Indian and negro race against civilization and the Anglo-American race" (*Austin Papers*, 3:345). Other Texans made similar observations a few months before

Texas independence. On December 2, 1835, the Beaumont Committee, which supported independence, wrote to Maj. Henry Millard, a member of the provisional government, with a request to begin establishing procedures to deport free blacks from Texas after independence. The committee stated, "We earnestly recommend that you bring before the Council a bill prohibiting all black free persons or persons whatsoever from emigrating to Texas or residing within its limits under any pretext whatsoever" (Binkley 1936: 160–161).

After Texas independence it became common for travelers and government officials to describe Mexican Tejanos as a mongrel black race.[7] For example, William Gray, a land agent for U.S. investors, traveled throughout Texas in 1836–1837 and characterized many Mexicans to be "nearly black but having straight hair" (Gray 1965:89). Joseph Eve, U.S. chargé d'affaires of the Republic, also commented in a report that "Mexicans are a race of 'mongrels' composed of Spanish, Indian and African blood" (cited in de León 1987: 9). Adolphus Sterne, justice of the peace and head of the Nacogdoches branch of the Texas independence movement, left a description in his diary characterizing Mexicans in Nacogdoches. He wrote, "If their hair would be a little curly they would be taken anywhere for negroes" (Ibid., 16).

In sum, the problem afromexicanos posed to Texas was the threat they posed to institutionalized slavery. Such Mexicans were considered to be sympathetic to the enslaved and could easily be convinced to help fugitives escape to Mexico. Once enslaved persons crossed the border they were free because Mexico did not allow the extradition of fugitive slaves (Schoen 1937: 267). In 1840 Texas government officials tried to resolve this problem by deporting Mexicans of African descent (Menchaca 2001: 228–233). Afromexicanos and other free blacks were warned that if they did not leave Texas they could legally be converted into slaves. Later that year, after many influential Anglo-Americans claimed the act was unjust, on December 12, 1840, the Texas Congress revised its position (Act for the Relief of Certain Free Persons of Color, December 12, 1840, in *Laws of Texas Supplement 1822–1897:* 549; Schoen 1937: 277). It decreed that if free blacks could prove they had never been enslaved under Spanish and Mexican rule they could remain in Texas and continue to be free. This act applied to all afromexicanos.

Although afromexicanos were allowed to remain in Texas, they and other Mexicans were viewed as a threat to institutionalized slavery, and legal measures were taken to stop them from helping fugitive slaves. In the 1850s slave owners complained to the federal government that Mexicans from South Texas had established networks to help slaves escape to Mexico (Appiah and Gates 1999; Tyler 1972: 6–7). This was a particularly serious problem for slave owners who lived in the coastal counties adjacent to South Texas. Allegedly enslaved people from the coastal counties of Calhoun, Jackson, Matagorda, Colorado, and Wharton were given refuge in South Texas and later smuggled into Mexico. Slave owners complained that once fugitives escaped into South Texas it was nearly impossible to apprehend them. In 1854 slave owners tried to dismantle the runaway networks and asked for federal assistance in the form of a slave extradition treaty with Mexico. They also demanded that Mexico capture and return the runaway slaves. The slave owners charged that approximately four thousand slaves had been given refuge in Mexico, and the practice had to stop. Federal officials replied that Mexico was firm on this issue and would not comply. In response to the federal government's failure to enact policy, slave owners turned to the state government, and on February 9, 1854, the Texas legislature passed a series of laws to punish anyone who gave assistance to a runaway slave (Offenses Against Slaves and Slave Property, in *Laws of Texas*, 3:67). The most serious offense became giving slaves advice on escape routes to Mexico, a crime punishable by death or life imprisonment. People were also prohibited from transporting, harboring, clothing or feeding, and forging emancipation papers for runaway slaves. Depending on the gravity of the offense, a person could be sentenced from two to fifteen years in the penitentiary.

Many slave owners believed that if Mexicans by law were prohibited from associating with blacks their problem would be solved. The citizens of Travis County took the lead and developed a model to deal with the Mexican problem. On October 7, 1854, the citizens of Travis County held a public meeting to discuss ways of stopping Mexicans from helping slaves. They charged that slaves were becoming insubordinate and discontented because Mexicans told them they should be free and encouraged them to run away to Mexico. To ensure this impudent act would stop, the attendees voted in favor of expelling all trouble-making Mexicans from the county and segregating the rest. Resolution 8 read:

> WHEREAS, We have amongst us a Mexican population who continually associate with our slaves and instill into their minds false notions of freedom, and make them discontented and insubordinate, therefore,
> Resolved 1st, That all transient Mexicans, or those not freeholders, in our midst, be warned to leave within ten days from the passage of this resolution.

Resolved 2d, That all remaining after that time be forcibly expelled, unless their good character and good behavior, be vouched for by some responsible American citizen.

Resolved 3d, That all citizens employing Mexicans as laborers, be requested to notify, them of the passage of these resolutions.

Resolved 4th, That we will not employ Mexicans as laborers, and will discountenance and discourage their presence among us.

Resolved 5th, That a committee of ten energetic gentlemen be appointed to carry 1st and 2d resolutions into effect.

(*Texas State Times,* October 14, 1854, p. 2).

Other counties soon adopted the Travis County model. On October 23, 1854, a Convention of the Counties of Western Texas was held in the courthouse of the town of Gonzales to discuss the threat Mexican abolitionists posed to slave owners (*Texas State Times,* November 4, 1854, p. 1). The main resolution adopted at the convention was to allow cities and counties to pass ordinances prohibiting Mexicans from speaking to blacks, and if Mexicans refused they could be expelled from the county (de León 1987: 51–53). From 1854 to 1857 many Mexicans broke this ordinance, and as a consequence hundreds of Mexican families were forced to leave their homes in the counties of Colorado, Guadalupe, Uvalde, Austin, and Matagorda and in the city of Seguin. In San Antonio a referendum was held to oust the entire Mexican community, but it was defeated after the German community voted against the measure. Mexicans instead were placed under military surveillance (Montejano 1987: 38).

The expulsion of Mexican families from several counties was merely symptomatic of the Mexicans' social and political decline in Texas. By then, few Mexicans were elected to high-level offices. From 1845 to 1860 only two Mexicans were elected to the state legislature (Texas Legislature 1962: 3–36). This pattern worsened over time, and it is an issue I examine throughout my narrative. Most Mexicans who were elected to government positions were restricted to county or city positions.

Socially the status of Mexicans also declined over the years and was manifested in the radical decline of intermarriage between Mexicans and Anglo-Americans. Mexican women were no longer sought after as marriage partners by Anglo-American men, a practice that at times had been common in San Antonio and Laredo (Dysart 1976). In 1855 the Texan land investor John Donelson Coffee noted in a letter to his cousin that Mexicans were no longer accepted in Anglo-American social circles (Boom 1966: 283). According to Donelson, Anglo-Americans socialized with four or five

Mexican families and considered the single women of these families the only acceptable Mexican marriage partners. The women were described as being of light complexion and racially differentiated from the rest of the Mexican women, whom Donelson derogatorily called greasers and described as racially mixed women who resembled dark mulattas. Corroborating Donelson's observations are the marriage records from San Antonio. By the late 1840s only a handful of Mexican women married Anglo-American men, and in 1850 of sixty Anglo-American marriages only four involved Mexican brides, a pattern that continued into the 1860s (Bean and Bradshaw 1970: 394; Dysart 1976: 369).

The Mexicans' social decline was also manifested in the lack of respect shown by Anglo-Americans toward the Mexicans' property. In this area, however, the courts stepped in and defended the Mexicans' property rights. The illegal usurpation of the property of Mexicans had become such a law and order problem that in 1853 the Texas Supreme Court had to put an end to the practice. In *Cook v. De La Garza* the judges ruled that confiscating the property of Mexicans without legal state authority was illegal, and those who broke the law would be imprisoned. Anglo-Americans also challenged the right of Mexicans to inherit property. Once again the Texas courts stepped in and protected the legal rights of Mexicans. The legal principles used to defend the right of Mexicans to inherit property, however, were complicated since the legal rulings involved international law and its applicability to U.S. state laws. Two inheritance cases are exemplary of how the political rights of Mexicans of different races were litigated. Through them I will also illustrate how the social position of Mexicans of Spanish descent served to shape the legal rights Mexicans of color held in Texas. As I discussed earlier, Mexicans who were of Spanish descent were given full political rights, and I argue in this section that the rights given to them set a legal precedent to protect the legal rights of Mexicans of color, including those who were of partial African descent. The case of Maria de Jesusa Smith will illustrate the higher social status Mexicans of full Spanish descent held within Texas, whereas the case of Margaret Guess, an afromexicana, will illustrate the low social opinion some Anglo-Americans held of Mexicans who were black. Both cases, however, attest to the fact that people who were considered to be Mexican were given superior rights to enslaved people.

Maria de Jesusa Smith was a native Tejana and came from one of the aristocratic Mexican families who claimed to be descendants of the Spanish Canary Islanders. Her family, the Curbelo-Delgados, were among the wealthiest property owners in San Antonio. Maria de Jesusa was among the handful of Mexicans in San Antonio who had sided with the Anglo-

Americans during the Texas Revolution. During Mexican rule Maria de Jesusa married John Smith, an American investor who, when the movement to separate from Mexico began, actively participated in the revolt. John fought in the Battle of the Alamo, and after independence he became the first mayor of San Antonio. Maria de Jesusa and John had three daughters who were well received by Anglo society and who married prominent Anglo-Americans. Upon John's death, Maria de Jesusa inherited his estate, including property valued at over four hundred thousand dollars, ten thousand dollars in cash, a monthly stipend based on the collection of tenant rents, and the profits of the labor of three seamstress slave girls whom the Smiths hired out.[8] In 1845, Samuel Smith challenged Maria de Jesusa's right to inherit John's estate on the grounds that, being John's son, he was the only legitimate heir. He charged that Maria de Jesusa's marriage was invalid. Samuel lost after being unable to prove his paternity.

Samuel appealed his case to the Texas Supreme Court the following year. In the second trial, *Smith v. Smith* (1846), Samuel's attorneys argued that Maria de Jesusa could not inherit John's estate because her marriage was fraudulent: it not only had been consecrated outside the customs and traditions of U.S. society but also had taken place during Mexican rule and was therefore invalid. Although the arguments were compelling, the Texas Supreme Court upheld the lower court's decision on the basis that Mexico's marriage laws were legally binding under U.S. law. The judges added that marriages were not void merely because they had been performed in Catholic ceremonies or had followed Mexican traditions.[9]

Maria de Jesusa's case was of paramount significance, as it became the precedent for upholding Mexico's marriage and inheritance laws. The legal and cultural arguments used in defense of the Smiths' interethnic marriage were later found to be equally applicable to interracial marriages. That is, although afromexicanos were viewed to be inferior to whites, under Texas law they held superior rights in comparison to enslaved African Americans, and they were granted some of the legal rights of Mexican citizens. For example, in 1851, *Guess v. Lubbock* became the first miscegenation case to appear before the Texas Supreme Court. The case was complicated because it involved Margaret Guess, a Mexican woman who was accused of illegally assuming the status of a free black. Margaret owned a boardinghouse in Harris County, and after her spouse, Adam Smith, an Anglo-American, died his estate administrator, a Mr. Lubbock, attempted to enslave Margaret. Lubbock charged that Margaret, her property, and a little black girl who lived with her were property of the estate. Margaret denied the charges. Before the judges could render a decision, they had to first determine if, during

Mexican rule, Margaret had been part of the free Mexican population and had been married to Adam.

After reviewing the arguments, the Texas Supreme Court ruled on Margaret's behalf. Judge J. Lipscomb ruled that Margaret was part of the free Mexican population who could not be converted into property. On the basis of Mexican law, even if she had been a slave, when Adam publicly recognized her as his legitimate spouse she became a free person. It did not matter if Margaret had been born a slave.

These cases reveal that race mattered in Texas. The lighter complexioned you were, the better chance you had of being treated decently. During this era race determined social status, political representation shrank, and inclusion within white social circles became nearly nonexistent for people of color. Mexicans, however, were a free people, and regardless of their color did not have to fear being enslaved or placed on reservations. Nonetheless, Texas remained a hostile place for Mexicans of African descent: it was not advisable for them to migrate to Texas unless they were prepared to endure the hardships of Texas slave society. By 1860 slavery had grown in Texas, and 182,566 people were enslaved there (U.S. Census 1864: 33). The growth of slavery in Texas, however, would prove to be a turning point in U.S.-Mexico relations. Texas became one of the states of the Union that depended on slavery at a time when many states were prepared to terminate the institution. For Mexico the stance Anglo-Texans took to defend slavery created an opportune moment to lobby in support of favorable naturalization laws for Mexicans.

U.S.-Mexico Relations During the Civil War

The early 1860s was a tumultuous period for the United States and Mexico. A civil war broke out in the United States, and Mexico found itself under siege by a European military threat. Both countries were embroiled in violent wars that changed the course of their history. Unlike previous encounters that had divided the two countries, this time political events led to the formation of an alliance between Union forces and the Liberal Party of President Benito Juárez of Mexico. The alliance came to benefit Mexico and Mexican immigrants. After the governments of the United States and Mexico vanquished their enemies, warm diplomatic relations developed, replacing the bad feelings caused by the Mexican-American War. During this diplomatic phase, the governments of Mexico and the United States introduced the legal infrastructure to dismantle racially biased laws barring

Mexican immigrants from applying for U.S. citizenship. As noted earlier, the Naturalization Treaty of 1868 was enacted for that purpose, and it introduced the legal principle that Mexican immigrants should be treated on the basis not of their race but of their national origin. Mexican immigrants thereby gained the ability to become U.S. citizens, which in turn gave them many political rights. They gained the right to vote and to run for public office since most states in the 1800s required citizenship to be an elected official (Keyssar 2000). Likewise, they gained employment opportunities since in those days the federal government limited federal employment to citizens, and many states required a person to be a citizen in order to enter the legal and medical professions or work as junk dealers, pool parlor operators, boiler inspectors, and architects (Konvitz 1946; Leibowitz 1983). In some states a person had to be a citizen to own land.

President Benito Juárez and the Confederacy

In 1860, following the election of President Abraham Lincoln, the southern states threatened to secede (Barr 2000: 6). The North and South were divided on many economic issues, but the immediate and primary issue was the South's support of and dependence on slavery and the North's increasing opposition to it. The North was becoming industrialized, and its economic growth depended upon the exportation of manufactured goods and the development of a domestic market that would consume what the factories produced (Takaki 2000). For the domestic market to grow, workers needed to purchase products, but slavery was an obstacle because enslaved people could not participate in the consumer market. The economic stability of the North also depended upon the ability of the federal government to impose protective tariffs on imported goods. U.S. industrialists needed consumers to purchase American products, not European goods. In contrast to that of the North, the South's economy was agriculturalist and depended on slave labor to plant and harvest food and other crops. Southerners were hesitant to industrialize, as their economy was robust and depended on the exportation of cotton and other agricultural goods. Because of the South's agrarian economic infrastructure Southerners favored low import tariffs to maintain a healthy trade relationship with their European partners. If the North demanded higher import tariffs this would cause the South's European traders to increase their tariffs for southern cotton.

During the presidential election of 1860, slavery became the main political issue of debate. Members of the political parties were divided. Republicans overwhelmingly favored abolition, while northern and southern Democrats were divided. Moral arguments advanced by northern abolitionist organizations had fueled the growth of an antislavery movement in the North, which in turned influenced Republican and Democratic elected officials to support the views of their constituencies (Gillette 1969). The southern Democrats disapproved of the abolitionist movement, and when Lincoln appeared to become the favored candidate of the majority of the people, the southern Democrats threatened to secede from the Union if a man who was sympathetic toward abolition was elected to office. Upon Lincoln's election, South Carolina took the lead and made good on its promise to secede, and within months Mississippi, Florida, Alabama, Louisiana, Georgia, and Texas followed suit. To prevent the disintegration of the Union Lincoln sent troops to end the rebellion, but the movement toward secession, instead of being suppressed, widened further as Virginia, Arkansas, North Carolina, and Tennessee seceded. On April 12, 1861, Confederate forces attacked federal troops at Fort Sumter in South Carolina, and the Civil War escalated (Appiah and Gates 1999: 457).

Texas played a pivotal role in the war largely owing to its proximity to the Mexican border. Texas shared a border that was hundreds of miles long. The Confederacy could easily gain economic and military advantage over the Union if it succeeded in forging an alliance with Mexico. After the war broke out the Confederacy's economy continued to depend on the sale of cotton to Europe. England and other nations had refused to support the Union's economic blockade of the South and continued to buy cotton from the region. The Confederacy consequently used the sale of cotton to fund the war and purchase arms. However, if the war's funding base was to continue unobstructed it was necessary to export cotton, and this became very difficult when Confederate seaports came under armed attack. By early 1862, Union forces had blockaded most southern seaports, and Texas became the main outlet for the exportation of cotton abroad (Thompson 2000; Tyler 1973). Seaports in Texas, however, soon fell under Union control, and the main route for the transport of cotton abroad became the Texas-Mexico border. To reach Mexico, cotton had to be transported from the interior of the South into Texas, then across the border by land, and finally end its journey when loaded onto European vessels in Mexican seaports. The most difficult part of the journey was getting the cotton to Texas. Once there, the cargo could be easily transported into Mexico because it was now under the protection of the Mexican government. Like most of Europe, Mexico had declared its neutrality.

For the Confederacy, shipping its cargo through Mexico was essential. The Mexican route was its main economic bloodline in its efforts to win the war. Mexico's support was also necessary to ensure that Union forces would not launch attacks into Texas, Louisiana, and Florida from Mexico. Immediately after the war broke out the Confederacy and the Union sent diplomats to Mexico. President Juárez assured the representatives that he would not allow either side to launch military attacks from Mexican soil. He also assured them that Mexico would continue doing commerce with both parties since he had issued a neutrality order.

The Confederacy Insults Mexico: A Turning Point

The first diplomat sent to Mexico by the president of the Confederacy, Jefferson Davis, was Col. John T. Pickett. In October 1861, Pickett was commissioned to convince President Juárez to recognize the Confederacy and end Mexico's neutrality pact (Mahoney and Mahoney 1998: 33). The Confederacy in exchange offered to return to Mexico part of the territories the U.S. government had taken from it. Juárez was interested in the offer but cautious, since his government's political philosophy was closer to that of Lincoln's party. The Union and the Mexican government both opposed slavery and favored increasing federal control over the states. Moreover, while Juárez contemplated the offer he was in communication with the Union's ambassador to Mexico, Thomas Corwin, who accused Pickett of making plans with Spain to reconquer Mexico (McCornack 1955; Schoonover 1991).

In the end Pickett failed to gain President Juárez's support, but not simply because Juárez was suspicious of the offer: Pickett's insolent and racist behavior toward Mexican officials indicated that the Confederacy did not see Mexicans as equals. When Pickett met with Juárez, he arrogantly ordered Mexico to comply. In addition, Pickett ignorantly assured Juárez that the two nations could work together because their economies depended on the maintenance of a hierarchical racial order. Mexico in fact practiced not a slave economy but a peonage system. It is unclear if Pickett was trying to insult Juárez with his comments or if he was truly unaware, first, that Mexico's Constitution prohibited slavery and, second, that Juárez was trying to dismantle Mexico's peonage system. Juárez, a full-blooded Indian, despised the peonage system since the groups most severely affected by it were Indians. When Juárez refused to rescind his neutrality order and hand over to the Confederacy all of Mexico's ports, Pickett became hostile. He warned the president that failure to comply was a serious mistake and would cost Mexico its political sovereignty.

Upon Pickett's return to the South, he reported to President Davis that Mexico was hostile toward the Confederacy and was prepared to support the Union in spite of Juárez's agreement to remain neutral (Mahoney and Mahoney 1998). Pickett's assessment was not far off. Within days of Pickett's departure Juárez granted the Union permission to move troops through Mexican territory. This allowed Union soldiers to make advances against the Confederacy and protect Arizona and New Mexico from coming under Confederate control (Lamar 1970: 426–435; Wagoner 1970: 7–16).

Juárez's support for the Union was also obvious in the manner in which he enacted agreements with it. On December 11, 1861, Mexico and the United States concluded the Extradition Treaty, which clearly was not in the best interests of the Confederacy (Extradition Treaty, in 12 *U.S. Statutes at Large* 1199–1203; Tyler 1972:11).[10] Under the Extradition Treaty Mexico agreed to protect and give legal sanction to fugitive slaves, prohibit the piracy of U.S. ships in Mexican waters, and extradite criminals who rape, murder, assault or commit burglary against civilians. All stipulations benefited the Union war effort and supported the Underground Railroad that allowed runaway slaves to reach Mexico. Juárez also made diplomatic arrangements to offer shelter to Union refugees fleeing from the Confederacy. The city of Monterrey became the main destination of southern refugees, in particular Texan dissidents (*Centinela del Rio Grande*, June 26, 1861, p. 1; Tyler 1973).

Although Juárez supported the ideals of the North, he did not terminate relations with the South. He allowed confederate cargo to continue passing through Mexico, which was unavoidably expedient, given that Mexico was bankrupt and dependent on the taxes it collected from the customhouses at the border and along the seaports. Mexico desperately needed commerce to generate income because the counterintelligence information the Union had given Juárez had been confirmed. Less than two months after Pickett was expelled, Juárez learned that Spain, England, and France were about to launch an invasion of Mexico.

The French Invasion of Mexico

On December 17, 1861, an armada sent by France, England, and Spain arrived at the Port of Veracruz (Mahoney and Mahoney 1998:50). President

Juárez knew of its pending arrival and ordered the Mexican navy not to launch a defensive attack. Instead, Juárez planned to deal with the aggressors diplomatically and negotiate a deal. He asked Minister of Foreign Affairs Manuel Zamacona to greet the foreign diplomats at the port and commence negotiations. Juárez knew why the armada had been sent. Lincoln's secretary of state, William H. Seward, had apprised Juárez that a tripartite agreement to invade Mexico had been signed. According to Seward, however, England and Spain were prepared to retreat if Juárez rescinded his recently enacted foreign policy orders. The ordeal had started after President Juárez called a moratorium on all European debts. Juárez chose to suspend payments for two main reasons: the Mexican government was bankrupt, and Mexico had made sufficient payments to remunerate the original loans. Juárez had expected retaliation but not a foreign invasion.

Secretary Seward had become involved in the Mexican conflict as a means of befriending Mexico and stopping the Confederacy from making a deal with Juárez. Lincoln instructed Seward to find a diplomatic solution to Mexico's economic problems and, if need be, to inform the invading nations that the U.S. government was prepared to pay the interest on the loans until Mexico was able to resume payment of its foreign debts (Vázquez and Meyer 1985: 67). While Minister Zamacona negotiated a repayment agreement, Seward cautioned Mexico and assured the invading forces that the U.S. government would not intervene with armed forces. Seward, however, informed all parties that his government favored finding a peaceful solution and would keep a watchful eye on Mexico. While Spain and England negotiated a deal and were close to accepting the U.S. offer, Seward learned through intelligence agents that Spain was planning on using its armada to remain in Mexico and renew its hold over some of its former Latin American territories. Because this was against the interests of the United States, Seward immediately wired Charles Francis Adams, the American ambassador in London, to inform the British government that the United States would offer Mexico and other Latin American countries armed assistance once the southern insurrection was suppressed. Upon receiving the U.S. warning, Spain and England withdrew their troops. France, however, refused to negotiate with Mexico, and Emperor Napoleon III ordered his officers to launch a land invasion of Mexico. They were to begin by forming alliances with Juárez's enemies.

President Juárez indeed had many enemies in Mexico. The Catholic Church and part of the Mexican elite opposed him because of a series of reforms his Liberal Party had recently instituted. From 1858 to 1860 Juárez and members of the Liberal Party fought to instate policies to reduce the economic and political influence of the Catholic Church in Mexico (Meyer, Sherman, and Deeds 2007; Scholes 1957). Until the reforms had been enacted some European nations had continued to exert foreign influence over Mexican affairs through their dealings with the Catholic Church. Although advocates of the Church launched armed revolts against Juárez's regime, they failed to gain the support of the masses. This civil discord came to be called La Guerra de Reforma de México (the Mexican reform war). When the revolt came to an unsuccessful end, those who had plotted against Juárez's ruling party were forced to retreat, and many found refuge in France. When Juárez's opponents lost, the power of the Catholic Church was struck a terrible blow. Under the Reform Laws Juárez was able to nationalize all Church holdings, abolish the monasteries, disband the secular brotherhood associations, and order a moratorium on the establishment of new convents. The Liberal Party believed that by limiting the numerical growth of the clergy the Church's influence over civil matters would decline, as fewer clergy meant less ideological and economic control of civilians.

At first, some members of the oligarchy welcomed the nationalization of Church property since they expected the government to redistribute the confiscated lands. When Juárez put the land up for sale and refused to give it to the oligarchy, not surprisingly his popularity among elite social circles declined. Juárez's popularity further deteriorated within other sectors of the ruling class after he authored a series of judicial reforms affecting all Mexicans. First, Juárez ordered the official separation of Church and state. He proclaimed that the Church's main function was to minister to the faithful and not to influence the government. He also suspended the legal privileges the clergy held in Mexico. No longer would the clergy and the secular brotherhood associations be exempt from civil and criminal law. Any crimes committed by priests or brothers were to be litigated within the government, not by Church investigators.

Juárez then proceeded to reform the judicial system by trying to reduce the influence the upper class held within the court system. Civil and criminal codes were revised to give ordinary citizens further rights, and a jury system was established to ensure that more people were involved in deliberating the outcome of cases. Furthermore, to reduce the power the Church exercised over the property of Indian communities Juárez dismantled the political rights that tribal councils held over tribal communities (Aguirre Beltrán 1991b). He considered this to be a necessary step because the Church controlled the tribal councils. Under the reforms all land owned by a tribe was to be partitioned among the families and no longer controlled by the tribal council.[11] Juárez envisioned that under these reforms the tribal councils, which he considered to be backward and traditional, would be less influential over the youth of the country. Likewise, he believed that the youth would have a better chance of being integrated within Mexican society because the Church was responsible for encouraging Indians to maintain many of their tribal customs. According to Juárez, the best way of converting Indians into Mexican citizens was to make them property owners and educate their youth to value citizenship above tribal affiliation.

Elites and the clergy were not Juárez's only enemies. Some of the state governors also distrusted Juárez. Although during the reform war most state governors sided with the Liberal Party against the Church, they disapproved of what they perceived to be the erosion of state powers. Juárez had warned the governors that they must honor the congressional decrees and abide by the rulings of the federal supreme court. He had agreed to respect the states' autonomy as long as the governors did not interfere with the rights and general interests of the Republic (Scholes 1957: 43). Thus, when France ordered the invasion of Mexico Emperor Napoleon knew that the Juárez administration was compromised and could easily be destroyed.

Napoleon's intelligence sources were plentiful and reliable. He benefited from the advice of Mexican exiles residing in France as well as from intelligence sources in Mexico. The exiles had informed Napoleon that many Mexicans favored ending Mexico's constitutional government and replacing it with a monarchy under the protection of France. Juárez's failure to pay Mexico's foreign debt opened the way for Napoleon's legitimate and opportune entry into Mexican affairs. When French troops arrived in Mexico, however, their real motive was not to negotiate a foreign debt agreement but to conquer the country. French agents disembarked onto Mexican soil with the full intention of making secret plans with the clergy and the proroyalist sympathizers.

On May 5, 1862, Juárez's enemies plotted with Napoleon and launched the first attack (Ibid., 69). French troops attacked the city of Puebla, one of Mexico's main centers of commerce and the residence of the oligarchy. The Mexican people patriotically responded by launching a counter-offense. Their call to arms was sparked by memories of having lost half of Mexico to the United States. History was repeating itself, and Mexicans were not going to allow another foreign power to take their land. Thousands of civilians joined Juárez's troops and fought a series of battles that ended in a resounding victory for the Mexicans and the retreat of French troops. Within a year, however, Napoleon had reinforced his troops and captured Puebla. After Puebla fell, French troops marched onward to capture other cities.

Juárez immediately asked the United States for help, requesting that

President Lincoln enforce the Monroe Doctrine, a U.S. policy that forbade European countries from colonizing land and interfering with states in the Americas. Juárez dispatched Matías Romero, interim secretary in charge of foreign affairs, to Washington, D.C. But Secretary Seward refused to render aid and informed Romero that the United States was in no position to enforce the Monroe Doctrine. The truth was that President Lincoln did not want to anger France. The Mexican incident could potentially cause France to support the Confederacy. Lincoln, however, personally assured Romero that he supported Juárez and pledged that after the southern insurrection ended American troops would be sent to Mexico (Schoonover 1991). Lincoln nonetheless allowed Romero to raise funds in the United States for the war effort. Romero moved quickly, finding many allies among Washington's social circles and forming many powerful friendships with members of Congress, who donated large sums of money and extended Mexico personal loans. They also pledged to keep a watchful eye on Seward. Many congressmen distrusted Seward and believed he was insincere.

As Romero was trying to convince Seward to change his position, President Juárez sent other agents to the United States to foster pro-Juárez public opinion. Their official commission was to establish clubs in support of Mexico, but their real mission was to raise funds and secretly purchase weapons with the donations (Mahoney and Mahoney 1998: 74). Gen. Palacio Vega and Gen. Gaspar Ochoa were sent to fulfill Juárez's orders. Ochoa worked with Spanish-speaking Mexican groups, and Vega established English-speaking Monroe Doctrine Leagues. Both generals, however, worked together to purchase arms and find ways to smuggle the contraband into Mexico. Arms were purchased in New York and routed through Union territory until they reached California. At that point, allies such as Don Victor Castro, a Mexican American resident of California, received the contraband and through his networks relayed it on to Mexico (Miller 1958).

The Political Struggle Over the Texas-Mexico Border

For the duration of the French invasion President Juárez enjoyed massive support from all sectors of Mexican society (Meyer, Sherman, and Deeds 2007). Divisions within the upper class notwithstanding, he was recognized by most to be the commander in chief of the nation. Among his supporters were nearly all the state governors as well as hundreds of wealthy ranchers who purchased arms and mobilized their workers to fight the French. These regional leaders, who came to be known as *caudillos,* organized large armies under Juárez's central command. In the United States and Latin America Juárez also became a popular symbolic figure, standing for the ideals of republican sovereignty and against the tyranny of European imperialism.

In early 1862, however, problems began to develop along the Texas–Mexico border. Regional battles to control the customhouses broke out between local politicians, and Juárez appointed the governor of Nuevo León, Santiago Vidaurri, to control the money flowing through the customhouses (Tyler 1973: 64). Unbeknownst to Juárez, Vidaurri had grander plans. During his appointment as commander of the north Governor Vidaurri secretly broke Juárez's neutrality order and aided the Confederacy by selling them food, arms, and ammunition and issuing personal loans. Vidaurri also allowed Mexican soil to be used to launch attacks against the Union.

Meanwhile, as Juárez tried to strengthen his hold over northern Mexico, his troops suffered devastating losses against the French, and the capital was ceded. This forced Juárez and his cabinet to flee Mexico City and to find refuge elsewhere (Meyer, Sherman, and Deeds 2007). Juárez chose to relocate to northern Mexico, where the blockade against the French was impenetrable and where he could be close to the customhouses. This would secure his safety and allow his administrators to take control of the customhouses. Juárez immediately sent an envoy to meet with Vidaurri and negotiate an agreement to set up a new command center. Vidaurri proved to be unreceptive but did not outwardly refuse to host Juárez. Vidaurri knew that if he failed to comply, retaliation was unavoidable (Tyler 1973).

Juárez's problematic relationship with Vidaurri worsened after the president failed to receive a prompt response and learned that Vidaurri was failing to follow orders from central command.[12] To end Vidaurri's treacherous actions Juárez solicited the aid of Juan Cortina, a popular figure who commanded the loyalty of Mexicans along both sides of the Texas-Mexico border. In late 1863 Juárez repealed Vidaurri's appointment and replaced him with Cortina as commander of the North (Thompson 2000: 74; Thompson 1996: 344). On November 2, 1863, Cortina began the process of terminating Vidaurri's hold over the border. With the aide of Union soldiers, Cortina entered U.S. territory and took control of the South Texas towns where Confederate cargo was passing through on its way to Mexico. Of strategic importance was the town of Brownsville, through which cargo was shipped to the port of Tamaulipas (Marten 1990: 123–125; Thompson 2000: 43). Once most of South Texas was under Union control Vidaurri's influence declined in the region, and Cortina was eventually able to force Vidaurri to leave North Mexico.

With the fall of the Texas border into Union hands, things worsened for *the* Confederacy. Losing control of the border had been preceded by a series of disastrous setbacks as, in the summer of 1863, the Confederacy had lost the battles of Vicksburg and Gettysburg (Mahoney and Mahoney 1998: 76; Schoonover 1991: 139).

Mexican Tejanos in the Civil War

During the Civil War approximately 9,950 soldiers of Mexican descent served in the Confederate and Union armies throughout the United States (Thompson 2000: 5). Most of these soldiers supported the Union, and over 40 percent of the troops came from New Mexico. In Texas, largely as a result of the Confederate conscription laws, the pattern seen in New Mexico was reversed. In Texas a total of 2,550 soldiers of Mexican descent were registered in the Confederate forces, and 958 in the Union (Marten 1990: 75; Thompson 2000: 84). Although in Texas more Mexicans fought on the side of the Confederacy, of the total number of Texans who joined the Union forces 44 percent (958 out of 2,164) were Mexican (Marten 1990: 75–77; Thompson 2000: 81).

Most Mexican communities in Texas tried to remain neutral, however. In South Texas many town officials refused both to obey conscription laws when they were ordered and to organize committees to force men into action. Although the Confederate military was aware of these flagrantly disloyal actions, the town officials were not placed under arrest. The Confederate administration ordered that Mexican communities failing to comply be left alone, as placing towns under martial orders would potentially spark rebellions and lead Mexicans to ask for Union support (Richardson, Anderson, and Wallace 1997).

Archduke Ferdinand Maximilian and the Closure of the Wars

By 1864 Juárez and Lincoln saw the course of their nation's war going in different directions. While the Union was nearing victory, the Juarista troops were losing control of most major cities. By then Napoleon felt sure that France could win the war and terminate Juárez's constitutional government. With the help of Mexican conservatives he attempted to bring legitimacy to his rule by holding a plebiscite election to end constitutional rule in Mexico and install a regency government. In April 1864 the Mexican ruling class voted to convert Mexico into a monarchy and invite one of France's political allies to be emperor of Mexico (Vázquez and Meyer 1985: 70). A Mexican junta then chose to invite Archduke Ferdinand Maximilian of Austria to be the emperor of Mexico. By inviting the archduke, France was released from paying the costs of the Mexican invasion, which had become a serious political problem for Napoleon. At home the masses had begun to rebel against financing Napoleon's wars in Mexico and across the old world. The archduke's appointment allowed Napoleon to defray costs and place a puppet emperor under his control.

Archduke Maximilian accepted the offer and received immediate approval from the Catholic Church in Rome, France, Austria, Belgium, Holland, Portugal, Prussia, Russia, Spain, and Switzerland; he was granted unofficial approval by Great Britain. Brazil was the only Latin American country that recognized the puppet government, as it too was under French-Austrian control, ruled by Maximilian's cousin Emperor Dom Pedro III (Duncan 1996: 36). The U.S. Congress regarded the appointment of Maximilian as an open violation of the Monroe Doctrine. The majority of the Congress was prepared to send troops into Mexico but was blocked by the executive branch. Secretary Seward advised President Lincoln to not take action until the Civil War was over. The Congress nevertheless voted to officially recognize President Juárez as Mexico's legitimate president and continued to pressure Lincoln to provide assistance to Mexico. Without compromising U.S. troops, Lincoln sent aid to Mexico by allowing arms and ammunition to flow freely across the border. He also withheld diplomatic recognition of Maximilian's government.

Within months of his arrival in Mexico Maximilian tried to gain the support of both the Union and the Confederacy. He was aware of the Union's impending victory and knew it was necessary to convince Seward to not enforce the Monroe Doctrine. His aides appealed to the secretary, arguing that it was in Mexico's best interest to be governed by a foreign nation. Allegedly only strong monarchical rule could end Mexico's regional factionalism, which, according to Maximilian's envoys, was the primary cause of Mexico's financial troubles. Seward, convinced by this argument, advised Lincoln against supporting Congress's pro-Juárez stance on Mexico. The Confederacy, on the other hand, formally recognized Maximilian and unrealistically expected formal recognition in return (Mahoney and Mahoney 1998:63).

Congress refused to accept Seward's policy of inaction and demanded that Lincoln intervene. Furthermore, as the impending victory of the Union drew closer, editorials increasingly appeared in U.S. newspapers urging the president to enforce the Monroe Doctrine. With Seward refusing to intervene, American supporters of President Juárez took their case to the public. Among them was Gen. Ulysses Grant, who was a close personal friend of Matías Romero. General Grant, being a popular war hero, carried significant political clout in Congress and within social circles in Washington. In support of Congress Grant charged that Seward's inaction was placing the future stability of the United States in peril. According to Grant, if the French were not expelled from Mexico, a second U.S. civil war would soon follow, as Archduke Maximilian was a proven Confederate ally. Allegedly the archduke and Confederate officials were already making plans to renew the war after the South surrendered. Maximilian had allowed hundreds of Confederate refugees to settle in Mexico, and they were in the process of establishing a command center. Unless Mexico's constitutional government was restored, Grant added, the United States would not see peace for many years. Grant's forceful support of Congress reached the news media and spread throughout the country, leading many newspaper editors to expect Lincoln to take immediate action. On April 15, 1865, all hopes for intervention ceased when Lincoln was assassinated (Mahoney and Mahoney 1998: 79). After Lincoln's death, Seward remained in control of foreign affairs, and he advised incoming president Andrew Johnson to not enforce the Monroe Doctrine (Schoonover 1991).

To everyone's surprise, less than two months after Lincoln's assassination Juarista troops made several unexpected advances. Newspapers across the country reported that the course of the war had changed in Mexico's favor. Editorials criticized President Johnson's disgraceful policy toward Mexico, charging that the Union could have sent military aid since most Confederate generals had signed cease-fire agreements by late June 1865. News articles also predicted that the archduke's armies would suffer further devastating defeats because Napoleon was planning to withdraw most of his troops from Mexico. Napoleon had to reposition them in Prussia, where troops were needed to avert losing a more important war.

Within a year of Juárez's military triumph and without the assistance of the U.S. government, Juarista troops led by General Mariano Escobedo retook control of northern Mexico and of most cities in the central region. Juárez's advances elated the U.S. Congress and led many congressmen to publicly censure Johnson for failing to assist Mexico. Johnson had tarnished the reputation of the United States and Congress wanted to let the international world know that they had never been in support of Maximilian (Mahoney and Mahoney 1998). Johnson tried to save face and immediately rescinded his neutrality proclamation. He also ordered that several shipments of arms be sent to Juárez and that a volunteer army be deployed to Mexico (Schoonover 1991).

In February 1867 Juarista troops under the command of Gen. Porfirio Díaz took control of Mexico City, where Maximilian's central command was located. Maximilian was forced to retreat (Scholes 1957: 117). Napoleon immediately advised the archduke to abdicate and leave Mexico, but he refused to surrender and two months later was captured and executed.

On July 16, 1867, President Juárez triumphantly entered Mexico City on horseback and restored Mexico's constitutional government. He immediately brought order to the country and began the process of rebuilding Mexico's finances, which had been left in ruins by Maximilian and Napoleon. To do so he reached out to his new American allies and began an era of warm diplomatic relations.

U.S. Liberal Racial Legislation in the Aftermath of the Civil War

A period of friendly U.S.-Mexico relations followed in the aftermath of the American Civil War. Mexico and the United States were prepared to negotiate unresolved issues stemming from the Mexican-American War. Both countries wanted to bring closure to the bad feelings caused by the war of 1848 and begin a new era in which diplomatic relations would regulate binational commerce and bring order to the movement of people crossing the border. Before any agreements could be reached, however, the presidents of both countries needed to settle domestic problems.

After the expulsion of the French, Juárez enjoyed overwhelming popular support. He was reelected to the presidency in December 1867 and again in 1871 (Scholes 1957: 149). While in office Juárez enforced the Laws of the Reforma and with the help of Congress obtained the power to veto legislation passed by the states. Juárez's main political agenda, however, was to modernize Mexico. To enact these plans the government needed money to build schools and introduce capitalist development. Juárez's plans were highly dependent upon developing close commercial ties with countries that had supported Mexico during the invasion, such as the United States, Italy, and Latin America (See *Derecho Internacional Mexicano*, vol. 1, 1877; Duncan 1996). The United States played a central role in these plans since Mexico needed to replace Great Britain as its main trading partner. Despite Great Britain's wealth, Mexico distrusted the British government and no longer wished to maintain the same level of trade. Juárez was suspicious of Great Britain because it was well known that the government had covertly supported France (Vázquez and Meyer 1985).

While Mexico was engaged in formulating its development plans, the U.S. government was in the midst of a horrific battle to unify the country, and international negotiations with Mexico had to wait. The majority in Congress favored extending African Americans some political rights and punishing the South. President Johnson, however, disagreed. Johnson favored a quick restoration of all rights and privileges to the Confederate states, whereas Congress did not, fearing the immediate restoration of power would impede or completely obstruct the passing of federal legislation to improve the political rights of African Americans (Gillette 1969). The core of the problem lay with Johnson's political views of African Americans: he believed they should remain an impoverished underclass without the right of suffrage. If his policy was to have any chance of succeeding it was necessary for the Confederate legislatures to regain full authority and be able to pass black codes.

It was not until the election of April 1866 that Congress was able to take political action to counter Johnson's agenda. That year voters elected congressmen who favored keeping the Confederate states under military control and giving blacks some political rights (Gillette 1969). Although Johnson vetoed most Republican resolutions, Congress was able to override the vetoes and pass resolutions to retain control of the Confederate states. Of central importance to the cause was the passage of the Military Reconstruction Acts and the Command of the Army Act. Most important of all, Congress was able to stop President Johnson from closing the Freedman Bureau (Richardson, Anderson, and Wallace 1997), which was essential in protecting the lives of emancipated blacks in the Confederate states.

The most important legislation that Congress passed over the objections of President Johnson was the Fourteenth Amendment Act. Congress passed it on June 13, 1866 (14 *U.S. Statutes at Large* 358).[13] The act was specifically designed to amend the U.S. Constitution and establish a legal procedure whereby African Americans could become citizens and voters. The majority of Congress considered this legislation critical to weakening the full impact of the discriminatory black codes. Basically, if ratified by the states, the Fourteenth Amendment would create a uniform citizenship law that gave all people born or naturalized in the United States citizenship in the country. This policy would create the infrastructure for black people to defend themselves. Once they became citizens they would be eligible to vote and run for office. The amendment would also clarify what the government meant by citizenship, an issue that had remained vague in the U.S. Constitution (Keyssar 2000). The amendment stipulated that a citizen of the United States was also a citizen of the states. The Confederate states, therefore, would be unable to argue that blacks had been made citizens of the nation, but not citizens of their states.

While the Fourteenth Amendment was deliberated by the state legislatures, Congress imposed strict requirements on the Confederate states to be readmitted by enforcing the Military Act (Richardson, Anderson, and Wallace 1997). The act required the rebel states to ratify the Fourteenth Amendment before they were readmitted with full congressional representation. Until then, the states would remain under military control. On July 28, 1868, the Congress gained enough votes to ratify the Fourteenth Amendment. The Confederate states of Tennessee, Alabama, South Carolina, North Carolina, Georgia, West Virginia, Arkansas, Florida, and Louisiana ratified the amendment (15 *U.S. Statutes at Large* 710). Texas refused.

Texas remained under military control because the legislature refused to ratify. Moreover, under the Military Act Congress had the right to remove the governor of Texas and the state officials. President Johnson had no option but to enforce the congressional mandate when he was pressured to appoint a new provisional governor. With the ratification of the Fourteenth Amendment Congress could now turn to other pressing issues and commence negotiations with Mexico.

The Naturalization Treaty of 1868

In 1868 the presidents of the United States and Mexico commissioned Seward and Romero, now the minister plenipotentiary of foreign relations (Miller 1965), to commence binational talks to strengthen relations and settle disagreements. They were to negotiate treaties and contracts concerning property claims, commerce, and the border. They were also charged with clarifying international naturalization laws, as neither country had as yet negotiated a treaty to determine the political rights of immigrants.

On July 4, 1868, the first session of the Reclamation Convention was held, and the opening order of business was to investigate citizen complaints associated with the Mexican-American War. The convention began with a preamble that stated, "Whereas it is desirable to maintain and increase the friendly feelings between the United States and the Mexican Republic, and so strengthen the system and principles of Republican Government on the American Continent . . ." (Convention between the United States and Mexico to determine the citizenship of immigrants of both countries, in Derecho Internacional Mexicano, vol. 1, 1877: 297).[14] The convention opened with Romero and Seward agreeing that citizens of both nations had lost economic resources during the war, and it was necessary for their governments to make reparations. They agreed to establish a binational reclamation commission to oversee the claims and establish an award process. A Reclamation Commission was constituted and mandated to investigate all complaints. As the talks proceeded it became obvious that Mexico was at a disadvantage. Seward demanded that all Americans who had lost their investments in Mexico during the war be compensated. He refused to compensate Mexicans for the land they had lost when the U.S. government acquired Mexican territory. He also refused to allow any of the Spanish or Mexican land grant claims to be litigated through the commission. This was an affair only the U.S. Congress could address. Romero recognized the unfairness of the deal, but he was willing to accept the conditions (Romero 1889; Schoonover 1991: 228). If he refused to concede, Romero predicted, the U.S. government would advise businessmen not to invest in Mexico. By accepting Seward's terms Romero believed the U.S. government would declare Mexico a solvent country, a country where foreign investments were secure. This was critical for Mexico if the Juarista government was to obtain the funds to modernize the economy and undo the damage the French had done. Most important, the talks needed to proceed since other pressing matters had to be negotiated. The land grant claims were therefore sacrificed for the good of the nation. The convention ended with the signing of the Reclamation Treaty of 1868, which outlined the grievance and award process.

Although Romero acknowledged that the Reclamation Treaty would leave Mexico in greater debt than it was in before the talks began, he had gained the confidence of the United States and was now able to address the next order of business President Juárez had commissioned him to negotiate. He was to conclude a treaty whereby Mexican immigrants obtained the right to apply for U.S. citizenship. This was a sensitive matter since U.S. law allowed only whites to apply for naturalization, and most Mexicans were people of color (see Naturalization Act of 1802, in 2 *U.S. Statutes at Large* 153).

A few days after the Reclamation Convention, Romero and Seward reconvened to negotiate a naturalization treaty. They met on July 10, 1868, and agreed in the Convention with Mexico that the immigrants of their respective countries had the political right to renounce their citizenship of origin and acquire the citizenship of their new country by naturalization. This was a major accomplishment for Mexico. Romero had changed a tradition that dated back to 1790 (Naturalization Act of 1790, in 1 *U.S. Statutes at Large* 103). By treaty, Mexicans had now become the only nonwhite immigrant group to be allowed to apply for U.S. citizenship. The agreement between Romero and Seward ended with the signing of the Naturalization Treaty of 1868, which proclaimed in its preamble,

> The President of the United States of America and the President of the Republic of Mexico, being desirous of regulating citizenship of persons who emigrate from Mexico to the United States of America, and from the Republic of Mexico have decided to treat on this subject, and with this object have named as plenipotentiaries, the President of the United States, William H. Seward, Secretary of State; and the President of Mexico Matías Romero, accredited as envoy extraordinary and minister plenipotentiary of the republic of Mexico near the government of the United States; who, after having communicated to each other their respective full powers, found in good and due form, have agreed upon the following articles . . . (Naturalization Treaty of 1868, in 15 *U.S. Statutes at Large* 687)

In article 1 the treaty stipulated that U.S. and Mexican citizens had the right to change their citizenship allegiance through naturalization. Article 2 stipulated the process. Article 3 stipulated that immigrants and naturalized citizens could be extradited to their country of origin if they had committed crimes in their home country. And article 4 allowed immigrants to renounce their naturalized citizenship if they planned to resume permanent residence in their country of origin; it also outlined the process for doing so.

In the treaty, Seward did not append any articles or language excluding Mexicans of color from the naturalization process. The treaty thus did not exclude Mexicans on the basis of race and was consistent with the spirit of the times, in particular with the Fourteenth Amendment. President Juárez ratified the treaty on December 28, 1868, and President Johnson on February 1, 1869. In sum, the treaty became part of the liberal racial legislation adopted by the U.S. federal government. Five months later, the U.S. Congress passed another liberal naturalization law, extending to black immigrants the political right to naturalize in the United States (16 *U.S. Statutes at Large* 256). Mexican and black immigrants became the only populations of color who were exempt from the racially discriminatory naturalization laws of the United States.

After the ratification of the Naturalization Treaty the Mexican Congress convened to deliberate how to execute the economic agreements made with the U.S. government. Romero presented a plan already endorsed by President Juárez and his cabinet. At first, the Congress, yielding to strong opposition from the states, rejected the plan. Most congressmen did not support

Romero's proposal because the main beneficiaries would be the Mexican federal government and American investors, with few benefits given to the states. The congressmen acknowledged that it was necessary to create generous incentives to attract foreign investors, but it was not necessary to give the federal government all the gains when the resources were to be taken from the states. In 1872 the Mexican Congress finally endorsed Romero's economic plan on the premise that U.S. corporations were projected to create local employment and reduce the states' unemployment rates. That year Mexico agreed to lease land to U.S. corporations for the purpose of extracting silver, gold, and other minerals. The corporations were to pay the federal government an annual fee of three hundred thousand pesos per mine (Scholes 1957: 170). The government was also to receive 5 percent of the mines' profits and was to levy taxes of 1 percent of the worth of the gold exported and of 8 percent on the silver. Except for the Federal District (Mexico City) and the state of Baja California, a state government could not levy a state tax. Instead, the federal government would share 5 percent of the tax revenues with the states.

In the end, this plan was disastrous for the states and the Mexican people. The vision of President Juárez and his administration was to share the profits with the states by using the funds to develop local economies. Unfortunately, Juárez was forced to step down from the presidency after suffering a heart attack. He died on July 19, 1872 (Scholes 1957: 176). The new administration had a different attitude toward the masses, preferring to invest in the cities, where the elites resided. Those who followed him betrayed Juárez's vision, and they used the infrastructure negotiated by Romero to establish a class structure in which the upper class depended on U.S. foreign investments to maintain their lives of privilege. This stimulated Mexican immigration to the United States and sparked among the immigrants a desire to change their nationality, an act the Naturalization Treaty allowed them to do. The exodus of the Mexican population was soon to begin on a grand scale.

Furthermore, when Mexico and the U.S. government began their negotiation of the land reclamation complaints Mexico was left in a weak bargaining position. Mexican members of the Reclamation Commission had to act with caution so as not to anger the U.S. representatives. The commission examined 2,075 claims, of which 1,017 were from the United States and 998 from Mexico (Vázquez and Meyer 1985: 74). Of these claims, 186 were upheld for the United States and 167 for Mexico. The Catholic archdiocese of California initiated the most controversial case, claiming that the Mexican government had illegally seized Church property and sold it at the outbreak of the Mexican-American War. Attorneys for the Mexican government countered that the property belonged to the Indians, not to the Church. The commission disagreed and awarded the archdiocese of California nearly one million dollars. At the conclusion of the hearings Mexico ended up paying out much more money than the United States even though most property damage had occurred in Mexico. Not only was Mexico left in greater debt, but Mexican Americans and Mexicans who lived along the border were not compensated for the territory they had lost. The U.S. Congress was not forced to pay for the land it had acquired and resold or granted to U.S. citizens. In total, Mexico paid $4,125,622.20 and the United States $150,498.42 (Ibid., 74–75). A paternalistic economic pattern had begun.

CHAPTER 2

The Politics of Naturalization Policy in Texas: The Case of Mexican Immigrants

In this chapter I examine the naturalization history of the Mexican-origin population in Texas from 1848 to 1892. I explore the social and political events that prompted Mexican immigrants to migrate to the United States and also consider how Mexicans were received in Texas, arguing that the political atmosphere of the period influenced whether they were granted or denied U.S. citizenship. During the U.S. Civil War and in the first years of Reconstruction Mexican immigrants were granted citizenship at an astonishing rate, a phenomenon that was not replicated at any time in the nineteenth and early twentieth centuries.

The First Naturalized Mexicans

Before the passage of the Naturalization Treaty of 1868 very few Mexican immigrants applied for U.S. citizenship, most likely because naturalization law clearly stipulated that citizenship was restricted to whites (Naturalization Act 1790). Nonetheless, there were a few Mexican applicants. From the end of the Mexican-American War in 1848 up to 1859, 21 Mexicans applied for U.S. citizenship. In 1848 Henry Voelcker became the first Mexican applicant (Index to Naturalization Records Found in Texas State, District and County Courts, 1846–1939, roll 1).[1] His case is quite different from those of other Mexicans because he was born in Germany. Voelcker filed his papers in the San Antonio District Court of Bexar County and was granted citizenship four years later (Bexar County Court, 4th Civil Minute Book B, p. 359). At first, Voelcker's petition was blocked because the county clerk questioned his eligibility, citing a problem with his nationality. Consequently, Voelcker was required to appear before a judge and explain why he was applying as a Mexican citizen when he had been born in Germany. Apparently Voelcker was a German immigrant who, before moving to the United States, had immigrated to Mexico and settled in the state of Tamaulipas. Although the court records do not explain why he settled in Tamaulipas, it is likely he was affiliated with one of the German colonies the Mexican government had recruited to settle in Mexico. In 1831, at the time of Voelcker's migration to Mexico, many provinces in Germany were undergoing severe economic hardships and concerned nobles sponsored philanthropic overseas voyages to resettle their tenants in the New World (Biesele 1987: iv). When the Mexican government made land available for colonization in north Mexico, German nobles took advantage of the opportunity to dispatch their tenants and thereby reduce the number of people dependent on their estates. When German immigrants arrived in Mexico, however, they had to naturalize to obtain land.

Regardless of whether or not a nobleman sponsored his journey, Voelcker, according to court records, remained in Tamaulipas until the outbreak of the Mexican-American War in 1846, at which time he moved to Texas and settled in a small northern town called Palo Pinto. Two years later he moved again and settled in a large German town called New Braunfels in Comal County, which was located in central Texas, next to Bexar County. New Braunfels was founded in the early 1840s as part of a settlement program initiated by the Republic of Texas. To attract white settlers to Texas the republican government granted land or sold it cheaply (see Act of 1839, in *Laws of Texas*, 2:35–36; Act of 1841, in ibid., p. 554). Such land policies attracted thousands of impoverished German immigrants who, upon arriving in Texas, commonly chose to live near their compatriots, and established several colonies in central Texas. New Braunfels became one of the largest and most important German settlements (Jordan 1982). After the Mexican-American War, the economy of New Braunfels prospered, and its stability attracted many German immigrants, including Henry Voelcker. Voelcker finally applied for U.S. citizenship in 1848, but, as noted, he had to apply as a Mexican citizen because during his temporary stay in Mexico he had naturalized and become a Mexican citizen (Bexar County Naturalization Papers, 1851–1859, book A).

One year after Voelcker sought U.S. citizenship, Christophe Metz applied in the County Court of Gonzales (TNR, roll 7), but was not granted citizenship. Very little information is available in Christophe's case since he was not asked to appear before a judge. We know only that Metz's surname is a common one in Germany and France and that in 1855 he reapplied but once again was denied citizenship. Generally, naturalization records leave detailed information about an applicant only when the clerk notes some problem and refers the case to a judge or when a file was expedited. Most naturalization records contain only copies of the application and, when citizenship was granted, a copy of the certificate verifying it. These forms provide limited information and at most note a person's place of birth and date of entry into the United States, the citizenship the applicant is renouncing, the name of the sheriff or deputy who acted as witness, and the name of the judge or clerk who processed the petition. Similar information is contained in the final certificate, except that the papers were solely issued and signed by a judge. It is rare for the forms to note a person's occupation, but some do since there were no standard forms during the nineteenth century. Each county in Texas also prepared a master index of all petitions and noted their disposition and history.

Olgin Maximiano was the third Mexican to apply for naturalization but the first applicant whose surname was Spanish. Olgin applied in 1852 in Bexar County and was granted citizenship five years later (TNR, roll 1). Unfortunately, I could not locate his records. During the 1850s, the number of applications by Mexicans were few, yet the number of counties processing applications increased considerably. By 1859 Bexar, Cameron, Webb, Medina, Nueces, and Uvalde counties had processed 19 applications, and 8 Mexicans successfully completed the process (table 2.1, 2.2). In other words, 42 percent of applications were granted (Nueces County Declarations 1852–1906; TNR, rolls 1–4, 8, 9, 10). Yet the successful applicants did not all have Spanish surnames. Among the applicants was Franc Ytawvia, whose surname was also of German origin. As time passed, the number of applicants with no Spanish surname was small. Generally, in each decade of the nineteenth century fewer than 10 Mexican petitioners had no Spanish surname. Nonetheless, last names such as Perry, Perris, Bason, Harambourne, Quiros, Gross, and Ferrino did occasionally appear throughout the nineteenth century.

In the 1860s the number of applications increased, and with the exception of 3 petitioners the Mexican applicants had traditional Spanish surnames like Garcia, Rodriguez, and Hernandez. During this decade a total of 273 applications were filed, and 243 of these, or 89 percent, were granted. Although in the 1860s there were many applications in comparison to the previous decade, nearly all these petitions were filed in two years in particular, 1862 and 1869, and were associated with important events surrounding the politics of the American Civil War and its aftermath. At this time the number of counties processing applications also increased significantly.

Table 2.1. Counties Processing Naturalization Certificates from Mexicans, 1848–1869

1848:	Bexar	1860s:	Bee
	Gonzales		Bexar
1850s:	Bexar		Cameron
	Cameron		Guadalupe
	Medina		Nueces
	Nueces		Robertson
	Uvalde		Starr
	Webb		Uvalde
			Webb
			Zapata
			Austin Federal Court
			Brownsville Federal Court

Source: Index to Naturalization Records found in Texas State District and County Courts, 1846–1939, rolls 1 to 10; General Courts Austin, Brownsville, El Paso, Galveston, San Antonio, Jefferson, Texarkana, Tyler, Waco.

Table 2.2. Overview of Mexican Immigrant Naturalization Applications and Success Rate, 1848–1889[a]

Date	Total Applied	Granted	Percentage Granted
1848–1849	2	0	0
1850–1859	19	8	42.00%
1860–1869	273	243	89.00%
1870–1879	4,952	37	.75%
1880–1889	8,469	17	.02%

[a]From 1848 to 1906, ninety-three applications have incomplete nineteenth-century dates. These applications were not included in the decade analysis. Only one of these applications was granted.

Sources: Index to Naturalization Records found in Texas State, District, and County Courts, 1846–1939, rolls 1 to 10; General Courts Austin, Brownsville, Galveston, San Antonio, Jefferson, Texarkana, Tyler, Waco; Nueces County Declarations; Southern District a; Southern District b; Webb County Declarations, vols. 1-3; Webb County Declarations, vols. 4–6, 1895–1900.

Naturalization During the Civil War and Reconstruction

The first surge of petitions occurred during the Civil War, on June 22, 1862. One hundred and two Mexicans applied in Starr County, and 101 were granted citizenship.[2] It is uncertain if the Confederacy or the U.S. government processed these applications, as copies of the certificates have been lost, and only the county clerk's index remains. The index contains information on the name of the applicants, their country of citizenship, the date the applications were filed, the name of the court where the applications were filed and granted, and the number of times an applicant appeared in front of a clerk or judge. As a means of obtaining information on the applicants I researched their names and found that many had served in the armed forces of both the Union and Confederacy (Marten 1990; Thompson 2000). I also found that when the applicants received their citizenship papers the Starr County Courthouse, where the applicants applied, was under Confederate control (Scott 1935). A Confederate county or district clerk, therefore, must have processed the certificates.

Civil War records corroborate this information. On June 17, 1862, five days before the citizenship certificates were issued, Noah Cox, the district clerk and Confederate sympathizer, formed a home guard volunteer army in Starr County (Election Registers 1860–1865) (Thompson 2000: 18). The company was composed of 100 men from Starr County, most being residents of the town of Roma. The men were subsequently transferred to Company F of the 12th Texas Cavalry.

The fact that some of the men whose names appear in Starr County's naturalization records are also found in Union soldier rolls does not invalidate the point that these men were given citizenship by a Confederate government. For example, in Texas during the outbreak of the Civil War many Mexican soldiers fought for the Confederacy and toward the midpoint of the war defected to the Union. The turning point came in 1863, when Juan Cortina, general commander of north Mexico, crossed the Texas-Mexico border to render military support to Union forces. It became widely publicized that at this time most Mexican Confederates defected and joined Cortina's troops (Scott 1935: 102–106; Thompson 2000: 87–89). Cortina, though he was a Mexican general, was highly regarded in South Texas and was considered a folk hero. Earlier, Cortina had lived in South Texas but was forced to leave when the Texas Rangers accused him of starting an insurrection movement. The incident came to be known as the Cortina Wars, and the charges raised by the lawmen were viewed by most Mexicans of South Texas as an abuse of power. Thus, when Cortina rode into South

Texas, Mexicans remembered him and fought on his side. Together, Cortina and his supporters captured many towns along the border, including Rio Grande City, where the Starr County Courthouse stood. The military takeover of Rio Grande City by Cortina helps to explain why some of the Mexicans whose names appear in the Starr County naturalization index are registered as both Confederate and Union soldiers.

In any case, regardless of the fact that the applicants most likely were granted citizenship by the Confederacy, it is certain that the U.S. government validated their naturalization papers. On July 14, 1870, the U.S. Congress decreed that all naturalization proceedings conducted during the Civil War and processed by courts of the United States were legal (16 *U.S. Statutes at Large* 255).[3] At the state level a similar act was passed after the Texas legislature regained its right to govern Texas. In 1870, the Texas legislature validated all laws and acts of government passed by the Confederacy as long as U.S. law had not been violated (Richardson, Anderson, and Wallace 1997: 226). By this act of the legislature the naturalization transactions that had occurred during the Confederate period, including those from Starr County, were legalized,

In 1869, during Reconstruction, the number of petitions filed by Mexicans once again surged and was associated with political events. At this time Texans were petitioning the U.S. Congress to reseat their congressmen and to end military control of the state government (Ramsdell 1970). The events that led the surge are thus embroiled in Reconstruction politics. As I discussed in chapter 1, when the Texas legislature failed to ratify the Fourteenth Amendment the state government was disbanded, and Texas was placed under military governance. This did not adversely affect Mexicans, as under Union control they did well politically. The federal government ratified the Naturalization Treaty of 1868, and at the state level the military commander appointed Union officials to run the government, including the judges who oversaw the naturalization petitions (Campbell 1992: 80; Nunn 1962: 28). Placing the courts under Union control benefited Mexicans in that their naturalization applications were favorably acted upon. In 1869 nearly all of the applications submitted by Mexican immigrants were accepted, a practice that was never again replicated. One hundred and forty-one applications were submitted and 134 were accepted, a 95 percent acceptance rate (TNR, rolls 2, 8). Most of the applications were granted on the eve of the November gubernatorial race of 1869 and are associated with the Texas legislature's attempt to restore its governance

In 1868 the U.S. Congress allowed Texans to begin the restoration of their state government (Ramsdell 1970). The expelled Texas congressmen assured the federal government that Texans were prepared to ratify the Fourteenth Amendment and abide by the laws of Reconstruction. They also promised Congress that African Americans would be allowed to participate in the Reconstruction Convention, to be held in two sessions beginning on June 1, 1868 (Winkler 1916: 107). The Congress instructed Gen. W. S. Hancock, the military commander, to organize an election and allow delegates to be chosen for the convention. Of the ninety elected delegates thirteen were African Americans and none were Mexican (Nunn 1962: 23).[4] At the convention the delegates were to determine the procedures enacted to run the government, revise the Texas constitutional suffrage amendment so that the Fourteenth Amendment could be ratified, deliberate on the question of whether Texas should be divided into separate states, and establish procedures to elect future government officials.

During the first session the delegates could not agree on how to revise the suffrage amendment and chose to table it until other issues of government were discussed. The delegates were divided on the type of suffrage African Americans would be given. Democratic delegates represented the sentiments of most ex-Confederates, whereas the Republican delegates represented African Americans, those in favor of ending military rule, and former Union sympathizers. The Republicans, however, were divided into Radicals and Conservatives. The Conservatives shared many of the views of the Democrats and were not in favor of extending universal suffrage to African Americans or of incorporating them as equals.

The first session of the convention explored dividing Texas into three states. One heated debate proposed making South Texas a separate state since the region was culturally different from the rest of the state. The plan was voted on and rejected. During the second session the suffrage question was finally addressed. On February 18, 1869, the delegates agreed to ratify the Fourteenth Amendment (Ramsdell 1970: 254), but they disagreed on the type of voting rights African Americans should be given. Democratic delegates proposed excluding black voters from the primaries as well as from special elections. Likewise, many delegates favored prohibiting immigrants from voting (Richardson, Anderson, and Wallace 1997: 227). Since 1845 the Texas constitution had allowed immigrants to vote as long as they were white and had filed a naturalization petition. The delegates finally reached a compromise and revised article 6 of the state constitution, which delineated who had the right to vote in Texas. The delegates removed the white racial prerequisite and extended suffrage to all male citizens of the United States aged twenty-one and over, including immigrants who had filed a naturalization petition (Texas Constitution, Article 6, in *Laws of Texas*, 7:23).

Once this issue was resolved, it was time to hold a general election and allow people to accept or reject the resolutions. If the voters accepted the delegates' resolutions the state government would be restored. In anticipation that the resolutions would pass, the military commander also allowed voters to elect a governor.

On November 30, 1869, a heated gubernatorial election ensued (Ramsdell 1970: 283). Most Texans thought the only candidates that realistically could be elected were Republicans since the Democratic candidate did not support the passage of the Fourteenth Amendment. Voters knew Congress would not end military rule if a Democrat was elected. Therefore, the voters' choices were A. J. Hamilton, a conservative Republican, or E. J. Davis, a radical Republican.

In South Texas, a week prior to the election, many Mexican immigrants filed naturalization petitions in Cameron and Nueces counties. Most of the applications in 1869 were submitted at this time, and approval of a petition allowed an applicant to vote. Between November 19 and November 26, 1869, 118 Mexicans filed naturalization papers in Cameron County (TNR, roll 2), and of these, 113 were granted citizenship that day.[5] Oddly, the applicants were issued their citizenship papers on the same day they filed and were not required to wait two years, as naturalization law required.[6] Generally, the residential requirement was waived only when a person had resided in the United States from childhood. In other South Texas counties, 18 Mexicans submitted petitions during that same week, and nearly all were given citizenship the same day they filed. Of these petitions, 16 were filed in Nueces County (TNR, roll 8).

The gubernatorial election was very close, and the candidates accused each other of voter fraud. Hamilton charged that Davis's followers prevented many Hamilton supporters from voting and stuffed ballot boxes with Davis ballots. Hamilton also accused some election officers of being crooked and not holding elections in some counties where the voters favored Hamilton. As a result of these accusations the military commander took control of the ballot boxes and did not release the election results until a month later. On January 8, 1870, the election returns were finally certified: Texans had overwhelmingly voted in favor of ratifying the Fourteenth Amendment and extending suffrage to African Americans, but they were evenly divided on the gubernatorial election. Davis, the radical Republican, won by a slim majority. The returns indicated that Davis had received 39,901 votes, Hamilton 39,092, and Stuart, the Democratic candidate, 380 (Ramsdell 1970: 286).

Mexicans, like other Texans, voted for a Republican, but they too were divided on the Republican candidates. The election returns in South Texas indicate that Davis won in Maverick, Medina, Presidio, and Atascosa counties, while Hamilton won in Live Oak, Nueces, Cameron, Hidalgo, Kinney, San Patricio, Starr, Uvalde, Webb, and Karnes (Kingston, Attlesey, and Crawford 1992: 58–61) (table 2.3). In the Texas counties with majority Mexican populations, such as El Paso and Presidio, Davis won by a large majority, and he also won in Bexar, where a large number of Mexicans resided.

On March 30, 1870, the U.S. Congress restored political representation in Texas and authorized the Texas legislature to govern the state (Richardson, Anderson, and Wallace 1997: 225). Nearly four months later military rule ended when the Congress received legislative reports proving that African Americans were allowed to vote in Texas and evidence was submitted that violence against African Americans was declining. Governor Davis assured Congress that Reconstruction policies were being enforced and that the military state police were protecting the freed population. At that time approximately 40 percent of the state police were African American. Davis also reported that he had reformed the judicial system (Campbell 1992) and that henceforth he personally would appoint all judges in Texas to ensure that they were sympathetic to Reconstruction laws. Furthermore, the governor said that the Texas legislature was in the process of abolishing the position of county judge to ensure that locals could not put pressure on the judges when they made decisions concerning African Americans. District judges would be assigned the duties of the county judge. During his term in office Governor Davis fulfilled his promise to Congress and appointed only former Union men to judgeships in all courts in Texas.

The End of Reconstruction in Texas: Elections, Judges, and Naturalization

Although Texans had complied with federal law, the majority of whites resented the intrusion of the U.S. Congress into their political affairs. Once the power of the legislature was restored, white citizens demonstrated their animosity toward the federal government by turning against Republican elected officials and converting Texas into a one-party state run by Democrats, the former Confederates. Republican politicians were aware of this political reconfiguration, and many began to shift their political alliances. Republicans who were unwilling to change their liberal racial principles either had to end their political careers or move to states where Republicans could be elected to office (Scarborough 1972). Many Republicans, however, merely chose to become Democrats and abandoned their support of civil rights for African Americans. In 1872 Democrats took over the legislature, and voters elected four Democrats to Congress. African Americans steadfastly supported Republican state and congressional candidates, but they were continually outvoted. A year later a new governor, Richard Coke, was elected, and he not only opposed the civil rights African Americans had gained in Texas, but also disapproved of allowing them to participate in the electoral process. Given that most state offices were under Democratic control, the new governor had a legislature that was willing to end Reconstruction (Barr 2005). The Thirteenth Texas Legislature began repealing most of the laws passed during Reconstruction and terminated the state's commitment to protecting African Americans from violence. The legislature rescinded the Police Act, which had appointed many African Americans as state police, ended state funding for African American schools, and reinstated the right of former Confederate officers to run for office. Furthermore, Governor Coke, who, as noted, publicly opposed African American suffrage, refused to protect black voters during elections. In addition, he began replacing Davis's judicial appointees with conservative Democrats (Ibid., 429).

Not surprisingly, in the elections of the early 1870s in Texas nearly all African American voters opposed the Democratic candidates. Voters of Mexican origin, however, were divided. For example, in South Texas, where the Mexican-origin population was concentrated, voters were divided in their support for Democrats and Republicans (Kingston, Attlesey, and Crawford 1992: 58–61). In the gubernatorial election of 1873, Hidalgo, Kinney, Nueces, Webb, and Zavala counties remained Republican, whereas Cameron, El Paso, Frio, Karnes, Live Oak, Medina, San Patricio, and Uvalde overwhelmingly supported the Democratic candidate. Atascosa and Starr, two of the larger counties, remained evenly divided (see table 2.3). Bexar also became a Democratic stronghold.

By 1876, however, most Mexicans overwhelmingly voted Democrat. Only those in Medina County remained in the Republican camp (Ibid., 60). The Mexicans' voting behavior mirrored a pattern found throughout Texas. By the late seventies the Republicans' influence in the legislature had diminished substantially (Richardson, Wallace, and Anderson 1997: 243). Their constituencies were primarily limited to African Americans, some German immigrant communities, and former abolitionists (Martin 1970). In the Texas House of Representatives only seven Republicans out of the ninety-two members remained in office and three out of thirty-one in the Senate (Legislative Manual for the State of Texas 1879: 230–232). The few

Table 2.3. Voting Patterns for Democrats and Republicans in Counties with Majority or Large Mexican Populations, 1869, 1873, 1876[a]

| | General Elections | | | | | | | |
| | 1869 Const./Gubernatorial Race | | | 1873 Gubernatorial Race | | 1876 Gubernatorial Race | |
County	Hamilton	Davis	Dem	Dem	Rep	Dem	Rep
Atascosa	482	998	0	913	912	1,677	750
Bexar	590	924	0	1,832	1,234	2,552	1,104
Cameron	328	220	0	433	221	1,190	91
Dimmit	NO RETURNS						
Duval	NO RETURNS						
El Paso	122	336	0	447	46	628	19
Encinal	NO RETURNS						
Frio	—	—	—	69	13	158	9
Hidalgo	49	14	0	60	72	141	13

County							
Karnes	135	31	0	185	88	331	0
Kinney	15	0	0	94	114	203	25
La Salle	NO RETURNS						
Live Oak	83	1	0	115	13	262	3
McMullen	NO RETURNS						
Maverick	17	35	0	71	65	312	74
Medina	10	230	0	326	76	234	297
Nueces	413	227	0	199	313	1,007	181
Presidio	15	19	0	—	—	239	22
San Patricio	30	10	0	91	12	208	6
Starr	82	14	0	100	97	248	70
Uvalde	29	8	0	148	22	252	3
Webb	110	23	0	91	512	646	6
Zapata	NO RETURNS						
Zavala	—	—	—	49	62	132	2

[a] Counties not organized in South Texas at this time: Brooks, Willacy, Jim Hogg, Kenedy, Kleberg, Jim Wells.

Source: Kingston, Attlesey, and Crawford 1992.

Republican representatives came from districts in which the African American population constituted 50 percent to 74 percent of the total number of voters (Martin 1970: 92).

Besides the changes in the party affiliations of the members of the legislature, the court system was restructured when Democrats took over the state government. Governor Coke replaced the district and state judges with former Confederates, and the legislature passed several reforms. In 1876 the judicial districts were redrawn, and African American counties throughout Texas were appended to white majority counties. The redistricting created districts in which African American voters were in the minority and would have little influence in the election of their district judge (Barr 2005), a highly powerful position at the local level. The district judgeship was also converted from an appointed to an elective seat. District judges could retry cases or hear appeals from the lower courts, decide on legal matters involving monetary disputes of one hundred dollars or more, have original jurisdiction of criminal and divorce cases, hear all suits to recover damages for slander or defamation, hold all trials concerning title of land or liens, and handle all cases involving state matters, including the processing of naturalization petitions (*Laws of Texas*, 8:196). Not surprisingly, throughout the nineteenth century all district judges were Anglo-American males (Election Registers 1838–1972a; 1838–1972b). Three years later the legislature enacted another major change in the court system and nullified former governor Davis's mandate on county judges by reinstating the position of county judge (Richardson, Wallace, and Anderson 1997: 230). Again, this was an act that undid Reconstruction law, as radical Republicans had fought to abolish the position of county judge because they believed African Americans could not obtain justice in county courts. Once the office was reestablished, the county judge was limited to hearing civil cases and disputes involving one hundred dollars or less. The county courts were also empowered to process naturalization petitions, a political right allowed by the U.S. Congress.

Mexicans in South Texas were not as extensively affected by the redistricting as African Americans were, largely because they were concentrated in one region, and any redistricting plan would not reconfigure the ethnic makeup of the counties. Only the counties along the borders of South Texas were affected by the redistricting (map 2.1). For example, the South Texas counties of Frio, Uvalde, Kinney, Medina, and Maverick were appended to counties in central Texas to form District 24 (Burke 1879: 137–138).[7] Likewise, the South Texas counties of Karnes, Live Oak, San Patricio, and McMullen were appended to central and coastal counties to form District 23.[8]

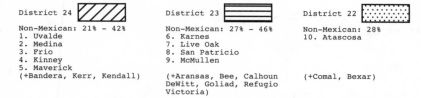

District 24	District 23	District 22
Non-Mexican: 21% - 42%	Non-Mexican: 27% - 46%	Non-Mexican: 28%
1. Uvalde	6. Karnes	10. Atascosa
2. Medina	7. Live Oak	
3. Frio	8. San Patricio	
4. Kinney	9. McMullen	
5. Maverick		
(+Bandera, Kerr, Kendall)	(+Aransas, Bee, Calhoun DeWitt, Goliad, Refugio Victoria)	(+Comal, Bexar)

Map 2.1. 1878: South Texas and Judicial Districts 22, 23, 24. U.S. Census 1872: 65, 372–373, for census population; Burke 1879: 135, for judicial districts; Arreola 2002: 38, and Gournay 1995: 95, for county boundaries.

Atascosa County in South Texas was adjoined to central Texas counties to form District 22.[9]

U.S. census data indicate that the counties that were redistricted and adjoined to regions outside of South Texas had large Anglo-American populations (table 2.4; cf. table 2.5). By the 1870s the borders of South Texas were populated by Mexicans, but also by European immigrants and settlers from the interior of the United States, of whom the majority were white. According to the U.S. Census of 1870, 33 percent to 42 percent of the residents of

Table 2.4. Non-Mexican Residents of South Texas, 1870

County	Population	Non-Mexican Foreign-Born	Born in U.S. Out of Texas[a]	Total No.	Total Percent
Karnes	1,705	240	540	780	46%
Kinney	1,204	39	464	503	42%
Live Oak	852	40	270	310	36%
Frio	309	7	101	118	38%
San Patricio	602	50	166	216	36%
Medina	2,078	665	177	842	41%
Uvalde	851	30	248	278	33%
McMullen	230	2	61	63	27%
Atascosa	2,915	72	747	819	28%
Nueces	3,975	396	622	1,018	26%
Zavala	133	0	32	32	24%
Maverick	1,951	59	345	404	21%
Dimmit	109	1	20	21	19%
LaSalle	69	1	11	12	17%
Cameron	10,999	706	676	1,382	13%
Starr	4,154	228	193	421	10%
Duval	1,083	52	53	105	10%
Webb	2,615	123	116	239	9%
Hidalgo	2,387	17	58	75	3%
Zapata	1,488	5	2	7	0.4%
Encinal	427	0	2	2	0.4%

[a]The census reported that those born in states other than Texas migrated from Alabama, Tennessee, Mississippi, Georgia, and Louisiana.
Source: U.S. Census 1872: 64–65, 372–373.

Kinney, Uvalde, and Medina were born either in Europe or in the southern states of Alabama, Tennessee, Mississippi, Georgia, and Louisiana (U.S. Census 1872: 64–65, 372–373). The same characteristics applied to 46 percent of the residents of Karnes, 36 percent of San Patricio, 36 percent of Live Oak, and 28 percent of Atascosa.

The judicial redistricting and its consequences for Mexicans are complicated issues and beyond the scope of this book. However, my research yielded two basic findings: all district judges elected to office in Texas during the nineteenth and early twentieth centuries were Anglo-American (Election Registers 1838–1872a; 1838–1872b); and the naturalization rate of the

Mexican immigrant population dropped substantially in most counties. The percentage of petitions granted fell from 89 percent in 1869 to .75 percent in 1879 (TNR, 1–10), a substantial drop-off (see table 2.2). Making matters worse, naturalization records indicate that 70 percent of the applications granted in the 1870s were processed before the changes in the court system took place (28 out of 37 applications were granted before 1877).[10]

The exact reason for the decline in the number of applications granted is uncertain, but one cannot ignore the historical context, which implies that redistricting and the reappointment of judges adversely affected the Mexican population. Moreover, the decrease cannot be attributed to a decline in the number of petitions, as Mexicans continued to apply in very large numbers. During the 1870s, 4,952 Mexican immigrants applied for naturalization (TNR, rolls 1–10). This was a radical increase from ten years earlier, an increase of nearly 1,714 percent.

In my review of records I found that after the Democratic takeover of the legislature District Judge Zacharia Norton in Robertson County was the only district judge who continued to approve petitions filed by Mexicans. He was the only Republican district judge who remained in office after Governor Coke replaced the district judges (Campbell 1992). In the 1870s Norton finalized the naturalization process of eight Mexican applicants and granted them citizenship (TNR, roll 8). This is not surprising since Norton's district was largely Republican and was approximately 74 percent African American (see Martin 1970). The race of the Mexican applicants was not noted, however.

Troubled Times for Mexican Immigrants Begin: California Disputes the Validity of the Naturalization Treaty of 1868

Besides the changes in the judicial system of Texas, two events in California shed light on why judges in Texas may have been hesitant to issue naturalization certificates to Mexicans. First, the California legislature refused to enforce the Naturalization Treaty of 1868 because it was the opinion of the legislators that unless Mexicans were white they were not citizens and thus ineligible to apply for citizenship. Attorneys for the state alleged that neither treaties nor the Fourteenth Amendment made Mexicans of Indian descent eligible for U.S. citizenship. Second, in 1870 in *People v. Pablo De La Guerra* the California Supreme Court concurred with the legislature when it upheld the state's interpretation of who was a citizen in the state. The De La Guerra case was of paramount significance to Texas because of the large number of people of Mexican descent living in Texas, including 54 percent of the Mexican immigrants in the United States (N = 23,020 out of 42,435) (U.S. Census 1872: 392). Moreover, the case was important to Texas because the California Supreme Court offered an opinion on the legal principles that could be used to deny or grant U.S. citizenship to Mexican immigrants of color. The arguments contained in the De La Guerra case basically proffered that regardless of treaty law, dark-complexioned Mexicans were not citizens and could not apply for citizenship for the simple reason that treaty law was vague on the subject of race, and the Fourteenth Amendment did not apply to Mexicans.

It is not surprising that the De La Guerra case came before the California Supreme Court two years after Congress ratified the Fourteenth Amendment since California was among the few states that had fought on the side of the Union but had voted against its passage. On March 3, 1868, legislators in California voted against passage, and only after Congress ratified the amendment did the legislature recognize African Americans had been made citizens (Shiesei 2003). The legislature, however, did not agree that the amendment applied to other racial minorities (*U.S. v. Wong Kim Ark* 1898).

The De La Guerra case involved Pablo De La Guerra, a wealthy Mexican rancher and former district and county judge who during the Civil War served as California's lieutenant governor. In 1870 the California legislature removed De La Guerra from his position of district judge. The state alleged he was not white and therefore not a citizen, which made him ineligible to vote or hold office. The De La Guerra case was being used by the state to set a precedent and reaffirm its position that only Mexicans who were white were U.S. citizens, and if they had immigrated they had to be white to be eligible for citizenship. The attorneys for the state argued that the California legislature had the authority to remove De La Guerra from office because the state constitution did not allow Mexicans of Indian descent to be citizens. They alleged that in the United States Mexicans had been made citizens of the nation by the Treaty of Guadalupe Hidalgo, but they had not been made citizens of the states. In California, therefore, the state government had the right to exclude certain types of Mexicans from U.S. citizenship because treaty law was null and void when it conflicted with state law.

The state attorneys then turned to naturalization and treaty law to further support their exclusionary position. They argued, first, that in California Mexicans who were of Indian descent could not apply for citizenship because federal naturalization law excluded that type of people. Then in regard to treaty law they argued that such compacts were enforceable only when state legislators chose to uphold them. Treaties could also be nullified by mandates of a state. Allegedly treaties could be broken because the federal government set a precedent in 1848 when it annexed the Mexican territories and allowed the states to incorporate Mexicans according to the decision of the state or territorial legislatures. On the basis of the congressional mandate of 1848, it became lawful for Mexicans throughout the United States to be either denied or granted citizenship. To illustrate their point, the attorneys compared the history of Texas with that of California. They argued that in Texas most Mexicans, including those of indigenous descent, were citizens because Congress accepted the Texas legislature's decision to adopt the citizenship laws practiced by the former Republic of Texas. Under the Republic's laws only blacks and tribal Indians were excluded from citizenship (see chapter 1). State law, therefore, not treaty law, was the basis for determining the status of Mexicans in Texas. In California, however, Congress accepted the legislature's mandate to exclude Mexicans who were not white and thereby created a legal precedent giving state law authority superior to treaty law.

De La Guerra's attorneys argued that the Treaty of Guadalupe Hidalgo and the Fourteenth Amendment had made Mexicans citizens. They maintained further that in addition to the status he was granted by federal law De La Guerra was eligible for U.S. citizenship because he was white and not part of the indigenous people of California.

The California Supreme Court handed down a convoluted decision in the case. The court ruled on behalf of both parties, opining that the U.S. Congress did not extend citizenship to Mexicans of Indian descent. However, the court overturned the legislature's action against De La Guerra because the state attorneys had been unable to prove he was of Indian descent. Nonetheless, the justices did uphold most of the arguments of the state attorneys. They ruled that treaties did not have power to nullify conflicting state laws. In the court's opinion no treaty had the power to make Mexicans citizens if the decision of the state was to deny them that status. Hence the justices concurred with the state that dark-complexioned Mexicans could not be made citizens by any federal law. Essentially, the justices ruled in favor of states' rights rather than recognize the authority federal treaties imposed upon the states. Furthermore, the justices interpreted the spirit of the Fourteenth Amendment as not applying to Mexicans of Indian descent.

In Texas, the courts were now left with competing precedents to follow. The De La Guerra ruling gave them the option of denying citizenship to Mexican immigrants of Indian descent on the basis of state rights. However, the Texas courts also had a conflicting legal precedent to follow in that the Naturalization Treaty of 1868 did not cite race as a determining factor in whether Mexican immigrants could become citizens of the United States. In everyday practice judges in Texas had the power to interpret citizenship law however they wanted. They had two problematic and conflicting legal precedents to follow and could choose either to use race as a legal barrier to citizenship or to ignore it altogether.

In looking back at naturalization patterns, one would be naive to think that after the De La Guerra ruling most judges did not consider race to be an exclusionary factor. How else can the drop in the acceptance rate of granted petitions to Mexicans be explained when it fell from 89 percent to .75 percent within ten years? On the other hand, the political atmosphere in Texas may have been an even greater factor given that the judicial system was restructured and the liberal Union judges replaced.[11]

Growth and Regional Concentration of the Mexican Immigrant Sector in Texas

During the 1870s immigration from Mexico to Texas continued to increase. When President Benito Juárez was in office, he tried to stabilize the country, but the task was very difficult because the war with France had devastated the economy. In turn, the economic depression generated conditions that prompted internal migration in Mexico and eventually led to large-scale immigration to the United States. Especially hard hit were small-scale farming communities that depended on subsistence crops to feed their families and to produce additional crops for market. Many families found themselves unable to make a living on their farms and were forced to abandon their homes and migrate to Mexico's urban centers, where the economy was less depressed. The federal government, burdened by an empty treasury and preoccupied with paying its foreign debt, was unable to create the jobs needed to employ its displaced rural populations. The federal treasury was consumed by the costs of running a bureaucracy and proving its financial solvency within the global economy. Paying its international foreign debt was necessary to prevent another confrontation like that which had occurred in 1861, when Juárez instructed the treasury to suspend its foreign debt payments and as a consequence provoked a counterresponse from the creditor nations. Exacerbating Mexico's financial troubles were the quarterly payments the country made to the United States. Mexico had borrowed heavily from the United States, and it was critical not to default on any loan if it expected more credit to be extended, which was likely since the economy was not recuperating (see Ludlow and Marichal 1998). The government was also burdened by the payments it had to make to settle the reclamation property claims American citizens had won through the U.S.-Mexico Reclamation Committee. Mexico, therefore, was focused on improving its global international standing rather than on investing in welfare programs or creating jobs (Vásquez and Meyer 1985). This dire economic situation left most Mexicans economically destitute, and those who were able to raise enough money to migrate north chose to relocate to the United States, where employment was available. By 1870 the U.S. Census estimated the Mexican foreign-born population in the United States had grown in the past ten years from 27,466 to 42,436 (U.S. Census 1864: 34; U.S. Census 1872: 372–373). Most of the growth occurred in Texas and specifically in South Texas, where the majority of the immigrants resided. In Texas, 23,020 Mexican immigrants were counted, and 75 percent (N = 17,170) lived in South Texas (Ibid.). The remainder were scattered mainly in Bexar and Presidio counties and in the city of El Paso. By 1870 about half of the counties of South Texas were heavily populated by Mexican immigrants. In Cameron, Starr, Hidalgo, Nueces, Maverick, Zapata, Duval, Encinal, and La Salle they came to constitute 48 percent to 81 percent of the total number of residents. In the other South Texas counties their numbers were lower, ranging from 2 percent to 22 percent.

Mexicans were not the only ethnic group living in South Texas. As previously mentioned, European immigrants and Anglo-Americans from the southern states of the U.S. had settled along the borders of South Texas counties, and the size of the non-Mexican population in most counties ranged from 46 percent to 33 percent of the total number of residents (see map 2.1; table 2.4). In Nueces and Cameron counties, two of the largest counties in South Texas, the percentage of Anglo-Americans was considerably less, but their total numbers were significant. Native-born Anglo-Americans and European immigrants numbered at least 1,382 in Cameron and 958 in Nueces (U.S. Census 1872: 372). (Most of the European foreign-born residents came from Germany, England, and Ireland.) As their numbers increased so did their political and economic control of the region. Although most of them were mid- to small-scale farmers, several ranching dynasties emerged and reached prominence. Two of the most influential heads of families were Richard King and Mifflin Kenedy, who founded successful agribusiness and cattle corporations in Nueces, Cameron, and Hidalgo counties (Alonzo 1998; Montejano 1987). King ultimately became the wealthiest cattle baron in South Texas. Dillard R. Fant also was a successful entrepreneur and landowner, controlling over 220,000 acres in Starr and Hidalgo counties.

People of Mexican descent, however, did not lose total political control of the region. During the 1870s the mayors of the towns continued to be of Mexican origin, and Mexicans held many positions as elected officials, including county and district clerks, county treasurer, county surveyor, assessor of taxes, inspector of hides, and county registrar (Election Registers 1838–1972a; 1838–1972b). Specifically, in Starr, Zapata, and Webb counties most of these offices were held by Mexican Americans. Yet in most counties Mexican-origin communities lost total control of the judicial system and the law enforcement domain. Only in Starr, Webb, and Zapata did Mexican-origin communities continue to be represented in these two areas.

In Webb and Zapata the residents elected county judges and local justices of the peace of Mexican descent throughout the late nineteenth century. In Starr, the county judge was an Anglo-American, yet nearly half of the local justices of the peace were of Mexican descent. In the law enforcement domain only Webb and Zapata retained partial control of the elected offices. For most of the late nineteenth century Webb and Zapata elected sheriffs of Mexican descent and sometimes constables. In the other counties, seldom was a sheriff of Mexican descent elected, and only on occasion were constables elected. In Duval, Cameron, Hidalgo, Kinney, Nueces, La Salle, and Starr counties constables of Mexican descent did serve but infrequently. Although at the local and county level Mexicans retained some control of their region, Anglo-Americans monopolized the higher levels of government. At the state and congressional levels, where money was needed to win an election, few Mexicans were elected to office. Anglo-Americans came to dominate these political domains.

Besides Anglo-Americans, people of African descent lived in South Texas. Their numbers were few, and they were scattered throughout the region. In 1870 blacks numbered a little over 2,000 (table 2.5). It is very likely that a large percentage of this population was of Mexican descent since Spanish censuses indicate that 155 afromexicanos settled in South Texas (Hinojosa 1983: 124). Likewise, the U.S. Census indicates that prior to the Civil War nearly half of Texas's free black population lived in South Texas (N = 148 out of 344), the majority residing in Cameron and Hidalgo counties (U.S. Census 1872: 65). Although it is very likely that part of the African-descent population was Mexican, without a doubt many others were emancipated slaves. Slavery in South Texas had been rare, but nonetheless it was practiced. Karnes, Nueces, and Atascosa counties had the largest slave populations (Ibid., 66).

In South Texas part of the black population was also foreign-born. How many there were is uncertain, however, since the U.S. census did not enumerate their numbers by county. We know only that the majority of foreign-

Table 2.5. Black Population in South Texas and Selected Counties, 1860 and 1870[a]

| | 1870 | | 1860 | |
	Total County Population	Black	Free Black	Enslaved Black
South Texas				
Kinney	1,204	418	15	0
Nueces	3,975	332	1	216
Maverick	1,951	281	21	1
Karnes	1,705	279	0	327
Atascosa	2,915	160	0	107
Cameron	10,999	157	66	7
Medina	2,078	92	0	106
Uvalde	851	73	0	27
San Patricio	602	64	0	95
Hidalgo	2,387	41	34	1
Live Oak	852	28	0	85
Starr	4,154	18	4	6
Frio	309	15	0	2
McMullen	230	12	0	0
Dimmit	109	8	0	0
Zavala	133	4	0	0
Duval	1,083	3	0	0
Webb	2,615	2	0	0
La Salle	69	1	0	0
Zapata	1,488	0	0	0
Encinal	427	0	0	0
Other Counties				
Bexar	16,043	2,303	2	1,395
Presidio	1,627	489	2	4
El Paso	3,671	306	14	15

[a]The U.S. Census Bureau did not distinguish the black population according to place of birth.
Source: U.S. Census 1872: 65–67

born blacks in Texas were Mexican. The U.S. Census of 1870 identified 841 foreign-born blacks, of whom 448 were Mexican (Ibid., 335–336). It is very likely that they settled in South Texas since that was the main place of entry for most Mexican immigrants.

Resentment Toward Mexican Immigration and Law Enforcement Along the Border

The incredible growth of the Mexican immigrant population in the 1870s came to be resented by many Anglo-Americans in Texas, despite the fact that at the federal level relations between the governments of Mexico and the United States were stable and friendly. U.S. commerce with Mexico was of particular importance to the federal government, and profitable contracts had been negotiated with American businessmen. In Texas, however, first the legislature and, later, Governor Coke became concerned with the federal government's failure to regulate Mexican immigration, and several measures were taken to patrol the U.S.-Mexico border.

Mexican immigrants, like U.S.-born Mexican Americans, were viewed by the Anglo-American population of Texas as a socially inferior mongrel race (Foley 1997). The consensus within the Texas legislature was that among the arriving immigrants were Mexican outlaws. Mexican bandits had supposedly begun to take over the open range, and it was necessary to regulate immigration. Mexican immigrants were accused of stealing cattle from Texan-Anglo ranchers and taking the herds back into Mexico. The first action to regulate immigration was taken by the Texas legislature in 1871, when it established a Bureau of Immigration to supervise and control all matters connected with immigration (*Laws of Texas*, 6:1029). A few years later, in 1875, Governor Coke took a more forceful measure and reinstated the Texas Rangers (Durham 1962: viii). The Rangers had been disbanded after the Civil War, but when the federal government refused to send federal troops to patrol the border, Coke recommissioned them.[12] When federal aid was refused, Coke took matters into his own hands and wrote to the U.S. Senate that the border would be protected at all costs, even to the extent of allowing the Rangers to cross into Mexico. In the letter Governor Coke warned Congress that he would allow the Texas Rangers to take over federal law enforcement functions even if international law was violated. Under U.S. law, only federal troops were allowed to conduct military missions across international borders. Coke's letter of May 1875 stated,

No state has surrendered the right of defense of its people in its own way against aggressions from neighboring states of people. . . . I apprehend that international courtesy, comity and amity have never been required by the law of nations, carried to the romantic extent of surrendering the great natural right of self-defense against the constant affliction of serious, permanent and wrongful injury upon the people of one nation by those of another, although the attacks may be unauthorized by the government of the territory from which it comes. (cited in Callahan 1932: 349)

In compliance with the governor's mandate, Capt. L. H. McNelly was placed in command of the Texas Rangers and ordered to keep peace in South Texas. His men were allowed to shoot anyone suspected of being a bandit. Unfortunately, the governor's orders were taken to heart, and the Rangers indiscriminately attacked people, instilling terror in Mexican communities. Mexicans were shot or arrested merely because they were suspected of being *bandidos* or because they were accused of protecting cattle rustlers.

Mexicans learned that when the Rangers rode into town everyone should hide or remain indoors. One incident committed against the Mexican community of Brownsville was so serious that it brought a public outcry and even reached the attention of the U.S. War Department. The incident began on June 12, 1875, when Captain McNelly led a posse of Rangers into Palo Alto, near Brownsville, and slaughtered thirteen Mexican *vaqueros* (cowboys) who were resting in their camp (Durham 1962: 65; Kingston 1988: 87). McNelly alleged the men were Mexican cattle rustlers who were planning to cross cattle into Mexico. When the vaqueros tried to surrender, the Rangers refused to listen and shot them on site. To teach Mexicans a lesson and show them what would happen if they disobeyed the Rangers, McNelly and his troop rode into Brownsville with the victims' bodies and hung them in the public square. He warned the observers that if any of the bodies were removed the assailants would be shot on sight. The sheriff of Brownsville immediately complained to the U.S. Army, and a few days later an investigation was held. McNelly claimed that a public display of the bodies was needed to instill fear in potential cattle rustlers because Brownsville was rumored to be the main crossing point for stolen cattle. During the investigation, the townspeople complained that the vaqueros were not Mexican cattle rustlers at all but residents of Brownsville who were returning from a stock-buying trip in north Texas. When the cattle were inspected for stolen brands, most were found to be unbranded, proving the vaqueros were not thieves. The investigation served to curtail McNelly's reign of terror, and from that day on he was ordered to turn in all suspects to the local judge. McNelly was no longer allowed to determine whether a suspect was guilty or not.

McNelly's ruthless campaign of brutality did not end, however, until a much larger, international incident caused the secretary of war to intervene. In November 1875 McNelly and his Rangers crossed the Mexican border without federal authorization and attacked the Mexican village of Cachuttas (Durham 1962: 114). To legally cross the border the Rangers needed authorization from the Mexican government and the U.S. secretary of war. When the Rangers arrived at Cachuttas, Mayor Juan Flores of Camargo asked them to leave, but they refused. Flores next returned to McNelly's camp accompanied by one hundred local men and ordered the Rangers once more to stop their investigation. McNelly again refused and this time began shooting, an attack that left the mayor mortally wounded along with eighty of the townspeople. After the shootout McNelly and the Rangers proceeded to raid local ranches and steal the Mexicans' cattle, leaving only after rounding up most of the local herds. Upon their return to Texas the Rangers deposited the cattle at the King Ranch, King being a close friend of McNelly and the employer of several of the Rangers.[13] The Mexican population, well aware that some of the Rangers worked at the King Ranch, called the Rangers "los rinches de la Kineña" (the Rangers of King Ranch) (Montejano 1987: 52).

A state investigation of the Cachuttas incident revealed that 250 of the 400 cattle were unbranded. Once again McNelly was warned, but he was not fired until a few years later when influential Anglo-Americans from South Texas accused him of shooting suspects rather than turning them in to local authorities. Although McNelly was fired, the Rangers continued to patrol the border. By 1876, however, owing to federal pressure they were no longer allowed to participate in any event dealing with immigration or international issues. President Ulysses S. Grant and the Congress agreed that border disputes must be settled diplomatically, not by force. The president also disapproved of Coke's ongoing request that he send more federal troops. Some congressmen charged that the violence along the U.S.-Mexico border was an exaggeration perpetuated by Texan politicians who wanted the federal government to declare war against Mexico. The alleged goal of these Texans was to persuade the U.S. government to invade Mexico and take the ranchland bordering South Texas (Callahan 1932: 350, 357, 375–377). Coke disputed the allegation and responded that declaring war on Mexico was a military necessity because several villages there had to be annexed to restore peace and order along the border. According to the governor, most of the Mexican bandits entering Texas came from a few villages in north Mexico. Coke further charged that Texans were accused of acting in their self-interest only as a distraction, when the real reason for the federal government's refusal to protect the border was financial. Allegedly, the Congress did not want to send federal troops into Mexico because American diplomats were in the process of closing several business deals for U.S. railroad corporations.

During Grant's administration, Governor Coke and the Texas legislature experienced several setbacks in policing the U.S-Mexico border. A few months after the governor was told that the government would not invade Mexico, the War Department warned Texas that immigration was a political right solely under the jurisdiction of U.S. Congress. The legislature had to disband the recently established immigration bureau, and the governor was pressured to ensure that the Texas Rangers did not abuse their law enforcement mandate (*Laws of Texas*, 8:834).[14] Several incidents had caused the War Department to caution Texas. The most serious violation of law and order led Congress to investigate the Rangers' involvement in the Salt War Riots.

The Salt War Riots erupted in El Paso on December 12, 1876 (White 1923: 99–119), when an angry mob of Mexicans from El Paso and from the Mexican city of Ciudad Juárez attacked a posse of armed Anglo-Americans, including District Judge Charles Howard, twelve of his hired gunmen, and a troop of Texas Rangers. According to the Rangers, the confrontation began when a priest named Father Borriga led a crowd of Mexicans across the border in Ciudad Juárez and was joined by a larger crowd in El Paso. The crowd walked to the El Paso salt lakes and began collecting salt without paying the fee owed to Judge Howard, who owned the lakes. Howard's men tried to stop the crowd, and fighting broke out between them and a group of armed Mexicans.

The dispute over the salt had begun a few months earlier. For centuries the salt lakes had been public property, but Judge Howard unexpectedly took legal possession of them under title granted to him by the Texas legislature. He then announced to locals that as the new owner of the salt lakes he was going to start charging a fee for harvesting the salt. People protested and took their complaint to their legislators. As part of the complaint locals charged that city and county officials were illegally taking title of government land in El Paso. The salt lakes, plus several roads and streets which had been recently built and paid for by the city, had suddenly been privatized and given to local officials. Louis Cardis, the representative for El Paso, tried to convince the judge to cede his title to the salt lakes and al-

Figure 2.1. Las Norias bandit raid: Texas Rangers with dead bandits, October 8, 1915. Runyon (Robert) Photograph Collection. Center for American History, UT-Austin (RUN 00096).

low public entry, but he would have none of it. Instead, he prepared for an armed confrontation and hired several gunmen (Timmons 2004: 203). As the Mexican community grew angrier, Cardis met with the judge and tried again to convince him to return the salt lakes to the city. Unfortunately, the meeting ended violently, and Judge Howard shot Cardis.

After the shootout, Judge Howard, fearing for his life, wired the federal government to send troops to control the angry Mexicans. When assistance was denied, he turned to the Rangers. Immediately a troop of Rangers was dispatched. A few days later, according to the Rangers, the Salt War Riots erupted. Howard had refused to give away his salt, and he assembled his gunmen to protect the lakes and charge everyone a fee. The trouble began when Father Borriga arrived with the townspeople. Allegedly among them were many armed men, who outnumbered and ambushed the judge's men. In the attack several Mexicans were killed along with Howard and three of the Rangers (fig. 2.1). A few weeks after the riot, Congress investigated the incident because it had become an international affair involving the death of Mexican citizens. During the congressional hearing a few Texas legislators tried to use the riot as evidence that federal troops were needed along the

U.S.-Mexico border. They warned the congressional committee that if the federal government did not protect the border, the state government would be forced to hire more Texas Rangers and deal with the border crossers. In response to the ordeal Congress agreed to establish Fort Bliss in El Paso and reduce the role of the Rangers in West Texas. For Congress, federal intervention was a compromise. It pacified Texas legislators and at the same time helped to maintain cordial relations with Mexico. If international business relations were to continue running smoothly Congress needed to assure Mexico that its citizens were welcome in Texas.

U.S.-Mexico Capitalist Ventures and the Porfiriato

In 1876 Porfirio Díaz assumed the presidency of Mexico and instituted programs that increased Mexican farmers' poverty and entrenched Mexico in a capitalist venture dependent on U.S. foreign investments (Miller 1985: 257). As Mexican capitalism matured, the wealthiest sectors of Mexican society prospered, while the common person became entrapped in a production process that Mexican elites recognized benefited foreign investors more than the country as a whole.

President Díaz maintained former president Juárez's financial solvency plan but devised legislation that ran contrary to the social welfare of the masses and to the spirit of the Juárez regime. To establish internal stability and stimulate economic growth Díaz gave capitalists incentives to invest in Mexico. Under his modernization program the presidential cabinet planned to lure capitalist investors by granting them government subsidies, giving them land grants, and awarding them generous tax breaks. Díaz envisioned that his plan would lead industrialists to expand factory employment, bring needed foreign capital into the country, and convince large-scale agribusinesses to increase food production. The outcomes of the development plan were projected to lower food costs and generate employment. This ideal capitalist environment, however, was dependent upon reinterpreting or dismantling the land and judicial reforms made during the Juárez administration. To enforce his modernization program Díaz cleverly created the legal infrastructure to gain control of the country by controlling the military and the police. He acquired the constitutional power to appoint the army officers' corps, the police, and the federal police.

Once Díaz had secured control of the military and police bureaucracy, he began to impose policies to destroy his enemies and reward his allies. Díaz enacted a policy called *pan o palo* (bread or the stick), by which he ordered that anyone who opposed his regime would be punished by being imprisoned, sent into exile, placed in work gangs, or shot. To ensure the complicity of the masses in the rural areas, where three-quarters of the population resided, Díaz hired a large federal police force and armed them with weapons that were superior to those of the state and local police. The mission of this federal unit, whose members were called *rurales*, was to maintain order in the countryside and ensure that Díaz's economic plan was followed. In the presence of massive unemployment in Mexico, Díaz was able to easily recruit a large military and rural police force. The rurales and federal soldiers were assured of an income to support their families.

In the rural areas, Díaz created the legal infrastructure that allowed large landowners to usurp their neighbors' ranches (Galarza 1964). He gave land concessions to wealthy Mexican ranchers and Anglo-American investors by transferring titles through eminent domain or merely by allowing the rurales to evict farmers. After people were removed from their farms the courts declared the property abandoned and issued new titles. Díaz and his supporters proclaimed that such harsh measures were necessary because the only means of increasing productivity was to consolidate the farmland and put it in the hands of a few investors.

The majority of the concessions, however, were given to the railroad companies. In 1876 the federal government began its modernization plan to improve the nation's transportation infrastructure (Callahan 1932; Lorey 1999). Six U.S. companies were invited to lay railroad track throughout Mexico. The problem with the modernization program was that massive land grants were given to railroad companies, and as track was laid thousands of families were displaced and their land expropriated. During the late 1870s the dislocation was gradual, but within a decade it was massive.

Mexican citizens were also adversely affected by reforms in the mining industry. By law, foreign companies were exempt from paying state taxes on the minerals they extracted. Although the tax breaks benefited both U.S. and British companies, Americans were Mexico's main investors in the mines. They controlled 80 percent of all foreign investments in this industry (Callahan 1932: 519; Gilly 1994: 48). Because the companies did not have to pay state taxes regional resources were ravished, while the state governments and its residents profited very little. The rationale for the tax system was that it would create jobs in the states and introduce new technology, which in turn could be replicated by Mexican investors. In theory this aid would allow Mexican industrialists to modernize the country's mining industry (Pletcher 1958). But Díaz's plan failed to protect workers, as foreign companies were not required to pay a living wage. Mexico was to be industrialized at the expense of the workers and without implementing any environmental protection policies.

U.S. investors also profited from the labor exploitation of urban populations. In the cities American businessmen established hundreds of new factories, and workers there, like rural workers, were not paid a living wage. To ensure that investors were content with their labor force the federal government did not protect Mexican workers (Miller 1985). Foreign and domestic employers were allowed to force their workers to labor twelve to fifteen hours a day, and when quotas were to be met workers did not have to be given a day of rest (Pletcher 1958). The federal government also failed to pass protective laws in hazardous employment and did not require employers to pay workers for overtime or compensate them when injured. Employers could also arbitrarily reduce their pay, and no governmental recourse was available to challenge the validity of the pay cuts. In rural areas workers were often not paid any wages, as it was legal for employers to pay them with overpriced goods purchased from the company store. Employers controlled the price of the goods that were exchanged for wages. To protect company managers from angry workers the federal government allowed companies to hire their own police, and if the contracted police were insufficient, then the rurales were at the disposal of the companies. When Díaz became president the repression of the workers commenced immediately but worsened in the coming decades because he destroyed all opposition through coercion and bribes. As Díaz's power increased, the Mexican Congress conceded to his demands and revised the Constitution to eliminate presidential term limits. This allowed Díaz to be continuously reelected and remain the constitutional president. Essentially Díaz and his supporters created a legal dictatorship that was protected by a well-paid military and federal police. To deter dissent, Díaz imprisoned, exiled, or assassinated anyone who questioned his administration's actions. In attempting to develop Mexican capitalism, Díaz lost his respect and sense of responsibility for the citizenry and created a cultural hierarchy that made the wealthy the only citizens with legitimate rights and claims to the wealth of the state.

Many Mexicans were unwilling to endure the dictatorship, and immigration to the United States became their main outlet to find a better life. By 1880 the Mexican foreign-born population living in the United States had grown to 68,399, 63 percent of whom lived in Texas (N = 43,161) (U.S. Census 1882: 495). A pattern began to emerge that supports the observations of Agamben's (2000) analysis of global migration, namely, that migration is a means of escape from oppression and crippling poverty. When nation-states are unable to protect their citizens or refuse to do so, those people who can escape the hardships of their native country will seek another nation to assure them of the necessities of life.

As a result of the Porfirian regime's capitalist ventures, Mexico became entrenched in a global capitalist system that mainly benefited domestic elites and foreign investors. As Eric Wolf (1982) observes, when states lose compassion for their citizenry, capitalist development becomes despotic and an infrastructure emerges that ravages the land, produces massive profits for the capitalist allies who control production processes, and forces workers into compliance through the use of state force. In particular, when the land is ravaged, whether by appropriation, alienation, or spoilage, the masses have limited recourses with which to resist exploitation: they can comply, revolt, or migrate.

Mexican Immigration and the Railroad Corporations

In Texas during the 1880s Mexican immigrants continued to settle in communities with high concentrations of Mexican-origin people (Arreola 2002: 41; White 1923: 128). But they began to move to other areas of Texas when railway track was constructed throughout the state.

In the mid-1870s, the Texas legislature commenced a statewide project to improve the state's transportation infrastructure. Cities and towns throughout Texas were to be connected by train. The railway industry was lagging behind in most states in the United States because construction had stopped during the Civil War and through the first years of Reconstruction. Before the legislature took action only 711 miles of track had been laid in Texas (*The Houston Post Almanac* 1897: 208). To attract investors, the legislature gave generous land grants to any corporation willing to lay track in Texas. The problem with the land concessions was that the legislature purchased or took by eminent domain thousands of acres belonging to small-scale farmers. This action produced major changes in Texas land patterns, leading to the growth of massive estates requiring immigrant labor to work the land.

Among the main investors laying track in Texas was Uriah Loth, who, with the financial support of his partners Richard King and Mifflin Kenedy, established in 1875 the Corpus Christi, San Diego and Rio Grande Narrow Gauge Railroad Company (Richardson, Anderson, and Wallace 1997: 55). The company was later renamed the Texas-Mexican National Railway Corporation. From 1876 to 1879 they built 162 miles of track across South Texas. The town of San Diego, located in the interior of South Texas, was connected to Corpus Christi, a small city on the gulf coast near the Mexican border. This southern route also connected Laredo, a border city, to San Diego. These train routes thus facilitated the movement of people from along the border into the interior of South Texas. A few years later these cities were connected by railway to San Antonio, Galveston, and Houston, thus allowing Mexicans to migrate to other parts of Texas (Callahan 1932: 483).

The U.S. Census indicates that by 1880, although 88 percent of Mexican immigrants in Texas lived in South Texas and in the counties of El Paso, Presidio, and Bexar (N = 37,868 out of 43,161), they had begun to settle in new areas (table 2.6) (U.S. Census 1882: 495, 528–531). Their dispersion was largely facilitated by the growth of the railroad industry. In central Texas the number of Mexicans increased to 2,212, and over 50 percent chose Travis, Wilson, Hays, and Llano counties as their homes (Ibid., 530). Mexicans were attracted to central Texas because the economy there was diversified. Farming employment as well as jobs in the service industry were available. Mexicans were also attracted to occupations in the herding and cattle industry (Jordan 1982).

In South Texas Mexican immigrants constituted 39 percent of the total population of the counties (N = 31,693 out of 81,490), and they remained a very important part of the region's economy, culture, and political life (U.S. Census 1882: 528–531). However, they were more concentrated in the counties adjacent to the border and in places where massive cattle ranches were established. In Cameron, Starr, Duval, Hidalgo, Maverick, Zapata, Encinal, and Webb counties Mexican immigrants numbered nearly half of the total population or more (see table 2.6). In other South Texas counties their numbers were smaller, yet still quite high, ranging from around 41 percent to 10 percent. By this time the number of black people had also risen in South Texas, increasing by at least 50 percent and numbering a little over 3,000 (U.S. Census 1885: 371). It is uncertain how many of them were Mexican immigrants since the census of 1880 did not identify the nativity of the black population. We know that a total of 803 foreign-born blacks lived in Texas, but where they lived and what their country of origin was are unknown.

By 1880 the Mexican immigrant population of West Texas and Bexar had also increased, yet their numbers were not as large as those in South Texas. In El Paso County the majority of the Mexican-descent population was born in the United States. Here, Mexican immigrants comprised 28 percent of the total population (out of 3,845) (U.S. Census Bureau 1882: 529), whereas Mexican Americans made up around 60 percent (de León and Kenneth 1997:12; White 1923: 187). Many of the immigrant families who

Table 2.6. Concentration of Foreign-Born Mexican Immigrants in South Texas and Selected Counties, 1880

	County Pop.	Mexican Foreign-Born No.	Mexican Foreign-Born % of Total	Non-Mexican Foreign-Born	Born in U.S.[a]	Born in U.S. out of Texas[b]
South Texas[c]						
Encinal	1,902	1,250	66	10	642	5
Zapata	3,636	2,295	63	9	1,332	12
Starr	8,304	4,827	58	174	3,303	410
Duval	5,732	3,258	57	131	2,343	195
Hidalgo	4,347	2,388	55	13	1,946	62
Maverick	2,967	1,613	54	135	1,219	235
Webb	5,273	2,608	49	159	2,506	310
Cameron	14,959	7,096	47	631	7,232	642
La Salle	789	320	41	14	455	69
Nueces	7,673	2,734	36	531	4,408	832
Kinney	4,487	1,403	31	481	2,603	1,087
Dimmit	665	149	22	6	510	107
San Patricio	1,001	189	19	72	740	162
Uvalde	2,541	447	18	99	1,995	577
Live Oak	1,994	273	14	72	1,649	412
McMullen	701	101	14	32	568	137
Atascosa	4,217	416	10	135	3,666	892
Frio	2,130	171	8	60	1,899	516
Zavala	410	30	7.3	4	376	97
Medina	4,492	77	1.7	772	3,643	611
Karnes	3,270	48	1.4	326	2,896	721
Total	**81,490**	**31,693**	**39**	**3,866**	**45,931**	**8,091**
Other Regions						
El Paso	3,845	1,082	28	70	2,693	248
Pecos	1,807	1,234	68	34	539	177
Presidio	2,873	1,595	56	62	1,216	550
Bexar	30,470	3,498	12	4,414	22,558	5,865

[a]The black population is included in this table. Blacks in South Texas numbered 3,108, in El Paso 47, in Bexar 3,867, Pecos 127, and Presidio 429 (U.S. Census 1882: 495; U.S. Census 1885: 371–375). It is uncertain what percentage of the Mexican foreign-born was black, as a racial category was not given.
[b]Most people born out of state and in the United States came from Alabama, Tennessee, Mississippi, Georgia, and Louisiana.
[c]Brooks, Willacy, Jim Hogg, Kenedy, Kleberg, and Jim Wells had not been organized. They were part of Nueces or Cameron counties in the 1870s. Val Verde also had not been organized.
Source: U.S. Census 1882: 495, 528–531, 544, 663; U.S. Census 1885: 371–375.

lived in El Paso came from Ciudad Juárez and lived only temporarily in the United States, as their farms were located in Mexico. Within the next ten years, however, as the political and economic situation worsened in Mexico their numbers increased, and they became permanent U.S. residents, working in the salt and mineral mines, in construction, and in farming. Only in Presidio County did the Mexican immigrant population outnumber the native born. In this West Texas county, however, the total number of residents was very small, and most people depended on subsistence farming. The presence of Mexican immigrants, who composed 56 percent of the total population, was largely attributed to the dispersion of extended families along the border rather than to individuals seeking employment in large-scale farms (U.S. Census Bureau 1882: 530). In Bexar County, Mexican immigrants accounted for a relatively small percentage of the total population, only 12 percent (N = 3,498 out of 30,470), and, like immigrants in central Texas, they were engaged in various types of occupations, not just farming and farm work (Ibid., 528; U.S. Census 1885: 371). Many immigrants who settled in Bexar were from the professional classes of Mexico and opened small businesses upon their arrival (de León and Kenneth 1997: 12).

As more railway track was laid in Texas, the ability of Mexicans to move beyond South Texas became easier. Many Anglo-Americans were displeased by their presence and saw them as intruders, a controversy that became more acute when Mexico laid its own track and U.S. investors connected the railway systems of Mexico to those of the border counties of Texas.

Railways and the Growth of Agricultural Estates in South Texas

By the late 1890s railroad corporations had helped to modernize Texas by connecting most major cities by railway, but thousands of Anglo-American farmers were angered by the power the corporations were given by the legislature. By then, 8,709 miles of track had been built (Houston Post 1897: 208). Corporations not only had the right to lay track through private property, but also gained the power to appropriate the land they needed, and once it was theirs they could in turn sell whatever acreage they did not use. The construction of the railway led to an economic era during which railroad investors became railway barons with political power never before seen in Texas. As their power grew, the open range diminished. Throughout Texas railroad companies received enormous grants, so excessive that the companies sold the unneeded land to private investors. It became common for cattle corporations to purchase the railroad grants and establish large cattle ranches (Clements 1955). This disrupted the open-range culture, as cattle corporations needed to fence their property, while farmers needed open space to graze their animals or to cross their neighbor's property when transporting goods or animals to market. Soon, however, railroad barons chose to establish cattle ranches rather than sell their land, and fencing became a bigger problem for the small-scale farmer.

For the Mexicans of South Texas this was a disastrous development because their livelihoods depended upon an agrarian and ranching economy in which neighbors did not fence their property and the government allowed grazing in vacant land. During this period King expanded his property holdings and built a cattle empire. He acquired part of the land by purchasing it, but in addition, because he was a railroad investor, he was given governmental land concessions. He profited from the railroad venture as the legislature gave him enormous land grants in South Texas. In turn King used his land concessions to increase the acreage of his family's ranches and cleverly manipulated the railway projects to benefit his ranching business. King and his partner Kenedy laid track along the San Diego route, which allowed them to transport cattle and farm products from their ranches to marketing centers along the gulf coast and the border (Montejano 1987).

While the railroad concessions allowed King and Kenedy to enlarge their landholdings in South Texas, they were not the only ones to hasten the end of open-range culture. Five Anglo-American cattle ranchers purchased thousands of acres in Hidalgo, Nueces, Cameron, Starr, and Duval counties (Alonzo 1998). In these counties the local economy changed from a small-scale dual system of farming and ranching to a large-scale corporate ranching economy. Many Mexican sheep and cattle ranchers were adversely affected by the economic changes because when the corporate ranchers bought the property they fenced off their ranches and blocked many of their Mexican neighbors' access routes to the watering spots (Arreola 2002). Exacerbating the problem, the corporate ranchers ordered their cowhands to construct fences without consulting their neighbors. A common outcome was that sections of the Mexicans' farmland, especially land where water was available for cattle, were usurped (de León 1987; Paredes 1957). The most feared corporate ranchers were King and Kenedy. Between 1875 and 1885 King gradually obtained, through purchase, intimidation, and government concessions, 614,000 acres of land in South Texas, while Kenedy acquired nearly 400,000 acres in Cameron and Hidalgo counties (Ashton 1996: 1064; Montejano 1987: 63–70). Kenedy also acquired his wife's property when he married Petra Vela de Vidal, a wealthy Mexican American widow who was part of the landed elite of South Texas. Many Mexicans retaliated by cutting through the fences. As fence cutting became a common practice, the cattle barons complained to state authorities and gained the right to have the Texas Rangers arrest offenders. This, however, did not end the conflict.

The fencing battles in South Texas were not unique to the area. Throughout Texas such battles broke out between small-scale farmers and cattle corporations. Outside of South Texas, the railroad corporations were a bigger problem, as most of the railway was built in north and central Texas. In South Texas, King and Kenedy retaliated by demonstrating their power and influence over the legislature. In 1884, the two men, together with other corporate heads, successfully lobbied the legislature to pass a law making fence cutting a felony (Kingston 1988: 92; Vásquez and Meyer 1985: 77). Within a few years of the passage of this law many Mexican ranchers were forced out of business because of the difficulty in feeding their herds. Approximately 50 percent of the Mexican stock herders switched to full-time farming or entered other occupations (Alonzo 1998: 228).

Unfortunately, a series of climatic events affecting South Texas debilitated the economy even further and made full-time ranching a problematic occupation. Between 1885 and 1887, a cycle of drought and blizzards hit South Texas and drove more Mexicans out of ranching (Alonzo 1998: 234; Anderson, Richardson, and Wallace 1997: 275). Many Mexican families had to sell their property to survive. The most severely affected were those from Nueces and Cameron counties. The corporate ranchers were also affected, but most did not go bankrupt. When Mexicans sold their property only the wealthy ranchers had sufficient funds to buy it (de León 1987; Montejano 1987). As more Mexicans found themselves destitute and pressured to sell their ranchlands, hundreds of thousands of acres became consolidated in the hands of a few corporate ranchers. The King family acquired the largest percentage of the property and by the early 1900s owned over one million acres in South Texas (Cheeseman 1996: 1108). At this time the King family, in partnership with the Kenedys, acquired most of the coastal land in Cameron and Nueces counties (Richardson, Anderson, and Wallace, 1997: 278). Other capitalists also did quite well, including Dillard R. Fant, Edward Lasater, A. J. Bloomberg, G. M. Raphael, Jeremiah Galvan, Francisco Yturria, and Henry M. Fields (Alonzo 1998: 252).

Although a large number of Mexican families sold their property because of the financial effects of the climatic changes, many were able to retain portions of their ranches (Richardson, Anderson, and Wallace 1997: 281). Such families survived the crisis but their acreage was reduced and their ranches were converted to small or midscale holdings (Montejano 1987). Mexican families who lost their property were forced to enter the wage labor market, most becoming farmworkers. Those who had greater resources and did not have to sell their labor entered into tenancy contracts with the new owners of their ranches. In Cameron, Hidalgo, Starr, and Zapata counties many Mexican families transitioned from ranch owners to tenant farmers (Alonzo 1998; Bulletin of the University of Texas 1915: 18).[15]

In sum, despite the fact that many Mexican families were devastated by the climatic disasters and the fencing legislation, others survived and made a decent living off their land. With the consolidation of land in the hands of a few corporate ranching families, however, corporate agriculture prospered in South Texas. This meant that corporations needed more labor to work the land and herd the cattle. This situation was ideal for President Díaz in that it solved the unemployment problems in Mexico that his modernization program was producing in the countryside. As employment in South Texas increased and unemployment in Mexico reached critical levels—for the powerless—the situation could be alleviated only by out-migration. The exodus continued.

Texas and Mexico Connected by Railway

The numerical growth of the Mexican population of Texas was facilitated by the construction of an international railway system connecting Mexico and Texas. The original intent of the project was to construct track to transport cargo between Mexico and the United States. Of particular importance was the shipment of silver and gold to the United States from Mexico and the export of U.S. manufactured goods to Mexico. For example, by 1889 Mexico was importing $36 million in U.S. manufactured goods (Vásquez and Meyer 1985: 91), and the United States imported over one million bullions of duty-free gold (Matías Romero Archives, roll 72).[16]

This economic relationship enflamed anti-U.S. sentiments in Mexico. Many Mexican intellectuals called it imperialism and protested against the uneven trade relations. In particular, they charged that the U.S. railroad corporations and the mining companies were corrupt. Mexican intellectuals complained that Mexico was paying for U.S. imperialism by allowing the mining companies to steal mineral resources and by permitting the railroad corporations to build track wherever they wanted (Callahan 1932: 504). Critics also protested that the railroad companies were out of control: not only were they given land grants and tax exemptions to build useless track, but on top of that the Mexican government paid the corporations $8,000 per kilometer of constructed track. The Mexican people in return received very little because railroad investors chose not to build track in most cities, choosing instead to lay track to connect the mines to the U.S. border and to Mexico City and Guadalajara, where there was high demand for U.S. manufactured goods.

In 1881, King, Kenedy, and Loth became the first railroad investors to lay track in Mexico (Ibid., 483). Their corporation, the Texas-Mexican National Railway Corporation, built the first branch connecting Mexico City to the city of Laredo, in Webb County. Two years later a second U.S. company, the Mexican Central, built additional branches connecting El Paso to Mexico City and to Guadalajara. And in the same year the Southern Pacific connected Eagle Pass to San Antonio, Galveston, Houston and to the Mexican city of Monclova (Ibid., 491). The following year, 1884, the Mexican Central constructed a fourth point of entry into Texas, this branch directly linking Brownsville (Cameron County) to its neighboring sister city of Matamoros, Tamaulipas. By then, the Mexican Central had built additional branches from El Paso to Colima and Tampico in southern Mexico (Coatsworth 1978). By 1892, U.S. railway corporations had invested $251 million in Mexico (Davids 1976: 180).

Though the primary function of the Mexican railway system was commercial, the American investors unwittingly created the infrastructure to rapidly move people from Mexico into the United States. By the time the Mexican railway system was established Texas was well connected to other parts of the United States, and since all of the tracks from Mexico led to Texas, a cheap source of travel became available (fig. 2.2). Other U.S. border states would not be connected by rail until the early twentieth century (Lorey 1999: 54). Though cheap train fares modernized travel for those who could afford first-, second-, or third-class coaches many Mexicans continued to cross the border to Texas on foot or in wagons.

The first Mexican train routes established through the counties of Webb, Cameron, El Paso, and Maverick caused the populations of these counties to boom (Morales and Schemal 2004). In particular, the cities of Laredo, El Paso, and Brownsville exploded. These counties, however, also grew in size as a result of the northern routes tying them to U.S. cities outside of Texas. El Paso, for example, attracted a large number of Anglo-Americans when it became connected to New Mexico and California. The city was soon transformed into a large urban center populated by newcomers prepared to invest heavily in upgrading their new homes. Hundreds of low-paying jobs were created as El Paso was transformed into a modern urban center with hotels, theaters, restaurants, schools, an opera house, club buildings, banks, saloons, stores, civic buildings, and recreational facilities (Metz 1994). The

Figure 2.2. Nineteenth-century border crossers, the Rio Grande, Texas. Aultman Collection A5650, El Paso Public Library, Border Heritage Center.

availability of employment led to the ongoing growth of a permanent Mexican immigrant population.

Growth of U.S. Imperialism in Mexico

Although many intellectuals criticized President Díaz's lack of regulation of foreign companies, their censures served no purpose since the federal government had the military power to do whatever it wanted. Díaz's regime maintained a tight hold on the population through its army and its rural police. By the late nineteenth century Díaz had spent one-third of the national budget on the military and law enforcement (Meyer, Sherman, and Deeds 2007: 396). To pay for its law enforcement and modernization programs the regime borrowed money from international banks. U.S. banks were willing to invest in Mexico but most chose not to lend money, and Díaz thus had to turn to European banks (Gilly 1994; Sloan 1978). British banks became the main lenders, but they placed strict conditions on Mexico, which angered Mexican intellectuals and many members of congress. The British banks agreed to issue loans as long as Mexico paid off the debts owed by Emperor Maximilian. The emperor had defaulted on many of the loans he incurred during the French invasion of Mexico (Zabludovsky 1998: 154). When Díaz agreed he was met with an uproar from his critics. The agreement placed the Mexican people in a very difficult position, as the total loan amount was over 22 million pounds and would be difficult to pay. The banks were satisfied with Díaz's generous agreement and payment plan, for if Mexico defaulted, British investors had been guaranteed public land to recuperate their losses.

Díaz eliminated opposition at the state level by replacing most of the governors with former Porfirista military generals. Although the masses feared Díaz's regime, he had many friends and fervent supporters. The modernization program was working in the cities, and it benefited both the upper-class and the urban professional middle class. These people enjoyed the luxuries imported from the United States and made use of the public works Díaz was carrying out in the urban areas (de la Peña 1993). Mexico City became the main beneficiary of the modernization program, as schools, parks, libraries, hospitals, a palace of fine arts, and the construction of new streets and drainage systems improved the ambiance of the city. Díaz built similar amenities in the cities where his main supporters resided. Most important were the transportation improvements made in the cities. To satisfy the demands of the elite, foreign companies built trolley systems in Mexico City and in the largest cities of Mexico. Several companies also began to build railway systems connecting Mexico City to various regions of the country.

The most controversial projects the Díaz administration implemented had to do with the mines and the countryside. The projects were designed not only to increase Mexico's economic productivity, but also to attract foreign investors. Before the programs could be implemented it was necessary to revise laws passed by the Juárez administration. In 1883 the Mexican Congress passed the Land Law Act, which affected thousands of small-scale farmers and detribalized Indian communities (Meyer, Sherman, and Deeds 2007: 398; Murillo 2008). The law required that all public land be surveyed for the purpose of development. Within a few years of its passage, one-fifth of Mexico's total land mass, or 68 million acres of rural land, was put into the hands of foreign corporations and Mexico's ruling class (Miller 1985: 272). Under the act Mexican and foreign corporations were hired to survey public lands, subdivide plots for settlement, and establish a transportation infrastructure. In return, corporations were to receive one-third of the land surveyed and be given the privilege of purchasing the remaining two-thirds. Owing to the corrupt surveying system established by the federal government many Mexicans lost their land when the corporations included privately owned ranchlands within the government's public property. The most coveted property was that on which an irrigation system had been built or which was located near water. Once the land was surveyed, Mexican farmers had to prove legal ownership in court or lose their ranches. Throughout Mexico the courts upheld the corporations' surveys over the farmers' claims. It was common for the courts to void a farmer's deed if it lacked a survey or if a registry of a deed could not be found. For many poor farmers the only recourse was to migrate north into Texas, a task made easier by the railroad infrastructure.

The company that benefited most from the land act was the American Hartford Company, which acquired several million acres (Davids 1976: 187). Other U.S. corporations with similar gains were La Esmeralda Plantation Company of Ohio, the Laguna Company of Delaware, the Vista Hermosa Company, the Palomes Land and Cattle Company, the T.O. Ranch, and the Huller Company. By the early twentieth century U.S. investors controlled 43 percent of all property values (Sloan 1978: 285).

Mexican Indians were disproportionately affected by the land act, as thousands of communities in Mexico had never received a deed following the Juárez administration's order that all tribal lands be subdivided and privatized (Cabrera 1914; Miller 1985). Under Mexico's Lerda Law the federal government had stripped the tribal councils of their legal authority over their community's land, and each family was given part of the tribe's communal holdings. The problem with the privatization program was that Juárez died, and the incoming administrations failed to register the changes or issue new deeds. Thus when the Land Law Act of 1883 passed, detribalized Indians were left at the mercy of the courts. Judges had the power to interpret property law and decide to support the surveying companies or recognize that the Lerda Law had been improperly executed. If the latter was the case, a deed issued by Juárez's administration was unnecessary (Murillo 2008; Orozco 1895). The Indians' legal defense rested upon the court's decision to uphold a series of property laws passed during the Spanish period (Aguirre Beltrán 1991b). Before Mexican independence, Spain issued Indians many land grants as either private parcels or communal land grants (see Menchaca 2001). The legal basis of the grants was to ensure that Indian communities had sufficient land to remain together as a collectivity. Indians who heeded President Juárez's orders and privatized their holdings but failed to disband their tribal councils could argue in court that although they were not given deeds the Spanish land grant titles were still valid since they were not detribalized communities (Stephen 2002). The judges, therefore, had the power to rule on behalf of these Indians and uphold their Spanish community land claims, but Indians who had disbanded their councils had no legal recourse because they were detribalized Indians. If they managed not to get evicted from their lands, the main option left to them was to remain in their homes and become tenant farmers. If they were expelled they had to migrate, and many of them chose to join the northern migration. Some detribalized Indians began a journey that would eventually transform them into U.S. citizens.

A second controversial policy benefiting American corporations was Mexico's subsoil property law. In 1884 foreign corporations were given the subsoil rights of the property they had acquired in Mexico. Ownership of the minerals and fuels was no longer reserved for the nation (Meyer, Sherman, and Deeds 2007: 387–389), a concession that would eventually prove to be Díaz's main political blunder and a rallying point against his regime. A corporation owned by the Guggenheim family, which had invested heavily in the mining industry and in turn acquired lands with minerals and petroleum, was the main beneficiary of the subsoil property law. The Guggenheim Corporation owned the American Smelting and Refining Company, which built plants in Coahuila, Chihuahua, Durango, and San Luis Potosí. The corporation also owned the majority of the stock in the Aguascalientes Metal Company, the Guggenheim Exploration Company, the Tecolote Silver Mines, the Esperanza Gold Mine, and several other mines in north Mexico. By 1888 the Guggenheims and other U.S. corporations had invested $30 million in the mines (Callahan 1932: 508).

The Farmers' Alliance: A Social Movement against Immigrants Is Set in Motion

During the late nineteenth century Mexicans were not the only ones affected by unjust land policies passed by their government. In the United States, state legislatures also passed land laws to attract capitalist investors. It became a common policy for state governments to lure investors by offering land grants (Barnes 1984; Hicks 1964). In Texas the legislature's land grant concessions attracted 41 railroad companies. The companies were awarded 10,240 acres for every mile of track they laid in Texas (Sitton and Conrad 1998: 11). Although most of the granted land was owned by the government, when routes passed through private property the companies were given the land they needed through eminent domain. Farmers throughout Texas were affected, but the most severely impacted were those whose homesteads were located along the routes where railroad track was laid connecting central Texas to Dallas, Houston, Nacogdoches, and Fort Worth. In the mid-1870s, the loss of farmland sparked a social movement against the railroad corporations. At first, the target of the angry farmers was the corporations, but as the movement matured immigrants became the farmers' scapegoats.

Small-scale farmers established an organization called the Green Backs. The first members were farmers from the counties where land was lost to the railroads, but as the legislature awarded railroad corporations more land the movement spread to other regions. Farmers whose homesteads were not in the path of the routes joined the movement when they saw that the land concessions were adversely affecting them.

Initially the main purpose of the Green Backs was to place pressure on the legislature to stop the land concessions and to establish a railroad regulatory board to oversee the shipping rates charged for cargo. Farmers alleged that once the towns and cities were connected by railway, train companies were free to charge whatever rate they wanted for shipping freight from farm to market. This caused an unfair economic imbalance between those who could afford to ship their goods to market by train and those who could not. Goods transported by train arrived at market sooner and fresher and could be shipped to far-off destinations, advances the traditional horse-and-cart method could not match. The train system was ruining many businesses and pushing some farmers into bankruptcy.

The Green Backs, unable to attract a large membership, were ignored by the Texas legislature. By 1880 many disillusioned Green Backs left the organization to join chapters of a newly formed national organization called the Farmers' Alliance (Barnes 1984: 49). The Farmers' Alliance had a platform similar to that of the Green Backs, but it had a larger networking base and a stable funding source. For the Green Backs, joining a national organization was a strategic political move, as within a few months of reorganizing, local chapters grew to over one thousand members. Now that a national organization was behind the farmers, the Texas legislature took notice. State legislators knew that farmers could no longer be ignored given that they were now being aided by outside professional organizers who were teaching them how to appeal to the general public. After alliance chapters launched a successful statewide campaign against the railroad corporations and gained the support of the public, the legislature was pressured to repeal the railroad land grant program in 1882 (Richardson, Anderson, and Wallace 1997: 255). By this time, however, railroad corporations had received over 32 million acres of land in Texas.

The Farmers' Alliance successful campaign against the railroad corporations attracted thousands of new members. By 1886, its membership grew to seventy-five thousand. A large number of railroad workers had also joined the alliance, as they too favored regulating the railroad industry. Their interests, however, differed. Railroad workers specifically wanted improved working conditions and higher wages, whereas farmers wanted cheap cargo shipment rates and other related farming demands. In August 1886 the Farmers' Alliance joined a labor union called the Knights of Labor, and the two groups organized a convention to discuss their common goals (Barnes 1984: 73). Their overarching plan was to pressure the legislature to regulate corporations and banks in Texas and to pass laws protecting industrial workers. Both organizations also supported the passage of a state law granting or selling cheap land to farmers (Richardson, Anderson, and Wallace 1997).

After the convention the Farmers' Alliance and the Knights of Labor aggressively pursued their platforms by participating in state-level electoral politics. Electing representatives who supported their platform became their goal. When the organizations were unable to convince sufficient legislators to support their agenda, labor and farm activists began running their own candidates. They also learned that to attract new members a more diversified political campaign was needed. A campaign emphasizing federal relief for farmers had failed to attract prosperous farmers and the merchant classes. Likewise, organizers knew that professionals and schoolteachers were sympathetic to the industrial workers' platform but would not support an organization whose agenda did not affect them directly. A grassroots campaign shared by the general public was needed. The leadership of the Farmers' Alliance therefore proposed launching a campaign against immigrants since at the national level many alliance chapters were attracting new members through their anti-immigrant campaigns. In Texas this strategy manifested itself in a campaign targeting Mexican and German immigrants.

Scapegoats: German and Mexican Immigrants

Although the Mexican population of South Texas shared many of the goals espoused by the Farmers' Alliance, the organization failed to gain acceptance in the region largely owing to its anti-immigrant campaign. The alliance also failed to attract German residents throughout Texas for the same reason. Germans and Mexicans, for exaggerated and sometimes unfounded reasons, had become the main scapegoats of the frustrations felt by poor and disempowered white farmers. German immigrants were viewed to be economic competitors, while Mexicans were considered a drain on the local economies. Any understanding of the Farmers' Alliance campaign against immigrants must be sought in an exploration of the sources of the farmers'

Table 2.7. Mexican and German Foreign-Born in Texas, 1850–1890

Decade	German	Mexican	Total Foreign-Born	Percentage Mexican/ German
1850	8,191	4,459	16,774	75
1860	20,553	12,443	43,422	76
1870	23,893	23,020	62,411	75
1880	35,347	43,161	114,616	69
1890	48,774	51,469	152,956[a]	66

[a]Of the total foreign-born, 99,425 were from Europe, Canada, and Newfoundland (Newfoundland was a colony of Great Britain at this time.)
Sources: U.S. Census 1854: xxxvii, 117–118; U.S. Census 1864: xxiv, 490; U.S. Census 1872: 321, 392; U.S. Census 1882: 493; U.S. Census 1885: 443; U.S. Census 1894: 669–675; U.S. Census 1897b: 9.

resentment toward Germans and Mexicans, who throughout the mid- to late nineteenth century constituted over three-quarters of the foreign-born population of the state (table 2.7).

The Farmers' Alliance and many native white farmers believed immigration was one of the root causes of their socioeconomic problems (Martin 1970). German immigrants were accused of conspiring with the corporations. They were denounced for purchasing property from the railroad companies, fencing off their farms, and not protesting against the unfair cargo fees charged by the railroad corporations. Germans were also accused of forming secretive ethnic clubs. In north Texas, alliance members charged that the clubs were used to form financial networks between German farmers, at the cost of excluding others (Jordan 1982). One of the main charges the alliance members raised against the Germans was their practice of fencing off their property. Allegedly, they erected the fences to prevent non-German farmers from moving their herds across the property and thus to make it difficult for them to take their cattle to market. In general, Germans were viewed as having become successful farmers at the cost of native whites.

For many native whites the German problem had developed gradually over the years but became severe in the early 1870s, when German immigrants arrived in Texas in large numbers (Richardson, Anderson, and Wallace 1997: 267). Many whites perceived their arrival to be part of a conspiracy between government and foreign corporations. The farmers' accusations were exaggerated but were based partially on facts. In 1871 the Texas legislature began recruiting German farmers through the state bureau of immigration, and to attract them promised to sell them fertile agricultural lands for cheap prices. As an added incentive the state paid for part of their voyage and upon their arrival had agents take them to their homesteads (*Laws of Texas*, 6:1030). Local farmers thought this treatment gave the Germans an unfair advantage. A few years later, after the federal government disbanded the Texas Immigration Bureau, native white farmers continued to believe that Germans were given an unfair advantage since the railroad corporations continued to sell them the best land. It had become public knowledge that wealthy Germans were buying large parcels of land in Texas and paid the passage of poor German farmers to work their land (Clements 1955; S.H.S. 1924).

Native white farmers also vilified German Americans. The prosperity of many families of German descent was attributed to their clannish ways and competitive nature. According to many native white farmers, the only reason Germans owned successful farms was that their grandparents had taken advantage of the land grant system in Texas and had purchased the most valuable land in the central and coastal regions. Their relatives had unfairly acquired this property, it was claimed, because they were financed by wealthy German investors, unlike the majority of the settlers of English descent, who did not have the same resources and had to settle for whatever type of land the government gave them (see Act of 1839, *Laws of Texas*, 2:35–36; Act of 1841, *Laws of Texas*, 2:554; Act of 1866 in Paschal 1874, p. 1445). The Farmers' Alliance agreed and charged that Germans had acquired the best land in Texas. Over the years this gave them an economic advantage, and when the railroad corporations began to sell property Germans had the financial assets to buy additional acreage. These structural conditions, according to the Farmers' Alliance, contributed to an unfair market economy and eventually caused the high bankruptcy rate of the poor non-German farmer. Alliance members, however, acknowledged that the railroad companies, not the German farmers, caused the white farmers' problems. German communities were nevertheless accused of supporting the railroad companies and being indifferent to the problems faced by the poor white farmer.

The charges raised by the Farmers' Alliance were exaggerated and were misdirected, but they were not entirely incorrect since it was a fact that thousands of white farmers had gone bankrupt. By 1880, 37 percent of farmers in Texas had lost their farms, and many were forced to turn to land tenancy (Gould 1973: 127); and a significant percentage of that land was resold to foreign corporations (Jordan 1982). Many German farmers also profited from the availability of cheap railroad land. Yet Germans were unfairly accused, since it was wealthy farmers in general who purchased the property from the railroad corporations. Germans were also mistakenly stereotyped as newcomers, when in fact many had arrived in the 1830s, and their success was largely a result of their knowledge of farming technology passed from father to son (Biesele 1987: iv).

The first wave of German immigrants settled primarily in central Texas in the counties of Gillespie and Comal. This region came to be known as the Verein Core, the heart of the German colonies. A large number of Germans also settled in the central counties of Bexar, Travis, and Fayette. Later waves of immigrants settled in the German colonies, but many became dispersed throughout Texas and formed large communities in east Texas and near the coast in the counties of Galveston, Austin, Washington, and Harris (see table 2.7). Most farmers established small, efficient farms based on a diversified crop and animal husbandry economy. On the average the farms owned by Germans were 183 acres, while those of native white Texans were approximately 260 acres (Jordan 1982: 98). Although most farms owned by Germans were small, their productivity led many to become prosperous commercial farmers. By the late 1880s, the success of their farms allowed German farmers to expand their holdings, and they began to purchase more property from the railroad corporations and from native white Texans whose farms went bankrupt. In central Texas German farmers became the most prosperous large-scale farm operators, while in east Texas their farms were small to midscale but successful. German farmers also established commercial associations to market their products and gain advantage over other local farmers. By 1890 the majority of people of German descent were prosperous farmers, and the immigrant population accounted for 50 percent of the total European foreign-born (N = 48,774 out of 97,677) (U.S. Census 1894: 669–675).

At the other end of the economic spectrum were the Mexicans. Members of the Farmers' Alliance nevertheless had equally compelling reasons to dislike them. After all, they too were immigrants. The nativist attitude toward Mexicans was of long standing and not limited to the Farmers' Alliance. To begin with, Mexicans were Catholic, not Protestant like most whites. Furthermore, ever since Texas gained its independence from Mexico, the loyalty of people of Mexican descent was suspect, and they were seen as a culturally and racially inferior people. Mexican immigrants were also seen as a drain on the economy. They kept coming to Texas, and it seemed as if there was no end to their migration. From 1880 to 1890 the size of the Mexican immigrant population grew from 43,161 to 51,469 (U.S. Census 1885: 443; U.S. Census 1895: 657–660). For the general white population immigration was not a problem as long as they remained in South Texas or in the traditional ethnic enclaves of San Antonio, El Paso, and Presidio counties. In the view of the Farmers' Alliance, however, Mexican immigration was a threat for two major reasons. First, immigrating Mexicans expanded the size of the population of Mexican descent, and this meant that they increased the numerical size of their ethnic vote. Since Mexicans were not supporters of their organization, they posed a political threat. Second, some farmers and industrial workers saw Mexican immigration as an employment threat because Mexicans were beginning to move into new areas and compete for jobs. It was better to stop immigration before they took jobs away from whites.

In the 1890s Mexican immigrants continued to be concentrated in South Texas and in the other traditional zones. However, their numbers began to increase in the western, central, and northern parts of the state. In the newly organized counties of west Texas they came to be seen as competitors because many worked for cattle corporations or for wealthy ranchers. Many were employed as farmworkers on the larger farms, whereas others worked in the cattle industry, which flourished in the area (Jordan 1982; Timmons 2004). Approximately 2,889 Mexican immigrants settled in Pecos, Val Verde, Reeves, Jefferson Davis, Brewster, and Tom Green counties (U.S. Census 1894: 669–672).[17]

Central Texas also experienced a considerable increase in the Mexican immigrant population. Here they were resented for becoming sharecroppers or tenant farmers on land owned by wealthy Germans. They were also often employed as farm laborers and seen as competitors with the locals (Arreola 2002; Foley 1997; Martin 1970). By 1890 the Mexican immigrant population of Travis, Hays, Wilson, and Caldwell counties had grown to a little over 3,000 (U.S. Census 1894: 669–672).[18]

Some Mexicans even found their way into north Texas, where traditionally few Mexican immigrants had ventured. They numbered 587, the majority residing in the counties of Dallas, Limestone, Tarrant, and Cherokee (Ibid.). The railroad corporations had established sixty-four sawmills in the northeast and needed cheap labor that was willing to perform dangerous tasks and work long hours for cheap wages (Sitton and Conrad 1998). Here

Mexicans were not viewed as economic competitors by the locals since work in the sawmills was dangerous; whites found employment in this sector undesirable and considered it a last resort.

The Farmers' Alliance and Their Anti-Immigrant Campaign: The Alien Land Act

In the early 1890s the economy of Texas experienced a temporary downturn, and immigrants became a political scapegoat (Gould 1973: 32). The most serious drag on the economy was the falling prices for cotton and agriculture, which in turn raised the cost of living. Because the majority of families in Texas depended on agriculture for their living, an unstable agricultural market threatened the livelihood of most Texans.[19] The falling agricultural market prices caused many small-scale farmers to go bankrupt and sell their property. By 1890 the percentage of impoverished farmers who turned to tenant farming reached critical proportions. By then, 41.9 percent of farmers were renting land from wealthy farmers and corporations (Bulletin of the University of Texas 1915: 12; Foley 1997: 65). Worst of all, many farmers had to abandon farming altogether and enter the migrant labor stream. Approximately 32 percent of African Americans were employed as agricultural workers, along with 55 percent of native whites and U.S.-born Mexicans, and 7.5 percent of the foreign-born, including Mexicans (U.S. Census 1897a: 612).[20] Although all groups were affected by the economic slump, farmers in the northeast were hit the worst, while German communities throughout Texas, whose diversified farming economy helped them escape the crisis, were able to weather the storm (Martin 1970).

The many whites in central and east Texas who found it difficult to obtain tenant contracts and were forced to turn to farm labor saw their financial condition worsen. Many blamed their impoverishment on Mexican immigrants and African Americans. Allegedly wealthy farmers preferred to rent to Mexicans and African Americans because they were willing to pay higher rents. Whites charged that these people drove up the cost of rents and forced poor whites out of farming. In Hays, Dewitt, Wilson, and Gonzales counties angry whites established organizations to stop prosperous farmers from renting land to Mexicans and blacks (Foley 1997: 37).

The Farmers' Alliance listened to the complaints of the displaced farmers and took action. They strategically used the labor market conflict to launch a recruitment campaign. The leadership, however, chose to focus on the problems Mexicans and other immigrants were said to produce. Mexicans were accused of taking away jobs and driving up the cost of tenant rents, while German immigrants and foreign corporations were depicted as invading America. Although many white farmers wanted the Farmers' Alliance to also take a position against African Americans, the organization refused to do so since at the national level African Americans were important in many regional political campaigns. Furthermore, at the national level the alliance was undergoing restructuring and merging with other labor and farm organizations that did not favor the exclusion of African Americans.

In the early 1890s most chapters of the Farmers' Alliance merged with other organizations and reorganized as the People's Party (Hackney 1971: 1). The main national platform became relief for farmers. The party demanded that state governments stop all farm foreclosures and if necessary use state funds to pay the farmers' debts. In Texas most chapters of the alliance also reorganized under the People's Party, and they endorsed the national agrarian campaign. This led to tremendous growth in membership. Although a few counties along the eastern coast welcomed African Americans, most chapters in Texas exclusively recruited native whites and purposely excluded racial minorities and immigrants (Martin 1970).

The People's Party became a national organization and gained considerable strength after its reorganization, prompting the Republican and Democratic parties to pay close attention to the party's activities. Throughout the country People's Party chapters were either running their own candidates for office or supporting Republican or Democratic allies; and they were winning elections. In Texas Gov. James Hogg, who was a Democrat, took notice. He pledged his commitment to farmers and demonstrated public support of the People's Party. Although he remained a solid Democrat and supportive of corporations, he advocated against alien landholdings and affirmed his belief that Texas belonged to native whites (Richardson, Anderson, and Wallace 1997: 255). He also concurred with the People's Party that in the past the legislature had not done enough to help the poor farmer against the powerful railroad corporations. Hogg promised to help by stopping bank foreclosures of farms and regulating the fees charged for railway cargo.

To implement his promises, Governor Hogg introduced legislation to regulate the railroad industry. He asked that a regulatory commission be established. The legislation passed in 1890 but was immediately challenged by the railroad industry (Ibid., 294). While the Texas Supreme Court deliberated the dispute, a commission was established but was not allowed to function until the court determined whether the state could establish such a commission. This angered the People's Party, and they threatened to push out of office any legislator who supported the railroad industry. To pacify angry farmers, many Democratic legislators supported other issues promoted by the party, specifically their anti-immigrant planks. The People's Party asked legislators to pass laws prohibiting aliens and foreign corporations from owning land in the United States (Hackney 1971: 5). This was critical since a study conducted by the Farmers' Alliance in 1890 indicated that in the United States aliens and foreign companies owned 150 million acres (Clements 1955: 210).

At the national level members of Congress concurred that there was a tenancy problem in the United States, but they were divided on whether the problem was caused by the tenant farmer or by foreign corporations. Some congressmen proposed that the foreign corporations who purchased property from the railroads and then became absentee landlords caused the main problem, while others held that the tenant farmer who was unable to make the land productive was at fault. On the basis of a federal study conducted in 1885 Congress concluded that tenancy grew rapidly in Texas, Colorado, Kansas, and Montana. The study also found that foreign corporations contracted a large percentage of the tenant farmers. Although Congress recognized that there was a problem, it could not intervene since tenancy legislation was a domain of the states. Congress could only offer the states advice.

In Texas, Governor Hogg reacted to the pressure of the People's Party and the findings of Congress by introducing legislation to address the tenancy problems caused by aliens and foreign corporations. In 1891, he proposed legislation to limit the rights of aliens to own land in Texas (Winkler 1916: 296). This strategic move allowed him to buy time to pacify the angry farmers, while the courts determined what authority the legislature held over the railroad corporations. Hogg's legislation was carefully crafted, however, in order not to alienate corporate investors. Hogg identified the alien farmer as the main problem rather than the corporations who had sold them land. He cited two main problems: tenants poorly maintained or underdeveloped their farms, and British corporations sold their American holdings to alien farmers rather than to Americans, an act that had created a tenancy and alien landownership problem in Texas. The Twenty-second Texas Legislature agreed, and to alleviate the state's land problems it revised the Texas Alien Land Law of 1854. Under the new Alien Land Law of 1891 aliens were required to become U.S. citizens to own land in Texas ("Aliens," in *General Laws of Texas, Regular Session, 22nd Legislature 1891*, p. 82). Immigrants had six years to naturalize to avoid having their land confiscated by the state. Under former law immigrants were allowed to own land as long as they had filed papers of naturalization, but they did not have to complete the process. Now finalizing of papers was necessary.[21]

The legislation was a major victory for the People's Party and their first successful campaign against aliens. Yet many members of the party were dissatisfied because they believed the legislature had not gone far enough. They favored limiting landownership to U.S.-born residents and prohibiting aliens from owning property in Texas, regardless of whether they naturalized. The victory of the People's Party was short-lived, however, as within months of the legislative mandate the Texas Supreme Court ruled that the Alien Land Law of 1891 was unconstitutional (*The New Handbook of Texas* 1996: 106). In the opinion of the justices the law had to be rewritten and made constitutional because it prevented foreign corporations from conducting business in Texas. According to the justices, aliens could be prohibited from owning land in Texas, but corporations could not be banned from conducting business in the United States. The act of prohibiting foreign corporations from owning land prevented them from leasing property to tenants, and this in turn obstructed their right to conduct business.[22]

The People's Party regarded the court's ruling as a setback but not a total defeat since the court upheld the state's right to prohibit aliens from owning property in Texas. Party members knew that they had to continue pressuring the legislature and the governor (Barkdsale 1932). The Party began to run its own candidates for state-level offices rather than support Democratic allies. In the gubernatorial election of 1892 the party ran its own candidate (Winkler 1916: 293, 315).

To dissuade voters from supporting the People's Party, Governor Hogg's campaign incorporated some of the party's agrarian reform planks. The intent was to demonstrate that the governor was solidly behind the farmers, while at the same time not alienate all foreign-stock families. On March 14, 1892, Hogg addressed the legislature, encouraging the representatives to write a bill that ensured that land in Texas would remain in the hands of U.S. citizens. He expressed disdain for alien landownership and argued that wealthy foreign investors should not be eligible to own land in Texas. The governor stated,

> After the hardships of a frontier life are passed and the resources of the country are known, then it is that aliens, without any intention of citizenship, are eager to lay their hands upon the richest soil at the lowest price possible to be held for speculative purposes. When it is possible for these lands to be collected and owned in large bodies by aliens, a swarm of foreign tenantry at once follows, and large estates dominated by alien landlords spring up to menace the peace and happiness of the citizen and to perpetuate a system of bondage on the tenants themselves. (*Journal of the Senate of Texas, 22nd Legislature, Extra Session*, 1892, p. 14)

He then asked the legislature to write a just but inflexible alien land law prohibiting immigrants from owning land in Texas if they did not plan to become U.S. citizens: "The law should be so drawn that within a reasonable specified time after an alien (a person not a citizen of the United States) acquires by purchase, inheritance or otherwise the deed or title to lands within this State, he shall either become a citizen to enjoy said land, or shall sell it to some citizen of the United States" (Ibid.). In his address Governor Hogg acknowledged that the state legislature did not have the power to prevent foreign corporations from owning or leasing land. He advised legislators, however, to restrict the amount of acreage corporations could acquire and to require corporate owners to become U.S. citizens. He did not believe either stipulation was unconstitutional since corporations would be allowed to conduct business in Texas. Moreover, corporate owners would merely be restricted more or less in the way immigrants were (Ibid., 15).

The next day the House of Representatives debated Hogg's proposals. The debates ranged from prohibiting all aliens and foreigners from owning property in Texas (House Bill No. 22, in *Journal of the House of Representatives, Texas, 22nd Legislature, Extra Session*, 1892, pp. 34–42) to more moderate resolutions restricting landownership to citizens and naturalized aliens (House Bill No. 23). Some resolutions even proposed plans to strip current owners of their land and require them to sell it to American citizens (Bill No. 40).

After two and a half weeks of debate in both houses, on April 12, 1892, the legislature reached a compromise (*Laws of Texas*, 10:370). The revised legislation expressed animus against alien ownership but not against foreign corporate investments. No prohibitive measures were placed upon foreign corporations.[23] They could continue doing business as usual. The new law placed restrictions on immigrants planning to purchase property and on those who inherited property from an alien. Land already owned by immigrants was exempt from the act. All immigrants purchasing property must have filed naturalization papers. Immigrants, however, could not purchase property in a nonincorporated area or in a nonplatted section of a city, town, or village. Basically the law prevented the sale of undeveloped land to immigrants outside of the places that were already settled and developed. This was an important restriction since at this time many new counties were being organized in south, west, and north Texas, and the boundaries of many counties were being redrawn (Coursey 1962; Gournay 1995). Heirs were required to file naturalization papers within ten years of inheriting property; if they chose not to become citizens they were required to sell their land. Only children who inherited property were given a longer period to resolve matters. After they turned twenty-one, heirs had ten years to naturalize or else sell their land. The inheritance law was designed to force non-U.S. residents to either resettle in the United States or sell their property since a person had to be a U.S. resident to file naturalization papers.

In the end, the reforms were moderate in comparison to the mandate Governor Hogg had proposed, and they were also a radical departure from the platform espoused by the People's Party. It is not surprising that the legislature passed a moderate alien land law since 1892 was an election year. Legislators needed to pacify native whites, but at the same time not alienate immigrant voters. In Texas the immigrant vote was important because immigrants could vote and also influence how their native-born children cast their ballots (Saunders 1971). Hogg was reelected, and so were most Democratic legislators. The People's Party lost the gubernatorial bid but did much better than expected. Eight People's Party candidates were elected to the lower house and one to the senate (Richardson, Anderson, and Wallace 1997: 297). This was a cautionary victory: the party learned that it had to be careful not to alienate the children of immigrant voters.

Electoral Politics and the Exclusion of Mexicans by the People's Party

After the campaign of 1892 the People's Party rethought its strategy and decided to court the German and African American vote. If the party secured these ethnic votes it could win elections in counties where native whites were evenly divided between Democrats and the People's Party (Martin 1970). Previous elections had indicated that African Americans were no longer solidly behind Republicans, and convincing them to join the party was a possibility. African Americans were voting according to local needs rather than solely on party lines. The party's agrarian platform was very likely to appeal to them. The German communities would be difficult to recruit but not impossible. They too were voting on the basis of local needs. Certainly the prosperous farmers would not be attracted to the party, but small-scale farmers might (Clements 1955). In the case of other voters, European immigrants were ignored because their numbers were insufficient to affect election results, and Mexicans were considered a lost cause since they were solidly in the Democratic camp. The People's Party decided that the best way to deal with voters of Mexican descent was simply to stop them from casting their ballots.

To gain the support of German Americans, the People's Party changed its anti-immigrant rhetoric and stipulated in their campaign propaganda that they were against Mexican Catholics and foreign corporations (Jordan 1982; Martin 1970). They were not against the older generation of European immigrants. Mexicans were stereotyped as newcomers and foreigners, while Germans and other European groups were characterized as valued members of the white race who during Texas independence and the Mexican War had fought against an inferior race.

Regardless of the party's change in attitude, people of German origin continued to distrust it. Furthermore, in some east Texas counties native whites did not follow the party line and continued to promote agendas that alienated German voters. Local liquor prohibition resolutions were proposed, and many chapters began to demand that the party adopt a prohibition plank. For many farmers of German descent this was a serious threat because they were the main manufacturers of beer in Texas and the owners of breweries (Gould 1973). The party had also miscalculated the effects of its anti-Mexican campaign on the German communities since their depiction of Mexicans as unpatriotic and superstitious Catholics angered many German Catholics. Likewise, many German communities resented the party for having spearheaded the lobbying campaign for the Alien Land Act. The legislation had restricted the purchasing ability of large-scale landowners.

When the next election came around in 1894, the leadership of the People's Party learned that they had been unable to win over the German vote. Regardless of this failure, party members were quite satisfied with the results of the general election. The party won nearly half of the native white and African American vote. This allowed them to declare victory. The election results shocked everyone, especially the Democrats, since the People's Party elected twenty-two members to the House of Representatives (Martin 1970: 210). The party was also content with the gubernatorial race, even though they lost. They had come close to winning, very close. The Democratic candidate, C. A. Culberson, won with 206,141 votes, and the People's Party candidate, T. L. Nugent, came in second with 152,731 (Kingston, Attlesey, and Crawford 1992: 69). Culberson was a clear winner but only because the remaining 61,742 votes were divided among three other candidates. The Democrats knew that the gubernatorial seat and the state legislature were in danger of being lost if in the next election they did not put an end to the People's Party appeal. The People's Party, on the other hand, knew they could destroy the Democratic Party or at least challenge its hold on the legislature. To do so the party had to either dismantle or win over the Democratic base. It needed to continue going after a larger percentage of the native white and African American vote, but it was also critical to stop immigrants from voting in Texas. The election results indicated that most immigrants voted Democrat. The only way to stop immigrants from voting was to change the state's voting laws and prohibit noncitizens from voting. Such a step, however, would have to be taken strategically in order not to alienate the American-born children of European immigrants. The party's specific target became Mexican immigrants and their children, who they believed constituted the majority of the voters of Mexican descent. If these sectors of the Mexican-origin population were prevented from voting, the party would be able to win key races in South Texas, El Paso, and Bexar. Of particular importance was winning Congressional District 11, as it covered all of South Texas and the eastern coastal counties. The party strategized that if Mexican immigrants and their children could be prevented from voting, they could win the district because they already had the African American coastal vote, and now they merely had to appeal to the white voters.

Mexican Immigrant Naturalization Patterns

The agrarian platform of the People's Party proposed radical reforms to benefit the common person in Texas. Mexicans easily could have been attracted to the party had they not been purposely excluded and treated like economic and political scapegoats. It is ironic that a party that espoused noble ideals embedded in a doctrine of social class equality could favor policies that discriminated against immigrants and people of Mexican origin. Rather than demanding equality for all Texans, the People's Party only wanted equality for some people. In the party's grand plan there was no room for Mexicans, as the economic interests and social mobility of the small farmer depended largely upon the creation of a social stratum that could be exploited. Cheap agricultural labor was the key to changing the small-scale farm from a subsistent operation to a commercial production. In the view of the small-scale farmers who composed the core and majority membership of the People's Party, families of Mexican descent, in particular immigrants, needed to be denied political rights if they were to be converted into a permanent peonage class.

By 1889 a total of 13,715 Mexican immigrants had filed naturalization papers in 1848–1889, 98 percent of them having filed within the last twenty years, and although they formed a small voting unit, it was large enough to be important in regional elections when voters were evenly divided on a candidate (see table 2.2). More important, the Mexican immigrant voting block was not limited to those who had filed naturalization papers, as the native-born children of immigrants could also vote and were their political allies. Likewise, in many communities there were influential immigrants who could convince Mexican Americans to vote with them. Of particular importance were the owners of Spanish-language newspapers, who in election season unified the vote.

The influence of the united Mexican-descent vote was acknowledged in political circles, yet it was also well-known that its full political potential was limited by financial constraints affecting eligible immigrant voters. Voting was beyond the reach of many Mexicans because they simply could not afford the naturalization application fees. For example, in 1889, the naturalization laws required that a person be twenty-one years of age or older to apply, have resided in the United States at least five years at the time of application, and pay several fees at different stages of the process (Naturalization Act of 1870 in *16 U.S. Statutes at Large* 254). After the first papers were filed, an applicant had to wait two years before a judge allowed them to file final papers and take the oath of citizenship. At minimum the total fee for naturalizing added up to at least $1.50 per family member, a significant expense at that time. The first fee cost 50 cents and was paid to the clerk for processing the initial papers (the declaration). The applicant also had to pay an additional 50-cent fee for the application certificate. If additional copies were needed, each certificate cost 50 cents. A final fee of 50 cents was collected when the final certificate was issued. However, if the applicant was required to come before a judge additional times, other fees accrued. Naturalization, therefore, was a long, expensive process that many Mexicans could afford only after they had acquired a steady paying job.

The People's Party was aware of the financial restrictions immigrants faced. Party members knew that if the naturalization process was made more strenuous, Mexican immigrants could be prevented from becoming U.S. citizens and in turn prevented from voting and purchasing property in Texas. Ultimately, by making the naturalization process more difficult, the size of the electoral body represented by people of Mexican origin could be reduced. The People's Party thus embarked on a political campaign to make naturalization nearly impossible for Mexican immigrants and to stop their native-born children from voting.

CHAPTER 3

Ricardo Rodriguez and the People's Party in the 1890s

During the 1890s a growing political movement in Texas sought to bar people of Mexican origin from obtaining U.S. citizenship. The movement was led by the People's Party but was strongly supported by Republicans and some Democrats. Few Democratic politicians formed alliances with the People's Party, and many who did were motivated by nativist or Populist ideals. The most fervent Democratic allies came from voting districts in west or South Texas, where the voting constituencies were ethnically mixed. In many of these districts it was difficult to get elected without the support of Mexican voters, and some politicians considered this fact a nuisance, one that had to be eliminated. Other Democratic politicians, however, supported the People's Party simply because they held nativist views and did not believe Mexicans of Indian descent were rational, responsible citizens.

The political alliance that formed to disenfranchise voters of Mexican descent began in the Texas legislature and then moved into the courtrooms before culminating in the federal court ruling *In re Rodriguez* (1897). What transpired went beyond Texas politics, however, and became one of the most important and formative moments in Mexicans' naturalization history, as the Populist alliance attempted to bar all people of Mexican descent from obtaining U.S. citizenship.

I use government archives, platforms of the parties' state conventions, news articles, and legal records to document the political movement launched against Mexicans. By examining newspaper accounts I also reconstruct the reaction of the community of Mexican origin to the public hostility expressed against them.

The Election of 1894 and the Twenty-Fourth Texas Legislature: The Anti-Immigrant Agenda Begins

By the early 1890s the People's Party was enjoying widespread support and some success, although it had failed to gain the governor's seat in 1892. In preparation for the upcoming election, the leadership of the People's Party began to forge a closer alliance with the Prohibition Party, which at that time was gaining a following in conservative communities across Texas. The parties shared two goals: ending alien ownership of property in Texas and reducing the influence corporations held over the state government. In 1894 the parties coordinated their state conventions to facilitate the attendance of their members at both. The two conventions, held in Waco, were scheduled for consecutive weeks in mid-June, so that when one convention ended the next would begin within a few days. This enabled the executive committee of the People's Party to meet with the leaders of the Prohibition Party to co-ordinate their political planks for the upcoming November election (Winkler 1916: 332–336).

When the state conventions ended, the leadership of the People's Party was divided on how close their alliance with the Prohibition Party should be. They had common goals, yet the positions taken by the Prohibition-ists were considered extreme and politically naive. The executive commit-tee of the People's Party was prepared to work together but was unwill-ing to endorse most of the Prohibitionists' planks against the manufacture, consumption, and sale of liquor. It feared such a prohibition would alienate many voters and negate all possible gains they might make within the Ger-man communities (Bryan 1896). Their fears were well grounded as it turned out because during the Prohibition Party's state convention of June 28 the party outlined an extremist platform that could well have alienated many voters. The party adopted several articles that the People's Party was un-comfortable with, among them banning the sale, manufacture, and con-sumption of liquor, ending all immigration to Texas, and revising federal naturalization laws in order to require immigrants to have resided in the United States for ten years before becoming eligible to apply for citizen-ship (Winkler 1916: 307, 335–337). Unlike the People's Party, which was targeting only Mexicans, the Prohibitionists alleged that all immigrants were a detriment to the welfare of the state, in particular Germans because they manufactured liquor and thereby contributed to the social ills associ-ated with its consumption (Gould 1973). According to them, liquor, im-migration, and poverty were interrelated because immigrants manufactured alcohol and wastefully consumed it. They believed that only by obstructing immigrants' path toward citizenship would Texans be able to combat the impact of their degeneracy.

Although the Prohibition Party was seen as an important ally, the executive committee of the People's Party decided that a close alliance should be formed only at the local level. They encouraged their members to work with Prohibitionists in communities where the majority supported the ban of liquor. Prohibition was a sensitive issue, and for now they could not endorse a statewide campaign. Instead they would continue to focus on their national campaign against corporations and find ways to dilute the impact of the Mexican vote. They believed such a campaign would continue to attract Democrats and Republicans to their party, but the strategy turned out to be a political blunder, as prohibition soon became a central rallying point of Texans of all walks of life.

Instead of using prohibition to rally votes, the People's Party focused on electoral campaigns that could realistically be won. One of the most important goals was to win Congressional District 11 in the general election of 1894, a victory that would give them their first congressional victory in Texas and bring them national attention. The only obstacle in their way was Mexican voters. Congressman William Henry Crain was running for reelection in District 11, and his seat was vulnerable. The district encompassed all of South Texas and also two gulf coast counties that contained large pockets of People's Party supporters. Crain was popular among immigrants, especially Mexicans, but he had begun to lose his political base among native whites. His ongoing opposition to making naturalization more restrictive and to limiting immigration won him many votes among immigrants, but it also cost him votes in native white districts. A year earlier, Crain had actively opposed unfavorable naturalization legislation pending before the U.S. Congress (Crain 1894). One bill proposed instituting a literacy requirement for all naturalization applicants, the intent of which was to prevent undesirable immigrants from becoming U.S. citizens. A second bill proposed to amend residency requirements for naturalization when applicants came from nations identified as desirable sources of immigration. Immigrants from desirable countries would be exempted from the five-year residency requirement and would be naturalized after they declared their intention to become U.S. citizens. Arguing that all immigrants should be treated the same, Crain opposed both revisions on the basis that the legislation was unfair. He also successfully lobbied against a constitutional amendment to limit voting to U.S. citizens. None of these bills made it through Congress.

In the election of November 1894 Crain campaigned for reelection against the People's Party candidate in his district, Vachel Weldon, who was benefiting from the party's backing and appeared to have an excellent chance of winning (Cantrell and Barton 1989: 669–671). Although Weldon was running as an independent, he had accepted the People's Party nomination and was included on their ticket. Capturing the majority of voters in South Texas would be difficult for him, but there was a good chance that the three large counties on the gulf coast, Wharton, Jackson, and Calhoun, would give Weldon the votes he needed.[1] A large percentage of the residents in those counties were African American, and the People's Party believed that voters there would support their party. Eighty-one percent of Wharton's population was African American, while in Jackson and Calhoun, it was 56 percent and 34 percent, respectively, while the rest of the residents were primarily native whites (Martin 1970: 92).

As noted earlier, People's candidates did well in the election of 1894 but lost the gubernatorial race as well as the District 11 race. The loss to Congressman Crain was a major setback, as the People's Party had expected Weldon to win an easy victory, one that they had regarded as their main opportunity to gain national prominence for the Texas chapters. Overall, 24 members of the People's Party were elected to the Twenty-Fourth Texas Legislature (*Southern Mercury*, January 31, 1895, p. 2). Of these, 22 were elected to the House of Representatives (out of a total of 128) and 2 to the state senate (out of 33).[2] Moreover, the People's Party gained a large percentage of the vote, and at the county level this growing appeal translated into an increase in local wins (Abramowitz 1953). Candidates won seats in counties and towns in north and east Texas, where People's and Prohibitionist candidates had traditionally done well. However, the main surprise in the election returns was that People's Party candidates were elected in many Democratic counties in central Texas, including Caldwell, Callahan, Blanco, Burnet, Lampasas, Hamilton, Wilson, Bosque, Burleson, Limestone, Raines, Bastrop, Lee, Bandera and Milam (Martin 1970: 61). Many African Americans also voted for People's candidates, although the majority remained divided between Democrats and Republicans (Ibid., 97). Germans and Mexicans, as expected, overwhelmingly supported Democrats (Ibid., 61; Cantrell and Barton 1989). People's supporters, however, surprisingly carried Dimmit County in South Texas. For Democrats, more surprising than this was the number of votes for governor the People's candidate received. As noted in chapter 2, the Democratic candidate, C. A. Culberson, won with 206,141 votes, yet the People's candidate, T. L. Nugent, did well as the runner-up, with 152,731 votes (Kingston, Attlesey and Crawford 1992: 69). The gubernatorial race basically signaled that the People's Party had replaced the Republican Party as the alternative party for native whites.

Republicans won only 2 state-level seats. It was now clear that the main opposition to the Democratic Party would come from People's candidates.

Although the elections of 1894 went well for the People's Party, they claimed that Crain's supporters cheated by stuffing the ballot boxes with illegal Mexican votes (Cantrell and Barton 1989). The party charged that Crain had won the election fraudulently since Weldon won in sixteen of the twenty-eight counties, and in nine of the counties won by Crain Weldon had received a large number of the votes.[3] The executive committee of the party issued a formal complaint and asked Weldon to challenge the election because they had proof that in Cameron County, where 2,216 votes were cast, a large number of Mexicans had cast illegal ballots. The party informed Weldon that they had witnesses who would testify that Mexicans had been illegally naturalized on the day of the election so that they could vote for Crain. This was a serious charge, as by law a person could not be naturalized on election day (see U.S. Naturalization Act 1870, in 16 *U.S. Statutes at Large* 254).

Weldon refused to challenge the vote and graciously conceded to the congressman. The allegations that Mexican immigrants voted illegally were never proven, and a review of Cameron's naturalization records does not support the charges. In 1894, 168 men applied for U.S. citizenship (TNR, roll 2), of whom 160 were Mexican, 6 were Anglo-Americans, and 2 were Spaniards. Of the Mexican applicants, 100 of the 160 had applied for citizenship at least six months before election day, and the remaining 60 had applied between October 23 and November 5, 1894. These individuals applied close to the date of the election but did not register on election day, as was alleged. Furthermore, the number of petitioners who filed papers close to election day could not have influenced the election results because the number of voters in Cameron was a small fraction of those who supported Crain. If fraud was committed and the election boxes were stuffed, the deception was committed by the election judges, not by Mexican voters.

When the newly elected Twenty-Fourth Legislature assembled in January 1895, one of the first orders of business was to address the best way to purify the franchise. The Crain controversy had vilified immigrants and identified them as an electoral problem. Legislation aimed at reforming the voting laws was introduced by Democrats, unanimously supported by members of the People's Party, and heatedly debated by Democrats. The two Republicans in the House of Representatives were divided. The Democrat Samuel B. McBride spearheaded the drive to prohibit immigrants from voting in Texas by introducing legislation in the House to revise Article 6 of the State Constitution to mandate that only U.S. citizens be allowed to vote in Texas. McBride represented District 98 (Blanco, Gillespie, Hays, and Comal), a mixed district composed of native Texans and immigrants. Although the majority of the residents in McBride's district were working-class native whites, affluent German immigrants engaged in the production of liquor and poor Mexican tenant farmers dependent on their German employers also lived there (Jordan 1982: 210).[4] The district was also home to one of the largest chapters of the White Caps, a secret organization resolved to stop German farmers from employing and renting property to Mexicans and blacks (Foley 1997).

On January 11, 1895, McBride introduced House Joint Resolution (H.J.R.) 3 to amend the Texas Constitution and extend suffrage strictly to U.S. citizens (*House Journal, Texas, 24th Legislature, Regular Session, 1895,* p. 16, 24). To defeat his bill, opponents introduced poll tax legislation requiring voters from the ages of twenty-one to sixty to pay a fee in order to vote. They rallied others to support McBride's resolution only if a poll tax was appended. McBride and his supporters opposed the amendment, charging that it was a transparent attempt to end debate, as no one would dare impose a tax on poor farmers (see Martin 1970; Strong 1944). McBride's bill died on the floor after failing to receive sufficient votes to continue.

While McBride's supporters caucused on ways to gain support to end alien voting, the official newspaper of the People's Party, the *Southern Mercury,* on February 14, 1895, commented on current resolutions supported by legislators representing the People's Party. Among the legislation were bills to increase the taxation of railroad and insurance companies and to allow women assistant physicians to work in asylums. The *Southern Mercury* also reported that one of the party's bills had angered Democrats because many legislators were in support of prohibiting Mexicans from voting in Texas. The *Southern Mercury* stated, "The attempt to protect the honest voters of the state against the illegal voting of 75,000 peons and greasers on the border aroused the ire of the Democrats greatly" (*Southern Mercury,* February 14, 1895, p. 8).

On February 22, 1895, McBride reintroduced his bill. Once again the bill failed to gain the necessary two-thirds majority to pass and it died (*House Journal, Texas, 24th Legislature, Regular Session, 1895,* pp. 353–354). The next day an unidentified reporter from the *Dallas Morning News* described the events leading up to McBride's defeat and commented on the status of other pending constitutional legislation. The news article also clarified misconceptions, described the heated debate, and stated that the constitutional legislation was aimed not at all immigrants but at Mexicans only. According to the *Dallas Morning News,* many Democrats charged McBride with trying to destroy the Democratic Party. He was accused of being a Prohibitionist and of opposing German immigrants. McBride denied the charges, arguing that he was being misunderstood because his bill was directed at Mexicans, not Germans. The *Dallas Morning News* reported as follows:

> Mr. McBride closed the discussion and took occasion to deny the charge made against him by a local German paper that he was a local optionist and that his resolution was a prohibition scheme. He stated that he represented more Germans than any other member of the house and that he had received a large majority of their votes at the last election. He recalled the fact that at his request consideration of the resolution had been postponed to give the German citizens of Texas a chance to protest against it if they did not like it, but that on the contrary many memorials and letters had been received from them favoring it. He said that the floating Mexican vote was what was aimed at. (*Dallas Morning News,* February 23, 1895, pp. 1–2)

According to the Dallas paper, when McBride clarified his position as being against Mexicans the debate exploded, and many serious charges were raised against Mexican immigrants and Mexican Americans. Many legislators rose to defend McBride and proposed several schemes to constitutionally deny people of Mexican descent the vote. Others counterattacked and rebuked the derogatory remarks, defending the honor of their Mexican constituencies and characterizing them as honest people. A few legislators tried to temper the debate by asking the members to stop their disorderly debate and try to calmly discuss why some believed Mexican voters posed a problem. One issue that remained unclear throughout the debate was whether the reforms would apply only to Mexican immigrants or if policies were being designed to stop all people of Mexican descent from voting. When legislators discussed why the voting reforms were needed, the general argument was that Mexicans spoiled the electoral process.

Those who participated in the debate represented districts throughout Texas, but those who defended Mexican voters were primarily from Bexar and South Texas. Interestingly, a few of the legislators who advocated unfavorable reforms against Mexicans represented counties containing large Mexican populations. These counties, however, had a mixed Anglo and Mexican voting constituency.

Some legislators attempted to temper the debate by moving away from racial issues and focusing on administrative complications. Their arguments ranged from a possible gubernatorial veto, as it was known that the governor supported immigrant voting, to charging that the McBride bill was fiscally irresponsible, given that it would cost the state twenty-six thousand dollars to hold a statewide election to disenfranchise Mexican voters.

The *Dallas Morning News* proceeded to report that after the House defeated McBride's bill the debate continued on the floor but took on an impolite tone. Representative Owsley, an ally of McBride, requested further debate and reconsideration of the McBride bill. Several representatives from southwest Texas supported him but Representative Monroe, who represented the counties of Starr, Cameron, Zapata, and Hidalgo (District 85), opposed reconsideration. He also reminded the representatives from southwest Texas that Mexicans had placed them in office, and if they continued to support McBride they would lose their seats in the next election. Monroe also demanded civility and asked the legislators to stop insulting the Mexican people. The *Dallas Morning News* summarized Monroe's admonishment:

> Mr. Monroe of Starr obtained the floor and paid his respects to the gentlemen who had been abusing the Mexican vote without which they would not now be occupying their seats in the twenty-fourth legislature. He predicted that the passage of the resolution would split the democratic party and addressing himself to some of the gentlemen from South west Texas who favored resolution he said that if it passed he doubted very much if they would ever occupy their seats again. (*Dallas Morning News*, February 23, 1895, p. 1)

Representative Martin, from District 96, which encompassed a mixed Anglo and Mexican district, responded to Monroe's threat. District 96 included the South Texas counties of Kinney and Maverick and the southwest Texas counties of El Paso, Jeff Davis, Presidio, Pecos, and Val Verde. Although all of these counties contained majority Mexican populations, the district also included the counties of Brewster, Foley, and Buchel, whose populations were predominantly Anglo-American. Martin defended himself by stating that he and other legislators representing counties with large Mexican populations had nothing against the Mexican race. Their support of the constitutional revision was merely an attempt to purify the vote because it was a well-known fact that to win elections in Mexican counties politicians found illegal ways to get the Mexican vote. By stopping Mexicans from voting the elections would be fair. The *Dallas Morning News* reported as follows:

> Mr. Martin of Kinney stated that it was unfair to make it appear that he and Mr. Turney and Mr. Tarver were making war upon the Mexican race, as they were simply contending for the purification of the ballot. He stated that he did not believe that Starr county was an exception to the rule prevailing in elections on the Rio Grande, and that he had it from good au-

thority that the Gentleman from Starr had himself stated that in the house. That the only way they got the Mexican vote down there was to corral it on the night before the election and to hold it until the ballots were cast. Going further, he stated the gentleman from Cameron had admitted to him that he opposed the resolution because it was impolitic and feared that if it passed his head would fall in the basket. (Ibid., 1)

These statements angered Representatives Monroe and Seabury, both of whom represented counties from South Texas, because Martin had in effect publicly accused them of illegally corralling Mexican voters. Seabury tried to interrupt Representative Martin and exclaimed the accusations were false. Martin merely disregarded the outburst and continued to describe how illegal Mexican votes were obtained along the border.

At that point, Representative Wurzbach, representing the central and south Texas counties of Bexar, Atascosa, Karnes, Wilson, and Live Oak (District 90), entered the debate and launched several serious personal attacks against Martin. He judiciously began by demanding that Martin present evidence to support his charges. When Martin admitted that he was simply surmising from personal observations and conversations with others, Wurzbach turned the debate around and accused Martin of political corruption. He charged that Martin was speaking of personal experience and that the examples presented by Martin only proved that he, and not others, was personally involved in obtaining illegal Mexican votes.

To end the acrimonious exchange, Monroe again jumped in and reiterated that the legislators must stop insulting the Mexican people. Based on his experience, he said, the Mexican vote was not corralled: when Mexicans cast their ballots they voted intelligently. In the words of the *Dallas Morning News,* "Mr. Monroe, in reply to Mr. Martin's allusions to Starr County, stated that the people of that county were not corralled, but voted intelligently and with a full knowledge of the men upon the tickets submitted to them and as a consequence the democratic majority there was healthy and on the increase" (Ibid., 2). Representative Blair, from District 89, representing the county of Bexar (San Antonio), concurred and asked for debate to close. Allegedly, Martin's remarks were not resolving anything and at best were unethical misrepresentations of the Rio Grande voters. The newspaper article concluded with an accounting of the House vote and reported that reconsideration of the bill failed.

A month later, on March 20, 1895, the supporters of the constitutional revision suffered additional setbacks when several bills proposing to amend Article 6 either failed to gain approval of the Committee on Constitutional

Amendments or eventually died on the speaker's table (*House Journal, Texas, 24th Legislature, Regular Session, 1895*, p. 521). The defeats did not dissuade supporters of the constitutional revision from continuing their battle.

Passing Anti-Immigrant Legislation

On April 1, 1895, the House representatives of the Twenty-Fourth Legislature reintroduced amendments to revise the suffrage article of the Texas Constitution (*House Journal, Texas, 24th Legislature, Regular and Called Sessions, 1895*, p. 641). This was the third attempt and, if the legislation failed to pass, most likely the last. Several proposals were reintroduced to require immigrant voters to pay a poll tax. The only bill to clear the House was Representative Tarver's H.J.R. 32. Tarver represented the South Texas counties of Webb and Encinal (District 36), and in spite of the criticisms of other South Texas representatives he had supported McBride. On April 10 the bill was voted on, and the legislature agreed to require immigrants to have filed their naturalization papers at least twelve months before an election to be eligible to vote in Texas (Ibid., 724–725). The bill passed with overwhelming support, only twelve legislators, eleven Democrats and one Republican, voting against it. Most of the legislators who opposed the bill were from counties with large concentrations of German voters. Oddly, most of the representatives from South Texas, Bexar, and southwest Texas were absent for the vote. It is uncertain if their absence was aimed at trying to ensure that insufficient representatives were present to avoid passage of the bill (a two-thirds majority approval was necessary for passage) or if they chose to abstain in order not to witness what was sure to be an unavoidable event. Perhaps the truth lay in what the African-American legislator Robert L. Smith (Republican) angrily exclaimed after the vote was taken: "The absentees have no business to be absent when important business is being transacted. Perhaps some of them are endeavoring to 'dodge a vote,' if so the Sergeant-at-Arms is paid to force attendance" (Ibid., 725).

The following day H.J.R. 32 was introduced in the Senate (*Senate Journal, Texas, 24th Legislature, Regular and Called Sessions, 1895*, p. 467). Hereafter opponents of the bill stood their ground and tried to kill it. On April 26, 1895, the Senate debated the bill. Senators J. B. Dibrell and E. A. Atlee, the main opponents, heatedly argued against it. Dibrell represented District 21, which contained central Texas counties composed of large immigrant German communities, and Atlee represented District 23, which was solely composed of South Texas counties.

When the bill was introduced in the Senate it failed to pass, not just on the first try but on the second as well. Finally, on the third try Atlee and Dibrell gave into the pressure, Atlee agreeing to support the bill if it was revised. Immigrants would be allowed to vote six months after they had filed their naturalization papers, not the twelve months Tarver asked for. On April 30, 1895, the House and Senate overwhelmingly approved Atlee's revision. Once the act had passed, it was up to the voters to accept or defeat it in the upcoming November election (Ibid., 677).

A few months later, on October 3, 1895, the Senate and House passed additional legislation affecting communities of Mexican origin when they outlawed bullfighting, a traditional Mexican sport. The governor refused to sign the act into law, but it became law when it was approved by both the House and the Senate and signed by the speaker of the House (*Journal of the Senate of Texas, 24th Legislature, First Called Session, October 1, 1895 to October 7, 1895*, p. 10; *Journal of the House of Representatives, Texas, 24th Legislature, 1895, First Called Session*, p. 23).

Whereas only the moderate version of the constitutional reform was agreed upon and was to be presented to the voters, members of the People's Party took it upon themselves to resurrect the political agenda McBride had introduced. Some members of the People's Party believed that if the legislature was unwilling to stop Mexican immigrants from voting, then it would have to be done through the courts. T. J. McMinn, an attorney from San Antonio and a member of the People's Party executive committee, took the lead. Launching policies that adversely affected immigrants was not new to McMinn. A few years earlier he had been part of the executive committee that created resolutions to end alien landownership (Winkler 1916: 296–297). McMinn's hostile stance toward people of Mexican descent most likely was not personal, but reflected his party's tactical strategy to reduce the number of immigrant voters. The tactic of supporting policies that would disenfranchise Mexicans only rather than immigrants in general antagonized fewer people and made the People's Party less threatening to European immigrants and their U.S.-born children. Before recounting the exploits of McMinn's political movement, a discussion of Populism is needed to elucidate how political alliances were forged against Mexicans.

Populism and the Republican Party

Many Texans were attracted to the People's Party because of its Populist philosophy. Populism advocated the fair distribution of wealth among farmers, workers, and capitalists (Hicks 1964; Pollack 1967a). Populists believed that it was the responsibility of government to pass laws to protect the common man from the abuses of banks, railroads, and capitalists. They also demanded that the government guarantee workingmen employment and ensure that there was sufficient land for those who wanted to farm (Pollack 1967b: xxx). Other tenets of the Populist philosophy depended on regional politics and belief systems. A person who held a Populist philosophy could belong to any political party or organization, but in general he believed in the above principles. The main organizations that promoted Populism were the People's Party, the Prohibitionist Party, and the Farmers' Alliance. Many Democrats too believed in Populist principles but chose to remain within the Democratic Party either because they disagreed with certain aspects of the Populist philosophy or because they did not believe a third party could win elections (Cantrell and Barton 1989).

In the southern states most Populists did not believe that their philosophy was applicable to blacks and other racial minorities. In the Midwest it was common for Populists to be inclusive of blacks, yet many were anti-Semitic and also favored policies to remove Native Americans from reservation lands (Bryan 1896; Hicks 1964). At the national level, members of the People's Party distinguished their association from other Populist parties and organizations by proposing tolerance of African Americans and support of some of their local demands (Pollack 1967b), but the party did not support social equality or advocate racial integration (Abramowitz 1953; Saunders 1971). The party's progressive attitude toward blacks created a social space for whites who wanted to be inclusive of other races, but it also drove away whites who did not sanction any reforms that benefited African Americans. For example, when many chapters of the Farmers' Alliance began to reorganize under the banner of the People's Party, chapters that refused to extend membership to blacks refused to regroup and retained their Farmers' Alliance affiliation. This was a common problem in the South, where most chapters of the Farmers' Alliance chose to remain independent. Most southern chapters chose to form political alliances with the People's Party rather than reorganize, and during election seasons they coordinated their campaigns.

In Texas, many people endorsed Populism, including Democrats and Republicans, although Populist policies were mainly carried out through the activities of third parties. The Prohibition Party primarily attracted conservative whites in favor of Prohibition, while the People's Party had mass appeal. For example, in 1892 after the Republican Party split, black Republicans in Texas began to join the People's Party in larger numbers (Saunders

1971: 65). That year, the executive committee of the Texas Republican Party reorganized and no longer welcomed blacks. Liberal whites who opposed the change protested but were unable to stop the official exclusion of blacks, and at the Republican convention held in Dallas on April 12 and 13, 1892, the executive committee officially voted to exclude blacks and renamed their party the Reform Republicans (Winkler 1916: 304). The goal of the reorganization was to rescue the Texas Republican Party from degradation by denying the goals of Reconstruction and thereby, the party's leaders believed, attract white Texans to the Republican Party again. They thought that an exclusively white membership would appeal to Democrats and members of the People's Party who disagreed with the party's inclusive stance toward African Americans. During the convention the executive committee officially outlined the reasons for the separation and announced that

> We have taken as a convention called together as a representative body
> of white Republicans of Texas, and we appeal to you to give us your aid
> in an attempt to rescue the Republican party in our state from its present
> degraded and helpless condition. . . . Therefore, the necessity has risen for
> the organization of the Republican party of Texas independent of its past
> history and upon the further recognition of the fact that only upon the in-
> telligence and manhood of the white American citizen can any party in this
> country hope for growth and success. (Winkler 1916: 303–304)

Those white Republicans who disapproved reorganized as the Regular Republicans and held a separate convention on September 13–14, 1892, in Fort Worth. The Regular Republican platform reaffirmed their party's commitment to advancing equal rights for African Americans, and in their speeches the delegates criticized the Reform Republicans for establishing a lily-white party (Ibid., 405). Although the Republican Party split in Texas, both factions continued to endorse the national Republican platform, but the fracturing led to the defection of many blacks and liberal whites.

After the split, many African Americans joined the People's Party. In the gubernatorial election of 1894, despite the fact that African Americans overwhelmingly favored Democrats, for the first time in Texas history they gave the People's Party a large percentage of their votes. In seventeen counties with African American populations of over 50 percent the election registrars of 1894 indicate that the Democratic gubernatorial candidate received 16,721 votes, the Republican 10,649, and the People's candidate 8,693 (Martin 1970: 97), the largest percentage of votes a People's candidate had ever received in majority African American counties. The People's

Party recognized the importance of African Americans' votes and actively competed for them (Saunders 1971). The leaders of the party demonstrated their sincere commitment to African Americans by asking them to serve on their state committees and by supporting African American leaders at the local level while also promoting progressive civil rights important to African Americans. Among the policies advocated in the party's platform were giving black communities control over their segregated schools and calling for governmental appointments of black judges (Cantrell and Barton 1989: 666). The position taken by the People's Party may have been honorable, but it was not altruistic. The party needed the black vote in order to launch successful election campaigns against Democrats, particularly in counties and cities where African Americans could influence the outcome of an election.

The admission of a large number of African Americans into the People's Party was welcomed by the leadership but resented by the majority of low-ranking party members. The Democrats took notice and attempted to attract whites who opposed the commingling of the races. They were aware of the common man's racism and used it to their advantage by stigmatizing the People's Party as the "party of the negro lover" (Abramowitz 1953: 279). Such calumny effectively drove many poor whites out of the People's Party and convinced others to remain within the Democratic camp.

The Political Battle over the Mexican Vote:
In Re Rodriguez (1897)

The People's Party political strategy to dilute the impact of the immigrant vote, but without alienating people of German descent, began on May 11, 1896, when McMinn and Andrew Jack Evans filed a petition to prohibit Mexican immigrants of Indian descent from applying for U.S. citizenship (*San Antonio Daily Express*, May 12, 1896, p. 5). They filed their petition in the U.S. Western District Court, a federal court, immediately after Ricardo Rodriguez submitted his final papers of naturalization in the Bexar County Court. Both courthouses were located in San Antonio. Rodriguez was trying to finalize a process that had begun in 1883, when he filed his declaration of intention to become a U.S. citizen.[5] At this time San Antonio had a large foreign-born population: 50 percent (N = 18,853 out of 37,673) of the residents were immigrants or the children of immigrants (U.S. Census 1895: 705), of whom nearly two-thirds were of Mexican and German descent (Ibid., 556, 709). McMinn's actions were not surprising to local San Antonians, as for several years he had publicly advocated his opposition to allowing people of Mexican origin to vote. McMinn had raised the issue in previous elections but had never taken action. An unnamed reporter for the *San Antonio Daily Express* has left a remarkable eyewitness account of the events surrounding McMinn's and Evans's petition. In the article the reporter included information not only about Rodriguez's naturalization application and the petition filed by McMinn and Evans, but also about Mc-Minn's political career, certain comments made by McMinn, and the clerks who accepted the petitions. According to the reporter, McMinn and Evans challenged Rodriguez's right to apply for naturalization on the grounds that Mexicans like him were not eligible to become U.S. citizens. They charged that Rodriguez was neither white nor black and therefore not of one of the races allowed to apply for U.S. citizenship.

The article stated that the county clerk had determined that Rodriguez fulfilled all federal requirements to naturalize. He had filed his application properly, paid all the fees, brought two witnesses to testify as to his character, and submitted an affidavit prepared by Attorney James Fisk attesting to the fulfillment of his state and county residency requirements.[6] McMinn and Evans acknowledged that the papers had been properly filed, but they challenged Rodriguez's right to apply for citizenship because they alleged he was of Aztec descent. The *San Antonio Daily Express* article summarized these points:

> The papers are all regular and form no part of the dispute, the issue being made on the nationality of the man, it being stated in court that he was of Aztec descent.
>
> When the application was presented Messrs. McMinn and Evans offered the following resistance:
>
> "Come now the undersigned as amicus courae and respectfully suggest to the court that the applicant, Ricardo Rodriguez, is ineligible to citizenship for this so wit:
>
> "That he is not a white person, and an African, nor of African descent, and is therefore not capable of becoming an American citizen, and of this they ask the judgment of the court." (*San Antonio Daily Express*, May 12, 1896, p. 5)

When McMinn and Evans filed their petition, the clerk asked them to personally hand it to Judge Thomas S. Maxey and summarize their arguments before the judge. When they met Judge Maxey, McMinn and Evans cited several precedents of the Texas Supreme Court, which rulings had concluded that only whites and blacks were eligible to apply for naturalization. They also cited a rare U.S. Senate record from 1848 on the Treaty of Guadalupe Hidalgo, which, they argued, proved that Mexicans were not given citizenship when the U.S. government annexed Mexico's northern territories. This allegation was very serious, as it affected all people of Mexican descent. They took the position that in 1848 many Mexican diplomats and U.S. congressmen were in favor of extending citizenship to Mexicans in the annexed territories, but the issue was not clearly stipulated in the treaty and was never resolved by Congress. They were of the opinion that Mexicans and their descendants had never been given citizenship. The newspaper article summarized Evans's argument:

> The records of the executive session of the Senate of which the treaty of Guadalupe Hidalgo was considered, were also taken up. The discussion centered around the eighth and ninth articles of the treaty, in which it was stipulated that the Mexicans living in the ceded territory of Texas might become citizens of the United States whenever Congress said so. Congress it was pointed out had not yet taken action in the matter. . . . Thus, under pressure from the Whigs, it was finally agreed that the Mexicans in the ceded territory should become citizens whenever Congress deemed it wise to act in the matter. (Ibid.)

Once McMinn and Evans completed their presentations, Judge Maxey assured them that their petition would be taken under advisement. The following Saturday he would hold a hearing to explore the petition's merits and to appoint an advisory committee to study the charges. Rodriguez would also be deposed that day. McMinn and Evans were assured that their petition was taken seriously but that no rushed decisions would be made merely because they wanted a ruling prior to the upcoming election in November.

After the reporter finished narrating Maxey's comments, he turned to McMinn's interview. According to McMinn, he and Evans had filed the petition at this time to specifically prevent Mexican immigrants from voting in the upcoming election. They acknowledged that their petition had greater implications, and if the court ruled in their favor all people of Mexican descent, including those born in the United States, would be prohibited from voting. The news reporter summarized McMinn's and Evans's response: "While, according to Messrs. McMinn and Evans the purpose of the proceeding is solely to prevent the newly arrived Mexicans from voting it is admitted that if successful it will result to the disenfranchisement not only of recent arrivals from Mexico, but of all resident Mexicans, even those who were born here, and will even extend to those residents some of whose parents are American" (Ibid.). The news article ended its description of the proceedings by critically commenting on McMinn's and Evans's questionable motives. Allegedly the Populist and Republican parties needed to stop Mexicans from voting because Mexicans did not support either party. The article stated,

> Next to Judge Maxey's decision interest centers in guessing what political party, if any, is responsible for the proceedings. The belief obtains that Messrs. McMinn and A. J. Evans are acting as attorneys for some political party that has not been getting a very large share of the Mexican votes, and is therefore anxious to have it eliminated as a factor in the politics of this section.
>
> Mr. McMinn is an ardent Populist and his associate, Capt. Evans, is a stalwart Republican. (Ibid.)

As previously mentioned, McMinn was a high-ranking officer in the state executive committee of the People's Party, and Evans too had a long history of holding high-ranking positions within the Republican Party. From 1867 to 1890 Evans was a delegate at the Republican National Conventions as well as a sometime member of the Texas Republican Party's executive committee (see Winkler 1916). Furthermore, during Reconstruction Evans was a member of the Republican Party's platform committee and was appointed by Governor Davis to serve on committees dealing with African American civil rights. When the Republican Party split he was not a member of either faction's executive committee.

In the Mexican quarters of San Antonio, news of McMinn's and Evans's charges alarmed many people. Pablo Cruz, the editor of *El Regidor,* a well-respected Mexican-language newspaper headquartered in San Antonio, reported on the events that had befallen Rodriguez. He cautioned the Mexican community that McMinn's petition placed them in peril because it affected all people of Mexican descent. Cruz added that McMinn's and Evans's actions were most likely personal because both men had previously run for office, and they attributed their losses to illegal Mexican voting (*El Regidor,* May 14, 1896, p. 1; *El Regidor,* June 18, 1896, p. 1). At this time Cruz was reluctant to accuse McMinn of acting on behalf of the People's Party, as he himself was an advocate of the party. On various occasions Cruz had asked his readers to vote intelligently and support Populist candidates if elected Democratic officials failed to fulfill their campaign promises. On many occasions Cruz had also praised the virtues of Populism. For example, three years earlier Cruz had written an editorial calling on Mexicans to join the People's Party. He proclaimed that People's candidates supported the common man, whereas the Democratic Party was the party of the capitalists. On October 14, 1893, Cruz wrote,

> As our readers have observed EL REGIDOR for a few days has been translating political articles published in newspapers affiliated with the People's Party, these articles are inspired by a true patriotism based on doctrines practiced by members of the third party, they are ones who support the aspirations of the majority, or in other words of the people. . . . the egotism of those business magnates who occupy power is apparent, as they have forgotten that the people elected them, yet they only support the capitalists . . . they blindly obey the corrupt capitalists, who destroy the welfare of the people by enriching themselves like ravenous vampires.
>
> The People's Party is destined to destroy the men who punish and exploit the party; consequently, we believe that all of the honorable workers in Texas of Mexican descent should imitate their German, Swedish, and French colleagues and work together to help the People's Party destroy their enemies for ever, in this way the people's welfare and dignity will be assured. (*El Regidor*, October 14, 1893, p. 1; my translation)[7]

Cruz's earnest support of the People's Party began to dwindle as the Rodriguez case progressed. Within a short time it became apparent that an official coalition had been formed between the Republican Party and the People's Party. At that point Cruz stopped publishing news articles praising the virtues of Populism and began writing editorials in support of the Mexicans' only political ally, the Democratic Party.

Fusion Politics

Cruz's fears became a political reality when the apologies extended by some members of the People's Party over the McMinn-Evans affair were proven to be false and a mere ploy to secure Mexican votes during the November election. Several events transpired during the People's Party state convention of 1896 that demonstrated the party was officially in support of McMinn. The alliances that were formed in Texas between Republicans and the People's Party provide a context to delineate why McMinn and Evans collaborated against Rodriguez.

At the national level the People's Party made great advances between 1892 and 1894. Many new chapters were established, and the number of voters supporting the party increased. The growth and surge of the party's popularity was attributed to the fusion agenda its leaders had set in motion. During the general election of 1894 the People's Party vote increased nationwide by 42 percent, reaching a total of 1½ million votes (Hicks 1964: 338; Pollack 1967b: xxxix). Republicans, Populists, and Democrats voted for the People's ticket. Across the nation candidates running on the People's ticket won state and local elections because alliances had been made across party lines. Owing to the success of the fusion movement the national committee of the People's Party directed all of its chapters to form alliances with any party willing to endorse their Populist agenda. Their goal was to elect Republicans and Democrats who held Populist ideals, but, more important, to elect People's Party candidates through crossover voting. Of particular importance were the state legislative and congressional races, as these offices controlled the direction of the country. Making alliances, however, though essential, was acknowledged by the leadership of the party to be complicated.

In the election of 1896, most of the reformers willing to make alliances with the People's Party were Democrats who feared losing the presidency and most of their congressional seats. President Grover Cleveland, who was running for reelection, was very unpopular and his candidacy had become detrimental to the Democratic Party (Baker 1998: 19). William McKinley, the Republican presidential candidate, on the other hand, was running a successful campaign and was the front-runner. His appeal was broad based and cut across social classes. McKinley promised the industrialist class expansion of foreign markets and assurance of their investments through foreign policy, while at the same time he agreed to exert less federal control of the South, specifically promising a hands-off policy in matters relating to race relations. This agenda appealed to whites of different parties and led them to favor Republican rule. On the other hand, President Cleveland's current policies were alienating all classes. Particularly harmful to his reelection was his stance on Independence Day (1894), when he sent federal troops to crush the Pullman Company strike. Many union members, who were protesting against reduced wages, were injured and several died in the four-day confrontation (Ibid., 21). Cleveland had also failed to relieve the depressed economies of several regions of the United States, and other domestic issues such as the Free Silver controversy plagued his administration. He had been unable to forge a national consensus on the debate over what monetary base U.S. currency should have. Industrialists favored basing U.S. currency on a gold standard, while popular opinion favored a silver standard. The result was that banks throughout the country were converting currency however they pleased, and as a result the common people were being cheated when they made payments or withdrew their savings. Winning the upcoming election was a huge challenge to Democrats. The best path to keeping Democrats in office, it was thought, was to make alliances with a third party.

The political struggle between Democrats and Republicans gave the People's Party leverage to negotiate political platforms that embraced their Populist agenda. To take advantage of this situation, the national committee of the People's Party advised its chapters to make political alliances with whatever party was willing to do so. This sounded like a reasonable directive, but in Texas and in most southern states the strategy was doomed to fail. In this region Democrats and Republicans were not friends of the People's Party. Making matters worse, while at the national level most chapters would make alliances with Democrats, in Texas and in the South the alliances would have to be made with the Republican Party because there the Democrats were not the underdogs; therefore they did not need to make deals with the People's Party. This meant that in Texas the People's Party would follow a path that was the opposite of the one they pursued elsewhere.

The fusionist mandate created immediate dissent in Texas. There were two major problems. First, their supposed allies, the Republicans, were still associated with the evils of the Civil War and Reconstruction. Second, although the Republican Party had split, many members of the People's Party refused to work with either the liberal or the lily-white faction. Progressive liberal whites were unwilling to support Reform Republicans because they had ousted their black members, while racist whites were unwilling to vote for Regular Republicans, who in many counties were black candidates or sympathizers of progressive civil rights politics. Other members of the People's Party were simply unwilling to work with Republicans. Many had joined the People's Party because of its Populist appeal against capitalists. For those who held Socialist beliefs, this was particularly troublesome and betrayed the main reason they had left the traditional parties (Hicks 1964).

In spite of the problems fusion politics caused, the People's Party state executive committee in Texas agreed to follow the national mandate and had their members make alliances with both factions of the Republican Party. Together they negotiated a joint ticket for the upcoming election. They agreed to support the People's candidate for governor and at the state and local level elect Republican candidates. The two parties agreed to remain independent in their choice for president since at the national level it was anticipated that the People's Party would endorse the Democratic candidate, William J. Bryan, whereas Republicans were in support of McKinley.

When news of the negotiations spread, many chapters of the People's Party threatened to defect. The party's leadership was concerned with a potential revolt but planned to defuse the conflict when they met during the state convention. As the election drew closer, in Texas fusion politics commenced, and the Rodriguez trial came to mark a milestone in the fusion agenda.

Ricardo Rodriguez on Trial

On May 16, 1896, Judge Maxey held a trial in U.S. Western District Court in San Antonio to address the charges raised by McMinn and Evans (*San Antonio Daily Express*, May 17, 1896, p. 11). He asked Rodriguez to testify on his behalf and explain why he sought U.S. citizenship. People present in the courtroom were expecting Judge Maxey to render his decision that very day. According to the *San Antonio Daily Express* the crowd was larger than any ever seen before in the city. A reporter for the *Express* described the courtroom spectacle:

> It was announced that Judge Maxey of the Federal Court would render his decision on the application of Ricardo Rodriguez for final naturalization papers yesterday morning and as a result the courtroom was well filled with people anxious to learn whether or not Mexicans were eligible to citizenship in this country.
>
> The case has created no little interest here and in this part of the State, for it is believed that the decision will affect the entire Mexican vote. (Ibid.)

Judge Maxey surprised the crowd when he announced that a final decision would be delayed. The seriousness of the challenge had prompted the judge to assemble a committee to study the charges. A decision would be rendered after the committee submitted its report. Four prominent attorneys were appointed: Thomas M. Paschal, Charles W. Ogden, Thomas Franklin, and Floyd McGown. Judge Maxey also requested that McMinn and Evans submit briefs. Of the four attorneys on the committee, Paschal and McGown were the most prominent and in addition had the most experience litigating cases involving Mexicans. McGown, a distinguished attorney in private practice, was a Republican but was not currently involved in politics.[8] He was a partner in the firm McGown and Shaw, and he had judicial experience involving Spanish and Mexican land grant disputes (Texas Archival Resources online, 2006). Paschal was a Democrat, but early in his career he had been a member of the Republican Party. During Reconstruction Paschal supported the radical wing of the Republican Party. At the time of Rodriguez's trial, Paschal, like McGown, worked in private practice. Of the committee members, Paschal was the most distinguished public figure. As a young attorney he began his career as a district attorney in South Texas and quickly moved up the ranks to become a judge in the Criminal District Court of Bexar County. He then became district judge of the Thirty-Eighth District, which covered several counties in South Texas. He later served as commissioner of the Western District of Texas, and most recently had completed a term in the U.S. Congress as representative from Texas (1893–1894) (Norton, 1912: 108). Paschal also came from a family of prominent Texas attorneys. One of his uncles was the distinguished legal scholar George W. Paschal, who was the leading expert in Texas on the incorporation of Spanish and Mexican civil laws within the legal system of Texas. George Paschal wrote many legal texts but was best known for *Paschal's Annotated Constitution* and *Paschal's Digest of Law and Decisions of Texas* (Scarborough 1972). Both texts were compilations of the history of Texas law and the rulings made by the state courts of Texas. In Judge Maxey's opinion, Paschal's experience as a district judge was perhaps the most valuable asset he brought to the committee. Paschal was the only member of the committee who had ruled on thousands of naturalization cases. In particular, he was remembered by many Texans for having made an unpopular ruling in *Ex parte Sauer* (1891) when he refused a German immigrant naturalization on the grounds that he was a Socialist. Paschal had ruled that such people threatened American democracy.

Ogden was not a distinguished public figure in the mold of Paschal and McGown, but he brought to the committee valuable personal experience on electoral politics and party warfare. He was the son of the late Texas Supreme Court Justice Wesley B. Ogden. In 1873, Justice Ogden served as chief justice of the Texas Supreme Court and presided over the scandalous *Ex parte Rodriguez* ruling (Ramsdell 1970; Campbell 1996: 1115). In this case the justices ruled in favor of Republicans and invalidated the gubernatorial election of 1873 under the charge that Democrats had committed fraud by allowing people to vote several times. *Ex parte Rodriguez* involved a Mexican man named Joseph Rodriguez who was hired by Republicans to vote illegally. Their intention was to prove that election clerks favored Democrats and often stuffed ballot boxes and allowed Mexican Democrats to vote more than once. When Republicans lost the election, a committee met with Justice Ogden and demanded that a trial be held to determine if the election was valid. When the Texas Supreme Court concluded its investigation it ruled on behalf of Republicans. The court ruled that Governor Davis, a Republican, be allowed to remain in office until a new election was held. The public protested and refused to accept the ruling. To control the protesters Governor Davis tried to get federal aid, but it was denied, and Richard Coke, the Democratic candidate who had won the election in a landslide, was seated as governor. Ogden's family experience enabled him to bring to the committee valuable insight into party politics.

After Judge Maxey made the unexpected announcement that he would delay his decision, he stirred the crowd even further by ruling that Rodriguez was allowed to vote in the upcoming November election. This meant that all eligible Mexican immigrants could vote. Judge Maxey then turned to the main issues the committee was to explore and announced that treaty law and naturalization law were to be the central points examined. But he did not consider the Treaty of Guadalupe Hidalgo to be the focus of debate. This was not good news for McMinn and Evans, as they had expected that their interpretation of the Treaty of Guadalupe Hidalgo would lead to an adverse ruling against Mexicans. Instead, Judge Maxey identified the Naturalization Treaty of 1868 as the main legal issue affecting the Rodriguez case. In that treaty, Judge Maxey stated, the U.S. Congress gave Mexican immigrants the right to become U.S. citizens based on an international agreement (see chapter 1). The problem was that it was uncertain if the treaty was still in effect. If it was, Mexicans had the right to apply for U.S. citizenship; if not, the committee had to determine if another treaty had been negotiated. It would also be necessary to determine if U.S. naturalization laws prohibited Rodriguez from applying for citizenship. The *San Antonio Daily Express* reviewed Maxey's announcements:

> Judge Maxey . . . said that from his judgment there could be no appeal except possibly by writ of mandamus from the higher court. He did not think there was any cause for haste as Rodriguez could vote on his intention papers. He thought the matter was one of much importance and he wanted the matter fully investigated before a decision was rendered. He therefore held the application in abeyance.
>
> In remarking upon the case Judge Maxey stated that if the treaty between the United States and Mexico of 1868 regarding naturalization was still in effect he would not hesitate a moment in granting Rodriguez final papers, but he was informed that treaty had terminated, and if such was the fact and another treaty had been entered into, he might be in doubt about granting the papers. At any rate if the said treaty had terminated the case was one of undue importance and one that he would not like to pass

without closely investigating the same. (*San Antonio Daily Express*, May 17, 1896, p. 11)

Both of these announcements were damaging to McMinn's and Evans's case. First, Judge Maxey had allowed Mexicans to vote in the November election. More devastating, however, was his opinion that the Naturalization Treaty of 1868 was the central point of study because this indicated that the judge was not persuaded by their arguments on the Treaty of Guadalupe Hidalgo. Their main contention, however, was still viable: they had the opportunity to submit briefs and convince the committee that Mexicans could be denied U.S. citizenship because they were Indians.

Following these announcements, Rodriguez was sworn in and questioned by the committee. A *San Antonio Daily Express* reporter described Rodriguez's appearance. He was characterized as an ignorant man belonging to the dark race of the Mexican peon class. When the questioning began, Rodriguez was asked to comment on his residency. Rodriguez replied that he was thirty-seven years old and born in the state of Guanajuato near a ranchería called Ojuelas. In Mexico it is commonly known that a ranchería is a village inhabited by the descendants of Indians.[9] Rodriguez later moved to Lampasas, Mexico, where he worked in the fields and then immigrated to Texas in 1883, entering through the port of Laredo. After living in Laredo for a short period, he moved to San Antonio, where he currently resides. Judge Maxey then asked Rodriguez to comment on his language, schooling, and ancestry. Rodriguez answered that he did not know how to read and write. Concerning his ancestry he said he knew very little, a brilliant response in that by making it he neither lied nor implicated himself in furthering McMinn's and Evans's case. Considering the legal challenge the two men posed, namely, charging that Indians were prohibited from obtaining U.S. citizenship, Rodriguez's response was appropriate. Rodriguez stated that he was uncertain of his race, but he knew he was not an Indian, a Spaniard, or an African male. He was a Mexican. The *San Antonio Daily Express* reported Rodriguez's response to the ancestry question: "When asked as to his ancestors, he said that as far back as he could remember, they were all Mexicans. He knew nothing of the Aztec or Toltec race. He said he was not a descendant of the aborigines of Mexico, was certain that he did not descend from Spaniards who had gone to Mexico from Spain and was very positive that there was not any African blood in his veins" (*San Antonio Daily Express*, May 17, 1896, p. 11). It is uncertain if Rodriguez's response was sincere or if an attorney coached him. In stressing that he was a Mexican Rodriguez gave the perfect answer because the Naturalization Treaty of 1868 had given Mexicans the right to apply for citizenship. Likewise, by stating that he was not an Indian, Rodriguez avoided being racially classified as Indian and thereby did not fall into McMinn's and Evans's trap. If he had acknowledged his Indian ancestry McMinn and Evans could have argued that U.S. laws affecting Indians also applied to Mexicans.

According to the *Daily Express* reporter, when Rodriguez was questioned about the structure of the U.S. government he knew little about it, yet he answered intelligently. He knew Porfirio Díaz was the president of Mexico and that Texas was a state, but not the names of the president of the United States or the governor of Texas. Rodriguez also informed the court that he was not a political man. When asked why he wanted to become a U.S. citizen he replied sincerely and simply that it was because he lived in the United States (*San Antonio Daily Express,* May 17, 1896, p. 11).

Following Rodriguez's questioning, his witness was sworn in. Attorney Fisk testified to Rodriguez's good character and employment history, stating that he had known Rodriguez for ten years. Rodriguez was a married man with no children, and he worked for the city of San Antonio digging ditches (Ibid.). Concerning his character, Fisk stated that Rodriguez had a very good reputation, in fact, above average, and was a remarkably peaceful, law-abiding citizen. Although Fisk was identified as Rodriguez's character witness, it appears that he was actually Rodriguez's private counsel, as he had prepared Rodriguez's final naturalization papers (*San Antonio Daily Express,* May 12, 1896, p. 5). At the time of the proceedings Fisk was neither publicly affiliated with any party nor running for public office, although in the past he had run and had held several elected positions in San Antonio (San Antonio City Directory 1885). He was a local attorney in private practice (*Texas Legal Directory for 1876–77,* p. 28). After Fisk's testimony, Judge Maxey concluded the depositions and dismissed the audience without announcing a date for his final ruling.

The First Reactions of the Mexican Community: Diplomacy and Violence

A few days after the proceedings people of Mexican descent began to organize against the potential legal troubles that might befall them. Fidel Valle, the editor of *El Cronista,* a newspaper published in Brownsville, wrote a letter to Matías Romero, the Mexican minister of the Mexican Legion in Washington, D.C., and the highest-ranking Mexican diplomat in the United States. Having been one of its authors, Romero was an expert on the Naturalization Treaty of 1868 (see chapter 2). Valle's letter read as follows:

May 23, 1896

Mr. Matías Romero
Mexico's Minister, Washington
My Dear Sir,
Pardon me for taking the liberty to request information regarding whether the Naturalization Treaty enacted in 1868 between Mexico and the United States is still in effect, or if there is another treaty in effect. We would like to address the issue of naturalization intelligently. At this time, in this country the federal district will be resolving the question, it is alleged that the Treaty of '68 is not in effect and that Mexicans under the law are "not white," has another convention been held on this issue.
    Sincerely,
    Fidel Valle
(Matías Romero Papers, roll 65, document no. 46304; my translation)[10]

There is no record of Romero's having responded. He may have done so privately, but international law forbade foreign consuls from intervening publicly in the domestic affairs of the nations they were residing in. We know that Romero, James L. Slayden, a Texas politician, and Judge Maxey were friends (see Slayden 1963), and, furthermore, that Maxey and Slayden were both Democrats and on occasion vacationed together in Mexico. Also certain is that at the time of the Rodriguez case Slayden was running for the U.S. Congress in District 12, which stretched from central Texas, including Bexar (San Antonio), to west Texas and also contained the South Texas counties of Kinney, Maverick, and Medina. In addition, we know that during Slayden's congressional campaign he publicly criticized McMinn and Evans, which made him popular among voters of Mexican descent (*El Regidor*, October 22, 1896, p. 9 ; *El Regidor*, October 13, 1898, p. 1; *El Regidor*, November 3, 1898, p. 1; *El Regidor*, November 10, 1898, p. 1).

Other people of Mexican origin who supported Rodriguez were less diplomatic than Valle. On July 1, 1896, a group of men most likely from South Texas addressed a rather comical but threatening letter to the San Antonio chief of police, W. D. Druse and to McMinn (*El Regidor*, July 2, 1896, p. 1). In the letter they asked for a city permit so that their organization of twenty-five members could hold a series of demonstrations against employers who exploited Mexican, Italian, and French immigrant laborers.

They warned Chief Druse that after he received the letter they would hold their first demonstration and begin shooting at gringos and Germans. They added that their protest had been delayed because several of their members were tired, having traveled a long way to get to San Antonio, but were now well rested and ready to get underway. They ended the letter by promising to disclose the name of their organization at their first rally.

The letter was reprinted in *El Regidor* with commentary by the editor. Cruz found the letter to be quite odd and concluded it was a public commentary against the abuses immigrants underwent in Texas. Cruz recounted the main points of the letter:

> The reasons for killing the gringos and sour krauts are the following: gringos and Germans are protected by Texas law when they rob their workers' salaries; they also kill them and force them to leave this nation. The courts should impart equal justice; to the Italian, Negro, and to the unfortunate Mexican, the Spaniard, the French, and Cuban, justice should not only be given to the Germans and gringos; in this way the statute would represent balanced justice and not infamy. . . . We will no longer ask Mayor Elmendorf for work, because we expect justice from God . . .
>
> McMinn and the police are alarmed, many of them cannot sleep or eat after hearing about the letter. (*El Regidor,* July 2, 1896, p. 1; my translation)[11]

Cruz also noted that McMinn had made a public announcement stressing that the letter stunned him, but he assured his supporters that nothing would stop him (Ibid.; *El Regidor,* July 4, 1896, p. 4). Cruz ended his editorial by questioning the authenticity of the letter, which he found to be odd and contradictory. The protesters had refused to name their organization, yet several members signed the letter. Surely, he believed, if the letter was authentic the organizers would not have disclosed their names because what they planned to do was against the law. Cruz also claimed the letter was written by someone who did not know Spanish well, as it was written in broken Spanish, another oddity in that one of the signers claimed to be a physician. The letter was signed by Julio Escobar, doctor; Pedro Ramos, agent; Tirso and his uncle Rojas; Refugio Moreno, counselor; Zodgo Cristino, secretary; Santiago Bagteyer, auditor; and Carlos Chengarari, commissioner. Cruz was uncertain as to whether the names were authentic or written in jest and whether the letter was a ploy intended to put Mexicans in a bad light. The secret organization never disclosed its name or staged a violent spectacle.

A day before Cruz published his editorial, the *San Antonio Daily Express* reported that a large crowd of Mexican Populists had held a political meeting in San Antonio to discuss the McMinn affair. It is uncertain if there is a connection between the letter and the meeting, or if the letter was sent by someone who wanted to ridicule the Mexicans who had organized the meeting. According to the *Daily Express,* on June 29, 1896, Mexican Populists held a meeting to demand a formal investigation of their party's involvement in the McMinn suit. They insisted that the executive committee of the People's Party confirm or deny its support for McMinn (*Daily Express,* July 1, 1896, p. 8). A. L. Montalbo, the organizer, announced that he had sent a letter to Jerome Kearby, who was running for governor on the People's Party ticket. In an adjoining article published in the same issue of the *newspaper* Kearby responded to Montalbo, agreeing to meet with him and other members of the People's Party but stating that he was neither involved in the suit nor knew anything about it. To his knowledge the People's Party had not officially endorsed McMinn or declared a public stance on treaty law. Kearby said he believed it was unlikely his party would support the suit. He assured Montalbo that this issue would be brought to closure in the upcoming People's Party convention, and it would be resolved in favor of the Mexican people.

The day after Kearby's letter appeared in the *Daily Express,* Cruz published a Spanish version of it which included public comments made by McMinn (*El Regidor,* July 2, 1896, p. 4). McMinn explained that his critics were malicious people who were too stupid to understand what he was trying to do. They were confused and had misinformed Kearby on the intent of his petition, which, he said, was aimed merely at trying to follow the law and prevent some Mexicans from illegally assuming citizenship. His petition would clean up the electoral process by preventing Democratic candidates from buying illegal votes. According to McMinn, Mexican teachers were largely to blame for the electoral fraud because they recruited Mexicans at election time and delivered them to the Democrats.

In mid-July 1896 Kearby, accompanied by Selig Deutschman, an attorney and local member of the People's Party, met with Montalbo (*El Regidor,* July 16, 1896, p. 16). After the meeting Kearby assured the Mexican delegation that McMinn was acting independently and that his party's executive committee would publicly censure McMinn's petition. Kearby and Deutschman would personally seek an official censure at the party's upcoming state convention.

Nearly two weeks after the meeting between Kearby and Montalbo, Mexican supporters of the People's Party held a rally in San Antonio to recruit members and garner support for Kearby (*El Regidor,* July 30, 1896,

p. 1; *San Antonio Daily Express,* July 29, 1896, p. 5). Apparently Montalbo and other Populist Mexicans felt comfortable with Kearby's apology and were confident that McMinn was acting on his own. At the rally Montalbo outlined the principles of Populism and explained its benefits to Mexicans. After Montalbo's speech, A. C. Valdes, the editor of *El Heraldo,* a Spanish-language newspaper, asked Montalbo to update the audience on what action Kearby was taking against McMinn. Montalbo responded defensively by saying that the People's Party should not be blamed for McMinn's actions, as the party had no control over its members' politics.

Unfortunately, it soon became apparent that Kearby's dealings with Montalbo were an exercise in hypocrisy and lies, a disclosure that left Montalbo feeling disappointed and angry. Montalbo's lobbying efforts, however, would not be wasted because the shame he felt for naively following Kearby would prompt him to take political action against the People's Party.

The People's Party State Convention, August 1896

The state convention of the People's Party was held in Galveston, Texas, on August 5 and 6, 1896 (Winkler 1916: 379). The executive committee of the party endorsed the national party's nominee for president, supporting the Democratic candidate, William Jennings Bryan, against the Republican, William McKinley (Cantrell and Barton 1989). The committee also voted in favor of supporting a state ticket with nominees from both the Republican and People's parties. Essentially, the fusion mandate of the national committee was followed, a decision that many members angrily protested because the national and state tickets were contradictory and appeared not to make any sense. At the national level a Democrat was being supported, while at the state level Republicans were endorsed. Many delegates also opposed Bryan because he had failed to formally accept the People's nomination (Bryan 1896; Hicks 1964). Disregarding the conflict, the state's executive committee and the majority of the delegates endorsed the party's schizophrenic coalition and moved onward with a bipartisan ticket. Before the nominations were made the executive committee announced that Republicans had agreed to back any gubernatorial candidate elected at the convention. Kearby was the overwhelming choice for governor.

The convention attendees also endorsed the national platform. The resolutions did not deviate from those of former years and included planks adopted in previous conventions, such as support for farmers, workers' rights, censure of corporations, demands that the government take full control of banks, and reaffirmation of the party's commitment to end alien ownership of land (see Bryan 1896: 275). The national platform also advanced new resolutions, such as removal of Indians from reservations to make room for qualified settlers and support for silverite reformers in the national debate over legal tender. In addition, other measures were adopted that applied only to Texas, including increasing the school year, reducing the number of judicial districts, supporting laws to protect laborers, reducing the work day to eight hours, and extending equal justice to all citizens irrespective of race, color, and nationality (Winkler 1916: 379–383). On the legal tender issue most delegates approved the national resolution, but the majority believed that debate over silver or gold was irrelevant. What was important to the membership was for government to force banks to guarantee the full value of paper currency. That is, when people made payments to the banks in paper currency, the banks should not be able to decide if the dollar was worth less than its face value because the price of gold or silver had gone up or down. The delegates simply did not want the common man to be cheated by banks and merchants.

In regard to the McMinn situation, the convention's executive committee refused to endorse any censure motion. Deutschman and others tried to pressure Kearby into introducing a censure resolution, but he refused. Deutschman then tried to introduce the resolution himself, but owing to a lack of support it was defeated in committee (*El Regidor,* August 6, 1896, p. 4). Exacerbating matters, Deutschman was unable to stop the party from nominating McMinn for the position of justice of the Supreme Court of Texas (Election Registers 1838–1972b; Winkler 1916: 380). In the end, a very public and official endorsement of McMinn was made. His nomination signaled the party's official support and essentially gave him the go-ahead to pursue his hostile anti-immigrant agenda.

After the convention, official support for McMinn appeared in the party newspaper, the *Southern Mercury,* which on October 8, 1896 (p. 8), published an article that devastated Mexicans, calling them undemocratic and charging that Mexican teachers were committing electoral fraud. It asked readers to stop this unjust travesty and called on white men to end Mexican supremacy in South Texas:

> To the voters of Texas. You are not invited to read this unless you hold integrity.
>
> All taxpayers are interested, but some taxpayers submit to known wrong rather than expose and resist peculation within their organization.
>
> The facts herein recited are only intended as appeal to Men of intelligence and integrity, with whom considerations of virtue—political and personal—are paramount.

On our state border school funds are paid to Mexicans—many of them—who can not either read or write the English language. The salaries are paid ostensibly to "school teachers." They can not teach and do not teach, but do control Mexican votes, and all the Rio Grande, as all Texas knows, is "the sheet anchor of democracy." . . . white men down there, who are outraged by Mexican supremacy, have not complained for fear of the torch and the assassin's knife. Names, dates and amounts are ready to be furnished the moment a tribunal, legal or legislative, will take notice and investigate these and kindred allegations. (Ibid.)

In a second article the *Southern Mercury* published a letter thanking Mc-Minn for his activism against the Mexican teachers. The anonymous fan pledged his support and advised McMinn on how to clean up electoral fraud in South Texas. He also identified the names of the troublesome teachers, but the newspaper redacted their names when the letter was published. The letter read as follows:

Hon. T. J. McMinn:

Yours of the 1st inst[ant] just received. I enclose herewith a list of the xxx county school teachers. All of those marked x are unable to read or write the English language. It is an open secret that the $15,000 county school fund is used for political purposes; that is to say all "school teachers" in the county who can control votes direct or indirectly are given schools regardless of their ability to teach. . . .

Say Mc, I do not want to be drawn into any controversy nor get into trouble. I am so disgusted that I am endeavoring to leave here. The above, however, are facts. You can understand how to use any information—use it judiciously.

Yours with Resp.,

———————.

(*Southern Mercury*, October 15, 1896, pp. 8–9).

The letter closed by encouraging McMinn to take legal action against the Mexican schoolteachers of South Texas.

People of Mexican Descent Organize

On October 8, 1896, Montalbo organized a meeting to denounce the People's Party and to inform people of Mexican descent that it was critical that they support the Democratic Party (*San Antonio Daily Express*, October 9,

1896, p. 5). Over two hundred people of Mexican origin attended as well as a few Anglo-Americans, including Deutschman. Reviewing the events that had taken place at the state convention, Montalbo recounted how the People's Party had unanimously endorsed McMinn, and he exclaimed that the party believed Mexicans should be treated like "pack animals" who had no civil rights. He warned the audience that if McMinn was elected to the Texas Supreme Court he would interpret U.S. laws in such a way as to deprive Mexicans of basic civil rights and deny them ownership of their property. The *Daily Express* summarized the issues discussed at the meeting in an article appropriately entitled, "The Mexicans are Very Angry: The Effort to Disenfranchise Them Denounced, Indignation Meeting Last Night—Responsibility for the Proceedings Charged to Pops [Populist People's Party] and Republicans—Severe Arraignment." Montalbo was quoted as saying the following:

> McMinn was designated by the Populist Convention at Galveston as a candidate for the judge of the Supreme Court. He was nominated by Stump Ashby, the highest member of the Texas Populists, and his nomination was unanimous. The delegates to that convention represented there with their voice and votes all of the Populists in Texas, and it is clear that the Populist party represented there approved the views of McMinn, and the McMinn views are that the Texas Mexicans should be reduced to the category of pack animals, who may be good enough to work, but not good enough to exercise any civil rights. . . .
>
> The election of the Populists to the State offices, among whom there is McMinn for judge of the Supreme Court will mean that the Texas Mexicans will be deprived of their civil rights, and as the law provides that aliens shall not hold possessions, it will also mean that they will lose with their civil rights their possessions also. (*San Antonio Daily Express*, October 9, 1896, p. 5)

Montalbo proceeded to warn the crowd that Republicans were backing Mc-Minn and that they too were in favor of limiting the civil rights of Mexicans in Texas. He explained the legal ramifications of the petition against Rodriguez and stated that McMinn acknowledged that the *Rodriguez* ruling would affect all Mexicans, including those born in the United States. Mexicans of mixed Anglo parentage would also be affected. Montalbo stated,

> T. J. McMinn, some years ago, insisted that the courts should declare that the Mexicans were not worthy of American citizenship. This he held should apply not only to those who intend to become naturalized citizens, but also

those born of Mexican parents in this country, even though one of those parents was not a Mexican. In other words, he intends to take the nationality away from a man for no other reason than that he has the least particle of Mexican blood. (Ibid.)

Montalbo urged the crowd not to support the People's Party because they were against Mexicans and entreated voters to support Democrats and not believe the false accusations voiced against them. Montalbo then informed the audience of the political battles that had recently transpired in the legislature: "Coming to the question of Mexican citizenship . . . 'At the last session of the Legislature there was presented a bill tending by some covert manner, to rob the Texas-Mexicans of their rights, and all of the Populist Representatives voted for the bill and all of the Democrats against it'" (Ibid.). Montalbo ended his speech by informing the crowd that Mexicans were being attacked from different political directions, and he exhorted people to vote Democratic since that was the only party that had a record of protecting the Mexicans' civil rights. At the end of the meeting a committee was formed to organize against the threat posed by McMinn. Blas Hernandes was nominated chair and Blas Mateo secretary. The committee's task was monumental, as Mexicans faced a terrible dilemma in the courts and at the ballot box. They had to not only organize to get a favorable ruling in the Rodriguez case, but also get out the vote to defeat the suffrage amendment to the Texas Constitution, which was to be voted on in the November election.

The November Elections of 1896 and the Demise of the People's Party

On November 3, 1896, Texans voted, and the outcome was disastrous for the People's Party as well as for the Republicans (Martin 1970: 246). Fusion politics had failed in Texas. The leadership of both parties underestimated their members' opposition and unwillingness to follow an incoherent mandate. Clearly Texans were unwilling to vote for candidates who were not part of their party and who did not have a record of supporting their issues (Abramowitz 1953; Cantrell and Barton 1989). Many whites were also unwilling to vote for black candidates. The election marked the disintegration of the People's Party in Texas and the rapid defection of its members, including the leadership. Most members turned to other parties, the vast majority joining the Democrats.

Kearby lost the gubernatorial race to the Democratic incumbent, Culberson, and the gains the People's Party had made in the previous two elections were lost. The party retained only six seats in the House and two in the Senate (*Texas Legislative Manual*, 1897: 56–61). The Republicans did better than usual but overall they too found the results disappointing. They elected one person to the Senate and three to the House. The African American legislator Robert L. Smith was reelected. At the national level Republicans did well, but their victory was not associated with fusion politics. McKinley defeated Bryan in the presidential race, and Republicans took over the Congress. At the national level most of the candidates the People's Party had endorsed lost, and in Texas the state candidates faced a similar defeat. The fusion ticket succeeded in only a few legislative races, winning a majority of the seats in the legislatures in Kansas, Nebraska, South Dakota, Montana, Idaho, and Washington; fusionists also won a landslide victory in North Carolina (Hicks 1964: 377). In the Congress fusion politics appears to have succeeded only moderately: some twenty-five members of the new House of Representatives classified themselves as Populists or fusionists and six senators were designated as Populists.

In Texas, members of the People's Party were divided on what caused the unexpected election results. White conservatives blamed blacks and Mexicans (Cantrell and Barton 1989; Martin 1970), charging that insufficient energy had been spent to prevent Mexicans and blacks from selling their votes to Democrats. Others charged that the party had become known as the "party of the Negro lover." A third explanation held that the main problem was corruption at the county level, where officials who in previous elections had run on the People's ticket were either incompetent or corrupt, or were religious zealots who had made alliances with prohibitionists against the will of the voters. People were fed up and chose to turn Democrat. Although the members disagreed on what had led to their party's disintegration, they concurred on one major issue: fusion politics had destroyed the People's Party in Texas. Voters perceived the party to have a split personality with no coherent philosophy or direction.

A few months after the election the People's Party in Texas reorganized. Immediately a new agenda was set that led many members to abandon the party altogether. Blacks were no longer welcomed or encouraged to be members, and all policies supporting African American civil rights issues were dropped from the party's platform. The party maintained its strong anti-immigrant stance and continued to support policies against immigrants, including placing a poll tax on immigrant voters. This move was largely fueled by the fact that the only plank in the platform that did well at election time was the constitutional reform to limit voting to immigrants who had filed their naturalization petition at least six months before an election. The Suffrage Amendment Act won by 268,262 to 51,649 (*Laws of Texas*, 10:956).

The new direction the People's Party took led its liberal faction to quit the party. Kearby became a Democrat. Others, who were devoted to labor rights and African American civil rights, formed the Socialist Party (Winkler 1916: 419). The Socialists focused their energy on forming an international workers' party and creating alliances with Socialists in other countries. Their party's main goals were to lobby for legislation prohibiting child labor and abuse of women's labor, but they also demanded regulations to protect the health and welfare of workers in general. The Socialist Party did not attract many members and within a few years had disbanded.

Members like McMinn remained solidly behind the People's Party and helped to set new policy directions. Although McMinn had lost the race for Texas Supreme Court justice by a landslide, he was confident the party could recuperate. In 1900 he became the People's Party main leader in Texas and was their gubernatorial nominee (Election Registers 1838–1972b; Winkler 1916: 647).

Congressional Immigration Politics:
Judge Maxey Awaits Federal Decisions

After the election Judge Maxey was expected to announce a ruling on the *Rodriguez* case, but nothing was heard. Under the law Mexican immigrants continued to be able to vote in Texas as long as they complied with the newly passed Texas Suffrage Amendment. Nonwhites, like Rodriguez, were also still eligible to vote. Moreover, despite the fact that the People's Party had been defeated at the polls, the few remaining Populist representatives in the House attempted to resuscitate the party by reworking their anti-immigrant agenda. When the newly elected Twenty-Fifth Legislature met in its first session in 1897, legislators representing the People's Party introduced bills to disenfranchise immigrants. Their old strategy of disenfranchising only Mexicans had failed, so now their aim was to eliminate immigrant voters altogether.

On January 15, 1897, several bills were introduced to end immigrant voting in Texas (*House Journal, Texas, 25th Legislature, Regular and First Called Session, 1897*, p. 34).[12] J. G. Burney, a member of the People's Party representing District 92 (Kerr, Kendall, and Banderas counties), introduced House Resolution (H.R.) 3 to make citizenship a requirement for voting in Texas. S. E. Holland, also a member of the People's Party and representing

District 37 (Burnet and Lampasas counties), introduced H.R. 5 supporting Burney but adding an amendment requiring that all voters pay a poll tax. Three Democrats also introduced bills requiring citizenship but disapproved of any poll tax amendment. All of these resolutions failed to pass the House and received unfavorable reviews from the Committee on Constitutional Reforms. The speaker of the House also recommended that they not be passed (Ibid., 138, 1447).

The failed resolutions were soon reintroduced in the House but failed to gain enough votes for reconsideration. During the House debates Representative Shelburne, a Democrat representing District 12 (Denton), tried to reach a compromise. He introduced H.R. 10 proposing that immigrants be allowed to vote as long as they could prove at election time that they could complete the naturalization process within one year of having voted (Ibid., 63). The proposal meant that if Judge Maxey failed to render his decision before the next election, Mexicans of Indian descent would lose their right to vote because they would be unable to prove they could acquire their naturalization papers within the required period. In the end, although Shelburne's resolution was supported by many and received a favorable review by the Constitutional Committee, it was defeated (Ibid., 279, 1448). The defeat was an important victory for immigrants and for the legislators who depended on the Mexican and German vote. If the bill had passed, immigrants besides Mexicans would have been affected because Congress was currently debating legislation to stop many immigrants from naturalizing or working in the United States if they were not literate in English. The pending changes in federal law would have placed the naturalization applications of many immigrants in political limbo and disqualified many Texan voters.

The federal congressional revisions over immigration and naturalization law had been debated for many years, but it was not until early January 1897 that Sen. Henry Cabot Lodge believed he had enough votes to place restrictions on immigrants from non-English-speaking countries. The primary intent of the legislation, which came to be known as the Lodge Immigrant Bill (H. R. 7864) (*Congressional Record, Proceedings and Debates, 54th Congress, Second Session*, vol. 29, part 2, 1897, p. 182, 1692), was to stop undesirable immigration by requiring English literacy of all incoming immigrants (Section 2 of HR 7864, Ibid., 1423–1433). If the legislation passed, all immigrants would be required to know some English and prove so by reading at least twenty words of the U.S. Constitution. The secondary aim of the legislation was to disqualify immigrants from working in the United States if they failed to acquire citizenship. Section 4 of the bill affected nearly all immigrants, as citizenship would be a requisite for working in manual labor occupations and the mechanical trades. Only immigrants employed in professional occupations were exempt. The legislation also placed pressure on immigrants to leave by adding a criminal provision under section 4. Any alien found working in the named occupations without holding proper naturalization papers would be fined, imprisoned, and deported.

The legislation passed the House and Senate on January 25, 1897, and was sent to President Grover Cleveland for his signature.[13] The congressmen anticipated that he would sign the bill, but to their amazement he vetoed it (*Congressional Record and Appendix, 54th Congress, Second Session,* vol. 29, part 3, 1897, pp. 2667–2668). No one expected this outcome because Cleveland had lost the presidential election in 1896 and, being a lame duck president, was expected to follow the Congress's wishes. Yet one of his last acts as president was to veto the Lodge Immigrant Bill, and he devoted his presidential message to the Congress to outlining his rationale. He charged that Congress had advanced the legislation on the false premise that the United States no longer had room for immigrants. Writing that the resolution was "harsh and oppressive," he argued that it was wrong to pass legislation that converted immigrants into criminals. Cleveland began his admonishment of the Congress by disagreeing that the United States was flooded with undesirable immigrants:

> I herewith return without approval House bill numbered 7864, entitled "An act to amend the immigration laws of the United States."
>
> . . . It is not claimed, I believe, that the time has come for the further restriction of immigration on the ground that an excess of population overcrowds our land.
>
> It is said, however, that the quality of recent immigration is undesirable. The time is quite within recent memory when the same thing was said of immigrants who with their descendants are now numbered among our best citizens. It is said that too many immigrants settle in our cities, thus dangerously increasing the idle and vicious population. This is certainly a disadvantage.
>
> It can not be shown, however, that it affects all our cities nor that it is permanent; nor does it appear that this condition where it exists demands as its remedy the reversal of our present immigration policy. (Ibid., 2667)

Cleveland argued further that the literacy section of the bill did not make sense. He disagreed that restricting immigration to the educated classes would protect the country from degeneracy, contending that laborers were good people and that violence and disorder never originated with the laboring classes. On the contrary, laborers traditionally were the victims of educated agitators. Illiteracy was merely a pretext to cover up other political motives.

Cleveland then moved on to criticize the unfairness of criminalizing employment. The United States had the right to pass labor laws, but it was wrong to convert aliens into criminals merely because they needed to work: "The prohibition against the employment of aliens upon any public works of the United States is in line with other legislation of a like character. It is quite a different thing, however, to declare it a crime for an alien to come regularly and habitually into the United States for the purpose of obtaining work from private parties . . . and to constitute any employment of such alien a criminal offense" (Ibid.). Cleveland then commented on the bill's international impact. Without a doubt, he proclaimed, other nations would consider the legislation unfair and it was highly likely to produce a reaction from Canada and Mexico. The policy also infringed, he said, upon the economic rights of the U.S. states bordering Mexico and Canada, as it was a well-known fact that the border states depended on immigrant labor.

Cleveland closed his message by declaring the bill oppressive and remarking on how such unwise legislation could cause international security problems:

> Such unfriendly legislation as is proposed could hardly fail to provoke retaliatory measures to the injury of many of our citizens who now find employment on adjoining foreign soil. . . .
>
> A careful examination of this bill has convinced me that for the reasons given and others not specifically stated, its provisions are unnecessarily harsh and oppressive, and that its defects in construction would cause vexation and its operation would result in harm to our citizens. (Ibid., 2668)

Immediately upon receiving the president's veto, the House began the reconsideration process. The following day, on March 3, 1897, the bill failed to gain a three-quarters vote to override the president's veto, and it died in the House. One hundred and ninety-five members voted in favor of reconsideration, while 37 were opposed, and 123 abstained (*Congressional Record and Appendix, 54th Congress, Second Session*, vol. 29, part 3, 1897, pp. 2946–2947). Most representatives from Texas opposed reconsideration and had been against the legislation.[14]

For now, the U.S. Congress chose to leave immigration enforcement to the states. Many congressmen felt it was wrong to place harsh restrictions upon immigrants.[15] Instead, it was given to the states to handle their immigrant populations, and the state legislatures would henceforth be allowed to pass laws to restrict employment to citizens, to require literacy for employment, or to no longer allow immigrants to vote. This was the era of massive European immigration to the United States, and the states were left to deal with the millions of Europeans settling in their regions. From 1880 to 1890, the size of the foreign-born population grew from 6,679,943 to 9,249,547 (U.S. Census 1897b: 50). The sheer size in growth was alarming in itself, but when scholars like Francis Walker, a professor at MIT and the superintendent of the Census Bureau, charged that the growth was mainly attributable to undesirable southern and eastern European immigrants, the states had more information to consider when drafting their policies toward immigrants (Feagin and Booher; Feagin 2003; Ngai 2004; Scupin 2003). By 1902, nine of the thirty states that had originally allowed immigrants to vote had rescinded that policy (Keyssar 2000: table A-12). Texas continued to allow immigrants to vote but placed restrictions on the franchise and made it more difficult for immigrants to qualify to vote.

The large waves of European migration in the United States in the late nineteenth century were not experienced in Texas, largely because most of the immigrants settled in the Northeast, Illinois, and California. For the most part, only Mexicans and some Germans continued to select Texas as their destination. Even though the U.S. Congress had temporarily ended the immigration debate, however, Mexicans encountered new political problems when the newly inaugurated president of the United States chose to revisit Mexico-U.S. relations. On April 26, 1897, President McKinley decided to enact a new treaty with Mexico over the U.S.-Mexico border. Part of McKinley's scheme was a proposal to purchase areas of northern Mexico and enact a new border treaty. This policy shift complicated politics in Texas and made it difficult for Judge Maxey to render a final ruling on Rodriguez. New border policies were bound to affect immigration and the political status of Mexican immigrants.

If You Take the Land, You Have to Take the People: Annexation Plans During the Rodriguez Deliberations

In the late 1890s relations between the United States and Mexico were amicable. Mexican immigrants were allowed to settle in the United States, and commerce between the countries continued to flourish. The United States was Mexico's main trading partner, investor, and political ally. By 1902 U.S. corporations had invested over $500 million in Mexico (Callahan 1932: 510), and U.S. investors regularly bailed out the Mexican economy when it was in financial crisis. For example, because Mexico was heavily in debt to European countries, U.S. investors loaned the Mexican government money as needed to pay installments on its foreign debts (Zabludovsky 1998). In turn, Mexico guaranteed U.S. lenders payment by using government-owned land as collateral. Furthermore, the flourishing trade between the two countries saw 80 percent of Mexican exports going to the United States, and 56 percent of Mexico's imports coming from the United States. Problems along the border had also been effectively addressed. President Díaz was satisfied that President Cleveland had stopped the Texas Rangers from entering Mexico along the border without federal authority (Callahan 1932: 436). Díaz had returned the favor by negotiating a treaty with the United States to allow U.S. troops to cross the Arizona-Sonora border in search of hostile Indians. Although relations were amicable, on one international issue Díaz was unwilling to concede: he would not negotiate any treaty to change the geographical border between Mexico and the United States. Since 1889 the U.S. government had tried to purchase parts of the northern states of Mexico, but Díaz steadfastly refused. In 1897 McKinley, upon entering office, tried to rekindle negotiations, notwithstanding Mexico's firm opposition. This annexation scenario helps to illuminate the political issues Judge Maxey had to consider before rendering his decision on Rodriguez.

In the late 1880s the U.S. Congress held sessions to discuss purchasing the Mexican states bordering the United States. The rationale was that because U.S. investors already owned a large part of this territory it was logical that U.S. law govern this region. Díaz rejected all of the annexation proposals and warned the U.S. Congress that the execution of any plan to purchase or colonize Mexican territory would be met by armed resistance. Nevertheless, the U.S. Congress began the process of buying Baja California in 1889 after the American investor Louis Hallen urged Congress to acquire the territory. Hallen already owned more than half of the peninsula. As the State Department and the Committee on Foreign Affairs of the Congress studied the annexation plan, Matías Romero, who at this time was living in the United States and acting as Mexico's foreign minister, published a scathing article outlining President Díaz's opposition (Callahan 1932: 430; *Congressional Record, Proceedings and Debate, 51st Congress, First Session*, vol. 21, part I, 1889, p. 2639). The article, entitled the "Annexation of Mexico," appeared first in the prestigious journal the *North American Review* and was subsequently reprinted in newspapers across the nation (see *Las Novedades*, May 23, 1889, in Matías Romero Papers, roll 72, document no. 50264; *Mailand Express*, May 18, 1889). Romero affirmed his country's opposition to any type of land acquisition, whether by purchase or by force. He proclaimed that Mexicans were prepared to meet any act of aggression with armed force, regardless of the U.S. government's superior military power. He denounced the annexation plan as an invasion and called it a cultural extermination plan. Mexicans, he warned, were ready to fight, and this time Mexico would not fall so easily. Romero also examined other practical issues and advised readers that any invasion plan had to consider how the acquired population would affect the U.S. economy. Romero wrote,

> I have purposely refrained from dwelling on the actual difficulties of the subjugation of 12,000,000 brave people, proud of their nationality, and ready to fight to the last extremity to preserve it, and on the difficulties of keeping subdued such a large number of people, because, although these considerations are very serious, and, in the opinion of many competent minds, should be enough to forbid such a conquest . . . I am willing to assume that the conquest of Mexico could be accomplished; but I think it opportune to mention that a great military authority has recently said that a war with Mexico now would be a quite different affair from the one of 1846 and 1847, and its consequences would be quite different. Although it is a law of nature that the stronger can subdue the weaker, there are several factors in a struggle between two nations which may affect the final issue, and often the result may not quite compensate the magnitude of the effort. . . . the whole country, to a man, is decidedly opposed to annexation, not only because they are proud of their nationality, but also because they have the conviction that annexation for them means extermination, and naturally they are not willing to contribute to their own destruction. (Romero 1889: 532, 536)

Through the article Romero hoped to raise public opposition to annexation by illustrating the problems the idea would create. He explained that any proposal to annex land must also include a plan to determine how the acquired population would affect the United States. Romero began by arguing that if the land was taken the Fourteenth Amendment required that the acquired population be incorporated as citizens. He stressed that because north Mexico was populated by full-blooded Indians Mexicans would create a tremendous race problem in the United States. Approximately twelve million people would be incorporated as citizens, and they would wield considerable power in elections. Mexicans would also exacerbate racial conflict in America because they would join African Americans to pursue equal rights:

Twelve millions of a heterogeneous, dissatisfied, unwilling people, with a representation in the Congress of the United States . . . and the corresponding number of votes in the Electoral College, the fate and future of this country would then be placed in the hands of that dissatisfied element, which would thus exercise a controlling influence in its destiny.

. . . But if the American Statesmen, whose task it is to pilot this great Nation to a safe port, undertake to increase the already existing difficulties of the situation, which in all probability will daily grow greater, by adding to them the introduction of a whole nationality of twelve million people of almost insuperable assimilation, at least for many generations to come, a people of a different race, speaking a different language and possessing very different habits and ideas, two-thirds of whom are pure-blooded Indians, who, although docile, peaceful, and law abiding, are, on the whole, ignorant, and will, beyond all doubt, present the same social and political problems that are now offered by the colored race of the South. (Ibid., 530, 532)

Romero proceeded to examine the effects on the labor market. His scenario assumed Mexicans would be extended the same rights a modern democracy guaranteed its citizens. He argued that the acquisition of Mexico meant acquiring a new labor force protected by the rights of citizenship: "At least three million able-bodied Mexican laborers, whose wages range now from twelve and a half to fifty cents a day, and who would be quite willing to come north or west for the purpose of earning higher wages, would be thrown on the market, clothed with the rights of citizenship, and without any possibility of closing the doors of the country to them" (Ibid., 532). Regardless of Mexico's opposition and its threat of armed resistance, the U.S. government pursued the transaction. The State Department charged Secretary of State John Foster with inquiring if Mexico would at least be willing to sell the property not owned by Hallen in Baja California.

Less than two years later, on December 16, 1891, Senator Matthew Quay submitted the completed petition to the U.S. Congress. The territorial acquisition plans, however, had grown to include the purchase of Baja California plus parts of Sonora, Chihuahua, and Coahuila (*Congressional Record, Proceedings and Debate, 52nd Congress, First Session*, vol. 23, part I, 1892, p. 66). Essentially the entire U.S.-Mexico border would move south. Although the petition met resistance and was voted against by the Senate Foreign Relations Committee, Congress continued to pursue the purchase (Ibid., 1224; Extracts from Congressional Record 52nd Congress, First

Session, vol. 23, no. 47, 1892 in Matías Romero Papers, roll 72, document no. 50264).

Throughout the United States newspapers charged that the annexation plan was immoral because Mexico was firmly opposed. In a report compiled by the U.S. Congress and entitled "Public Opinion in the United States on the Annexation of Mexico" fifty newspapers published articles firmly opposing annexation (Matías Romero Papers, roll 72, document no. 50259).

Some newspapers also added that annexation would be injurious to both countries because thousands of people with different cultures and traditions would be absorbed. On February 8, 1892, the *Washington Post* offered a critical indictment of the annexation plan and commented that Mexicans were not a people that could be assimilated:

> As for the absorption of the entire republic of Mexico by the United States, it is a thing not to be thought of for a moment. The acquisition of Canada would be advantageous. The acquisition of Mexico would be injurious. The Mexicans differ from the Americans in blood and language, and in many respects the civilizations of the two countries differ. They would not unite. One government might be extended over both, but the two great sections would remain distinct. It would require hundreds of years to make the Mexicans and the Americans alike and to establish English language in the place of the Spanish. It is doubtful if it could ever be done. These conditions forbid all thought of union between Mexico and the United States, whether peaceably or by force. (*Washington Post*, February 8, 1892, p. 4)

With Mexico's ongoing refusal to negotiate a purchase deal and public opinion against annexation increasing, the U.S. Congress temporarily abandoned its plans. However, as noted earlier, when President McKinley took office, within a few months of his appointment he resumed the purchase proposal (*Congressional Record, Proceedings and Debate, 55th Congress, Special Session*, vol. 30, part 2, 1897, p. 1434). He asked Senator Lodge to head a committee to explore changing the boundaries between Mexico and the United States and to prepare a treaty dealing with all matters of annexation.

Indeed, these matters were serious and implicated Texas tremendously, as the boundary between Texas and Mexico was potentially about to change. Republicans were in control of the presidency and the Congress, and they had the power to make all of the decisions over the border, the U.S.-Mexico Treaty, and the acquired population. In this political climate, Judge Maxey had a difficult choice to make: wait for the new border to be negotiated by Republicans and have Congress legislate the political rights Mexicans would hold in the United States; or rule on the Rodriguez case and set a precedent.

Judge Maxey Makes His Decision

Judge Maxey rendered his decision on May 3, 1897 (*In re Rodriguez* 1897: 337), a week and a half after President McKinley appointed Senator Lodge to head the annexation committee (see chapter 4). It is uncertain why Maxey did not wait for Congress to decide on McKinley's resolution since any annexation plan would have included a statement on the political rights Mexicans were to be extended. This discussion certainly would have affected the outcome of the *Rodriguez* case. On the one hand Maxey may have made his decision because negotiations with Mexico could take time. Perhaps, on the other hand, he chose to legislate from the bench. In other words, Maxey's decision preempted congressional politics.

Throughout Texas articles announcing Judge Maxey's ruling appeared in newspapers. The headlines ranged from "The Naturalization Law: The Rodriguez Case Decided by Judge Maxey Who Makes an Exhaustive Review of the Law" (*Dallas Morning News*, May 4, 1897, p. 2; *Houston Daily*, May 4, 1897, p. 2) to "A Famous Case Decided: Judge Maxey's Decision in the Mexican Naturalization Case" (*Austin Daily American Statesman*, May 7, 1897, p. 1). The *San Antonio Daily Express* offered the most detailed overview of the ruling. The title of its news article also succinctly captured Judge Maxey's decision: "Treaty Rights to Mexicans: Are Eligible to Citizenship in the United States" (*San Antonio Daily Express*, May 4, 1897, p. 5).

To ensure the accurate dissemination of the court's decision Judge Maxey issued an official statement of the ruling to the media. News reporters were given the statement of the facts, which contained a copy of McMinn's and Evans's petition, part of Rodriguez's response at trial, and a copy of Maxey's opinion. Only the *San Antonio Daily Express* published sections of these documents plus Judge Maxey's entire opinion. A condensed version of the documents and of Judge Maxey's ruling were eventually published in the *Federal Reporter*.

In the final ruling Judge Maxey offered an exhaustive review of federal and state laws to support his decision. He also reviewed the history of U.S. naturalization law and treaty law as they applied to Mexicans. The first issue Maxey addressed was whether Mexicans were disqualified from U.S.

citizenship because they were not white. He began his deliberation by partly concurring with the opinion advanced by McMinn and Evans in their original petition against Rodriguez. Maxey believed that Mexicans were not included in the ethnological meaning of white. Using Rodriguez as the example, he wrote,

> If the strict scientific classification of the anthropologist should be adopted, he would probably not be classed as white. It is certain he is not an African nor a person of African descent. According to his own statement, he is a "pure full blooded Mexican," bearing no relation to the Aztecs or original races of Mexico. Being, then, a citizen of Mexico, may he be naturalized, pursuant to the laws of congress? If debarred by the strict letter of the law from receiving letters of citizenship, is he embraced within the intent and meaning of the statute? If he falls within the meaning and intent of the law, his application should be granted, notwithstanding the letter of the statute may be against him. (*In re Rodriguez* 1897: 349; *San Antonio Daily Express*, May 4, 1897, p. 5)

Although Maxey believed that Mexicans were not white, he proposed that color did not disqualify them from holding U.S. citizenship. In the United States blacks were citizens and African immigrants were allowed to naturalize even though they were not white. People prohibited from obtaining citizenship, Maxey argued, must be named explicitly by statute. Mexicans cannot be treated like Indians and Asians merely because of their color. If Congress intended them to be part of the races prohibited from holding U.S. citizenship, they would have been named in the provisions excluding Asians and Indians.

Then, in an unprecedented move, Maxey proceeded to explain why Mexicans under citizenship law were included in the meaning of "Free White Person." Yet he was careful to stipulate that his opinion applied only to the meaning of who is a citizen and not to other areas of the law. Maxey argued that although Congress did not consider Mexicans to be white, it negotiated several treaties with Spain and Mexico giving them and their descendants U.S. citizenship. Beginning in 1819, when Florida was acquired from Spain, Maxey concluded, Congress did not exclude from citizenship any of the annexed peoples. The Treaty of 1819 was subsequently extended to the peoples of Louisiana when Spain ceded this territory to the United States. The same rights of citizenship were extended to Mexicans when the United States acquired Mexico's northern region following the Mexican-American War. In 1848, when the Treaty of Guadalupe Hidalgo brought closure to the war, Congress agreed to extend citizenship to the Mexican population. The same agreement was later negotiated in 1854, when the Gadsden Treaty was executed and the purchase of southern Arizona was finalized. Maxey emphasized that under none of the treaties with Mexico or Spain did Congress limit citizenship to free whites.

Maxey then added that because Congress agreed to extend citizenship to the annexed populations this agreement also applied to their descendants. He affirmed that the law was clear on this issue as the eighth article of the Treaty of Guadalupe Hidalgo stipulated: "In the said territories, property of every kind, now belonging to Mexicans not established there, shall be inviolably respected. The present owners, the heirs of these, and all Mexicans who may hereafter acquire said property by contract, shall enjoy with respect to it guaranties equally ample as if the same belonged to citizens of the United States" (*In re Rodriguez* 1897: 351).

After Maxey concluded his interpretation of treaty law, he clarified one other related issue raised by McMinn and Evans. They had argued that people who were of Indian descent and were not descendants of the annexed population of 1848 were ineligible to apply for citizenship. This applied to dark-complexioned people of Mexican descent, regardless of whether they had been born in Mexico or the United States. On this issue Maxey affirmatively said no. Maxey argued that although Mexicans were part of the Indian race, they could not be treated in the same way as the Native American populations of the United States because Mexicans were a detribalized people. Only tribal Indians from the United States and their descendants were disqualified because they had been excluded by statute and by the U.S. Supreme Court ruling *Elk v. Wilkins*. Mexicans, on the other hand, were protected by the Fourteenth Amendment. Maxey stated,

> While the amendment as held in the authorities fact cited was intended primarily for the negro race, it also confers the right of citizenship upon persons of all other races, white, yellow, or red, born or naturalized in the United States and "subject to the jurisdiction thereof." The language has been held to embrace even the Chinese, to whom the laws of naturalization do not extend. . . . Mexicans, therefore, born in the United States, and who at the date of birth, were subject to the jurisdiction of our government,—as all were, except children of Diplomatic officers, and a few others, not necessary in this connection to notice (*In re Look Tin Sing,* supra),—are citizens of the United States and of the state wherein they reside. The intimation of some of the briefs of counsel that *Elk vs. Wilkins,* 112 U.S. 94, 5 Sup. Ct. 41, excludes Mexicans from citizenship, is not maintainable. That case

refers exclusively to tribal Indians born and residing within the territory forming a part of the United States . . . The dissimilarity between the Elk Case and the one at bar is so pronounced that further reference to it is not deemed essential. (*San Antonio Daily Express,* May 4, 1897, p. 5; *In re Rodriguez,* 1897: 353)

Maxey then moved on to discuss the specific laws applied to immigrants. This was necessary since his general discussion had centered on why the annexed Mexican population, their heirs, and American-born Mexicans were not part of the prohibited populations denied U.S. citizenship. Now he had to elaborate on why the racial restrictions in naturalization law did not apply to Mexicans when the law clearly stipulated that only free white immigrants and Africans were allowed to naturalize. Here he had to prove that Congress allowed Mexican immigrants to naturalize whether or not they were part of the Indian race. On this issue Maxey invoked the Naturalization Treaty of 1868. According to Maxey, when the Naturalization Treaty of 1868 was enacted the president of the United States and the U.S. Congress knew most Mexicans were Indian, yet Congress chose not to include a clause to exclude such people. To strengthen the validity of his opinion Maxey argued that because the treaty was enacted during the same congressional session that the Fourteenth Amendment was adopted, Congress enacted the treaty to clarify the political rights all Mexican immigrants possess in the United States and to place them under the jurisdiction of the amendment.

Maxey concluded his analysis of U.S. law by proposing that although the treaty was no longer in effect it is part of a historical body of law that affirms that Mexicans, irrespective of their race, are allowed to naturalize. Maxey wrote,

When all the foregoing laws, treaties and constitutional Provisions are considered, which either affirmatively confer the rights of citizenship upon Mexicans or tacitly recognize in them the right of individual naturalization, the conclusion forces itself upon the mind that citizens of Mexico are eligible to American citizenship and may be individually naturalized by complying with the provisions of our laws. (*In re Rodriguez* 1887: 354)

One last issue Maxey had to address was McMinn's and Evans's allegation that Rodriguez could be disqualified from obtaining U.S. citizenship because he was illiterate and an ignorant man. Surprisingly, on this point Maxey concurred that they had raised a strong argument, since to qualify for citizenship an individual had to be of sound mind and character. In response, Maxey rhetorically asked: Was Ricardo Rodriguez's character so loathsome that he did not meet the minimum social requirements of a person seeking to naturalize? Maxey conceded that although Rodriguez was illiterate and not knowledgeable about U.S. laws he was a man of good character, and since there were no federal laws requiring immigrants to read and write he could not be disqualified. His final comment addressed the recent literacy legislation vetoed by President Cleveland:

> That the man is lamentably ignorant is conceded, and that he is unable to read and write the testimony clearly discloses. But the testimony also disclosed that he is a very good man, peaceable and industrious, of good moral character and law abiding to a remarkable degree. And hence it may be said of him, notwithstanding his inability to undergo an examination on questions of constitutional law, that by his daily walk during a residence of ten years in the city of San Antonio, he has practically illustrated and emphasized his attachments to the principles of the constitution. Congress has not seen fit to require of applicants for naturalization an educational qualification and courts should be careful to avoid judicial legislation.
>
> In the judgment of the court, the applicant possesses the requisite qualifications of citizenship, and his application will therefore be granted. (Ibid., 355)

Maxey finally rendered his opinion and declared Ricardo Rodriguez qualified to be naturalized. D. H. Hart, the clerk of the U.S. Western District Court, was ordered to prepare Rodriguez's final papers of naturalization (U.S. District Court, book D, no. 1478 1/2, pp. 5–7). McMinn's and Evans's efforts to deny U.S. citizenship to people of Mexican descent failed. Under treaty and naturalization laws race could not be used to exclude Mexicans from U.S. citizenship. Likewise Judge Maxey ruled that Native American exclusion laws did not apply to Mexicans because they were a detribalized people.

Judge Maxey's Advisory Committee: Legal Arguments Accepted or Rejected

Based on Judge Maxey's opinion it appears that he prudently assessed the legal briefs submitted by his committee but agreed mainly with the arguments advanced by Thomas M. Paschal. Paschal's central argument was that

Mexicans were not limited to acquiring citizenship in only one way. U.S. law allowed them to qualify for citizenship via four procedures: birth, naturalization, constitutional amendment, and by treaty. In his report Paschal outlined all of the treaty arguments used in Maxey's ruling (*In re Rodriguez* 1897: 339). Maxey, however, disagreed with Paschal's opinion that Mexicans were part of the Caucasian race. Paschal unsuccessfully argued that Mexicans came from one of the finest Caucasian races of Europe, and when they mixed with the Aztec race the Indian blood melted into the Spanish race (Ibid., 342).

On the issue of race Maxey concurred with Floyd McGown's assessment that on the basis of scientific logic Mexicans were not white. McGown cited many ethnological studies indicating that Indians were not included as part of the Caucasian race. On the contrary, McGown argued, ethnologists had proven that Indians belonged to the Mongolian race (Ibid., 345). McGown's intent in drawing this racial genealogy was to argue that although the U.S. Congress had not named Mexicans in any statute prohibiting them from naturalization—because they were Mongolians—the Chinese Exclusion Laws applied to them. On this issue Maxey disagreed. He reaffirmed his opinion that Mexicans needed to be named by statute.

Maxey also disagreed with most of McGown's persuasive arguments on state law. According to McGown, throughout the country state supreme courts had ruled that nonwhite immigrants were excluded from citizenship and, in his opinion, these rulings had created a precedent that also applied to Mexicans. McGown had advanced this argument to support McMinn's and Evans's original petition that Mexicans were part of the prohibited races denied the right to naturalize (see *San Antonio Daily Express*, May 17, 1896, p. 11). Offering several precedents in which racial minorities had been denied the privilege of naturalization, McGown argued that the federal government had made it very clear that only Africans and whites were eligible. Specifically, he argued the first precedent denying Mexican immigrants the right to apply for naturalization was set in 1878 *In re Ah Yup*. In this case the Circuit Court of California ruled that the Chinese were not white and therefore were ineligible. He then argued that since it was a well-known ethnological fact that Mexican Indians were part of the Mongolian race, *Ah Yup* applied to Mexicans. He then moved to discuss legal rulings on mixed-race Caucasians to argue that Mexican mestizos were ineligible to apply for naturalization. McGown stated that *In re Camille* (1880) the Circuit Court of Oregon had ruled that half-breed Indians were not white and therefore not eligible for naturalization. Using *In re Camille* as the precedent, McGown further argued that the court had ruled that mixed-race Caucasians could be considered white only if they were at least three-quarters white, and opined that since most Mexicans were full-blooded Indian they were ineligible. Employing *In re Kanaka Nian*, a case involving a Hawaiian immigrant, McGown once again argued that only whites were allowed to naturalize, as the Utah Supreme Court in 1889 had ruled that only European immigrants qualified. The final case used to challenge Rodriguez's naturalization was the U.S. Supreme Court case *Elk v. Wilkens* (1884). McGown argued that Congress made all Indians, including detribalized Indians, ineligible. Mexicans were Indian; therefore, they must be included under the U.S. Supreme Court ruling.

Maxey disagreed with all of McGown's arguments and upheld Paschal's counterarguments. Paschal stated that none of these cases applied to Rodriguez because Mexicans were not Chinese, Japanese, or tribal Indians. Camille also could not be applied to Mexicans because the case dealt with a legal argument over a birth at sea.

McMinn's and Evans's arguments on treaty law were also rejected by Maxey. In their briefs they echoed the same positions they had taken at trial, reiterating their opinion that a treaty cannot nullify a state law when in conflict and that the Treaty of Guadalupe Hidalgo had not made Mexicans U.S. citizens (*In re Rodriguez* 1897: 346–347). Maxey disagreed and concurred with Paschal. Mexicans born in the United States, Mexican immigrants, and the annexed Mexican population had been made citizens by treaty law and the passage of the Fourteenth Amendment.

The same day that Judge Maxey made his ruling, on May 3, 1897, Ricardo Rodriguez appeared in the San Antonio Western District Court of Texas in front of Clerk Hart. Rodriguez came to take his oath of citizenship and to obtain his naturalization certificate. Lorenzo Galvan and J. H. Ducas accompanied him and served as witnesses (U.S. District Court, San Antonio, Minute Book D, pp. 5–7). His friend and attorney James Fisk also accompanied him. After Rodriguez took his oath of citizenship he signed the clerk's naturalization logbook by using an "x" as a mark of his signature. The clerk wrote Rodriguez's name beside the mark. Clerk Hart recorded Rodriguez's confirmation and oath:

No. 14781/2 Order granting naturalization papers
Ex Parte Ricardo Rodriguez
On this the 3rd day of May, A.D. 1897, came on to be Heard the application of Ricardo Rodriguez, filed herein on the 11th day of May, A.D. 1896 to be admitted to become a citizen of the United States of America (said application being accompanied by a copy of the affidavit of the ap-

plicant and files in the County Court of Bexar County Texas, January 25, 1893, in which he declared his intention to become a citizen of the United States) which said application is as follows, to wit:

In United States District Court of Western District of Texas, at San Antonio Texas, setting:

Ex Parte

Ricardo Rodriguez

Comes now Ricardo Rodriguez and making application for final papers and admission to citizenship, on oath says:

That he will support the Constitution of the United States, and that he absolutely and entirely renounces and abjures all allegiance and fidelity to every foreign prince, potentate, State or sovereignty and particularly to the President of the Republic of Mexico, Porfirio Díaz, and his successors in office, of which said Republic applicant was formerly a citizen.

his

(Signed)   Ricardo x Rodriguez

mark

After overcoming a strenuous political campaign launched by members of the People's Party and by Republicans and enduring a slanderous trial in which he was debased and humiliated, Ricardo Rodriguez finally became a U.S. citizen. This persistent man, who wanted to become a U.S. citizen for the simple reason that he lived in the United States, clarified federal law and cleared a path toward citizenship for other Mexicans of color. His victory may have been personal, but it was a triumph for American democracy, as racial ideology was not allowed to destroy the principle of law.

CHAPTER 4

From the Spanish-American War to the Outbreak of the Mexican Revolution

Judge Maxey's ruling in favor of Ricardo Rodriguez indisputably clarified the political status of people of Mexican descent under U.S. law: they could not be denied U.S. citizenship on the basis of race. Although the Rodriguez case was a legal triumph for people of Mexican descent in its protection of their voting rights, Mexican immigrants in Texas nearly stopped applying for U.S. citizenship. In this chapter I explore the circumstances that led to the decline in Mexicans' applications and continue to examine the political status of Mexican immigrants in Texas. The discussion will be set in the context of political changes occurring in the United States and Mexico, especially in the aftermath of the Spanish-American War as events which strengthened the economic and political bonds between the Mexican and the U.S. governments unfolded and strongly shaped the U.S. government's open-door immigration policy toward Mexico.

Although I argue that amicable U.S.-Mexico relations followed the Spanish-American War, in Texas many Anglo-Americans did not share the federal government's positive attitude toward Mexico, and open hostility was demonstrated against Mexicans, including a legislative attempt to reduce the number of voters of Mexican descent. My narrative of the aftermath of the Rodriguez case concludes with an analysis of the conditions that led to the outbreak of the Mexican Revolution. The Revolution was a turning point in U.S.-Mexico immigration policy in that the U.S. government lost its economic hold on Mexico and was no longer willing to retain its open-door policy. This shift in policy echoes Eric Wolf's (1982, 1969) and David Harvey's (2006) observations that historically U.S. foreign policy is predicated upon economic self-interest. When U.S. capitalism no longer flourished in Mexico, the country and its people became a problem, to be treated as impudent neighbors with limited negotiation outlets.

Table 4.1. Counties Processing Naturalization Applications from Mexican Immigrants, 1870–1899

1870s	Aransas, Atascosa, Austin Federal, Bee, Bexar, Brownsville Federal, Caldwell, Calhoun, Cameron, DeWitt, Frio, Galveston, Galveston Federal, Gonzales, Harris, Hidalgo, Kendall, Kerr, Kinney, La Salle, Mason, Matagorda, Maverick, Nueces, Robertson, San Patricio, Starr, Travis, Uvalde, Val Verde, Victoria, Webb
1880s	Aransas, Atascosa, Bandera, Blanco, Bee, Bexar, Brownsville Federal, Burleson, Caldwell, Cameron, Colorado, Dallas, DeWitt, Dimmit, Falls, Fayette, Frio, Galveston, Galveston Federal, Harris, Hidalgo, Irion, Karnes, Kerr, Kimble, Kinney, La Salle, Mason, Matagorda, Maverick, Milam, McLennan, Nueces, Palo Pinto, Robertson, Refugio, San Patricio, Shackelford, Starr, Tarrant, Travis, Tyler, Uvalde, Val Verde, Victoria, Webb, Wharton, Wilbarger, Wilson, Zapata, Zavala
1890s	Anderson, Aransas, Atascosa, Bandera, Bastrop, Blanco, Bee, Bell, Bexar, Bosque, Brazos, Caldwell, Cameron, Collins, Colorado, Comal, Comanche, Cooke, Crockett, Dallas, Dimmit, DeWitt, Duval, Edwards, El Paso, Falls, Fayette, Frio, Galveston, Gillespie, Goliad, Gonzales, Grayson, Guadalupe, Hamilton, Harris, Hidalgo, Irion, Jefferson, Karnes, Kendall, Kerr, Kimble, Kinney, La Salle, Lavaca, Limestone, Madison, Matagorda, Maverick, Medina, McCulloch, McLennan, McMullen, Menard, Milam, Nueces, Refugio, Robertson, San Antonio Western District Court, San Patricio, Shackelford, Starr, Sterling, Sutton, Tarrant, Taylor, Throckmorton, Travis, Uvalde, Val Verde, Victoria, Webb, Wilson, Zapata, Zavala

Source: Index to Naturalization Records found in Texas State District and County Courts, 1846–1939, rolls 1 to 10; General Courts Austin, Brownsville, El Paso, Galveston, San Antonio, Jefferson, Texarkana, Tyler, Waco.

Naturalization Applications Filed by Mexicans Decline

After the Rodriguez ruling, Mexican immigrants, rather than flocking to the nearest court to declare their intention of filing for citizenship, did the opposite. The personal reasons individuals failed to apply are uncertain. What is definite is that naturalization records in Texas indicate that the submission rate fell radically from 1897 to 1899. Before the ruling the application rates had actually peaked, as eighteen new counties began to process petitions from Mexicans (table 4.1).

During the 1890s the number of petitions rose to 12,688, an increase of over 4,000 applications from the previous decade (TNR, rolls 1–10), but after Judge Maxey issued his ruling this trend ended. Of the total applications filed in the 1890s, only 295 were filed after the ruling, most from Webb County (N = 179, TNR, roll 10). Furthermore, after the ruling the granting of citizenship to Mexicans failed to increase,[1] and the state of affairs actually got worse.

Various factors contributed to this outcome. First, the Rodriguez case was a public spectacle that signified the antagonism many Anglo-Americans felt toward Mexicans. Rodriguez's challenge, rather than becoming a blueprint for Mexicans to follow in demanding their rights, most likely frightened them. Having to endure the ordeal Rodriguez experienced was a discouraging factor rather than a motivating one, and Mexicans decided that the best way to avoid problems was not to challenge Anglo-American citizens.

Second, Mexicans continued to have little control of the naturalization process. With the exception of two county judges of Mexican origin in Webb and Zapata counties, the judges who oversaw the naturalization application process were Anglo-Americans, and they had the power to interpret the law however they wanted (Election Registers 1838–1972a; Election Registers 1838–1972b). People of Mexican descent were elected to judicial positions in some South Texas counties, but they served in the lower courts as justices of the peace. A justice of the peace could not process naturalization documents, as this was the domain of the federal, state, district, and county courts.

The absence of Mexican Americans in the higher-level courts does not mean they were excluded from all state-level governance in Texas. During the 1890s Thomas A. Rodriguez was elected for one term to the Texas House of Representatives in 1893–1894 and later reelected in 1901 for one term (Texas Legislature 1962: 156). He represented District 90, which covered counties ranging from central to South Texas, including Bexar, Atascosa, Wilson, Karnes, and Live Oak. And in South Texas during the 1890s Mexicans continued to be elected to positions at the county level, including the offices of district attorney, county attorney, justice of the peace, county treasurer, county surveyor, assessor of taxes, sheriff, constable, and inspector of hides and animals.[2] Moreover, in the counties of Webb, Starr, and Zapata Mexicans held most of the county government positions. According to the research of David Montejano in his classic book *Anglos and Mexicans in the Making of Texas, 1836–1986* (1987), Mexicans were also elected to city council positions throughout South Texas. Thus by the 1890s in some regions of Texas Mexicans continued to wield political influence, yet in the higher-level courts, where naturalization decisions were made, their power was nearly nonexistent (Garcia 1998; Martinez 1993).

A third factor—likely the most important one—leading to the decline in the submission of applications was the outbreak of the Spanish-American War in 1898 (Hamilton 2006: 117). That is, because Mexico and the United States had conflicting laws about the rights and obligations of its naturalized citizens and their families, during wartime the preexisting conflicts became more salient and it was best for immigrants not to apply and in this way avoid serious legal problems. Conflicting clauses in U.S. and Mexican naturalization law dated back to the enactment of the first policies drafted after the two countries gained independence from their respective European colonial governments. Since 1790, under U.S. law when a father applied for naturalization the entire family acquired his legal status (see Commission on Naturalization 1905: 40–41).[3] By contrast, under Mexican naturalization law when a person renounced his or her citizenship Mexico recognized the change in the legal status of the applicant only, not in that of the entire family. The sons and daughters of a Mexican immigrant remained Mexican citizens whether they had been born in Mexico or in a foreign country (*Código de Extranjería*, chap. 9, article 30, 1886–1902, in Rodriguez 1903: 93). A person of Mexican descent whose parents were immigrants could renounce his or her Mexican citizenship only upon reaching the age of twenty.

During time of war this was a serious problem for the sons of Mexican immigrants, as they were obliged by both countries to bear arms in defense of their nations (see *Yale Law Journal* 1971: 77). Prior to the outbreak of the Spanish-American War, the U.S. government had tried to negotiate a treaty with Mexico to create a uniform international law on naturalization. The U.S. government wanted Mexico to release from citizenship the children of Mexican immigrants born in the United States as well as the children of naturalized citizens, but Mexico refused to change its citizenship laws (Callahan 1932: 400, 407). Furthermore, Mexico insisted that the sons of Mexican immigrants must fulfill their military duty in the armed forces of Mexico and, if necessary, be drafted in time of war. They could be released from military duty only when they turned twenty and formally renounced their Mexican citizenship (Código de Extranjería, chap. 1, article 3, in Rodriguez 1903: 96). If a male had not complied with his military obligations, he could be arrested and imprisoned if found on Mexican soil.

Mexican immigrants who had applied for citizenship and were waiting for their final papers also faced potential legal problems. They were left in limbo, citizens of neither country. Under Mexican law, a declarer was not considered a citizen of Mexico, and in the United States an applicant was not a U.S. citizen until final papers were issued. Thus, during wartime there could be serious implications for Mexican immigrants. If Mexican immigrants who had applied for U.S. citizenship were forced to return to Mexico they would not be eligible to receive any social services. Likewise, if they became embroiled in legal problems while residing in the United States, Mexico would not render them legal protection because they had renounced their citizenship (*Derecho Internacional Mexicano*, vol. 3, 1880: 590).

The Spanish-American War and Mexico

Even before the Spanish-American War broke out relations between the governments of the United States and Spain were strained. Spain suspected the United States of clandestinely interfering in its colonial affairs in Latin America. At that time Cuba and Puerto Rico were Spain's last two colonial possessions in the New World. Spain also believed U.S. businessmen were encouraging Cubans to revolt and were financing a revolution as a means of obtaining control of Cuba's sugar industry. Relations between Spain and the United States reached a boiling point on February 15, 1898, when a U.S. Navy ship, the *USS Maine*, exploded in Havana harbor (Corry 1998: 29). A few weeks earlier the U.S. government, fearing that insurgents might destroy the American sugar plantations if a revolution broke out, had sent the *Maine* to protect American investments in Cuba.

When the *Maine* exploded the U.S. Congress immediately suspected Spanish sabotage and within hours began preparing for war. President McKinley, however, refused to declare war until he had clarified various matters to his satisfaction, one of which was the need to determine which countries were U.S. allies. Of utmost significance to him was gaining Mexico's allegiance or at least its agreement to remain neutral. Mexico's geographical location placed the United States in harm's way should Mexico choose to support Spain.

In many ways the conflict between Spain and the United States benefited Mexico politically because during wartime it was prudent for the U.S. government to demonstrate its goodwill toward Mexico. In the months leading up to the explosion of the *Maine* Congress had realized that there was a strong possibility of going to war with Spain and that it was necessary therefore to repair its relations with Mexico (see Rhodes 1922). To do so Congress abandoned all plans to force Mexico to sell the northern states of Baja California and parts of Sonora and Chihuahua. For many years this had been a sensitive point of disagreement and a problem that had led President Díaz to call the United States an aggressor nation who preyed on its weaker neighbor. On the eve of the Spanish-American War, the U.S. government needed Mexico as an ally, not as a hostile neighbor. To close matters on the annexation plan, McKinley issued a confidential report on January 12, 1898, and informed Congress that the Office of the President would no longer pursue plans to remake the U.S.-Mexico border (*Congressional Record, Proceedings and Debate, 55th Congress, Second Session*, vol. 31, part 1, p. 559).

By April 21, 1898, the day McKinley declared war against Spain (Hamilton 2006: 117), the U.S. government had not only negotiated a series of agreements with Mexico dealing with extradition, water rights, and the maintenance of a free tax zone along the border, but also reestablished an international claims committee to settle financial disputes over the border (Davids 1976; Gilmore 1963). Mexico, in turn, agreed to remain neutral during the war. Four days after McKinley declared war Díaz ordered all governors in Mexico to maintain a state of neutrality and mandated severe punishments for the smuggling of arms to Spain. He assured Gen. Powell Clayton, the U.S. minister to Mexico, that all border towns would be vigilantly guarded to prevent individuals from rendering aid to Spain. Several regiments were dispatched to the Mexican ports of entry bordering the counties of Zapata, Uvalde, and Webb and the town of Eagle Pass (*San Antonio Express*, April 23, 1898, p. 6; *San Antonio Express*, April 28, 1898, p. 1).

Not everyone in Mexico shared Diaz's enthusiastic support for the United States. In fact, dissent spread throughout the country. For the first time since Díaz had taken office members of the ruling class publicly aired their anger as seeds of discontent were sown among the most trusted allies of the Porfirian dictatorship. Mexican aristocrats who retained social and economic relations with Spain expressed their anger and refused to support Mexico's embargo against Spain. Many merchants, especially those of Spanish birth, clandestinely set up networks to smuggle provisions into Cuba and continued to render aid to Spanish troops. They also helped Cuban refugees who sympathized with Spain to settle in Mexico. Some merchants went so far in their defiance of Diaz's neutrality order as to refuse to sell coal and other merchandise to U.S. ships docking in Mexican ports. When General Clayton heard about this, he immediately complained to Díaz, prompting the president to force merchants to comply via military orders.

Mexican intellectuals as well as the masses were ambivalent. They supported independence for Cuba but feared the U.S. government planned to make Cuba a possession of the United States. Their suspicion was not groundless because several decades earlier Mexico and Colombia had expressed their willingness to help Cuba gain independence but were forcefully told by the U.S. government not to interfere (Romero 1897). Many Mexicans remembered the hostile stance of the United States toward Cuban independence and distrusted their northern neighbor. It was widely believed that U.S. investors wanted Cuba as a possession in order to expand their lucrative sugar industry on the island.

President McKinley was aware that most nations believed the United States was insincere (Center for Military History 1993). To obtain international support for the war effort and to demonstrate that the United States was not a predatory nation, McKinley supported passage of the Teller Amendment, in which Congress agreed not to annex Cuba (Hamilton 2006: 109). After the Teller Amendment was signed, international criticism subsided. Germany and Great Britain, who, the United States feared, posed the largest military threat if they rendered aid to Spain, agreed to remain neutral, while Austria, France, Italy, and Russia supported Spain and adopted a wait-and-see attitude.

Within days of the U.S. government's formal declaration of war U.S. forces launched successful attacks against most of Spain's colonies in the New World and in the West Pacific. Spain suffered devastating losses and nearly lost the war. On April 29, 1898, the U.S. military defeated Spanish forces in Manila, the capital of the Philippine Islands (Ibid., 106). After Spain's defeat, the Filipino insurgents, who for decades, like the Cubans, had been fighting for independence from Spain, expected the U.S. government to declare the Philippines independent. The U.S. Congress, however, refused to cede the Philippine Islands and declared the people there incapable of self-rule. Under the Teller Amendment, Congress had agreed to not take possession of Cuba; the accord did not apply to other Spanish colonies.

Spanish troops in Cuba were the next to surrender, on July 17, 1898 (Ibid., 190, 193). Four days later Puerto Rico fell to U.S. troops and Spain was forced to concede defeat. The U.S. government, however, refused to enact an armistice agreement until all U.S. demands were met. Spain agreed to give up possession of Puerto Rico, Cuba, Guam, and the Philippine Islands in return for $100 million, but the U.S. government felt that such an amount was unfair and refused to end the war until Spain lowered its price to $20 million. The Spanish-American War officially ended on December 10, 1898 (Ibid., 322).

After the war Congress honored the Teller Amendment by not annexing Cuba, although the island remained a semi-independent state under the political and financial control of its liberator. The U.S. government also reserved the right to control Cuba's foreign affairs, oversee its governance, and establish a military base on the island, but Cuba did not, unlike Puerto Rico, Guam, and the Philippine Islands, become a formal colony of the United States.

Although countries around the world criticized the United States for its actions in Cuba, President Díaz endorsed U.S. policy. A large part of the Mexican aristocracy was also displeased with the outcome, yet they mourned Spain's defeat quietly and continued to do business with their neighbor across the border. Amicable relations between Mexico and the United States eventually resumed and led to mutually beneficial agreements. Under these conditions Mexican immigration continued to flow as usual, and U.S. investments in Mexico continued to enrich American investors and their Mexican partners. Likewise, at this time national policy toward immigrants improved. Two weeks after the *Maine* exploded in Cuba, the U.S. Supreme Court handed down an unprecedented ruling clarifying many issues on the rights and obligations of citizens and immigrants. In *U.S. v. Wong Kim Ark* (1898), the justices ruled that the law protected immigrants who pledged their allegiance to the government and obeyed U.S. law.[4] The justices also offered a uniform resolution on race, decreeing that it did not disqualify a person from citizenship. For Mexicans the implications of this ruling were monumental, as it prevented the overturning of the Rodriguez decision.

U.S. v. Wong Kim Ark, 1898:
Why the Rodriguez Case Was Not Challenged

With the passage of the Wong Kim Ark ruling a national precedent was created, and *In re Rodriguez* (1897) could not be overturned, not by members of the Populist Party, not by McMinn, not by anybody. Throughout the United States, before the *Wong Kim Ark* ruling, individuals and organizations that believed people of color were not citizens or could not be made citizens brought legal challenges before the courts. Because the rulings were not uniform and judges offered varying opinions, citizenship law needed to be standardized to clearly delineate the political status of nonwhite groups (*Elk v. Wilkens* 1884; *In re Look Tin Sang* 1884; *Nevada v. Ah Chew* 1881). On the eve of the Spanish-American War, it became extremely important to resolve this issue, as it was in the best interests of the United States to determine the rights and obligations of the U.S. population, including resident immigrants. It was particularly critical to determine a person's obligation to bear arms for the country. The government did not know how long the conflict would last, as Spain had many powerful European allies. When the Wong Kim Ark case was deliberated the justices addressed unresolved legal issues pertaining to immigrants and people born in the United States. On the question, Who was a citizen of the United States? the justices ruled that a child born in the United States acquired citizenship by the virtue of the Fourteenth Amendment. Most important of all, it decreed that race and national origin could not be used to deny a person the rights of citizenship. Opponents of this interpretation had argued that only whites and blacks had been made citizens by the amendment. The judges, however, ruled that U.S. tribal Indians were exempt from the ruling. The reasoning behind their exclusion was allegedly based not on race but on the protected status of U.S. American Indians. According to the justices, tribal peoples were excluded because they were part of dependent nations which were governed by different U.S. laws. Although this was an obvious setback for American Indian civil rights, for people of Mexican descent the justices clarified U.S. law and ruled that race did not disqualify a person from citizenship as long as they were not part of a U.S. dependent nation. In spirit, the Wong Kim Ark decision reaffirmed Judge Maxey's opinion that Mexicans were a detribalized people and could not be governed by the laws that applied to U.S. tribal nations.

The Wong Kim Ark ruling also delineated the political privileges and obligations immigrants were subject to in the United States. The justices ruled that "every citizen or subject of another country, while domiciled here, is within the allegiance and the protection, and consequently subject to the jurisdiction, of the United States" (Ibid., 694; *Yale Law Journal* 1971: 779). In other words, U.S. laws protected resident aliens if they obeyed the law and pledged allegiance to the U.S. government, an important stipulation during a time of war. The Wong Kim Ark decision gave Mexican immigrants, however, superior legal rights in comparison to other nonwhite immigrants. Because the justices did not declare the "White Only" racial prerequisite in the Naturalization Act of 1790 unconstitutional, naturalization remained the exclusive privilege of whites and blacks. However, by not overturning Rodriguez and ruling that Judge Maxey's interpretation of treaty law was wrong, the justices upheld the right of Mexican immigrants to apply for U.S. citizenship. Their Indian blood quantum did not disqualify them from naturalizing, and, like black immigrants, they were exempt from the White Only naturalization racial prerequisite. Indeed, the Wong Kim Ark decision benefited Mexican immigrants and made the United States an attractive country to migrate to. The ruling also benefited the Mexican government in that the justices chose not to include any stipulations that discriminated against its citizens. Mexican immigrants were assured protection under U.S. civil rights laws.

Mexican Immigrants Prove Their Loyalty During the Spanish-American War

Although federal law protected Mexican immigrants in Texas, such security did not spare them from the effects of the racial panic the Spanish-American War provoked vis-à-vis people of Spanish descent. At the local level many Anglo-Americans felt that Mexicans could not be trusted, and they turned against them. In response, Mexicans and Mexican Americans had to change public opinion and prove they were loyal Americans. President Díaz's neutrality in the war placed Mexico in the position of being an ally but did not obviate the suspicion many Americans harbored against Mexican Americans and Mexican immigrants. It is ironic that during the recent Rodriguez spectacle Mexicans had been vilified because of their Indian descent but once the war broke out their Spanish heritage linked them to the enemy.

The problems began in March 1898, when Mexicans experienced a series of violent incidents across Texas. The first took place in New Braunfels, where Mexican residents reported being violently attacked, the harassment becoming so extreme that families were forced to stay indoors and people had to stop working. Twenty-five Mexican men tried to persuade their tormentors to halt their aggression by publishing an open letter, the intent of which was to elicit public sympathy and prove that Mexicans were law-abiding citizens. The men asked Pablo Cruz, the editor of *El Regidor*, to publish their appeal, which he did, in Spanish and English, on March 31. He asked that the Mexican community of New Braunfels be left alone. The letter was written to the good people of New Braunfels, and it stressed that the Mexican community of the city was a peaceful, orderly one. But the writers of the letter also warned their tormentors that they would no longer tolerate the threats and were prepared to defend themselves by any legal and justifiable means (*El Regidor*, March 31, 1898, p. 3). In April more Mexican communities were harassed in the counties of DeWitt, Gonzales, and Karnes. They were accused of intending to conspire with the enemy. In Gonzales County the White Caps began to force Mexican families whom they suspected of sympathizing with Spain to leave the county. In DeWitt, some Anglo-Americans became so angry that they asked the governor to place Mexicans under house arrest. Their representative, Capt. Fred House, asked the governor to give the county permission to organize a home guard to place Mexicans under arrest. A reporter for the *San Antonio Express* summarized the chaos:

THREAT FROM MEXICANS: DE WITT, COUNTY
CITIZENS FEAR THEY WILL ATTEMPT VIOLENCE

April 25—Capt. Fred House left this afternoon for Austin, where he has gone to try to get a commission from Gov. Culberson to raise a company of home guards for the protection of the citizens in De Witt, Karnes and Gonzales. He told a correspondent of the Express that over in the corner of these counties the citizens were very much alarmed at the movement of the Mexicans. . . .

Austin, Tex., April 26—Col. Fred house, a veteran of De Witt county, arrived here this morning and notified Gov. Culberson that the Mexicans of that county are threatening to commit depredations on American citizens and property. He applied for authority to raise a troop of cavalry for the purpose of maintaining order among the lawless element.

"As soon as Mexicans of that section learned that war existed between the United States and Spain," said Col. House to the Express correspondent, "they became insulting and arrogant toward Americans. They assert openly that Texas rightfully belongs to Mexico and that they are going to take advantage of the present opportunity of getting it again. . . . The Mexicans who are making this threatening talk are all desperate characters and many of them are refugees from justice. A number of the leaders were recently run out of Gonzales county by the White Caps and if immediate steps are not taken toward placing them under control they will cause a great amount of damage and bloodshed. I simply want authority to organize a troop of cavalry and be allowed to perform military duty in preserving order." (*San Antonio Express,* April 26, 1898, p. 1)

The news report does not relate how the governor reacted, and no mention of his response was published by the *San Antonio Express,* but it is unlikely that the White Caps or any other group was given permission to openly harass Mexicans. The Mexican government was an ally of the United States, and it was rendering its neighbor assistance. The harassment of Mexicans continued nonetheless, but it appears to have consisted of acts committed by individuals independent of organized government. The *San Antonio Express* also reported that in Dimmit County and in the city of Laredo some Mexicans were under suspicion, but they were left alone and not placed under surveillance (*San Antonio Express,* March 26, 1898, p. 5).

A month after President McKinley declared war against Spain, the mayor of San Antonio, Bryan Callaghan, called upon the U.S. government to deport all Mexicans who openly sympathized with Spain (*El Regidor*, May 19, 1898, p. 1). Cruz reported on May 19 that many Anglo-Americans had echoed Mayor Callaghan's sentiments. The *San Antonio Express* reported a similar story. A reporter from the *Express* added that the mayor had fired a Mexican schoolteacher, Albert Martinez, for openly criticizing U.S. wartime activities. Martinez, who was also a journalist working for the Spanish-language newspaper *El Cronista,* spoke out against the harassment Mexicans were reporting across South Texas. Apparently groups of Anglo-Americans from San Antonio had organized a home guard and were patrolling the lower Rio Grande. Martinez was fired for merely stating that instead of riding along the border harassing Mexicans these men should join the military and go to Cuba, where they were needed (*San Antonio Express*, May 6, 1898, p. 6).

By late May the hostile incidents across Texas alarmed many Mexican civic leaders, and they met to discuss how best to defuse the conflict. They agreed that the best way for Mexicans to protect themselves was to demonstrate their loyalty to the United States. Cruz was one of the main organizers of the meeting, and he assisted several organizations in coordinating a time and place to hold a convocation. On May 26 several Mexican civic organizations, including La Unión, Sociedad Benevolencia Mexicana, Sociedad Hidalgo, and Por Los Hijos de Mexico, held a public meeting and rally to discuss the implications of the Spanish-American War for people of Mexican origin (*El Regidor,* May 26, 1898, p. 2). At first many Mexicans expressed their anger at having been unjustly harassed and considered unpatriotic Americans. Cruz reported on the event as follows:

> As a result of a convocation held last Saturday by citizens of this city, it was necessary for the Mexico-Texanos to hold a meeting on Sunday at 8 o'clock at the "Sociedad Benevolencia Mexicana" salon to protest against the hatred that was proclaimed against the Mexican race. These views are prejudicial and are aimed to provoke hatred. . . .
>
> This meeting is being held to prevent bad actions that could be launched against our race and to publicly dismiss the improper and calumnious lies . . . many of these prejudices that have been expressed can cause serious harm to the people of our Mexican race throughout the United States.[5] (Ibid.; my translation)

Although many grievances were debated, in a spirit of friendliness they concluded by setting an agenda to prove to Anglo-Americans that Mexicans were loyal American citizens and residents. As part of the program several attendees gave speeches on Latin American colonial history and argued that Mexicans should support the United States, as for centuries Spain had exploited Latin America. Others, preferring not to criticize Spain, focused on the hospitable treatment Mexican immigrants received in the United States. Among the speakers was a man named Treviño, who at the end of his speech received a tremendous applause. Treviño, focusing on U.S. citizenship and the meaning of naturalization, proclaimed that Mexicans had the right to abdicate their Mexican citizenship, as there was no shame in the act of changing one's political allegiance. Mexicans had come to the United States in search of a better life, he said, and now that they were here the United States was their country:

> I will try to deal sensibly with a very important point, that being that every adult male has the right to select the citizenship that best pleases him, as long as that choice is based on a noble aim. To call a person a renegade because he chooses to accept the citizenship of this country or any other country based on legitimate reasons is not an appropriate label to apply, for he has a clear consciousness of the laws he is following and of the constitution which he chooses to follow and desires to respect and defend. All rational people of different nationalities see this as just; a person can abdicate the nationality which they were born with so long as that person is conscious that they are contracting new ties with the nation they are adopting, and if not, they commit a grave error that is censurable and possibly punishable.[6] (Ibid., my translation)

He concluded by reminding the audience that it was an opportune time for Mexican immigrants to prove their American patriotism. Following Treviño's speech, the meeting took a festive turn when Professor Carlos Batista's orchestra entertained the audience with patriotic American songs. All evening long the orchestra played American tunes, the audience enthusiastically singing along. At the end of the event the organizers announced the names of the committee members who had been elected to resolve the crisis. Captain Cardenas, a veteran of the Civil War, was elected president, Pablo Cruz, secretary, and Ramón Guerra, from Starr, sergeant-at-arms.

A few days later Guerra organized a series of meetings to recruit Mexican volunteers to join the forces going to Cuba. He succeeded in organizing several units. (*El Regidor,* June 2, 1898, pp. 1, 3; *San Antonio Express,* May 29, 1898, p. 9; *San Antonio Express,* March 26, 1898, p. 5). Two units were formed in Bexar County, and one unit was composed of recruits from the counties of Uvalde and Starr. Following the May convocation, Cruz published a series of editorials asking the Mexican public to remain calm and not show support for Spain in any manner. In an editorial published on June 2, 1898, Cruz advised his readers to take the time to publicly demonstrate their patriotism (*El Regidor,* June 2, 1898, p. 3). He acknowledged that these were stressful times, and it might seem logical to sympathize with Spain, but before they did so, he asked them to think about what Spain had done to Mexico. They should not forget that Spain had caused great harm to Mexicans when in 1829 it tried to reconquer Mexico as well as when it supported Maximilian during the French invasion. On the other hand, he argued, the United States had proven to be a great friend to Mexico, repeatedly aiding its neighbor, especially during the French invasion.

Cruz continued to write editorials warning Mexicans of the retribution they would experience if they helped Spain. On June 23, 1898, he reported that in San Diego, Texas, the editor of *El Socialista,* a Spanish-language newspaper, was beaten for writing news articles supporting Spain (*El Regidor,* June 23, 1898, p. 1). Cruz also reported that on the border of Tamaulipas and Texas two plots to support Spain were uncovered and the conspirators arrested and imprisoned. Cruz warned individuals to be cautious of anti-Spanish vigilantes, as on June 1, 1898, Joseph Schueldo, a man who hated Spanish-Mexicans, was arrested for threatening them with a knife (*El Regidor,* June 2, 1898, p. 1). Cruz also warned the parishioners of San Fernando Cathedral not to support Archbishop Forest's dangerous appeals. The archbishop had asked them to support Spain because it was in the best interests of Catholics (*El Regidor,* June 23, 1898, p. 1; *San Antonio Express,* May 5, 1898, p. 6). Cruz also admonished a group of Mexicans who were organizing a Spanish club to help Spain, a group that, according to Cruz, had accused him of being a traitor to Mexico and Spain. In essence, Cruz warned his readers not to join any pro-Spanish clubs because such action could provoke retaliation against the entire community of Mexican origin.

A few days after Guerra organized the meetings to recruit Mexican volunteers a series of articles appeared in *El Tiempo,* a newspaper published in Mexico but circulated in the United States, accusing him and the Mexican community of San Antonio of being hypocrites, Yankified Mexicans, and traitors to the Mexican homeland. The editor of *El Tiempo* sympathized with Spain and asked Mexican Tejanos to take up arms against the imperialist Yankees. Cruz reprinted the news articles in *El Regidor* in order to rebut the accusations and to warn Mexicans not to support the views espoused in *El Tiempo.* He collaborated with *La Crónica,* a newspaper from Laredo, to disseminate his message. Jose Agustin Escuadron, a journalist with *La Crónica,* wrote most of the rebuttals.

El Tiempo responded by charging that Cruz was an apologist for U.S. imperialism and a tyrannical ideologue who unfairly attacked his opponents without giving them the opportunity to publish their opinions (*El Tiempo* in *El Regidor*, June 9, 1898, p. 1; *El Tiempo* in *El Regidor*, June 23, 1898, p. 4; *El Tiempo* in *El Regido*r, July 14, 1898, p. 1). He was denounced for silencing his opponents. In response, Cruz continued to vigorously defend the United States and praise the patriotism of Tejanos. Although *El Tiempo* was correct that Cruz was unwilling to personally criticize U.S. policy toward Cuba, he did publish several critical articles written by Escuadron.

On June 16, one month before the United States took possession of Cuba and Puerto Rico, Cruz published one of Escuadron's strongest critiques. Although Escuadron echoed Cruz's assimilationist sentiments, emphasizing that the United States was the Mexican immigrants' new homeland, he outwardly disagreed with U.S. foreign policy in Latin America (*El Regidor*, June 16, 1898, p. 1). Escuadron began his commentary by delineating the principles of the Monroe Doctrine and informing his readers that it was vitally important for all Latin American countries to uphold this doctrine. To emphasize his point he examined the significant role the Monroe Doctrine had played when French troops invaded Mexico. He argued that the U.S. Congress and most Latin American countries supported Mexico during the invasion because they agreed with the anti-imperialistic principles of the Monroe Doctrine. However, he also acknowledged that the United States must not be allowed to misuse the doctrine for its own imperialist aspirations. Cuba, he said, must be given self-governance, and the international community must not allow the United States to expand its borders and conquer this territory as it did when it took advantage of Mexico in 1848. Any form of annexation would be wrong, because the outcome, Escuadron commented, always culminates in converting the annexed populace into an oppressed people who are treated as foreigners in their native land and despised by those who have conquered them. Escuadron tried to end his analysis on a positive note by acknowledging that although a capitalist system can indeed exploit the weak, not all Americans hold imperialist attitudes toward Latin America. There are many, he argued, who believe the Monroe Doctrine is not about war and exploitation, but about colonizing Latin America by sharing its civilization, sciences, industry, and commerce. Escuadron concluded,

Well, this is what the Monroe Doctrine proclaims, it recognizes the rights of every citizen on the soil which they are from: nationals must exercise their authority over their government, so that only they should intervene in their country's public affairs without the intervention or influence of outsiders, because America can only be the mother of those who are its true sons.

We have said that there is no fundamental basis—or reason to believe—that the United States pretends to annex the Pearl of the Antilles or our own territory, because we are sure that our neighbors are reasonably trying to extend their sincere confraternity and share their ideas and common interests.

They do not want the Latin race to be conquered in a barbaric way because this naturally would provoke our hatred toward them and our people's resentment and censorship; instead they seek a civil and peaceful colonization where they extend their progress, industry, work, and their sciences and commerce. (Ibid.)[7]

Escuadron's editorial signified the dilemma people of Mexican origin were experiencing at that time. Even though many Mexicans acknowledged that U.S. international politics might be imperialistic, the United States was their new country, and it was their patriotic obligation to support it in spite of the racial prejudice they were experiencing.

On June 23, Escuadron continued to educate the public on the problems European imperialism produced in Latin America (*El Regidor*, June 23, 1898, p. 4). This time, however, he spent more time discussing U.S. immigration than criticizing U.S. foreign policy. He claimed that immigrants had made the United States the greatest nation in the world and went on to praise it for being a country of laws and for having produced the U.S. Constitution. He argued that in the United States the Constitution was upheld by the government, and it prevented the wealthy from exploiting the common person. He also commented that at this time the Constitution was moving the government toward extending equal rights to all people, regardless of who they were, and this, he claimed, was a model that needed to be replicated in Mexico, where the poor had few civil rights. Escuadron concluded by affirming the need to reform Mexico's government and make it accountable to the people.

A few months later, with the war at an end, Cruz stopped publishing commentaries on it and its aftermath. He merely reported facts, described the negotiations between Spain and the United States, and informed the public that the Spanish possessions now belonged to the United States. No apologies or criticisms were published. Cruz's newspaper abandoned its focus on international affairs and focused on local news only. In particular, he returned to electoral issues, to the matters he had covered in previous years, and continued to advise his readers to register to vote. During this period he wrote several articles urging his readers to reelect Congressman James Slayden, whom he credited with having stopped the Populist campaign to deny Mexicans the vote (*El Regidor,* October 13, 1898, p. 1; cf. *El Regidor,* November 10, 1898, p. 1). In his commentaries on Slayden, Cruz reported that on November 10, 1898, a social gathering of civic leaders was organized by Mexican Tejanos to thank Slayden for his support in opposing the Populist campaign. Oddly, Cruz did not praise Ricardo Rodriguez or A. L. Montalbo for their roles in defeating McMinn (see chapter 3).

U.S.-Mexico Relations: Anarchist Provisions Following the Spanish-American War

During the first decade of the twentieth century thousands of Mexicans continued to enter the United States in search of work, and their numbers continued to rise. In 1890, they numbered 74,761, and by 1900 the number had increased to 103,393. Most continued to live in Texas (N = 71,062 or 69 percent) (U.S. Census 1913b: 804). After the Spanish-American War many members of Mexico's ruling class joined the intellectuals to depose President Díaz, and when they ran into trouble they crossed the border into Texas. In 1903 the U.S. Congress became alarmed about the lack of regulation over Mexican immigration and began to pass legislation to address the issue. Most congressmen favored an open-door policy for Mexico but feared that dissidents might be accompanying ordinary people, and this had to end.

Congress's concern with Mexican immigration and the entry of political radicals was part of a larger preoccupation with immigration in general. European immigration had more than doubled at the beginning of the twentieth century, the largest increase being attributed to people from southern and eastern Europe, specifically Italy and Russia (Meyerink and Szucs 1997: 445; see Scupin 2003). Many congressmen were apprehensive about the newcomers because they differed in culture and traditions from the old stock of immigrants who had arrived from western and northern Europe, mainly from Great Britain, Ireland, and Germany. A second problem was the fear that among the immigrants were anarchists and socialists who did not believe in the American capitalist system.

The congressmen were divided on whether Mexicans were a problem or an asset. The majority favored an open-door policy for Mexico and Canada because a liberal immigration policy was necessary if U.S. goods were to continue flowing into the neighboring countries. Canada and Mexico were seen as important commercial trading partners, especially Mexico. In general congressmen agreed on the need to establish a system to register all people crossing the borders from Mexico and Canada. Setting up such a system was deemed necessary and urgent, as it was commonly believed that European and Mexican anarchists were entering the United States at the Canadian and Mexican borders. Registration, it was felt, was also fiscally necessary because many Europeans were trying to evade paying the head tax they owed by entering via the borders (Meyerink and Szucs 1997: 450–451). At that time Mexicans, Canadians, and Cubans did not have to pay a head tax to enter the United States, while the rest of the immigrants were required to pay one dollar per head of household (*Congressional Record, 57th Congress, Second Session,* vol. 36, part 1, p. 29).

After much debate Congress passed moderate reforms to police the Mexican and Canadian borders in an attempt both to stop the entry of anarchists and socialists and to ensure that Europeans paid their head tax. Congress also agreed not to tax Mexicans, Canadians, and Cubans. The majority of the members of Congress agreed that open borders must be maintained (Ibid., pp. 96, 128). Cuba was also included as part of the favored countries exempt from the head tax since its political status remained somewhere between a colony and an independent allied nation. Cuba had recently been given independence but remained technically a U.S. possession since the government retained the right to intervene in its political governance.

To protect the borders of the United States all railroad passengers entering the United States from Canada and Mexico would be inspected, registered, and counted (*Congressional Record, 57th Congress, Second Session,* vol. 36, part 3, p. 2806, 2894). No specific legislation was issued for those crossing on foot. Common laborers were allowed entry as long as they were Mexican or Canadian. The new legislation placed the responsibility on the railroad companies to ensure that all passengers complied with the new law. If the passengers were not Mexican, Canadian, or Cuban, they had to pay an entrance tax, raised now to two dollars per head of household. The companies were also required to prohibit entry to anarchists, as the new legislation added them to the classes of excluded populations together with convicts, prostitutes, idiots, the insane, those with contagious diseases, polygamists, persons convicted of political offenses, and persons likely to become public charges. If a railway inspector failed to collect the head tax or allowed a disqualified person to enter, the railroad company would be fined and forced to pay the violator's deportation costs. The same policies applied to passengers arriving from Cuba on steamships docking in U.S. ports, but in addition they were required to pass a medical and mental exam conducted by a licensed professional (33 *U.S. Statutes at Large* (part 1) 1216–1217).

The anarchist provision was clearly passed in order to benefit Díaz's dictatorship (Coerver and Hall 1984). After the Spanish-American War, political dissent within the Mexican ruling class spread, and Díaz asked the U.S. government to deny refuge to anarchists and socialists. To assist Díaz the U.S. Congress passed concurrent legislation prohibiting American residents from knowingly assisting anarchists (Ibid., 1221–1222). Anyone rendering aid to anarchists would be fined and imprisoned.

President Díaz's main political headache was news reporters, and his principal enemies were the Flores Magón brothers, Ricardo and Enrique, who since 1890 had been fueling anti-Díaz sentiment in the pages of the newspaper they had founded, *Regeneración* (Gilly 1994: 75). *Regeneración* opposed the Porfirian regime, and it became highly popular, circulating throughout Mexico. Many of its articles—particularly those decrying the growth of the hacienda system and its dislocation of indigenous populations—questioned the efficacy of the development programs enacted by the Díaz regime. Because Ricardo was closely associated with scholars and labor activists his news articles were very powerful, as he provided the masses with proof that the president's development programs were a failure.

Ricardo's network of allies also included members of the liberal democratic clubs that had existed since the 1890s but flourished after the Spanish-American War among the upper and middle classes. By 1900, 125 such clubs were established (Davids 1976: 200). Because the clubs were illegal the members met in secret. The ultimate purpose of these organizations was to recruit sufficient members to openly establish a political party that would support a presidential candidate willing to run against Díaz. At this time, Díaz continued to be Mexico's constitutional president because there was no opposition party as no one was willing to run against him. At the end of each term, to comply with the Constitution Díaz held an election to legally reelect himself.

By 1903 Ricardo had become Díaz's main political foe and repeatedly embarrassed the president by publicly calling for free and open elections. That year Díaz banned *Regeneración* and arrested Ricardo and his staff, but owing to political pressure the men were released within a few days, and their supporters clandestinely helped them escape into Texas. The staff of *Regeneración* was smuggled into San Antonio, where locals gave them housing and helped to reestablish the newspaper. Within a year, however, a series of political difficulties prevented the brothers from publishing their newspaper, and they were forced to leave San Antonio. Soon, however, they and their staff were invited by the Western Federation of Miners and the Industrial Workers of the World to relocate to St. Louis, where there was open support for them in the form of financial assistance to reestablish *Regeneración*. Díaz again tried to shut the newspaper down but, as earlier, was unsuccessful. Attorneys representing the newspaper staff argued in federal court that under the First Amendment of the U.S. Constitution *Regeneración* could be published on U.S. soil (Gilly 1994). Díaz then tried to have Ricardo and the rest of the staff extradited to Mexico, but immigration authorities refused to comply because none of the men had broken any immigration law. Díaz's attorneys responded by charging that all of the newspapermen were known anarchists, and under the Immigration Act of 1903 such people could not reside in the United States. The Mexican government, unable to prove the charge, was forced to momentarily stop legal action. The immigration reforms of 1903 proved to be useless in the case, as long as the Flores Magón brothers were not found to be anarchists. They continued to publish *Regeneración* and through their network of allies to smuggle the newspaper into Mexico, where it served to fuel dissent. Although the U.S. government protected the brothers' First Amendment rights it continued close surveillance of the newspaper staff. Díaz was reassured that U.S. Neutrality Laws prohibited immigrants from initiating a revolutionary movement against an organized government. As long as Díaz remained Mexico's constitutional president the United States would support his administration.

The Introduction of Poll Tax Voting Laws in Texas

Even though the federal government retained its open-door policy toward Mexico and the federal courts passed rulings to clarify and protect the citizenship rights of Mexican immigrants, concurrent events in Texas set back the gains Mexicans had earned in the United States. For many state legislators Mexican voting rights had become a nuisance. Mexicans were welcomed as a source of cheap labor, but their participation in the electoral process was not. Between 1901 and 1905 the Texas legislature passed a series of election reforms that adversely affected Mexican immigrants. The state imposed voting poll taxes, reduced the number of precincts, mandated primary elections, and allowed the parties to determine who could attend conventions and meetings. Thus despite the fact that at the federal level U.S.-Mexico relations were amicable and Mexican immigrants were given the right to naturalize and vote, voting became very difficult for Mexicans in

**Table 4.2. Counties Processing Naturalization Applications from
Mexican Immigrants, 1900–1906**

Aransas, Atascosa, Bandera, Bee, Bexar, Brazos, Caldwell, Cameron, Crockett,
DeWitt, Dimmit, Duval, Edwards, El Paso, Frio, Galveston, Gonzales, Guadalupe,
Hidalgo, Harris, Karnes, Kinney, La Salle, Limestone, Maverick, McCulloch, McMullen,
Nueces, Starr, Tarrant, Taylor, Travis, Tyler, Uvalde, Val Verde, Victoria, Washington,
Webb, Wilson, Zapata, Zavala

Source: Index to Naturalization Records found in Texas State District and County Courts,
1846–1939, rolls 1 to 10; General Courts Austin, Brownsville, El Paso, Galveston, San
Antonio, Jefferson, Texarkana, Tyler, Waco.

Texas. After the reforms the participation of Mexican immigrants in elections declined, and so did their naturalization application rates. (The granting of citizenship did not increase and remained consistently low, as in previous decades).[8] County data reveal that from 1900 to 1906 the number of
naturalization applications from Mexicans had fallen to 2,101 (TNR), and
in addition the number of counties processing applications fell drastically.
In the 1890s, seventy-six counties received applications from Mexicans, but
by 1906 that number had fallen to forty-one (see tables 4.1, 4.2, 4.3). The
fall in the application rate was directly related to the election reforms since
the main reason Mexican immigrants chose to naturalize was to have the
right to vote. When state voting laws changed it became very difficult for
Mexicans to vote, and the most compelling reason for naturalizing disappeared. It was a sad time for Mexicans who wanted to exercise their rights
as citizens. They had left their country in the first instance because of political and economic chaos. Díaz's dictatorship had devalued the worth of their
vote, as his electoral machine was designed to keep him in power. Once in
the United States many immigrants had tried to regain the right to vote by
abdicating their citizenship and becoming part of the American polity, only
to encounter prejudices and obstacles similar to the ones they thought they
had escaped.

The aim of the legislated election reforms of 1901 was to purge bad ele-
ments from the elective franchise by excluding the corrupt, the illiterate,
the ignorant, the disinterested, the trifling, and those who sold their votes
(Strong 1944). Many legislators believed that Mexicans, African Americans,
and poor whites caused the main problems because they sold their votes
to wealthy politicians (Hine 2003: 81; Strong 1944: 701). Some politicians
also charged that the levying of poll taxes would stop wealthy Germans

from bribing poor people to vote their way. They alleged that Germans paid agents to get people to vote against prohibition and placing restrictions on their brewery associations (Gould 1973; Taylor 1987). On March 6, 1901, the Texas legislature passed a voting poll tax requiring males under the age of sixty to pay a fee of $1.75 at least eight months before an election (*Laws of Texas*, 11:1026). The House passed the bill by a two-thirds majority, or eighty-seven in favor to fifteen opposed, while in the Senate twenty-three voted in favor and six opposed (Ibid., 322–323).[9] The representatives and senators of Bexar County and El Paso supported passage. The main opposition to the bill was voiced in the House and came from representatives from South Texas, all of whom voted against passage (*House Journal, Texas, 27th Legislature, 1901, Regular Session*, p. 481). A few other House members voiced opposition but not for the same reasons as the South Texas legislators. Several legislators charged that the poll taxes would actually empower Mexican immigrants because they were protected by wealthy politicians (*House Journal, Texas, 27th Legislature, 1901, Regular Session*, p. 482). In the Senate little opposition was raised, but the senators representing South Texas counties were divided (Texas Legislature 1962: 185–187). Three who represented counties from South Texas but whose districts were primarily composed of counties from central and west Texas voted in favor of the poll

Table 4.3. Counties Granting Mexicans Citizenship, 1900–1906

	Applied	Granted
Bexar	111	46
Cameron	198	3
DeWitt	4	1
Duval	2	2
Galveston	11	4
Kendall	6	4
Maverick	46	10
Starr	52	1
Val Verde	295	1
Wilson	0	2

Source: Index to Naturalization Records found in Texas State District and County Courts, 1846–1939, rolls 1 to 10; General Courts Austin, Brownsville, El Paso, Galveston, San Antonio, Jefferson, Texarkana, Tyler, Waco.

tax (*Journal of the Senate of Texas, 27th Legislature, 1901,* p. 267), while only one, D. McNeill Turner from District 23, opposed passage. His district, unlike the other three senatorial districts, was entirely contained within South Texas.

When the legislation was placed before the voters in the election of November 1902 the poll tax resolution passed by a margin of two to one: 200,650 voted in favor and 107,748 against (Barr 2000: 205; Gould 1973: 7). Counties with majority populations of Mexican origin voted nearly unanimously against the tax (Gould 1973: 693; Texas Almanac 1912: 42–43), as did counties with large African American populations (Barr 2000: 205). The poll tax was also rejected in counties with active labor union associations.

Terrell Election Laws and the White Primary System

After poll taxes were instituted, many Texas legislators felt other reforms were needed to ensure the elective franchise was left in the hands of white men. Some legislators favored limiting voting to the educated white classes, while others favored voting reforms to limit the participation of blacks and Mexicans. By federal law, however, people of color could not be prohibited from voting. States did have the power, however, to establish election procedures and in this manner affect the elective franchise. Using the White Man's Union Association model practiced in many counties throughout Texas, Rep. Alexander W. Terrell introduced legislation to require the executive committees of each party to determine their party's voting rules.[10] The intent of the legislation was to allow white men to establish rules to limit the participation of African American and Mexican voters. The most important power given to the executive committees was the right to eliminate any person from voting during primary elections, a model that had been established by the White Man's Association in 1878 for the specific purpose of excluding African Americans (Barr 2000: 196).[11] By the beginning of the twentieth century the White Man's Association controlled party politics in many areas of Texas and effectively excluded African Americans from primary elections in the counties of Leon, Navasota, Wharton, Jefferson Davis, Washington, Harrison, Matagorda, Brazoria, Franklin, Grimes, Milan, Bell, Dallas, Hill, Jackson, and Grayson (Ibid., 201). Only in Gonzales County were both African Americans and Mexicans excluded (see White Man's Union Associations).

Representative Terrell, who did not make any secret of his white supremacist views, often stated in public that the vote should be reserved for the

Anglo-Saxon American white man (Hine 2003: 82; Kingston, Attlesey and Crawford 1992: 186). He publicly acknowledged that his legislation was directed at eliminating the menace "Mexicans and Negroes" posed during election times (Montejano 1987: 143). When the legislation was introduced, the state executive committee of every party in Texas except for the Socialist Party endorsed the Terrell legislation (Cantrell and Barton 1987; Montejano 1987; Winkler 1916). The Prohibition Party felt that the representatives had not gone far enough to purify the vote.

On April 1, 1903, the Texas legislature formally endorsed the white primary system (*Laws of Texas*, 12:153). The legislation passed unanimously in the House and Senate.[12] The change went into effect on January 1, 1904, and section 85 of the state election laws was revised to read, "Each political party shall determine for itself in each county whether it will nominate candidates for office by primary election or convention, and due notice of the method chosen by such party shall be given in writing to the county judge by the chairman of the county executive committee" (Ibid., 149). Immediately following the reforms the state executive committee of the Democratic Party issued a mandate requiring the counties to allow only white Democrats to participate in the primaries (Montejano 1987). This directive was of paramount significance since Texas had become a one-party state, the rest of the parties holding little influence. Nonetheless, the People's Party, the Prohibition Party, and the Republican Party also instituted Terrell's election reform (Winkler 1916: 473, 477).

By 1904 the reforms effectively excluded most African Americans from participating in the primary elections (Barr 2000: 196). The Democratic Party did not officially name people of Mexican descent as one of the excluded groups, but election data indicate that voters of Mexican origin were adversely affected by the reforms. The number of voters dropped radically in 1904, and by 1908 the participation of voters of Mexican origin in primaries declined by nearly half. The reforms did not devastate the Mexican electorate to the same degree it did African American communities. For example, in 1896 the number of African American votes had peaked at 100,000, but by 1906, as a result of the reforms, their numbers had fallen to 5,000 (Kingston, Attlesey, and Crawford 1992: 55–57, 187).

Voting Patterns in South Texas, 1904

The presidential election of 1904 illustrates the widespread effects the reforms had on voters. As noted, at this time people of Mexican descent were not specified as one of the populations excluded from the primaries, yet they were negatively affected by the poll tax. A comparison of voting results in Texas in presidential elections prior to and after the passage of the poll tax legislation reveals that people in general were adversely affected, as the number of voters declined by 37 percent. In 1900, 449,329 people voted in the presidential election, but by 1904 the number had declined to 279,881 (Kingston, Attlesey, and Crawford 1992: 80). In many counties the decline was even sharper: some reported a decrease of over 50 percent (Barr 2000: 208).

In the case of voters of Mexican origin the decline was significant. In South Texas, where the majority of the residents were of Mexican descent, only Kinney, Zavala, and Karnes counties did not experience a significant drop (table 4.4). Election data from South Texas counties indicate that the total number of votes declined from 29,702 in 1900 to 12,937 in 1904 (Kingston, Attlesey, and Crawford 1992: 79–83). Most of the counties experienced a drop ranging from 28 percent to 72 percent. In the west Texas counties of El Paso and Presidio, where people of Mexican origin were the majority, the total number of votes declined much more. In 1900 the total number of votes cast in El Paso and Presidio was 4,177, and in 1904 the number declined to 2,866, a decline of 32 percent (Ibid.).

Voting data also show that counties with large numbers of Mexican immigrants were affected in much the same way as counties with a lower percentage. For example, Hidalgo County experienced a 72 percent decline in the number of voters from 1900 to 1904 and the total percentage of Mexican immigrants numbered 35 percent, while in San Patricio, where they constituted only 16 percent, the number of voters declined by 56 percent. Personal finances, not country of origin, determined who could afford to vote in Texas.

Ethnic Change in South Texas and the White Primary System

Although the executive committee of the Democratic Party never issued a formal request to disenfranchise Mexican voters, election results from the primary elections of 1908 to 1912 reveal further deterioration in the ability of voters of Mexican origin to participate in the primaries. The decline, however, followed in the aftermath of another major restructuring of election procedures. This time precinct locations were reconfigured.

In 1905 Representative Terrell once again was able to garner support to revise election laws in Texas: in this instance he aimed to change the precinct system.[13] In restructuring the precinct system, Terrell empowered the

Table 4.4. Presidential Election Results for El Paso, Presidio, and South Texas Counties, 1900 and 1904

County[a]	Votes Cast 1900	Votes Cast 1904	Percentage Decline	1900 Census Total Pop.	1900 Census Mexican Immigrants
Atascosa	1,127	808	28	7,143	563
Cameron	3,126	1,163	63	16,095	4,906
Dimmit	258	214	17	1,106	141
Duval	819	380	54	8,488	2,628
Frio	742	600	19	4,200	488
Hidalgo	1,823	512	72	6,837	2,366
Karnes	1,196	1,150	4	8,081	829
Kinney	369	410	—	2,447	484
La Salle	503	268	47	2,303	512
Live Oak	463	405	13	2,268	172
Maverick	823	502	39	4,066	1,514
Medina	1,416	1,025	28	7,783	842
McMullen	222	114	49	1,024	121
Nueces	1,601	727	55	10,439	1,986
San Patricio	500	220	56	2,872	452
Starr	2,106	1,230	42	11,469	4,262
Uvalde	838	530	37	4,647	601
Val Verde	798	583	27	5,268	1,576
Webb	2,873	1,542	46	21,851	10,755
Zapata	564	397	30	4,760	2,165
Zavala	161	157	3	792	40
El Paso	3,499	2,495	29	24,886	8,368
Presidio	678	371	45	3,673	1,468

[a]Brooks, Jim Wells, Willacy, Jim Hogg, and Kenedy had not been organized at this time. Encinal was annexed to Webb in 1899 (U.S. Census 1901: 41).
Source: Texas Almanac 1910: 47-53; U.S. Census 1901: 40–42, 787–788; Kingston, Attlesey, and Crawford 1992: 80–83.

classes who could afford to pay poll taxes and made it more difficult for the poor to vote. One of the most damaging changes affecting the poor, including voters of Mexican origin, was the elimination of precincts in areas where poll tax revenues were low. Section 9 of the election laws specified that the number of voting precincts and their location were to be determined on the basis of how many people had paid their poll taxes in the previous election

(*Laws of Texas,* 12:520). This clause allowed precincts to be placed in areas of towns and cities where the affluent lived and removed them or reduced their numbers in the poorer neighborhoods and counties. The placement of the precincts also had another serious implication. Because section 106 of the election laws mandated that a party's county executive committee be composed of representatives from each precinct, the placement of the precincts benefited the affluent. This mandate appeared to be very democratic, yet in practice the location of the precincts allowed the affluent to more easily elect representatives of their choice, while it placed hardships upon those who lived in areas where there were few precincts or none at all.

Terrell's reforms also gave additional power to county officers. The County Commissioners Court was given the authority to determine the location and boundaries of the precincts, determine when precincts were to be closed, elect the precinct judges, and monitor the elections (secs. 7, 109 to 111). For people of Mexican descent in most South Texas counties, within two years this reform placed the election machinery solely in the hands of Anglo-Americans since by 1907 few people of Mexican descent held county commissioner positions (Election Registers 1907–1912). Only in Duval, Zapata, and Starr did Mexican Americans hold the majority of the county commissioner seats.[14] By 1910 all county commissioner seats in the region were held by Anglo-Americans.

In South Texas the participation of voters of Mexican origin in primaries fell radically after the Terrell election changes were instituted. It is uncertain if the parties' county executive committees excluded them or if the decline was the result of some other factor. What is certain is that election returns for the governor's race from 1908 to 1912 indicate that in nearly all South Texas counties fewer people voted in the primaries in comparison with the general elections (table 4.5). For example, from 1908 to 1912 approximately one-half to two-thirds of those who voted in the general elections in South Texas did not participate in the county primaries in Dimmit, Kinney, Live Oak, Maverick, Medina, San Patricio, Val Verde, and Webb counties. Webb appears to have been affected the most, as less than 10 percent of the eligible voters there participated in the primaries. Cameron, Duval, and La Salle counties exhibit similar patterns in the elections of 1908 and 1910; however, in 1912 the number of voters did rise during primary time. Unfortunately, little research exists on the actual mechanisms in place that may have affected the election results in these counties. Only in Gonzales, Dimmit, and Duval counties has research shown that Mexicans, like blacks, were excluded from the primaries (Barr 2000: 201; Kingston, Attlesey, and Crawford 1992: 185; see Taylor 1970: 404; see White Man's

Table 4.5. Comparison of Primary Election Voting Patterns in South Texas, El Paso, and Presidio, 1908–1912

County	1908		1910		1912	
	Gov. Gen.	Gov. Prim.	Gov. Gen.	Gov. Prim.	Gov. Gen.	Gov. Prim.
Atascosa	780	685	698	782	770	1,217
Brooks[a]	—	—	—	—	595	301
Cameron	2,185	853	2,938	1,222	2,439	1,721
Dimmit	254	45	470	85	489	152
Duval	1,302	618	548	773	1,020	698
Frio	510	451	392	608	492	696
Hidalgo	590	588	982	733	1,377	912
Karnes	864	1,128	549	1,433	826	1,594
Kinney	448	120	396	95	280	56
La Salle	564	147	271	282	407	419
Live Oak	399	64	371	126	401	91
Maverick	545	162	448	114	406	94
Medina	1,295	226	1,263	754	1,122	808
McMullen	120	118	51	138	63	139
Nueces	1,092	808	1,053	1,261	1,284	1,339
San Patricio	415	101	575	298	880	329
Starr	1,324	350	957	643	928	537
Uvalde	1,205	526	1,195	854	758	1,015
Val Verde	580	276	624	149	585	168
Webb	1,345	110	1,030	295	1,566	426
Willacy	—	—	—	—	103	74
Zapata	428	0	462	0	199	0
Zavala	171	0	196	0	411	0
El Paso	3,291	2,371	2,479	2,777	4,053	4,954
Presidio	378	309	325	155	347	194

[a]Brooks was formed from Starr, Zapata, and Hidalgo in 1911, and Willacy from Hidalgo and Cameron in 1911 (Gournay 1995: 117–120).
Source: Texas Almanac 1910: 48–53, 55–57; Texas Almanac 1914: 49; Kingston, Attlesey and Crawford 1992: 80–83, 201–203, 276–283.

Union Associations). It is unlikely that the decline is attributable to African American voters since in most counties less than 2 percent of the eligible voters were African American males twenty-one years of age and over (U.S. Census 1901: 999–1002).[15]

In South Texas, demographic shifts also caused a drop-off in the participation rate of populations of Mexican origin at election times. As many newly arrived Anglo-Americans settled in South Texas, they immediately began to challenge the influence Mexicans and their Anglo allies had at election time. Demographic shifts in South Texas began in 1904, when the region's landed elite once again broke up their massive landholdings and began to advertise the sale of cheap land in Midwestern newspapers (Montejano 1987: 107). Most landowners sold their property for ten dollars an acre, considerably below the fourteen-dollar average market price in Texas (U.S. Census 1913c: 612–615). Within a few years South Texas experienced tremendous growth and change in its cultural and spatial landscape. Many of the large ranches were converted into small commercial farms of approximately 200 to 310 acres in size (Ibid., 620). By 1910 the region's population had grown to 205,958 from 133,939 in 1900 (U.S. Census 1901:40–42; U.S. Census 1913a: 243–245) (table 4.6).

Researchers have attributed most of the growth to Anglo-American newcomers because census data on the region's land base indicate that many new farms were established throughout the region (Bulletin of the University of Texas 1915: 29–30; Montejano 1987: 110).[16] The counties of Cameron, Kinney, La Salle, Maverick, San Patricio, Starr, Uvalde, and Val Verde experienced the greatest increase in the number of farms operated by owners, each county averaging a growth of over 45 percent (U.S. Census 1913c: 658–677). The rest of the counties experienced an average increase of around 20 percent. In general the newcomers contributed to the growth of the Anglo-American population of the region, which since 1870 had accounted for at least 28 percent of the residents in the counties bordering central Texas as well as in Kinney and Maverick (see chapter 2).

Mexican immigrants also continued to settle in South Texas, yet, unlike the Anglo-Americans, most came as laborers rather than farm owners. In 1910 only 23 percent of Mexican immigrants in Texas were farm owners (see Bulletin of University of Texas, 1915:27–29). In Zapata, Starr, and Duval counties, however, Mexican immigrants contributed to the growing number of farms operated by owners (table 4.7). In Starr County 302 immigrants owned farms, that is, nearly 50 percent of farms operated by owners. Census data reveal that most of the farms owned by foreign-born residents were purchased by Mexican immigrants since only fifty-three European immigrants lived in the county. A similar ethnic pattern is found in Duval and Zapata because nearly all immigrants in these two counties were Mexican.

Nonetheless, irrespective of the fact that some of the Mexican immigrants were economically stable, when thousands of Anglo-Americans moved to South Texas they became involved in local politics and came to

Table 4.6. Demographic Growth in South Texas Counties, 1900–1910

	1910		1900	
County	Total Pop.	Mexican Immigrants	Total Pop.	Mexican Immigrants
Atascosa	10,004	1,013	7,143	563
Cameron	27,158	8,617	16,095	4,906
Dimmit	3,460	556	1,106	141
Duval	8,964	2,235	8,488	2,628
Frio	8,895	2,397	4,200	488
Hidalgo	13,728	5,202	6,837	2,366
Karnes	14,942	1,528	8,081	829
Kinney	3,401	532	2,447	484
La Salle	4,747	1,084	2,303	512
Live Oak	3,442	385	2,268	172
Maverick	5,151	2,188	4,066	1,514
Medina	13,415	3,147	7,783	842
McMullen	1,091	103	1,024	121
Nueces[a]	21,955	2,828	10,439	1,986
San Patricio	7,307	1,071	2,872	452
Starr	13,151	3,444	11,469	4,262
Uvalde	11,233	1,170	4,647	601
Val Verde	8,613	2,948	5,268	1,576
Webb[b]	22,503	10,654	21,851	10,755
Zapata	3,809	1,541	4,760	2,165
Zavala	1,889	230	792	40

[a]Brooks, Willacy, Jim Wells, Jim Hogg, and Kenedy had not been organized at this time.
[b]Encinal was annexed to Webb in 1899 (U.S. Census 1901: 41).
Sources: U.S. Census 1901: 40–42, 788–789; U.S. Census 1913a: 805–850.

influence how elections were run. The newcomers refused to obey local rule and challenged the ways in which the local Anglo elite manipulated the Mexican vote to retain political control of the region. In particular, the political machines controlled by the Democrats Jim B. Wells Jr. and Rudolph Kleberg were challenged by the newcomers (Gutiérrez 1995; Weeks 1930).

Wells and Kleberg were wealthy, powerful men who besides owning large ranches had successful private law practices. Kleberg served as the representative for South Texas (District 11) from 1896 to 1903 and during his congressional campaigns he built a powerful coalition. His political

Table 4.7. Farm Owners by Foreign Nativity in South Texas, 1910

County	Total Foreign-Born		Total Farms Owned			1900 Total Farms Owned
	European Immigrants	Mexican Immigrants	Foreign-Born	Native-Born	Blacks	
Atascosa	161	1,013	90	504	28	574
Cameron	360	8,617	24	324	—	161
Dimmit	59	556	11	83	1	70
Duval	58	2,235	214	105	—	253
Frio	56	2,397	22	310	5	294
Hidalgo	138	5,202	100	268	3	308
Karnes	545	1,528	160	567	29	596
Kinney	100	532	10	102	2	57
La Salle	36	1,084	12	132	—	71
Live Oak	35	385	22	208	2	176
Maverick	110	2,188	14	21	1	15
Medina	405	3,147	100	646	23	685
McMullen	13	103	5	70	3	65
Nueces[a]	759	2,828	148	457	2	565
San Patricio	120	1,071	21	188	1	116
Starr	53	3,444	302	349	—	302
Uvalde	122	1,170	21	452	1	206
Val Verde	158	2,948	34	116	—	63
Webb[b]	312	10,654	93	184	—	200
Zapata	7	1,541	201	65	—	195
Zavala	25	230	10	99	—	84

[a]Brooks, Jim Wells, Willacy, Jim Hogg, and Kenedy had not been organized at this time.
[b]Encinal was annexed to Webb in 1899 (U.S. Census 1901: 41).
Sources: U.S. Census 1913a: 805–850, 1913c: 658–677.

network actually predated his time in office, since his law partner, Congressman William Crain, had established it many years earlier (Coolidge 1897: 108; Halford 1902: 108). Kleberg inherited District 11 when Crain died. Wells was equally influential, holding throughout his career a series of prestigious positions, including state district judge, chairman of the State Democratic Committee in 1900–1904, and cofounder of the most powerful political club in South Texas, the Democratic Club, which restricted its membership to prominent ranchers. In South Texas it was a well-known fact that to get elected to office candidates needed the support of the Democratic Club since its members had the finances to run successful elections and knew how to get out the vote. For years it had been rumored that the club purchased votes and that its members intimidated people by warning them to vote their way. For example, it was alleged that Mexican voters were fired from their jobs if they failed to comply with the club members' orders. Wells repeatedly dismissed these allegations as lies and distortions. He told reporters that he knew how to mobilize the Mexican vote without resorting to violence and intimidation. According to Wells, Mexicans voted for his ticket because they supported politicians who looked out for their welfare.

Nonetheless, although the Democratic Club controlled a large percentage of the votes in Texas, the arrival of a new ethnic population, one that was economically better off than Mexican voters, changed the political balance of power. The newcomers used the Terrell election reforms to challenge the old guard and the influence of the Mexican vote.

The Election of 1908: Boss Rule or Getting Out the Vote?

The general election of 1908 illustrates the setbacks that Wells and his political allies experienced as South Texas became more and more ethnically diversified. Although it is difficult to find fault with the reversal in the fortunes of the political bosses, one of the unfortunate outcomes of this change was the decline in the number of voters of Mexican descent and in their participation in the primaries (see table 4.5).

In 1908 Wells's political ticket was very unpopular among Anglo-American voters (Anders 1996a: 877). They refused to reelect Joseph Bailey for the U.S. Senate, and they openly campaigned against Wells's reelection as the regional delegate to the Democratic National Convention. Never before had Wells encountered such strong opposition. His troubles began when he backed Senator Bailey for reelection, knowing that Bailey was probably guilty of serious political corruption. Bailey was Wells's close friend and business associate, and he was not willing to abandon his lifelong friend. Bailey was under investigation for corruption because he had sponsored legislation to benefit oil and railroad companies without disclosing the financial gains he had made in doing so. His legislation benefited companies in which he was a board member, including H. Clay Pierce, Standard Oil, Southwestern Oil, and Kirby Lumber (Winkler 1916: 509).

To undermine the anticipated voting block forming against Bailey, Wells pressured his political allies to mobilize their Mexican constituency. Not only was a massive voter turnout necessary for Bailey to win, but the outcome of the election represented a symbolic barometer of Wells's influence in South Texas. How the election of 1908 played out and how Wells accessed the Mexican vote in that election are revealed in a series of letters written by Francis W. Seabury to Wells's political inner circle. One may describe these letters as evidence of boss rule, while a different interpretation can argue that they illustrate how Wells got out the vote. The letters are also insightful in that they describe how Seabury mobilized the Mexican community to get out the vote. In general, people of Mexican origin liked Seabury, for he had represented them well while serving as their state representative from 1895 to 1906.[17] While in office, Seabury gained a reputation as an advocate of the Mexican voter. He had fought against the legislative movements to deny Mexican immigrants the right to vote in Texas (see chapter 3). Throughout his tenure Seabury also stopped the state comptroller's office from seizing the property of Mexicans who were unable to pay delinquent taxes (see letters in Francis W. Seabury Papers, Center for American History, 2G/53).[18] And several times Seabury represented Mexican families in international incidents involving the imprisonment of young men while visiting relatives abroad. In sum, Seabury had a proven record of support and was trusted by people of Mexican origin in South Texas.

One of the letters concerning the election of 1908 was written by Seabury to Wells. On April 28, 1908, Seabury informed Wells that he was getting out the vote by mobilizing local Mexican *políticos*. The two men also strategized on which Mexican American political leaders needed to be mobilized. Seabury wrote,

April 28, 1908
Hon. James B. Wells
Brownsville, Texas

Dear Mr. Wells,
I am writing today to a large number. I suggest also that you write a letter to Lino Treviño at Falfurrias, asking him to do all he can in the matter; and also that you get word to Mr. Truitt to have your people go and vote. . . . (Francis W. Seabury Papers, Center for American History, 2G/53)

In a letter to Jesus Maria Ramirez, written in Spanish, Seabury describes how Wells was depending on Mexican voters to elect him as the delegate to the national convention and to help destroy the opposition to Bailey's reelection. According to Seabury, the election was not important only to Senator Bailey, as the honor and reputation of Wells also rested upon a successful outcome. In the letter Seabury tells Ramirez that a mass turnout in Starr County, particularly in the towns of Grulla and Salineño, was necessary if the opposition against the Wells ticket was to be diluted. In the letter Seabury asked Ramirez to get out the vote:

April 28, 1908
Sr. Jesus Maria Ramirez
San Pedro del Medanito, Texas

On May 2, 1908, the primary election will be held to elect the delegates to the national convention. Attorney Wells is very interested in this election and has asked us, as a special favor to him, to get out the vote for the ticket headed by Senator Joseph Bailey. In the rest of the precincts we will do our best to get out the vote, but in your precinct we are completely relying on you. In Falfurrias, many people will be voting against Mr. Wells's ticket, and for that reason it is important to get the majority of the votes in the rest of the county. Manuel Guerra is doing the most that he can in Roma and Old San Antonio, and I, Monroe, Jacob Guerra and the rest of us in this precinct, [and] others are working in Grulla and in El Salineño. This election is more important than it appears, because a majority against Bailey, or a small win for him, would be a triumph for our opponents. They will see this as evidence of the little influence Mr. Wells has within his own party. . . . We should help him as he has helped us on different occasions. This is not a matter of incurring debts, but rather of getting out the vote among our friends and dependents. . . . [19] (Ibid., my translation)

The letter closes by subtly reminding Ramirez that he needs to return the favors Wells has done for him and others. The letter also discloses the network of Mexican American allies Seabury was mobilizing. Among them was J. T. Canales, a Mexican American from Webb County, who in the last election had replaced Seabury as representative of District 95. Wells and Seabury had supported Canales.

In a third letter, this one to Benjamin B. Ramirez, Seabury further describes how Mexicans were involved in Wells's political network. Ramirez was the election judge of Precinct No. 6 for the town of San Pedro del Medanito in Cameron County. Seabury gave Ramirez instructions on his duties as judge and reviewed his responsibilities as organizer of the precinct convention. He also, however, reminded Ramirez to be faithful to Wells. Overall, the letter illustrates the politics of the period but informs one as well that Seabury was in favor of Mexicans participating in the primaries. Seabury tells Ramirez that all Democrats could participate in the election. The first part of the letter read,

> April 28, 1908
> Mr. Benjamin B. Ramirez
> San Pedro del Medanito, Texas
>
> Dear Sir,
> I enclose herewith a call for primaries, precinct conventions, and county conventions. You have been appointed presiding judge of Precinct No. 6 to hold the primary election, and also as chairman of the precinct convention. Both are held next Saturday, May 2, 1908. Your duties are simple. You appoint two judges and two Clerks to assist you to hold the primary election. This is open from 8 in the morning to 7 in the evening. All Democrats can vote. The precinct convention is held at three o'clock in the afternoon. All you have to do there is elect delegates for the county convention. (Ibid.)

Besides the letters to his political allies, Seabury wrote a series of letters to C. M. Laughlin, one of his opponents, charging him with being unfair to Mexican voters. In a letter to Laughlin at Falfurrias (Starr County) dated April 7, 1908, Seabury admonished him for refusing to hold a primary election in Starr County. Seabury did not offer details on exactly what Laughlin was doing wrong, but he did mention that the precinct head must follow the rules outlined in the state Democratic pamphlet. In the end Starr County held a primary election.

Seabury's letters indicate that the elections involved a degree of paternalism. Seabury asked for support because locals owed him favors. On the other hand, the letters also reveal that voters of Mexican descent were acting strategically because they supported a trusted ally. Seabury had a long history of advocating for his district.

The Redistricting of South Texas

Wells's allies did well in the election of 1908, he himself was elected as regional delegate to the Democratic National Convention, and Bailey won the Senate seat, but nevertheless Wells's political influence, already weakened, continued its decline (Texas Almanac 1910: 57; Winkler 1916: 504). In 1911 the Texas legislature dealt Wells's political machinery a hard blow by redistricting South Texas (Weeks 1930). Unfortunately, the redistricting also hurt elected officials of Mexican descent: their political influence at the county level nearly disappeared in the entire region.

Redistricting began when Anglo-American residents lobbied the legislature to reconfigure the boundaries of the counties in South Texas. Their intent was to create political districts that were separate from those controlled by Wells and his political allies. The boundaries they favored separated towns that had large numbers of Anglo-American residents from towns that were predominantly Mexican (Montejano 1987: 134). At first Wells was against the redistricting, but in 1911 he supported some of the plans. In particular, he favored the division of Cameron County because it would allow him to retain control of most of the county while placing the majority of the Anglo-American population in a separate county named Willacy (Montejano 1987:134).[20] Likewise, that same year Brooks County was carved out of Starr, Zapata, and Hidalgo counties. The pattern of redistricting South Texas continued throughout the 1920s. Towns where Anglo-Americans were the majority were redistricted into separate counties (see Gournay 1995: 117–123). For example, Nueces was subdivided into Jim Wells and Kleberg; Cameron and Hidalgo were once again subdivided to organize Kenedy; and the county of Jim Hogg was carved out of Brooks and Duval.

For Mexican Americans the redistricting immediately resulted in the loss of elected positions at the county and district levels. By 1911 persons with Spanish surnames were no longer elected to the county commission (Election Registers 1907–1912).[21] Likewise their representation in county and district offices nearly disappeared. At the district level people of Mexican descent were found in only a few counties serving as district clerks. And at the county level only a few people of Mexican descent acted as county clerk, tax collector, and treasurer. The number of county sheriffs also declined. Whereas in the past many sheriffs with Spanish surnames had been elected, now only Brooks, Zapata, Starr, and Webb counties had one. Only in Webb and Starr did a few Mexican Americans continue to serve in higher-level county positions. In Webb they were elected to county attorney and county judge, while in Starr they served as county attorney, school superintendent, assessor, and treasurer. The absence of Mexican Americans in the county commissions, however, was the most serious blow to their political repre-

sentation, as the commissioners had the power to determine electoral precinct locations and directly influence the manner of holding elections.[22]

The Mexican Revolution Begins

While people of Mexican descent experienced severe political setbacks in
Texas during this period and many lost their right to vote, civil disobedi-
ence against President Díaz's dictatorship broke out throughout all sectors
of Mexican society. Ironically, in both places the main problem affecting
Mexicans was the people's inability to vote freely. In Texas, poll taxes kept
many Mexicans from voting, while in Mexico the dictatorship had made a
mockery of the electoral process and effectively created the infrastructure to
keep the poor and the discontent politically powerless. On November 20,
1910, Francisco I. Madero called for armed resistance against the Porfirian
dictatorship, and the Mexican Revolution began (Gilly 1994: 81). Madero
was part of Mexico's ruling class, and he benefited from Díaz's development program, as he came from one of Mexico's wealthiest families, a family that had prospered under the regime. Madero conspired against Díaz for
the same reasons the Flores Magón brothers had bravely spoken out against
it before their exile in the United States. He opposed domestic and international corporate greed and believed workers should be paid a fair living
wage. Madero's main motivation, however, was to restore Mexico's constitutional democracy and allow free elections to determine the nation's governance. The irony in this sad drama was that the United States was simultaneously the engine driving the dictatorship and a haven for the politically
disenfranchised. Although the U.S. government and American businessmen were openly in support of Díaz's regime, U.S. law gave political exiles
the power to invoke the First Amendment of the U.S. Constitution and
from a distant land create dissent through the publication of their grievances. It was a complicated scenario, one in which the United States was
both a friend and a foe of Mexican democracy.

The Mexican Revolution marks an important phase in the Mexican immigrants' naturalization history because it resulted in the exodus of thousands of people seeking refuge in the United States. At first, most refugees
believed that their expatriation would be temporary, but they soon realized
that they were in the United States to stay and that their destiny was to
remain there and become permanent legal residents. Many refugees had
expected the revolution to last for a short time only because all sectors of
Mexican society were calling for Diaz's resignation, and the fall of his dic-

tatorship was only a matter of time. The problem that soon took center stage in the drama of the Mexican Revolution, however, was the victors' inability to agree on what direction Mexican capitalism should take. This prompted long-term conflicts which destabilized Mexico and within a decade of the call to arms caused a mass exodus of its citizenry. The Mexican immigrant population of the United States doubled.

Public criticism of Díaz's development program sparked debate and eventually led to organized armed revolt. The most effective conduit for disseminating proof of Díaz's failed policies was Ricardo and Enrique Flores Magón's newspaper *Regeneración*, which, as noted above, continued to expose the hypocrisy, corruption, and incompetence of the regime even after its removal to the United States. As the economy worsened, the Flores Magón brothers gained prominence, and the network of activists who smuggled their newspaper into Mexico expanded. The Mexican government found it difficult to refute the brothers' charges in the face of an economy that was clearly faltering. Exacerbating matters for the government were independent scholars like Esteban Calderón and Wistano L. Orozco, who also opposed Díaz's economic programs and in the early 1900s advanced studies that corroborated the brothers' news reports. They and others concluded that Díaz's land grant policies, rather than leading to an increase in the acreage under cultivation, had radically reduced the production of crops. Taking land from the peasantry and giving it to American investors and Mexican hacendados had not stimulated the economy (see Gilly 1994). On the contrary, the actual amount of cultivated acreage had decreased because the land either was no longer under cultivation or the new owners had converted the peasants into tenants, who in turn had less money to invest in farming.

The economic studies of Orozco were particularly damaging, as his results proved that in towns and cities where the courts had extinguished the land rights of the peasantry and turned the titles over to Díaz's corporate friends the cultivated acreage decreased and the local economy deteriorated (Ramirez 1974). Because people in such communities were converted into tenant farmers and were now required to pay rent, less money was available to purchase merchandise, and the consequence was the financial ruin of local businesses. In contrast to this scenario, Orozco found that in towns where the courts ruled in favor of the peasantry and elites were not allowed to expand their haciendas by usurping their neighbors' property the economy was strong. The prosperity of these towns was attributed to the circulation of cash. When farmers did not have to pay rent they reinvested their profits and spent the extra cash in the local shops.[23]

Díaz's regime could not hide the fact that by 1905 the sixty-nine million acres that had been given to U.S. and Mexican investors had not produced the expected results and the production of food had fallen to a critical level (Gilly 1994: 79; Knight 1986: 80). Elites were also displeased with Díaz's failure to negotiate favorable trade agreements. U.S. and European investors continued to trade with Mexico, but they lowered the amount of imports and negotiated lower rates for the purchase of henequen, coffee, and mineral resources. Likewise, many believed that Díaz was giving away Mexico's oil reserve in the Maya region, where thousands of acres of oil fields had been discovered. He was giving enormous land grants to foreign investors in return for their establishing of an oil-drilling infrastructure, an improvement which many believed could be realized by national industrialists (Callahan 1932). Worst of all, these generous concessions were displacing thousands of Maya and creating dissent. Overall, the failure of the development programs had resulted in high unemployment and exorbitant food costs, which together spelled disaster. This led members of the ruling class to question whether Díaz's administration was equipped to continue governing the country. Mexican industrialists like Madero began to question whether Díaz's cabinet members, appointed governors, and military generals were too old to govern the country. They were all over seventy years of age, and some were in their eighties (Callahan 1932: 530; Davids 1976:195; Knight 1986:17). Díaz himself was seventy-nine.

Throughout Mexico workers responded by establishing labor unions, while intellectuals and members of the middle class defied Díaz and established democratic clubs demanding free presidential elections. Open opposition to Díaz gained momentum when the labor unions formed solidarity alliances with the democratic clubs. In 1905 Díaz responded by once again breaking up the clubs and outlawing unionization (Gilly 1994: 62). Upon hearing of this, the Flores Magón brothers published a series of editorials supporting workers' right to unionize. They also exposed the government's violence toward the indigenous populations of Mexico and condemned the genocidal wars against the Maya and Yaqui Indians of Sonora, who had been punished for refusing to abandon their tribal lands. They reported that throughout Mexico Indian communities that attempted to protect their land were, if they survived the slaughter being committed by the military, apprehended, imprisoned, and given life prison sentences to be worked out in the haciendas owned by Díaz's friends. When Díaz read these latter charges he immediately wired the U.S. government and accused them of breaking U.S. Neutrality Laws (Coerver and Hall 1984). The brothers and their staff were temporarily arrested but released since there was insufficient evidence a revolutionary conspiracy was under way.

The Cananea Labor Strike and the Call for Revolution

The momentum that was building to depose Díaz's regime escalated when news spread throughout Mexico that the government had allowed a U.S. corporation to dispatch American troops onto Mexican soil. The mission of the troops was to end a peaceful labor strike that had been called on June 1, 1906, in the mining town of Cananea in Sonora. (González Ramírez 1974: xxiv). The mines were located close to the Sonora-Arizona border. Although most members of the Mexican ruling class were unsympathetic toward the strikers, many joined the national protest against what appeared to be U.S. intervention in governmental affairs, not to mention its trampling of Mexico's sovereignty. Many elites feared Mexico was losing its political autonomy.

The strike began when the Cananea Consolidated Copper Company, owned by the American investor William G. Greene, switched its wage system from direct payment to workers to a labor contractor system. The workers in the mining towns of Cananea, Buenavista, and El Ronquillo were affected by the new policy. To the miners this was an oppressive action and an intolerable misuse of power. They believed Greene was trying to punish them for forming a committee to arbitrate disputes between labor and management. Their pay scales had been downgraded after the committee asked to meet with Greene. Far from capitulating, the miners joined the Liga Minera de Los Estados Unidos and again demanded a meeting with Greene. They joined the miners' national union after meeting with Esteban Calderón, the founder of the union, who happened to be visiting the mines in Sonora (Calderón 1975) and had come to Cananea to conduct research on the labor conditions there. Calderón was an activist scholar who was in regular contact with the Flores Magón brothers. He was also responsible for smuggling *Regeneración* into Mexico and distributing it through the miners' networks.

On June 1, 1906, a large group of miners marched to El Ronquillo's headquarters and presented their demands to the office managers. Alvaro L. Diéguez, their spokesman, demanded that the company rescind its labor contracting policy. Under the new system, he argued, the company allowed labor contractors to keep part of the workers' wages. Diéguez then presented additional demands. Complaining that Anglo-American miners were unfairly paid twice as much as Mexican workers for performing the same tasks, he asked that workers be given equal pay for equal work. Anglo-Americans were also paid in gold rather than in pesos, like the Mexican workers. He also charged that the highest-paying jobs were reserved for

Anglo-Americans, regardless of their seniority. Diéguez made additional demands of the company: it should limit the workday to eight hours, pay a minimum wage rather than by the piece, prohibit the hiring of children under fourteen, keep the workplace clean, pay workers in cash, not force employees to buy their merchandise at the company store, and give Mexican and foreign workers with the same skills the same opportunity to compete for promotions.

Instead of negotiating, the management team ordered the men to return to work and called the police of El Ronquillo to arrest their spokesman. The police refused to arrest Diéguez. To assuage the strikers a group of influential locals from Buenavista tried to intercede. The mayor, the aldermen, the county judge, and the local doctor of Buenavista asked the miners to take their complaints to the county court rather than call a strike. The miners refused to listen and called the strike. The following morning, on June 2, some 1,200 miners met in Cananea and demanded to speak with Greene (Ibid., 61). At that point management knew the company had to negotiate and met Greene at his home. Greene read the demands but refused to meet with the miners or concede. He issued an official statement saying it was ludicrous for Mexicans to get paid the same wages as Anglo miners. He also stated that an eight-hour workday was unreasonable and that perhaps he was willing to reduce the workday from fourteen to twelve hours if the contracting system remained in place. Greene also admonished the workers and told them they should be thankful for having jobs. Instead of conceding, Greene telegraphed the governor of Sonora, Rafael Izábal, and ordered him to personally end the strike. Toward the end of the second day, fighting broke out between the miners and supporters of the company. One of the strikers set the company sawmill on fire.

By nightfall Greene's house in Cananea was barricaded by armed bodyguards and by dozens of Anglo volunteers who were awaiting reinforcements from across the border. Earlier that day Greene had asked the governor of Arizona to send state rangers, but the governor refused, as this was a personal matter. Nonetheless, by nightfall Greene was able to recruit around 500 Anglo-American volunteers from Arizona. Furthermore, Capt. Tom Rynning, an officer of the Arizona Rangers, disobeyed the governor's orders and crossed the border, bringing with him 275 rangers and hundreds of Anglo-American miners (Ibid., 97). Izábal had given the rangers permission to cross the border. When they arrived they joined the governor's state troops as well as federal troops sent by President Díaz.

The next morning, on June 3, another 2,200 Mexican miners joined the strike (Ibid., 86). The miners, however, were outnumbered, as thousands of

Mexican federal troops had been deployed. The fighting continued sporadically until the morning of the fourth. At that point Gen. Emilio Kosterilsky, the head of the federal troops, apprehended the last men suspected of organizing the strike and suppressed the rebellion. When the strike ended, 19 miners and 4 Anglo-American volunteers were dead, and 10 Mexicans were seriously wounded (Ibid., 108–109). General Kosterilsky issued a local ordinance warning citizens that any person suspected of organizing a meeting would be arrested and shot.

News of the strike spread throughout Mexico. Thousands of citizens were incensed that Governor Izábal had illegally authorized American troops to enter Mexico, an order that only the president and Congress were empowered to issue. To many this signified that Mexico had finally become a colony of the United States. From every corner of Mexico influential citizens asked President Díaz to place Izábal under arrest. To calm the people's furor Díaz held a trial. Unfortunately for Díaz, he failed to heed the public's warning, and this mistake soon proved to be his downfall. Díaz held the trial, as the people asked, but he mocked them by overturning the rulings. Although Izábal was found guilty, Díaz dismissed the charges and exonerated him. Worst of all, he gave amnesty to the Anglo-Americans who had been found guilty of killing unarmed Mexican miners, while on the other hand he refused to pardon any of the miners. Instead, he ordered the convicted miners to be executed by a firing squad. Díaz also ordered that the mining towns be placed under police surveillance and that anyone suspected of organizing a union or a democratic club be shot on sight. He then ordered a public execution of Calderón and the other strike leaders. When people heard of Calderón's pending execution, protests erupted throughout Mexico, and Díaz was pressured to suspend the executions. Instead he sentenced Calderón and the other leaders to fifteen years in the federal prison of San Juan de Ulúa.

Díaz's cruel actions backfired. Instead of provoking fear in the masses his impulsive behavior caused dissenters to defy federal law throughout Mexico and openly begin to organize labor unions and democratic clubs. A series of labor strikes ensued soon after. Workers from the textile, railroad, and mining industries coordinated their efforts and organized massive strikes. Making matters worse for Díaz, the Cananea strike inspired the Flores Magón brothers to take radical action. Thirty days after the strike, Ricardo Flores Magón published "El Manifesto Liberal," calling on people to organize against the dictatorship and outlining the rights that labor should be guaranteed in Mexico. Part of this treatise addressed the situation of Mexican immigrants abroad and proclaimed that the exodus of the Mexican people would end only when Díaz was forced to return the land he had stolen. To stop the flow of migrants, agrarian reform was ultimately necessary. The manifesto circulated widely and became an inspiration to Mexicans of all social classes. Díaz was irate and in his determination to destroy Ricardo ordered the Mexican government to resurrect its charges against Ricardo for violating U.S. Neutrality Laws, citing the manifesto as a call to arms. Government attorneys also charged that Ricardo had collaborated with Calderón to organize the strike at Cananea, and this proved that he had violated U.S. law because it was illegal to organize an armed rebellion from U.S. soil (Callahan 1932: 523). Ricardo was found guilty of conspiracy and sentenced to eighteen months. Díaz had finally won the battle of words. *Regeneración* was subsequently forced to go underground.

By 1908 Díaz had been unable to stabilize the country, and his close friends asked him to resign from office (Gilly 1994:80). He had lost the support of a large part of the bourgeoisie, as they feared that unless free elections were permitted at all levels of government they would lose control of the country. The governor of Nuevo León, Bernardo Reyes, a trusted and longtime friend of the president, was persuaded by Díaz's inner circle to ask the president to hold free elections (Niemeyer 1963). Díaz refused to take his friend's advice and forced Reyes into exile. A few months after the governor's departure, Madero took over Reyes's role as arbitrator between the discontented bourgeoisie and the Díaz administration. To pressure Díaz into resigning, Madero reinvigorated the network of well-financed democratic clubs that Reyes had established among members of Mexico's ruling class before his exile. He also asked the bourgeoisie to hold their meetings in public, an act that inspired further dissent. Díaz had to tolerate Madero because his family was well connected internationally and enjoyed the support of the wealthiest families in Mexico and Europe. However, by October 1910, when he learned that Madero had established an opposition party called the Partido Nacional Antirreeleccionista (National Antireelection Party) and announced that he was running for president, Díaz had had enough (Davids 1976: 213). He ordered that Madero be arrested immediately. Yet within days Madero was released, as the president's advisors informed Díaz that Madero's imprisonment had divided the ruling class and was influencing European investors to oppose the administration.

Madero knew this was a temporary situation and expected to be executed at any moment. Immediately upon his release from prison he organized secret meetings to set a timeline for revolutionary action. Madero and his allies began a draft of the Plan de San Luis Potosí outlining their vision of a democratic Mexico. When Madero learned that he and several of his associates were about to be arrested, they fled to Texas, where arrangements had been made in San Antonio to secretly allow them to continue writing the plan. When Díaz learned that Madero had been smuggled into the United States he asked the U.S. government to find him and initiate extradition procedures.

While in San Antonio Madero met with other exiled refugees and put into action the Plan de San Luis Potosí, which called upon Mexicans to revolt against the Porfirian dictatorship and initiate armed resistance on November 20, 1910 (Gilly 1994: 81). Pancho (Francisco) Villa, Pascual Orozco, and the governor of Chihuahua, Abraham Gonzales, acted on Madero's call to arms. On the day set for the revolution to begin their forces went into action, and together they captured many cities in the state of Chihuahua. By February 1911 most of the northern states were under the control of the revolutionary forces. In southern Mexico, Emiliano Zapata emerged as the people's general. By early May 1911 most cities in southern Mexico had either sided with Zapata or been captured by the revolutionary forces. At that point Díaz's cabinet advised him to turn the government over to Madero in order to save the current administration; otherwise, the most powerful generals, Villa and Zapata, would take over and immediately institute radical land reforms. If Madero, who was a capitalist and not necessarily against the status quo, were given the presidency he would favor moderate reforms and retain most of the laws benefiting the ruling class. Madero's land reform policies were also moderate, as he favored litigating agrarian cases in the courts rather than by executive order or military force. This would permit the bourgeoisie to litigate their land claims and allow them to liquidate their assets in the meantime. In sum, to keep the federal and state bureaucracies in place Díaz must abdicate to Madero.

At first Díaz was hesitant to relinquish power since he had been assured by U.S. Ambassador Henry Lane Wilson and the American consul, Gen. Alfred M. Gottschalk, that President William Howard Taft was in full support of the president. After Zapata took over the south, however, and all of the states had been captured by the revolutionary forces, Díaz had no choice but to step down. On May 20, 1911, he resigned, and Madero triumphantly entered Mexico City on horseback, signifying a change in administration (Ibid., 94). The revolutionary forces had won.

A few months later, on October 11, 1911, Madero was officially elected constitutional president of Mexico. Ambassador Wilson was relieved that neither Villa nor Zapata laid claim to the presidency, but he was nevertheless displeased with Madero's ascent to power. Wilson feared Madero's liberalism, especially his support for agrarian reform, as this directly affected American investors. Madero favored returning all of the land President

Díaz had awarded his allies, and Wilson doubted that American investors would be compensated. This was a serious problem for the United States in that American businessmen owned 43 percent of Mexico's land, either as absentee landowners or as Mexican residents (Sloan 1978: 285). Wilson personally believed it was best to remove Madero from office and seat one of Díaz's allies because a friendly president would protect U.S. investments in Mexico and continue trade. This was the advice he gave President Taft (Davids 1976; Meyer, Sherman, and Deeds 2007). At that time American investments in Mexico had grown to nearly \$1½ billion (Callahan 1932: 519; Vásquez and Meyer 1985: 97). They exceeded the total amount of all other foreign investments in Mexico and included 58 percent of the mines, 72 percent of the smelters, 58 percent of the oil, and 68 percent of the rubber businesses.

Mexican Immigrants in Texas

President Madero's ascent to power did not end the revolution in Mexico. Most of his generals refused to obey his order to disarm. Political factionalism soon followed, as the generals disagreed on how the government should be run and how much power the federal government should give the states. They also disagreed on another very serious matter: How should agrarian reform be implemented? The new leaders knew that land had to be returned to the people, but there was no agreement on what land had been stolen. Zapata favored immediate distribution of farmlands to the peasantry via executive order. In the state of Morelia, where Zapata refused to disarm his army, agrarian reform was instituted through his military orders (See Gilly 1994). On the opposite end of the ideological spectrum was Gen. Venustiano Carranza, who favored institutionalizing all federal and state reforms through the courts. Land should be distributed to the peasantry, he thought, only when the courts ruled that Díaz had taken it illegally. Zapata thought such a process betrayed the Revolution. People needed land now, and involving the courts in land reform would take too long. The courts were corrupt, and they would have to be reformed before land cases were litigated. He also disagreed that land titles predating Díaz's policies should be respected and not included in the distribution plans. In Zapata's view, the peasantry's displacement began with Spain.

In short, the generals disagreed on how to make the Mexican government accountable to the people, and the Revolution thus continued. As the violence escalated in Mexico, many people chose to escape by migrating to the United States, and Texas continued to be the primary refuge zone. The Texas legislature responded by asking the U.S. government to regulate Mexican immigration and place federal troops along the Texas-Mexico border. Nativism targeting Mexicans also heightened at this time, and the Texas legislature reacted by introducing legislation to revise the Texas Constitution and no longer allow noncitizens to vote. An unprecedented number of Mexicans were crossing the border, and under Texas law these people would soon be eligible to vote.

CHAPTER 5

Mexican Women and Naturalization: The Era of the Woman Suffrage Movement

Throughout this narrative I have advanced an analysis of the naturalization history of Mexican immigrants in Texas and examined why obtaining citizenship was closely intertwined with electoral politics. Following this thematic approach, I examine here the woman suffrage movement in Texas because in 1918 a new chapter in the Mexicans' naturalization history began. When women gained the right to vote in Texas, Mexican women who were naturalized or had filed intention papers became important political actors.

Unfortunately, although the extension of suffrage to women was a landmark event, in Texas this history is blemished, as within this story there is an underlying account of racist politics and social class biases against people of color and against immigrants. When white suffragists launched their campaign to gain the right to vote, they concurrently initiated a movement to stop Mexican immigrants from voting in Texas. The political stance white suffragists took against Mexicans, however, was complicated because they were merely reacting in the same way as the rest of the nation. That is, this period coincided with the outbreak of the Mexican Revolution, and the ousting of American corporations from Mexico. Thus, when U.S. capitalist investors were made unwelcome in Mexico, the U.S. government was displeased and no longer felt obliged to welcome Mexican immigrants. For suffragists the Mexican Revolution complicated matters and influenced how they shaped their political planks on immigration, voting, and naturalization. To elucidate why suffragists in Texas adopted political positions to make naturalization and voting difficult for Mexican immigrants, including Mexican women, it is necessary to first examine naturalization law specific to women.

Naturalization Law and Women, 1790–1906

In 1790, when the first naturalization act was passed, eligibility was limited to free white persons, but it was not limited by sex. The law was clear that women were allowed to apply for naturalization (Naturalization Act of 1790, in 1 *U.S. Statutes at Large* 103). The act also stipulated that the minor children, but not the adult children, of naturalized fathers were citizens. Adult sons and daughters had to apply on their own. The law, however, did not address the legal status of wives or widows whose husbands had naturalized or filed declaration papers. In 1804, as many cases were coming before the courts and different judicial rulings were being rendered on the political status of widows and their orphaned children, the U.S. Congress was forced to formulate a uniform policy. That year Congress decreed that when a man filed a declaration of intention to become a citizen but died prior to completing the process, regardless of his death, his widow and minor children became citizens. The only action they had to take was to appear in court, take the oath of allegiance, and renounce their former citizenship (Naturalization Act of 1804, 2 *U.S. Statutes at Large* 292). The revision of 1804, however, did not entirely clarify the political status of married women. Most courts assumed that if Congress agreed to give the children of naturalized males citizenship, the spirit of the law also applied to the legal spouse. Some judges disagreed and denied citizenship to married women because naturalization law did not specifically mention them by statute (See *Ex parte Pic,* Federal Case no. 11,118, 1 Cranch C.C. 372, in *American Digest,* 1898: no. 122).[1] The lack of judicial uniformity on the status of married women led Congress to revisit naturalization policy. In 1855, under "An Act to Secure the Right of Citizenship to Children of Citizens of the United States Born out of the Limits, thereof," Congress decreed that an alien woman married to a U.S. citizen was also a citizen, as long as she was eligible (Act of February 10, 1855, in 10 *U.S. Statutes at Large* 604). This meant that she needed to be of one of the races allowed to apply for citizenship. In Texas the act of 1855 was interpreted by the courts as a mandate giving married alien women the same legal status as their spouses (*American Digest* 1898: no. 157). Alien women married to U.S. citizens (naturalized or native born) were considered citizens, and the immigrant spouses of men who had filed papers of naturalization acquired the same legal status. The status of women born in the United States and married to an alien, however, remained ambiguous in Texas, as it did in other states. The U.S. Congress finally resolved this issue in 1907.

Before women acquired the right to vote throughout the United States, it was rare for a woman to apply for naturalization on her own; usually only single or orphaned women applied. Women had few reasons to apply for naturalization because, unlike men, they could not vote. For most women, due to the expense, applying for naturalization was a luxury (Smith 1998). The main protection single women gained if they naturalized was the right to apply for a homestead grant, but naturalization also prevented their being deported and, in states requiring citizenship for government jobs, expanded their employment opportunities. Women also naturalized when they desired to be independent from their husbands. For example, women who were separated or divorced needed their own certificates to prove they were U.S. citizens since their names were not necessarily registered in any government document. In those days women proved U.S. citizenship by presenting a marriage certificate and their husband's birth certificate or naturalization papers. For women who were separated or divorced these documents were not accessible.

Although most women who applied for naturalization were single, some married women paid the court fees to officially register their names in the naturalization indexes and to obtain a separate naturalization certificate. It was not until the passage of the Cable Act of 1922 that the names of all alien women applicants were officially entered. Before then, the registry indexes offered only a partial listing of the actual number of naturalized women. In Texas the naturalization records indicate that very few Mexican immigrant women applied on their own (TNR 1 to 10). As mentioned in my discussion on the politics of Reconstruction (see n. 6, chap. 2), Adelaida Cantu and Luz Espinoza were the first Mexican women to apply for naturalization in Texas. They both applied on November 19, 1869, in Cameron County during Governor Davis's heated gubernatorial reelection race. Their applications were among those of about one hundred Mexicans submitted that week. Only Adelaida was granted citizenship.

The exact number of Mexican women who naturalized in Texas is uncertain for the same reason that a complete registry is unavailable for immigrant women in general. The courts simply did not register the names of the spouses of most male applicants. Only women who applied on their own or paid to have their name entered on the registry are identified in the naturalization records. In addition, in the case of Mexican immigrants in Texas identifying women in the records is sometimes difficult because the gender of the applicant was not noted. In Mexican culture some names are not gender specific, and this makes it difficult to determine if an applicant was male or female. The names Encarnación, Guadalupe, and Cruz are of-

Table 5.1. Mexican Female Naturalization Applicants

Decade	First Name Common Only to Females	First Names Common to Males and Females[a]	Total
1860	2 (g1)[b]	0	2
1870	21 (g1)	12	33
1880	48	35	83
1890	53	39	92
1900–1906	7 (g1)	15 (g2)	22
ND	3	1	4
Total	134	102	236

[a]Names in this category: 1870: Guadalupe appeared 9 times, Encarnacion 2, Cruz 1; 1880: Guadalupe 28, Encarnacion 7; 1890: Guadalupe 25, Encarnacion 10, Cruz 4; 1900–1906: Guadalupe 10, Encarnacion 5; ND: Guadalupe 1.
[b]g = number of women granted citizenship. In 1880, Carmen Garcia applied in the Federal Court of Galveston. She is the only Mexican woman who applied in a federal court.
Sources: Index to Naturalization Records found in Texas State, District, and County Courts, 1846–1939; U.S. District Courts, Southern District of Texas, Galveston Index to Declarations, 1871–1905; General Courts Austin, Brownsville, El Paso, Galveston, San Antonio, Jefferson, Texarkana, Tyler, Waco, El Paso Naturalization Records, Declarations of Intention, 1890–1906.

ten given to both boys and girls when parents choose to name their children after a religious holiday or event (Lansky 2007; Woods 1984). The name Encarnación is related to the resurrection of Jesus Christ, Guadalupe venerates the Virgin of Guadalupe, and Cruz recalls the crucifixion of Christ. To estimate the number of women applicants who filed papers I present two tabulations (table 5.1). One list includes only traditional female first names and indicates that 134 women applied, of whom only 3 were granted citizenship. The second list includes the names of Encarnación, Guadalupe, and Cruz, which lengthens it to 236, of whom 5 were granted citizenship.

Overall, an analysis of Texas naturalization indexes reveals that from 1870 to 1899 there was a steady flow of applications from Mexican women. The number of female applicants declined at the beginning of the twentieth century, following the pattern of Mexican men. The only difference between the male and female applicants was that most Mexican women applied in Webb and Bexar counties.

After 1906 there are few data available on the number of Mexican women applicants in Texas since that year the federal government made major revisions in naturalization law and removed from the states the responsibility of maintaining naturalization records (see appendix 1). They did so for several reasons, but the most troublesome one was to remove county judges from the granting process, as the federal government suspected that county judges were manipulating the process to gain reelection (U.S. Commission on Naturalization 1905). Under the Naturalization Act of 1906, the U.S. Congress established procedural safeguards to uniformly gather information on the applicants and create a standard granting procedure (34 *U.S. Statutes at Large* [part 1] 596).[2] The Bureau of Immigration and Naturalization was also established for the specific purpose of centralizing all naturalization and immigration records, producing standard application forms, and enforcing the states' compliance with federal law. In Texas the problem with the restructuring is that it destroyed an important source of American history because the county courts were one of the main governmental institutions that kept records on immigrants, including Mexican women. Furthermore, because the Bureau of Immigration and Naturalization initiated new data collection and reporting procedures, it chose to evaluate the data based only on a national tabulation of the number of granted or denied petitions. Reports on the national origin of the applicants and the state where they applied were eliminated from the database (see appendix 1).[3] In sum, the Naturalization Act of 1906 restructured the court processing system and removed the record keeping from the states, which in turned changed the preservation of archival data on naturalization, including data on women.

Implications of the Naturalization Acts of 1906 and 1907

Between 1906 and 1907 Congress revised the naturalization laws and radically altered the naturalization process for Mexicans. Besides the record-keeping changes enacted by the act of 1906 three of its other provisions made it very difficult for Mexicans to qualify for citizenship, whereas the reforms of 1907 specifically affected Mexican women.

In 1906, Congress required all applicants to speak English after September 27 of that year, petitions were given expiration dates, and registry at port of entry was required to qualify for citizenship (34 *U.S. Statutes at Large* [part 1] 596). For immigrants in Texas, including Mexicans, the language requirement was devastating since the majority did not speak English. The U.S. Census estimates that in Texas in 1900 over 63 percent of male immigrants who were not citizens did not speak English (U.S. Census 1901: ccxvi).[4] The second provision of the act was particularly damaging to

Mexicans since petitions were null and void if they had not been completed within seven years after filing. This provision nullified most petitions, as from 1848 to 1906, 28,597 had been filed but only 416 granted. Only 2,027 petitions fell within the active time limit allowance because they were filed from 1900 to 1906. The rest were immediately voided by the provision.

The registry provision of the act also disqualified many Mexican immigrants. Many became ineligible to apply because they had not registered upon entry (Lee 2004: 126). Their disqualification, however, was not caused by their actions, but rather was owing to inconsistencies in the immigration and naturalization laws. Immigration law pertaining to Mexicans was designed to make entry easy for laborers. For example, if Mexicans crossed the border on foot they did not have to register or pay a fee (see chapter 4). Only Mexicans entering by steamship or train were required to register. So in 1906 when naturalization law changed and all immigrants were required to prove they had registered upon entry, the special laws designed to ease the entry for Mexicans may have led to their disqualification. My review of naturalization records in Texas indicates that the entry law was troublesome for many Mexicans since it was common for people to enter through the ranches or small towns rather than through official ports. Popular points of entry were Rancho Davis and Rancho Arrairo in Starr County, Rancho Jardin in Hidalgo, and the town of Carrizos in Dimmit (table 5.2; fig. 5.1).

Less than a year later, in March 1907, Congress passed additional laws, laws which buffered the full impact of the reforms of 1906 upon immigrant women. Congress acknowledged that further reforms were necessary to clarify the political status of married women because courts were rendering conflicting decisions. Under the Naturalization Act of March 2, 1907, all women acquired their husband's nationality (34 *U.S. Statutes at Large* [Part 2] 1220). This law removed all ambiguity pertaining to married women. The law came to benefit many immigrant women, but at the same time it made the political identity of all married women dependent on that of their husbands. Married women could no longer apply for citizenship on their own, and American-born women were stripped of their U.S. citizenship if they were married to men who were not naturalized or were ineligible to become a U.S. citizen (i.e., Asians or U.S. tribal Indians) (Smith 1998:2). On the other hand, immigrant women who were married to U.S. citizens automatically became citizens, and the wives of men who had petitioned to become citizens acquired the same status. The language requirement and the other stipulations found in the act of 1906 did not pertain to the wife of a U.S. citizen or applicant. In Texas the law was a mixed blessing since a very large part of the population of Mexican origin

Table 5.2. Places of Entry of Mexicans, 1848–1906

Ports: 1903	Towns and Ranches Commonly Cited: Non-Ports[a]
Brownsville, Cameron County	Rancho Davis, Starr County
Corpus Christi, Nueces County	"Un rancho" in Hidalgo County (common phrase)
Del Rio, Val Verde County	Rancho Arreiro, Starr County
Eagle Pass, Maverick County	Rancho Jardin, Bensten State Park, Hidalgo County
El Paso, El Paso County	Redmonds Ranch, Zapata County
Laredo, Webb County	Rancho Opposon (unknown ranch)
Presidio, Presidio County	San Pedro, Cameron or Starr County[b]
Rio Grande City, Starr County	Puente (most likely a ranch)
Roma, Starr County	Pass (most likely a ranch)
	Santa Tomas (most likely a ranch)
	Rancho Fravila (unknown ranch)
	Canutillo, El Paso County
	San Ignacio, Zapata County
	Carrizo Springs, Dimmit County
	Edinburg, Hidalgo County
	Guerra, Brooks County
	Presidio Del Norte, Presidio County
	Fort Davis, Jeff Davis County
	El Paso Del Norte, El Paso County
	Santa Maria, Cameron County
Ports-Post 1903 Boquillas, Brewster County (Big Bend National Park Mountains)	

[a]Other ports used primarily by Europeans include Port Bolivar, Texas City, Freeport, Port Arthur, Port Aransas, Port Lavaca, Sabine Pass, Galveston.
[b]There are many ranches named San Pedro in Cameron County. San Pedro could also stand for the nineteenth-century name of the city of Roma. Its original name was San Pedro de Roma.
Source: *List of Aliens Arriving at Brownsville, Del Rio, Eagle Pass, El Paso, Presidio, Rio Grande City, and Roma Texas, May 1903–June 1909; Index to Naturalization Records Found in Texas State, District, and County Courts, 1846–1939; *Texas Almanac* 1914: 144–150.

Figure 5.1. International Bridge 1917. Runyon (Robert) Photograph Collection. Center for American History, UT-Austin (RUN 03738).

was of mixed nativity. For example, in 1910 the U.S. Census estimated that 34,182 people of Mexican descent were part of mixed households in which one parent was born in Mexico (U.S. Census 1913b: 799). The law thus allowed many Mexican women to gain citizenship, while in other cases it caused U.S.-born women to lose it.

In retrospect, the acts of 1906 and 1907 changed and complicated the political status of Mexican immigrants. Most immigrant men lost their status as naturalized petitioners, while many immigrant women indisputably became U.S. citizens. In Texas this change had serious implications, as Texas was one of the few states in the nation that allowed immigrant males to vote. Once the applications of immigrant males were nullified, they were no longer eligible to vote, and the number of voters of Mexican origin declined. However, because this was also the era of the woman's suffrage movement, the reforms of 1907 had another major implication on election politics in Texas because suffragists were fighting for the right to vote, and if they were successful, then Mexican immigrant women would be able to vote. This scenario complicated suffrage politics in Texas, as extending Mexican women the suffrage would alienate male allies who opposed adding more immigrants to the electoral registries. This was a particularly troublesome

and complicated issue to resolve because the revolution in Mexico was causing thousands of immigrants to flee to Texas in an attempt to escape their
country's economic and political troubles.

The Mexican Revolution and World War I:
Background to the Woman Suffrage Movement in Texas

The woman suffrage movement in Texas dates to 1868, but it did not gain
popular support until 1912 following a state convention held in San Antonio (Taylor 1987: 13). The convention stimulated interest, and within a couple of years twenty-one chapters of the Texas Woman Suffrage Association
had been formed boasting a total membership of twenty-five hundred. The
association received a boost when the Texas Federation of Women's Clubs
endorsed equal suffrage and led many more women to join the association.
However, while the woman suffrage movement was gaining ground in
Texas, the Mexican Revolution, as noted, caused Mexican immigration to
surge, and suffragists had to take a position on immigration to demonstrate
their political knowledge and prove that they could be responsible voters.

By 1914 the leaders of the Mexican Revolution had resolved many issues
but were still divided on how to distribute the property former president
Díaz had usurped and given to foreign companies and Mexican elites. By
then several political battles over the presidency had also led to continuous
warfare. The most significant political development was the assassination of
President Francisco I. Madero by Gen. Victoriano Huerta, who, with the
support of the U.S. government, briefly ascended to the presidency (Gilly
1994). In retaliation, Emiliano Zapata, who continued to control southern
Mexico, removed Huerta from office with the aid of generals Pancho Villa
and Venustiano Carranza, who controlled the north. In 1914 Carranza rose
to power and took over the presidency (Ibid., 197). The three men continued
to disagree on agrarian reform. Within a year, President Carranza learned
that Villa and Zapata were prepared to remove him from office. They were
opposed to his agrarian reform plans, which, like Madero's, called for the
courts to adjudicate the distribution of land. Unlike Madero, he held a more
conservative position vis-à-vis the property that predated Díaz's regime. He
believed that the hacienda deeds that had been issued before Díaz's administration should not be included in the agrarian claims. This angered Zapata
and Villa, who saw this plan as benefiting only the bourgeoisie. They also
opposed any court intervention and demanded the immediate distribution
of land through executive order and military enforcement. In the regions

they controlled Villa and Zapata had already implemented agrarian reform. Carranza had warned the generals to stop and decreed those land transactions null and void. He had attempted unsuccessfully to disarm and arrest Villa and Zapata.

The U.S. government preferred to see Carranza in power rather than Villa or Zapata since his plan of litigating land claims in the courts would allow some U.S. businessmen to keep their property or at a minimum obtain compensation for it. President Woodrow Wilson officially recognized Carranza's presidency, which gave his administration political stability. In the view of the United States it was also important to destroy Villa's mass appeal, as he had publicly denounced the United States as an imperialist nation and the primary cause of Mexico's problems (Coerver and Hall 1984). After Carranza secured the support of the U.S. government, his appeal deteriorated further, and the masses overwhelmingly backed Villa and Zapata. Carranza knew his presidency was in trouble and thought it necessary to appeal to the masses. The only means of changing public opinion was to prove he was not only against U.S. imperialism, but also in favor of agrarian reform. In 1917 Carranza approved the passage of Article 27 of the Mexican Constitution and began the legal process of redistributing land. Under the Constitution the federal government was empowered to confiscate and claim any property for the purpose of instituting agrarian reform. Accompanying this mandate was the nationalization of oil and mineral resources, which stipulated that only Mexican nationals and naturalized citizens could own property containing oil and mineral resources. The federal government also declared ownership over all future discoveries of oil and mineral resources in undeveloped lands (Meyer, Sherman, and Deeds 2007: 474). The governments of the United States and Europe saw these reforms as hostile and philosophically to be communist in principle. President Wilson declared Article 27 illegal and protested against the nationalization of the oil industry since American companies owned most oil fields. American businessmen also took exception to Carranza's move and asked Wilson to send armed troops into Mexico. Wilson immediately demanded restitution but refused to intervene militarily, as he had more pressing matters to deal with. The United States was on the brink of entering World War I, and fighting two wars at the same time would have been unwise. Carranza knew as much and worked to convince his allies that restitution was unnecessary.

Tensions between Mexico and the United States produced anti-Mexican sentiments in the United States. Mexico was becoming a hostile neighbor while at the same time doing nothing to stop the waves of refugees from entering the United States, especially into Texas. Since the start of the Mexi-

Table 5.3. Mexican Immigrants in Texas and the United States, 1900–1920

Date	U.S. Total	Texas No.	%
1900	103,393	71,062	(68.7)
1910	221,915	125,016	(56.3)
1920	486,418	251,827	(51.7)

Source: U.S. Census 1913a: 804; U.S. Census 1922a: 309.

can Revolution the size of the Mexican immigrant population in the United States had radically increased. By 1917 it was estimated that the Mexican population had more than doubled during the war years and had increased to over four hundred thousand (U.S. Census 1922a: 309). The close proximity of Texas and Mexico had led the majority of the war refugees to settle in Texas, and this became a national problem (Truett and Young 2004; table 5.3; fig. 5.2).

President Wilson may have been unable to send troops into Mexico, but he did implement policies to punish Mexico. For example, Wilson supported congressmen who no longer felt obliged to extend to Mexico the special immigration status it had enjoyed under the Porfirian dictatorship. Wilson signed the Immigration Act of February 5, 1917, to cut down on Mexican immigration by imposing an entry fee on heads of households and requiring immigrants to be literate (39 *U.S. Statutes at Large* [Part 1] 877).[5] Mexico would no longer be exempt from immigration policies imposed on other countries. These two provisions were designed to radically reduce legal immigration from Mexico. Mexicans, however, were not excluded from entry, as most Asians were at that time. Within six months of the passage of the act, farmers in California and Arizona protested and lobbied successfully for a temporary delay. They argued that if Mexicans were prohibited from entering legally the agricultural industry would experience a tremendous labor shortage, with disastrous results (Romo 1975). Congress agreed that sanctions against Mexico would have to be delayed until the end of World War I, as farmers needed to increase the food supply during the war years. By this time, Mexican immigrants had become an important source of labor in California and Arizona.

On April 16, 1917, President Wilson finally made the decision to enter World War I (Gilly 1994: 249). The U.S. declaration of war and the federal government's hostile stance toward Mexico initiated a series of events in Texas that were highly problematic for immigrants, in particular for the two largest immigrant groups, Mexicans and Germans. The national political atmosphere cast doubt on the desirability of these peoples and tarnished their allegiance to the United States. Mexicans were also seen as a nuisance and no longer pawns in trade relations with Mexico, and Germans were distrusted for being alien enemies. Over the previous twenty years in Texas people of German descent had successfully assimilated, and many of the anti-German stereotypes had been laid to rest, but the war resurrected negative sentiments. Germans were stereotyped as clannish, duplicitous, irresponsible citizens, promoters of vice, and fraudulent voters (Gould 1973). Their breweries were also blamed for causing an alcoholism problem in Texas. In essence, people of German and Mexican descent were seen as the enemy. Unfortunately, the emergence of these attitudes coincided with the rise of the woman suffrage movement in Texas and influenced how suf-

Figure 5.2. Charity House refugees. Runyon (Robert) Photograph Collection. Center for American History, UT-Austin (RUN 02467).

fragists perceived immigrants. Germans had money and influence to protect themselves, but Mexicans did not.

Woman Suffrage and the Anti-Alien Campaign

A month after the United States entered World War I the Seventh Annual Convention of the Texas Equal Suffrage Association was held on May 15–17, 1917, in Waco. Many prohibitionist males attended (Jane Y. McCallum Papers, box 32, file 5, "The 7th Convention Waco, 1917"). The Texas Equal Suffrage Association (the new name of the Texas Woman Suffrage Association) had forged a close alliance with prohibition organizations, as suffragists and prohibitionists recognized that they held mutual interests. Together they formed the Texas Women's Anti-Vice Committee, whose purpose was to make Texas a dry state. They then established the Texas Social Hygiene Association to coordinate activities to stamp out saloons, prostitution, and venereal disease.

At the convention a resolution on women's suffrage was formalized and plans were prepared on how to convince state legislators to support it. It was agreed upon that representatives who favored prohibition would be the suffragists' closest allies. During the convention strategies to obtain suffrage took on a very negative stance against immigrants. Texas suffragists, however, were only echoing the official platform taken by the National American Woman Suffrage Association (NAWSA), their league's national association. Given that the United States was in the throes of a violent war against Germany NAWSA made full propaganda use of the concept of the alien enemy. NAWSA advised all of its leagues to advance an anti-immigrant agenda in efforts to push forward women's suffrage. The slogan to be promoted was, How could an "alien enemy" vote, while loyal American women could not (McArthur and Smith 2003: 61).

At the convention the anti-alien campaign took on a local southwestern expression. The two largest immigrant populations in the state were vilified. Germans were characterized as alien enemies, whereas Mexicans were depicted as ignorant refugees unworthy of American citizenship (Cox 2005). Both populations were deemed to be a threat to women's suffrage and must be politically disenfranchised before Texans voted on an equal suffrage referendum. In the convention sessions, Germans were identified as the main obstacle to women's suffrage because they owned the brewery associations and they funded campaigns against equal suffrage. Germans were said to oppose suffrage because women would favor prohibition if given the vote

(*Waco Morning News,* May 17, 1917, in Jane Y. McCallum Papers, box 32, file 5, "The 7th Convention Waco, 1917"). Mexicans were tied to the German problem because they were stereotyped as drinkers and ignorant people who allowed Germans to pay their poll taxes (Gould 1973).

At the convention suffragists adopted several anti-immigrant political planks. They endorsed women's suffrage, of course, but voted in favor of stopping noncitizens from voting in Texas. They also favored requiring immigrants to prove they were loyal Americans before naturalizing and raising the U.S. residency requirement to ten years before allowing immigrants to apply for citizenship. The resolution on suffrage was entitled "Democratic Platform on Woman Suffrage: With Citizenship Clause." It proposed the following:

> We recommend that the legislature submit an amendment to the State constitution giving women the right of suffrage on the same terms as men. We favor the submission of an amendment to the federal Constitution to various legislatures giving the right of suffrage to women on the same terms as men, and that the legislature ratify the same when so submitted.
>
> We believe that America should be for Americans, and therefore recommend the submission to the people of an amendment to the constitution granting the right of suffrage to persons of foreign birth only when they shall have acquired full citizenship in this country, by compliance with all naturalization laws of the nation and the state, and shall have first resided in this country ten years (Jane Y. McCallum Papers, box 32, file 5, "The 7th Convention Waco, 1917").

After the convention the Texas Equal Suffrage Association grew to ninety-eight chapters, and its president, Minnie Fisher Cunningham, immediately launched a legislative campaign to enfranchise women and end noncitizen voting in Texas. The campaign was called "All American Democracy." It openly advocated that voting should be a privilege enjoyed only by American citizens. Cunningham and the Texas suffragist chapters also became involved in the impeachment campaign against Gov. James Ferguson, who at the time was under investigation for fraud (Taylor 1987: 30). Ferguson was a longtime opponent of women's suffrage and of prohibition, and as long as he remained in office the two voting propositions had little chance of succeeding. If Ferguson were removed, Lieut. Gov. William Hobby would become the acting governor. Unlike Ferguson, Hobby was an advocate of women's suffrage. After a long and bitter investigation of Ferguson's finances, women's suffrage appeared to be closer to becoming a political reality when, on September 24, 1917, Ferguson resigned to avoid impeachment. Hobby was named acting governor, and white suffragists suddenly found that they had a powerful friend in state government (Gould 1973: 211).

White Primaries and the Exclusion of Mexican Immigrant Women

For the woman suffrage movement it was important that Hobby remain in office. The Texas Equal Suffrage Association therefore became actively involved in his reelection campaign and established hundreds of Hobby Women's Clubs. Cunningham expected him to easily win the Democratic nomination in the primary election. However, Governor Ferguson unexpectedly announced a bid for reelection, and it seemed likely he would receive the Democratic nomination, as he had been a very popular governor, firmly opposed to prohibition, and a friend of the common person. His allies affectionately called him Farmer Jim.

For Hobby to win the nomination it became necessary to immediately give white women the right to vote in the upcoming primary election. A resolution to revise the Texas Constitution to give women full suffrage in all elections would have to wait because the implementation of such an article would involve a long process and require legislative and voter approval. On the other hand, a short-term solution was to give women the right to vote in primary elections, as this could be mandated legislatively, without obtaining voter approval. In March 1918 Governor Hobby called a special session of the legislature and asked that suffrage be given to women in primary elections (Taylor 1987: 38). In the meantime, Cunningham initiated a lobbying campaign among legislators sympathetic to prohibition, promising them that if women were given the right to vote they would vote in favor of prohibition and support their reelection (McArthur and Smith 2003: 61).

On March 12, 1918, Rep. C. B. Metcalfe of San Angelo introduced House Resolution (H.R.) 105 asking members to extend suffrage to women at primary elections. He was a strong supporter of Hobby and a prohibition activist. In the legislative deliberations that ensued members of the House and Senate were overwhelmingly in favor of extending suffrage to white women, but most were reluctant to approve a bill that gave immigrant women voting rights (*House Journal, Texas, 35th Legislature, Fourth Called Session, 1918*, pp. 274, 330). They were not concerned about black women since current election codes prohibited most African Americans from attending the primaries. In the House the debate echoed the anti-immigrant spirit of the Waco suffrage resolution. Legislators openly tried to exclude alien women. As a means of denying immigrant women the vote Representative Butler from Bell County introduced concurrent H.R. 107 proposing that only U.S. citizens be allowed to vote in primary elections and participate in primary conventions.

H.R. 107 met strong opposition since it would affect male as well as female immigrants (Ibid., 333, 378). Legislators from South Texas and counties with large German populations opposed the amendment. Because H.R. 107 threatened male voters, Representative Canales from South Texas proposed that the bill specifically name only immigrant women. His amendment died. After three days of deliberations those who favored eliminating immigrants in general from the primaries won. Not surprisingly, H.R. 107 passed the same day legislators adopted H.R. 105 and supported giving women voting rights in primary elections.

When the resolutions reached the Senate on March 19, senators representing counties with large Mexican and German populations voted against H.R. 107 but were unable to block passage (*Journal of the Senate of Texas, 35th Legislature, Fourth Called Session, 1918,* p. 402). Furthermore, senators who did not support Hobby and were aware that H.R. 105 was designed to give him the votes he needed to win the primary nomination responded by asking that a poll tax amendment be added. This was an unexpected development and an effective way to prevent women from voting since the authors of the legislation knew that they could stop debate if legislators believed that continuing with the election reforms would culminate in forcing families to pay two poll taxes. After three days of heated debate the Hobby supporters were able to convince enough senators to compromise on a temporary solution. Women would not be given a permanent exemption from paying poll taxes. Poll taxes would be debated later. For now, eligible women would be given a onetime waiver of the poll tax fee (Ibid., 317). To receive the waiver, they would have to apply and receive a certificate. To obtain the certificate, however, women would need to be able to read and write, as they had to fill out the application without any assistance, including translation aid. In front of the election registrar, women were to write the name of their county and post office, identify their precinct, include a local address, and note the number of years at their current address. They also needed to write down their color, race, and occupation. The exemption certificate was an obvious informal English literacy test and a strategic compromise between prosuffragists, Hobby supporters, prohibitionists, and anti-immigrant senators.

The House accepted the Senate amendment, and the bills were sent to

Governor Hobby for his signature. On March 26, 1918, the governor approved the suffrage bill and a few days later approved the exclusion of immigrants from the primaries (House Bill no. 105, no. 107 signed by Governor Hobby, no. 2-13/63, Lorenzo de Zavala State Archives and Library). Women had finally become important players in gubernatorial elections. Ironically, H.R. 107 effectively denied immigrant women the electoral rights they had just gained in H.R. 105. The reforms enfranchised many women but also disqualified more groups of people from participating in primary elections. Many Mexican and German immigrants joined African Americans in being totally excluded from the primary process. Partial suffrage mainly enfranchised white women since African Americans were excluded by the Terrell election laws (see chapter 4).

Although Mexican American women born in the United States and Mexican women married to U.S. citizens were technically eligible to vote, their chances of voting were limited by the registration certificate. Cunningham, the president of the Texas Equal Suffrage Association, confided to Carrie Chapman Catt, president of NAWSA, that the matter of discouraging the ignorant foreign vote along the border had been handled by the legislature. She personally did not think that was fair, but she chose not to protest. The legislature expected that along the border the registration process would discourage women of Mexican descent from voting. The certificate had been designed to be a de facto English literacy test aimed at stopping them from voting (McArthur and Smith 2003: 79). On March 25, 1918, one day before the governor signed H.R. 105, Cunningham wrote to Chapman: "The bill carries a registration restriction that I am not wholly pleased with (copy in the newspaper clipping attached) but it is aimed at the ignorant foreign vote on the border and the situation is so acute that I could not ask our friends to fight for its defeat, the time was so short too" (Minnie Fisher Cunningham Collection, Houston Metropolitan Research Center, Houston Public Library, in Taylor 1987: 167–168). In the same letter Cunningham also comments on pending legislation and rejoices that resolutions to further disenfranchise immigrant voters will be considered: "A statutory prohibition law, for the entire state, and certain zone laws for the elimination of vice and bootlegging with special reference to the camp towns, a literacy test for all voters in the primary election and a law prohibiting any but American citizens taking part in the elections (primary). These are some of the most important but by no means all. I will try to get the complete list to you" (Ibid.). On July 27, 1918, women voted in the primary gubernatorial election (Winegarten and McArthur 1987: 172). The election went as expected. With the female vote swelling the electorate, Hobby received 461,479 votes to Ferguson's 217,012 (Gould 1973: 245). Having a powerful friend in state office now, the suffragists felt confident they would soon gain full suffrage.

The Election of 1919: Enfranchise Women and Disenfranchise Immigrants

After women were given the right to vote in the primaries white suffragists were divided on the role women of color should play within the Texas Equal Suffrage Association. The association agreed that immigrant women should not be allowed to vote, as this was part of their larger anti-immigrant voting campaign. Suffragists, however, disagreed on whether African American and Mexican American women should be allowed or encouraged to vote.

In San Antonio, Rena Maverick Green, the chair of the San Antonio chapter, believed that Mexican American women should be allowed to vote and in the gubernatorial race of 1918 initiated a campaign to register them (Winegarten and McArthur 1987: 169). She translated campaign literature into Spanish to educate women on electoral issues. Maverick Green also believed that Mexican immigrant women should be assimilated and eventually converted into voters. Through her participation in the Texas Federation of Women's Clubs she joined other suffragists to launch a campaign called "Stranger Within the Gates." It was part of the clubs' charitable attempt to Americanize Mexican immigrant women (Ayala 2005).

The welcoming activities of the San Antonio chapter were rare. The leadership of the Texas Equal Suffrage Association neither wanted Mexican American women to vote nor favored accepting members of Mexican descent (see correspondence, in re Jane Y. McCallum Papers, boxes 5, 6, 33).[6] Throughout the association's existence not a single woman with a Spanish surname was enrolled as the chair of a county chapter or served as an officer (Jane Y. McCallum Papers, box 7, file 2, "Instructions for Precinct Petitions and Related Material, n.d."). It is uncertain if the exclusion was for racial reasons or motivated solely by political considerations. That is, it was pragmatic for suffragists to make it difficult for Mexican American women to vote because it was public knowledge that Mexican women's clubs had a history of advocating for the rights of immigrants, and the agenda of the suffragists was directly in opposition to the goals of many Mexican American women.

One of the earliest Mexican women's clubs, La Liga Femenil Mexicanista (Mexican women's league), was established by women of Mexican descent in Laredo in 1911 ("Primary Suffrage," Texas State Library and Archives Commission; Garcia 1996: 194). The club's focus was not political but social and charitable: it helped poor children in South Texas with their education and provided food and clothing for the needy (Limón 1974). A large sector served by the club were war refugees from Mexico. Most other women's clubs of Mexican origin were branches of mutual aid organizations or were affiliated with churches. By 1920 many of the church clubs had evolved into chapters of Cruz Azul Mexicana (Ayala 2005: 97).[7] Within a year of the establishment of the first chapter in San Antonio the organization had expanded to fourteen chapters in South Texas as well as in the cities of Asherton, Castroville, Charlotte, Mackay, Lulling, Phelan, and Malakoff. As the membership of the organization grew and attitudes toward immigrants worsened, the women turned from charitable activities to advocacy for the rights of immigrants.

Because it was public knowledge that the Mexican women's clubs were concerned with the plight of the immigrant sector, white suffragists thought it counterproductive to include them within the suffrage movement, even if the women were born in the United States. In 1919, Edward Idar, the editor of *Evolución*, a newspaper in Laredo, commented on the suffrage campaign in Texas. He focused on the suffragists' "American Democracy" campaign, which publicly proposed ending immigrant voting in Texas. Idar supported women's suffrage in principle, but he was highly critical of their anti-immigrant campaign. He praised suffragists for sponsoring history and English Americanization classes, as he agreed that education benefited Mexican communities, but he disagreed with the English-only campaign currently sponsored by the Texas suffrage chapters and promoted by their national organization (*Evolución*, May 8, 1919, p. 3). During the congressional hearings of May 1919 Idar warned his readers that NAWSA was lobbying Congress to pass a bill requiring that English be the only language spoken in public and in the schools. Idar was also critical of the voting legislation the suffragists were promoting in Texas. He believed that many suffragists were not anti-Mexican and that they were merely complying with the agreements they had made with the Texas Prohibition Party. Idar reported that suffragists supported ending immigrant voting because they had struck a deal with the Prohibition Party. Unfortunately for Mexicans, Idar added, it was only a matter of time before the suffragist-prohibition coalition gained enough power to revise the Texas Constitution (*Evolución*, March 16, 1919, p. 3). According to Idar, within the Texas legislature only Representative Canales openly opposed the constitutional revision, as the rest of the Mexicans' political allies had abandoned them for fear that suffragists would vote against them in the primaries (*Evolución*, March 18, 1919, p. 3). Idar proposed that once white women obtained the right to vote in primary elections they had also gained the power to pressure legislators to vote their way. Idar's views would prove to be prophetic, as he was correct that a deal had been struck.

But to examine further the role racial politics played in the woman suffrage movement one might ask, how did suffragists interact with African American women? Leaders of the suffrage movement racialized the membership of their organization and developed networks to ensure that only white women participated in and shaped the course of women's voting rights.

Letters written by the officers of the Texas Equal Suffrage Association demonstrate that owing to their racist beliefs African Americans were excluded from the association. Again, however, not all suffragists shared the same beliefs. For example, the chapter from El Paso deviated from the norm and supported African American membership. In 1918 several members of the El Paso Equal Franchise League suggested to E. Sampson, an African American, that her club should apply for membership in the Texas Equal Suffrage Association as well as in NAWSA. When Sampson applied for state membership, however, she failed to inform headquarters that her club was composed of African Americans (Letter from Mrs. Critchett to Mrs. White, July 8, 1918, in Jane Y. McCallum Papers, box 5, file 10, "TESA/Edith League to various, n.d., 1919"). Headquarters encouraged her to pursue state and national membership. Later, when the Texas association officers discovered that Sampson was black they tried to stop her from completing the applications. Edith Hinkle League, the secretary of the Texas Equal Suffrage Association, was given the task of politely discouraging Sampson. In a letter Belle Critchett wrote to League she discusses the confusion. Apparently they were waiting for official orders from national headquarters to formally ask Sampson to withdraw her applications. Critchett bemoaned the ordeal and was angry with Sampson and the El Paso League for having placed her in an embarrassing position:

El Paso, Texas
July 1, 1918

Mrs. Edith Hinkle League,
Headquarters Secretary,
Galveston, Texas

My dear Mrs. League,
Your letter of July 1st is at hand. The note from Ruth White, Congressional Sec'y has nothing to do with our recent unpleasant experience in the League.

It is not a surprise to me for I knew that Mrs. E. Sampson who is a colored woman, President of the Colored Woman's Club has intended to make application as an auxiliary of the National Branch. Twice several members of our League here have been guests of the Colored Women's Club where they have given programs and we have assisted.

One of our members suggested the idea of writing with the National Branch, hence this note. They are not affiliated with our League here. I find one has to go slowly here with movements among the colored people. It seems that Mrs. Sampson did not state in her application that she was colored. She is a well-educated woman and is desirous of recognition from the white people.—I was asked a few weeks ago by our Democratic Executive chairman to suggest names of women for clerks at the coming election. As he wanted a large number I suggested three or four colored women to serve in their own precincts. I had asked Mrs. Sampson to furnish a few names but the chairman was indignant so I had to tell her we couldn't use the names this time.

I felt it was not best nor advisable at this time, our first election to rouse any trouble about the "colored question." I know Mrs. Sampson was disappointed but I told her I was not authorized to select the clerks, only to suggest some names. This has nothing to do with the vote, however. The application was made quite a while ago. I don't know what the ruling of the National Association is with reference to colored members.

I imagine they are admitted. We want to help the colored people but just now it is rather a hard question. Registration is going on in a satisfactory manner. I find I'm out of note-paper but I'll send this rather than to keep you waiting. With best wishes to you, to Mrs. Cunningham and to all workers I am

Sincerely yours,
Belle C. Critchett
(Ibid.)

On July, 17, 1918, Catt personally took charge of the embarrassing situation and responded to League, writing that NAWSA did not prohibit African American women from joining. According to the bylaws of the national association, the officers of each state league could determine whether African Americans might join (Ibid.). County chapters were, in turn, obliged to follow state policy and thus were not free to determine local membership. Catt concluded that the Texas association was free to adopt whatever policy it liked, but she advised against admission of blacks since it was not condoned in southern states. If the Texas clubs allowed African American women to join, suffragists would lose credibility for failing to maintain the color line.

Only in some northern states, she said, were a few educated African American women allowed to join when it was clear that they were nearly white. She advised League to tell Sampson to stop embarrassing the association and help the suffrage cause by removing her application:

July 17, 1918

My dear Mrs. League:—

Miss White has forwarded to me the copy of the letter from Mrs. Sampson of El Paso asking membership in the National American Woman Suffrage Association. She tells me that she referred the matter back to Mrs. Cunningham and that you have now asked the question as to what is the policy of the National Association.

In reply I will say that the question of auxiliaryship within the state is one for the state itself to decide. I presume that no colored women's league are members in southern states, although I do not know positively that this is true. There are a great many clubs in different northern states and they have been members for many years. I think in some northern states, individual colored women are direct members. Of course these women in the North are women with a good deal of white blood and are educated women, otherwise they would not be asking auxiliaryship.

Of late, however, there is a movement among the colored women and men everywhere to insist upon recognition and to get into all kinds of places that seem to have been closed to them before. This woman may desire to enter because she wishes to help the cause and she may merely be desirous of the recognition of her race. I am sure if I were a colored woman, I would do the same thing they are doing. The question has not been publicly fought out in our association, for the reason that the memberships come through the state and the states have not found it difficult to settle their own problems along this line. The constitution was amended last year, so that such a club as Mrs. Sampson's could not come into the National Association directly.

In some southern states it would be an impossibility to have a colored league without gravely upsetting the work and ruining the influences of the suffrage association. Whether this is true in Texas or not, I do not know, but I suggest that if you find it is so, you write Mrs. Sampson and tell her that you will be able to get the vote for women more easily if they do not embarrass you by asking for membership and that you are getting it for colored women as well as for white women and appeal to her interest in the matter to subside.

I return the letter which was forwarded to me with the correspondence and I will ask you to give some kind of an answer to Mrs. Sampson telling her that the matter has been turned over to you by the National Association.

Cordially yours,

Carrie Chapman Catt

President

(Ibid.)

Needless to say, neither Sampson's club nor any other African American women's club in Texas was awarded membership in the state or national organization (McArthur and Smith 2003: 62). Cunningham dealt with Sampson by simply ignoring her application and failing to present it for a vote.

Even though African American women's clubs were not allowed to affiliate with the Texas Equal Suffrage Association and were prohibited from joining the Texas Federation of Women's Clubs, African American women's clubs flourished (Winegarten 1996: 292). During the early 1900s they established hundreds of clubs in Texas, the great majority of which elected schoolteachers as their presidents (Winegarten 1995). The main objective of the clubs was to help African American communities by establishing community centers, girls' homes, homes for the elderly, nurseries, and other charitable activities. Many of the clubs were also concerned with suffrage and with organizing the black vote. African American women in Texas also established the Texas Association of Colored Women's Clubs and affiliated with the National Association of Colored Women's Clubs.

The Campaign for Full Suffrage

In January 1919, a few months after Hobby was elected, he began lobbying the legislature to extend full suffrage to women (*Journal of the House of Representatives, 36th Legislature, Regular Session, 1919*, p. 54). To gain legislative support for women's suffrage he appealed to those legislators who for years had tried to end alien voting in Texas (Gould 1973: 254; Winegarten and McArthur 1987: 183). Hobby informed the legislators that he planned to introduce an equal suffrage bill that also limited voting to citizens. In this way Hobby expected to gain the support of legislators who otherwise would not favor equal suffrage.

Some suffragists opposed the provision in the belief that immigrants and their allies would defeat women's suffrage. Jane Y. McCallum, who was in charge of legislative matters at the Texas Equal Suffrage Association, convinced Cunningham to support the governor. McCallum believed Hobby's move was a daring one but was bound to stimulate support for equal suffrage. Cunningham remained ambivalent, but they proceeded to work together nonetheless to convince the officers and the rank and file that support for their cause was created at the national level by broad campaigns against immigrants. Moreover, NAWSA encouraged chapters to utilize the anti-alien ambiance generated by the war to get out the vote. The Allies had recently won the war (November 11, 1918), and the American nation found itself eager and willing to champion causes to protect the homeland from foreigners. NAWSA had advised Texas headquarters to act now. Apparently in Kansas, Nebraska, and South Dakota similar legislative provisions had recently terminated immigrant voting and bolstered women's suffrage (Letter January 3, 1919, from Nettie R. Shuler of the National Headquarters, NAWSA, to Mrs. Nonie B. Mahoney, Texas Director and Mrs. A. N. Jane Y. McCallum, Auditor of the Texas Equal Rights Association, in Jane Y. McCallum Papers, box 6, file 2, "Correspondence 1919"). At this time only Arkansas, Indiana, Missouri, and Texas allowed immigrants who were not citizens to vote (Keyssar 2000: table A 12). It was also important for the Texas chapters to proceed with the voting legislation, as this would enhance support for NAWSA's national campaign (McArthur and Smith 2003: 79). In essence, national headquarters supported Hobby's plan.

Cunningham and McCallum encouraged suffragists to back the legislation because Hobby was planning to introduce a concurrent bill to make Texas a dry state (Gould 1973: 254). A prohibition bill would certainly help suffragists gain more votes since in Texas and throughout the United States sentiments had changed in favor of banning the production and sale of alcohol.

The Texas legislature began its deliberations on women's suffrage on January 15, 1919, when Hobby sent a message asking the representatives to begin debate (*Journal of the House of Representatives, 36th Legislature, Regular Session, 1919*, p. 54). Hobby favored equal suffrage because, as he argued, during the war women helped the troops in many ways, and this was sufficient evidence that they had the capability to vote. Hobby then took the opportunity to juxtapose the injustice of Texas's voting laws, asserting that loyal American women were not allowed to vote at the same time that immigrants, who had not proven their loyalty to America, held that right. Hobby wrote,

The useful part performed by women in all war activities and in helping so signally to speed the victory furnish additional reason for hastening the day of their equality as citizens. The bestowal of such equality will be a fitting reward for duty well performed and at the same time involves a broader Americanism. The amendment I have suggested not only extends the ballot to women who are equal with men with respect to Americanism, but also limits the ballot to others who are not equal with respect to Americanism. (Ibid., 56)

Several joint resolutions were introduced. Senate Joint Resolution 2, introduced by A. C. Buchanan of Bell County (District 27) and subsequently defeated, proposed extending women the suffrage but did not remove the right from immigrants. (Ibid., 73, 98). One month later, on February 15, House Joint Resolution 3, which, following Hobby's original version, proposed giving women the suffrage and ending alien voting, passed in the House and Senate and was sent to the governor for his signature (Ibid., 141). Although no legislators in the House had voted against the resolution, most legislators representing South Texas and counties with large German counties were absent from the vote.[8] In the Senate no opposing votes were recorded. A prohibition amendment also cleared the legislature and was signed by the governor (Ibid., 98). Both amendments were to be presented to the voters in a special election to consider suffrage and prohibition (*Senate Journal, Texas, 36th Legislature, Regular Session, 1919*, p. 245).

Once the legislature approved the suffrage amendment white suffragists launched an energetic campaign coordinated by Cunningham and with McCallum as the secretary of the press. Cunningham doubted they could win since immigrants were allowed to vote while women were not because the legislature had authorized women to vote only in primary elections, not in special or general elections. The campaign received financial support and political guidance from national headquarters and replicated strategies used in other states with similar referendums (McArthur and Smith 2003). As part of their political activities suffragists organized women at the county level to initiate petition drives in support of women's suffrage. They also lobbied politicians, published a weekly suffrage paper, held public meetings, and passed out hundreds of thousands of pamphlets. McCallum asked newspaper editors across the state to publish articles educating the public that a vote to disenfranchise aliens was a vote in favor of giving loyal American women the right to vote. She also urged news editors to publish advertisements to discourage immigrants from voting. In a general letter sent to editors on March 13, 1919, McCallum wrote,

My Dear Sir:

A visit to Equal Suffrage Headquarters would indicate to you that the State organizing is taking nothing for granted. . . . This we are also asking our friends to do, especially our newspaper friends; because we thoroughly realize and agree with all that has ever been said or written concerning the "Power of the Press." . . .

    To you especially we appeal to use all the power of your paper to see that the foreign and near-foreign men in Texas, most of whom were exempted from military service, do not, in the absence of our soldier boys, vote themselves into power, and at the same time disenfranchise the mothers, wives, sisters, and sweethearts who have stood behind these boys unreservedly, unflinchingly and without counting the cost. . . . Realizing that our only need now is to fully arouse Texas men to the actual situation, and confidently counting on your hearty co-operation, I am,

    Cordially Mrs. A. N. Jane Y. McCallum,
    Sec. press & Publicity Department
(Jane Y. McCallum Papers, box 6, file 2, "Correspondence 1919")

McCallum also sent letters to supporters in Medina and Uvalde to get out the vote, as in these counties the Mexican voting block could be defeated. Suffragists were told to ask voters to sign a petition and pledge that America should only be for citizens (Jane Y. McCallum Papers, box 6, file 12, "Correspondence April 10, 1919"). In this way voters would learn what the upcoming constitutional proposition was about.

On the day of the election, May 24, 1919, the Texas Equal Suffrage Association had hundreds of suffragists armed with leaflets and instructions on how to challenge alien voters watching the polls (Jane Y. McCallum Papers, box 33, file 8, "Voting"). Outside of the polls suffragists were to greet voters with a smile and give them a leaflet stressing that the war was over, but aliens still posed a problem. The leaflet was titled "The Amendment to enfranchise American Women and disenfranchise alien enemies." They were also instructed to keep an eye on the polls and challenge voters who needed translation assistance to cast their ballot. Mexicans were the target population. McCallum reminded suffragists that Governor Hobby had recently signed an emergency law prohibiting any person from giving voters assistance in any language other than English.[9]

Although Texas suffragists followed the national association's campaign strategies, they were defeated by over twenty-five thousand votes; the prohibition amendment succeeded (Winegarten and McArthur 1987: 183). NAWSA claimed that the referendum had failed because suffragists had miscalculated the amount of resentment citizens harbored against immigrants. In Texas, unlike the other states where immigrants had lost the vote, there was no comparable level of resentment. Cunningham partially agreed but believed they lost because their male allies failed to mobilize their constituencies and did not deliver the vote as promised. Their campaign was also crucially short of time and funds.

Within two weeks of the campaign suffragists held a mass meeting in Bexar County to discuss their defeat and to admonish those who had supported the alien voter. The city of San Antonio was selected as the location of the rally since Bexar County had played a strategic role in defeating the referendum. Bexar had the largest number of voters in Texas, and the vote there overwhelmingly went against revising the state's suffrage laws. At the rally women gave speeches casting serious doubts on the patriotism of aliens, while at the same time characterizing the female relatives of the boys who went to war as true loyal Americans. Aliens were unfairly labeled draft evaders. Furthermore, in their anger the suffragists went to the extreme of insinuating that during war alien males were either cowards or enemy sympathizers. They admonished the pro-immigrant sympathizers of Bexar County and accused them of supporting undesirable aliens. At the rally the women adopted several resolutions to censure all Texans who supported immigrant voting. In a "Resolution Passed at Mass Meeting of Women of Bexar County, June 5, 1919," they proclaimed,

> Whereas, the present constitution grants the right to vote to "every male person of foreign birth*** [asterisks in original] who at any election shall have declared his intention to become a citizen of the United States in accordance with the Federal Naturalization Laws and shall have resided in this State for one year"; which class includes 16,482 aliens in the United States between the age of twenty-one and thirty-six who escaped military service under the recent draft law. . . . Whereas the voters of Bexar County, by a large majority, did vote to retain the undesirable class of alien voters and draft evaders as electors in preference to granting this franchise to the patriotic women of Bexar County, who sacrificed their sons and loved ones on land and sea in defense of our nation, thereby reflecting upon the patriotism of the men in Bexar County and putting us in an unfortunate light before our Nation and the people of the world . . .
> THEREFORE BE IT RESOLVED:
> (1) That we here, in mass meeting assembled, declare that we deeply deplore and are humiliated by the votes cast in Bexar County. (Jane Y. McCallum Papers, box 33, file 7, "Resolutions Women of Bexar County, 1919")

Overall, the suffrage resolution failed in most counties and was overwhelmingly defeated in counties with voters of German descent. For example, in the German-majority counties of Comal, Fayette, and Austin it was defeated, respectively, by 1,089 to 116, 3,242 to 535, and 1,840 to 361 (Winegarten and McArthur 1987: 189–192). In South Texas the resolution won in almost every county, but it was a close election, nearly splitting the vote in half. Only in Medina, Starr, Jim Wells, and Live Oak was it defeated. Dallas was the only large city where the resolution did well. On May 31, 1919, Idar wrote an article on the election results in which he attributed the success of the suffrage amendment in South Texas to changing ethnic patterns. Apparently the new wave of Anglo-American settlers had grown, and they now constituted a large percentage of the total population. The newcomers differed politically from the Anglo landed elite and did not share the old-timers' views (*Evolución*, May 31, 1919, p. 1) (see chapter 4). The old politics, he stated, no longer worked. The landed elite could not deliver on their promises anymore, and it was necessary for the younger generation of Mexican voters to develop new political strategies, possibly following the example of the ethnic voters in New York and Chicago. In a later article, Idar reflected on the effects of the time-limit provision of the naturalization law of 1906. According to Idar, in the recent election many Mexicans found that they were no longer eligible to vote (*Evolución*, June 6, 1919, p. 4). When they appeared at the polls they were told their papers were invalid. Many immediately rushed to the courthouse and filed new papers, but a great number were unable to apply, as they were told the new laws required that they speak English.

Cunningham was so incensed by the results of the election that she filed charges of electoral fraud, claiming that in counties where brewery and distilling industries were located the election judges mismanaged the ballot boxes. She also blamed the German and Russian communities for losing the election (McArthur and Smith 2003: 82). McCallum, too, was very angry, but she blamed the German, Mexican, and black vote for having united and defeated the referendum (Letter to Mrs. Mabel Lee Elbridge and others from Jane Y. McCallum, June 17, 1919, in Jane Y. McCallum Papers, box 5, file 12, "Correspondence McCallum re TESA 1919"). She charged that former governor Ferguson and Senator Bailey of South Texas had traveled throughout Texas and organized the vote against the resolution (Gould 1973). Many supporters of Cunningham and McCallum asked them to calm down and withdraw the election challenge, maintaining that their efforts were futile and that they needed to concentrate on the national campaign to ratify the Nineteenth Amendment to the U.S. Constitution. The amendment, if passed by Congress and ratified by the states, would prohibit states and the federal government from denying eligible voters the right to vote on account of sex. Ratification of the Nineteenth Amendment would obviate the hostile attitude toward equal suffrage in Texas.

The friends of Cunningham and McCallum were correct. A month after the election in Texas, on June 13, 1919, the Nineteenth Amendment received congressional approval and was presented to the states for ratification. Although his critics opposed the move on the grounds that the voters had spoken, Governor Hobby convened an emergency session of the legislature to introduce the legislation and consider ratification. Since the resolution had no anti-alien provisions it easily passed both houses, and on June 28, 1919, the House and Senate in Texas ratified the Nineteenth Amendment, becoming the ninth state to do so (McArthur and Smith 2003: 84). It was now only a matter of time before three-fourths of the states ratified passage.

The ratification of the Nineteenth Amendment occurred during the same years that the Mexican Revolution neared its end. By April 1919, most people in Mexico were tired of fighting and wanted peace, the main leaders of the Revolution had ceased fighting, and their constituencies had either put down their arms or fragmented into ineffective civilian militias. Scholars disagree on exactly which month the Revolution ended, some claiming it was when Zapata was assassinated on April 10, 1919, others putting it a few months later when Pancho Villa retired, and still others when Carranza was assassinated on May 21, 1920 (Miller 1985: 308). Whatever date one uses to mark the end of the Revolution, it is clear that after Carranza's death a new era in U.S.-Mexico relations began when Alvaro Obregón became the constitutionally elected president on December 2, 1920. Obregon's presidency coincided with the ratification of the Nineteenth Amendment: by August 26, 1920, three-fourths of the states had ratified the amendment, and it was adopted as part of the U.S. Constitution (Winegarten and McArthur 1987: 196).

These two events marked a turning point for Mexican immigrants in Texas. On the one hand, women gained the right to vote and the power to determine whether aliens should continue voting in Texas. On the other hand, the U.S. government took a forceful position against Mexico and pressured President Obregón to return the property that had been expropriated from American investors. To force Mexico into compliance the U.S. government threatened to deport Mexican immigrants. Obregon was warned that anyone who had entered the United States without officially registering at a port of entry, as well as Mexican people who had become

indigent or were unemployed, could be deported. Only those who had naturalized would not be affected. The occurrence of these two events in the
early 1920s thus had the effect of making life more difficult for Mexican
immigrants. Mexicans who were not U.S. citizens were about to lose the
right to vote, and many of them also faced deportation to a country where
they had nothing to return to. They had no land and not even the promise of
a land grant because under Carranza's administration, which had mandated
that agrarian reform proceed through the courts, the redistribution process
had stalled, and less than 5 percent of the land taken by Díaz had been returned to the people (Gilly 1994: 260).

Poll Taxes, Mexican Immigrant Women, and the End of Alien Voting in Texas

On July 23, 1921, a referendum to end alien voting in Texas was held, and
Mexicans who were not U.S. citizens lost the right to vote (*General Laws of
Texas, 37th Legislature, Regular Session 1921*, p. 276). This process was preceded by a series of hostile events that began with the legislature's attempt
to impose a poll tax on immigrant women, was followed by deportation
raids, and culminated in national reforms over Mexican immigration.

Within weeks of the passage of the Nineteenth Amendment suffragists
began to lobby for the state government to waive the voting poll tax for
women. Most legislators responded positively to their proposal, but many
disapproved of giving alien women the same privilege. Those legislators
who for years had tried to disenfranchise immigrants now faced a larger
problem since women had expanded the number of immigrant voters. The
Nineteenth Amendment had made at least 33,749 foreign-born women eligible to vote in Texas (U.S. Census 1922b: 816; U.S. Census 1922c: 986),[10]
either because they were married to a U.S. citizen (32,800) or because they
had filed papers of naturalization on their own (Ibid., 949). An additional
10,000 foreign-born women could now vote because their husbands had
filed their papers to naturalize (U.S. Census 1922c: 986). In the case of
the community of Mexican origin, according to the U.S. Census, 6,045
Mexican immigrant women twenty-one years of age and older qualified,
either by being married to a U.S. citizen or by naturalizing on their own
(the total number of Mexican immigrant women twenty-one and over
was 71,223) (U.S. Census 1922b: 816). Their enfranchisement expanded
the number of Mexican immigrant voters in Texas since at that time few
Mexican immigrant males were eligible to vote. In 1920 only 3.4 percent

of foreign-born Mexican males were naturalized and eligible to vote (N = 3,104 out of 91,483).[11] In the previous ten years the number of eligible male voters had fallen radically. In 1910, 7,219 Mexican males reported they were naturalized and 1,928 that they had filed naturalization declarations (first papers) (U.S. Census 1913d: 1072, 807). The decline in voting eligibility was closely interrelated with the federal reforms of 1906.

The enfranchisement of immigrant women became a political nuisance for many legislators because, as I noted above, they enlarged the eligible pool of foreign voters. The representatives who opposed aliens' suffrage had to find a way to block their votes. In September 1920, when Governor Hobby officially supported the suffragists' proposal to exempt women from paying a poll tax, many legislators objected to the governor's call because he did not offer a plan to disenfranchise alien women. The governor merely stated that many spouses could not afford to pay two fees and that it was necessary to waive the poll tax for women.

Ten days after Hobby asked the attorney general's office to study the constitutional merits of his proposal, an unfavorable report was returned. The plan was found to be unconstitutional since it discriminated against male voters (Letter from E. F. Smith, Assistant Attorney General to Governor W. P. Hobby, in *Senate Journal, Texas, 36th Legislature, Fourth Called Session, 1920*, pp. 7–13). The attorney general's office reported that the only legal method of waiving the fee for women was to give all other voters the same opportunity; in other words, poll taxes in Texas would have to be eliminated. Such a resolution would never pass because legislators would never overturn Terrell's poll tax law and allow poor people and blacks to vote again in great numbers.

Governor Hobby disregarded the recommendation and proceeded to ask the legislature to find a legal way to exempt women from paying a poll tax (Ibid., 4–6). On September 22, 1920, the Senate began debate. Various resolutions were presented, but only one survived. Sen. W. L. Dean of Walker County (District 15) introduced Senate Joint Resolution (S.J.R.) 1, a very clever resolution that would waive the fee only for white women who were U.S. citizens. He proposed that only the class of persons who had received a poll tax exemption in the primary election of 1919 would not be required to pay a fee. This meant that immigrant women, since they did not qualify to vote in a primary election, would have to pay a poll tax and so would the Mexican American women who had been disqualified because they were not literate in English. The resolution also disqualified African American women since they had not been exempted from a poll tax because most blacks were prohibited from voting in primaries. The resolution read as follows:

All said articles relating to the levy and collection of a poll tax fixing the qualifications of voters to be eliminated from provisions of all the said Articles the word "male" as to levy and collect from all persons, both male and female, poll taxes, and fixing the qualifications of voters so as to include all persons, both male and female; and providing for the issuance of exemption certificates to persons not subject to the payment of poll tax on January 1st, 1919. (Ibid., 4)

On September 23, 1920, when the resolution was sent to the Senate's jurisprudence committee the legislation was partially amended to clarify its language to ensure that only those who were U.S. citizens and previously qualified for the exemption would not pay a poll tax. Section 5 of the resolution read as follows:

All persons who are citizens of this state who possess the qualifications of a voter under the Constitution and laws of this State and of the United States, and who were not subject to the payment of a poll tax on the 1st day of January, 1919, are hereby authorized to participate in all elections, general and special, held throughout the State of Texas prior to February 1st, 1921, by obtaining from the Tax Collector of the County of which they are residents exemption certificates as hereinafter provided. (Jane Y. McCallum Papers, box 33, file 10, "Poll Tax Campaign," copy of committee report, Senate Chamber, September 23, 1920)

When S.J.R. 1 reached the House it was overwhelmingly rejected (*House Journal, Texas, 36th Legislature, Fourth Called Session, 1920*, p. 120). By then the resolution had also lost support in the Senate. The only consensus the legislators could agree upon was to levy a poll tax on all voters. As of November 20, 1920, women in Texas who planned to vote were required to pay a state fee of $1.50 (Texas League of Women Voters 1922: 18; *Laws of Texas*, 20:11).[12]

Neither Governor Hobby nor the suffragists gave up. They knew there was a legal way of waiving the fee for some women, so they resorted to their old tactic of mobilizing legislators opposed to alien voting.

The End of Immigrant Voting in Texas: A Poll Tax Relief Act

In 1921 the Texas Senate began proceedings to deny immigrants the right to vote. Newspapers across Texas reported that Mexicans were the targeted group since only 5.6 percent of Mexican immigrants were U.S. citizens (see Ayala 2005: 56). The newspapers also reported that most German immigrants would not be affected since 70 percent were naturalized. For the most part, the papers were correct. In 1920 the U.S. Census reported that in Texas, with the exception of Italian immigrants, who were a fraction of the European immigrant populations, the majority of European immigrants were U.S. citizens. The rate of naturalization for European ethnic groups ranged from 56 percent to 70 percent (U.S. Census 1922: 816). Mexicans constituted 61 percent of the total immigrant population, and only a small percentage of them were naturalized. Unlike other groups, most Mexicans would be affected by the reforms.

In January 13, 1921, Sen. William H. Bledsoe of Bullock (District 29) and Sen. Richard M. Dudley of El Paso (District 25) (*Journal of the Senate of Texas, 37th Legislature, Regular Session 1921*, p. 40) found a way to finally end alien voting in Texas. They introduced a new resolution, S.J.R. 1, which proposed, first, that voting in Texas be limited to U.S. citizens, and, second, that a married couple would pay one poll tax fee for both spouses. This brilliant proposition would satisfy advocates of both tax relief for women and immigrant reform and was bound to be popular since it provided economic relief to families. Voters did not necessarily have to harbor negative feelings toward immigrants for the measure to be appealing. On March 2 the Senate passed the resolution, 24 voting in favor, 0 against, and 7 abstaining (Ibid., 400). Most of those who abstained represented counties in South Texas and counties with populations that had German majorities. The senators representing counties with Mexican majorities, however, were divided. Of the three senators representing South Texas counties, only Archie Parr did not support the measure. His District 23 was entirely contained in South Texas, while the other two senators' districts were distributed across regions that mainly covered counties outside of South Texas.

The same day the resolution was voted on by the Senate, it passed the House with 116 yes votes, 3 nos, and 10 abstentions (*Journal of the House of Representatives, Texas, 37th Legislature, Regular Session, 1921*, p. 645). Overall, there was massive support for the legislation, even from counties with Mexican and German populations. Representatives from counties with German majorities were divided, and in South Texas only J. F. Leslie, representing the counties of Starr, Brook, and Hidalgo, did not vote in favor of the legislation. The representatives from El Paso, Presidio, and Bexar favored passage. By this time there was no legislator of Mexican descent in office. In the previous election Representative Canales had been replaced, and the new Anglo-American representative for Cameron and Willacy supported passage.[13]

In 1919 Idar warned the readership of *Evolución* that the arrival of Anglo-American settlers in South Texas would change the demographics and evaporate the Mexicans' political clout there, and now his prediction was apparently becoming a reality. It was only a matter of time, he said, before the suffrage was withdrawn from Mexican immigrants since they were gradually becoming a smaller proportion of the total number of voters in South Texas (*Evolución*, March 15, 1919, p. 1; *Evolución*, March 16, 1919, p. 3). I agree with Idar's analysis but would add that it was not only a demographic shift that changed politics in South Texas. The Act of 1906 also had enormous consequences since the seven-year time limit imposed on naturalization applications nullified most of the immigrants' certificates and thereby eliminated their ability to vote. In turn, the imposition of the English-language requirement in order to apply for naturalization made it difficult for many Mexicans to renew their papers because they did not speak English. In 1920, 49.4 percent of Mexican immigrants in Texas were unable to speak English (U.S. Census 1925: 84). The naturalization reforms were not a secret, and legislators were aware of these legal changes. They knew it would be difficult for Mexican immigrants to regain their voting eligibility. It was common sense for them to support the constituencies that had elected them to office.

Interestingly, on the same day the anti-immigrant suffrage resolution passed the House, Representative Rogers of Harris County, seemingly not satisfied with the removal just of Mexican immigrants from the electoral process, introduced legislation to disenfranchise African American men and women also. Under H.R. 29 he proposed that voting be limited to citizens who could read and write (*Journal of the House of Representatives, Texas, 37th Legislature, Regular Session, 1921*, p. 782). The only people exempt from this requirement would be people who voted before 1866 and their descendants, and since only whites were allowed to vote before the Civil War the provision would exclusively affect African Americans. The House took no vote at this time, and the measure was referred to the Committee on Constitutional Reforms, where it died because of its obvious unconstitutionality. Rogers's actions were so transparent because in Harris County 23 percent of the population was African American, a voting block large enough to change election results (U.S. Census 1922c: 1000).[14]

S.J.R. 1 was presented to Governor Patrick M. Neff, who had replaced Hobby, on March 3, 1921. He opposed the legislation, and ninety days later it became law without his signature. Because the legislature treated the resolution as an emergency measure, it was presented to the voters at the earliest possible moment, July 23, 1921 (*General Laws of Texas, 37th Legislature, Regular Session 1921,* p. 276).

The Deportations of 1921:
Naturalized Mexicans Will Not Be Deported

After S.J.R. 1 was adopted by the state legislature, a series of deportation raids began in Texas. Because governments' antipathy toward immigrants at this time was widespread at both the state and national levels, the timing of the raids may have been associated either with the Texas electoral referendum or with a federal directive. In March 1921, the same month Texan legislators passed the resolution to end alien voting, the U.S. Congress was debating a bill to limit worldwide immigration to the United States (McLemore and Romo 1998). The bill was considered an emergency measure to stop the wave of European immigrants who, after World War I, were trying to escape their countries' economic troubles. A quota of 350,000 was proposed for the Eastern Hemisphere, and preferential entry was given to British, Irish, and northern Europeans (Ngai 2003: 2). Only a small number of southern and eastern Europeans would be allowed entry, as legislators maintained that immigrants from these regions were undesirable (Feagin and Booher Feagin 2003; Meyerink and Szucs 1997). Although the target of the legislation was Europeans, the newly elected president, Warren G. Harding, took advantage of the anti-immigration climate to announce that he planned to reform Mexican immigration policy and deport undesirable Mexicans.

The raids began across the country in April 1921, after President Harding took office. The president was making good on a campaign promise. He had pledged to reform U.S. immigration law and pressure Mexico to pay for losses that American investors had incurred during the Mexican Revolution (Vázquez and Meyer 1985). Harding informed President Obregón that Mexican males entering the United States would have to pay an entry fee. This fee had been instituted in 1917, but, as noted earlier, had been waived by the former president in response to pressures imposed by farmers (Romo 1975). The powerful agribusiness lobby had fought the fee provision, arguing that if it were enforced a labor shortage would be created in Arizona and California. This, in turn, would harm the entire U.S. economy. Harding also warned Obregón's government that Mexicans who had failed to pay a port of entry fee and were unemployed would be deported. Finally, indigent immigrant families would also be deported. Obregón suspected that the deportation threat was Harding's way of forcing the Congress of Mexico to pay reparations (*La Prensa*, April 28, 1921, p. 1). Carranza had initiated talks on the matter but had refused to compensate U.S. corporations for most of their losses. His administration refused to pay particularly for any of the confiscated land, as it concluded that U.S. corporations had illegally appropriated the land in the first place (*La Prensa*, April 11, 1921, p. 1; *La Prensa*, April 13, 1921, p. 1; *La Prensa*, April 30, 1921, p. 1).

President Obregón tried to negotiate a stay of deportations but informed the U.S. government that finding a solution would take time. President Harding refused to wait and warned Mexico that mass deportations would begin in Texas, California, Arizona, and Oklahoma. Those targeted for deportation had already been sent a letter by the secretary of the exterior (*La Prensa*, April 7, 1921, p. 1; *La Prensa*, April 24, 1921, p. 1). To prepare for the deportations, Obregón instructed the consular offices in the United States to aid the deportees (*La Prensa*, April 11, 1921, p. 1; *La Prensa*, April 14, 1921, p. 1). He also advised the consular agents to encourage people to leave voluntarily before being deported to avoid being apprehended by city police or county sheriffs and placed on a train bound for Mexico. A deportee's passage would be paid as far as the border and no farther, so if families did not want to be stranded in unfamiliar border towns they would have to pay the rest of their fare in order to reach their destinations (*La Prensa*, April 25, 1921, p. 1). The consular offices were also instructed to inform Mexicans of their rights and make it known that those who were employed and those who were naturalized or had filed papers would not be deported.

In Texas the deportations began in San Antonio on April 9, 1921 (*La Prensa*, April 10, 1921, p. 1). Although only a few people were rounded up, the apprehension of Gregorio Rios, a successful businessman, garnered attention from the local media. Apparently Rios was apprehended for being an anarchist and a troublemaker. A few days later the deportations escalated as over 5,000 people were deported or repatriated through the custom ports of Laredo, El Paso, and Brownsville (*La Prensa*, April 17, 1921, p. 1).

Throughout Texas the consular offices worked together with charitable Mexican American organizations, among which the most active were Cruz Azul Mexicana and Sociedad Honorífica Mexicana, to aid the deportees. The clubs raised money to help families pay for their train fares, and members handed out food to the families boarding trains. In many cities Sociedad Honorífica Mexican held meetings informing immigrants of their rights and encouraged them to establish chapters of Cruz Azul or the Sociedad.

In El Paso and Brownsville panic set in when thousands of Mexicans were apprehended. People feared being deported and left in the middle of nowhere. *La Prensa* reported that by April 12, 1921, consular diplomats who were observing the situation estimated that approximately twenty-two trains carrying deportees and voluntary repatriates had left Texas (*La Prensa*, April 12, 1921, p. 1). As the news of the deportations spread, thousands of Mexican immigrants in San Marcos, Fort Worth, and Dallas approached the consular offices to ask for aid so that they could leave voluntarily (*Dallas Morning News*, April 23, 1921, p. 11; *La Prensa*, May 4, 1921, p. 1). Due to the high number of requests many consular offices turned people away and gave assistance only to those who could prove they were Mexican. People were required to show birth certificates and passports in order to receive financial assistance, and they were informed that they needed to make arrangements for shelter since the Mexican government was not providing homes for the deportees. Apparently a rumor had spread that the Obregón government was about to start a temporary emergency agrarian program (*La Prensa*, April 20, 1921, p. 3).

Some U.S. officials felt the deportations were unfair and tried to assist the distressed families. In Congress, Sen. Morris Sheppard and others intervened and negotiated reduced train fares for voluntary repatriates. The train companies agreed to comply, but the agreement fell apart when the U.S. Department of Interstate Commerce refused to pay its portion of the subsidy (*La Prensa*, May 6, 1921, p. 1). The roundups continued in El Paso, and in May they began in Fort Worth, where 350 more people were expelled by force or left voluntarily (*Dallas Morning News*, April 23, 1921, p. 11; *La Prensa*, May 5, 1921, pp. 1, 4). Fifteen days later the deportations began in Dallas and some 579 Mexican immigrants left (*La Prensa*, May 20, 1921, p. 1). A few dozen people were also deported from Hillsboro and San Marcos (*La Prensa*, April 19, 1921, p. 5; *La Prensa*, May 7, 1921, p. 8).

By May 1921 over 60,000 Mexicans had been deported from the United States, but even this was insufficient to force President Obregón to negotiate, so President Harding placed an embargo on U.S.-Mexico trade (*La Prensa*, April 20, 1921, p. 1; *La Prensa*, May 4, 1921, p.1; *Dallas Morning News*, May, 10, 1921, p. 1). At that point Obregón began to concede and responded to the embargo by stating that the Mexican Supreme Court would be asked to determine if Article 27 violated international law (*La Prensa*, May 17, 1921, p. 1). At the same time the negotiations began, Texan farmers became alarmed over the deportations and collectively complained to the U.S. government. They also met with the Mexican Consulate of San Antonio to explore ways of ending the deportations and then organized a conference to identify solutions. On May 16, 1921, the San Antonio Chamber of Commerce held a conference attended by chambers of commerce across Texas to discuss the deportations (Ibid.). The central issue became the farm labor shortages caused by the deportations. If the raids continued, the farmers feared, their crops would be lost. Throughout Texas farmers reported that Mexicans were leaving voluntarily, and their supply of labor had fallen to the point where they did not have enough workers to harvest the fields. In response to their findings the representatives of the chambers of commerce drafted a plan outlining the problems and offering solutions. They wrote Congress that in Texas the federal plan to deport an estimated 11,000 unemployed Mexicans failed because it created panic and produced a farm labor shortage. Mexicans with jobs were leaving the countryside for fear that their families would be deported and left stranded. They asked for the deportations to cease and suggested that the best way of dealing with unemployment in Texas was to relocate Mexicans from the cities to the farming communities. To encourage Congress to adopt their plan, the chambers of commerce agreed to create temporary jobs and help with the relief of the unemployed.

By early June Harding announced that talks with Mexico were running smoothly and that he was satisfied with the progress they were making (*La Prensa*, June 8, 1921, p. 1). He had decided to call off the raids since the Mexican Supreme Court was expected to issue a favorable verdict. At a minimum U.S. oil corporations would be able to recover their oil field property. Two weeks later the U.S. Department of Exterior Relations informed the Mexican consular offices that all deportations would cease on July 1, 1921 (*La Prensa*, June 22, 1921, p. 1). The secretary of labor was also authorized to continue waiving the entry fee for Mexican laborers, and Congress chose not to limit immigration from the Western Hemisphere, including Mexico. Only countries from the Eastern Hemisphere would be assigned a quota (Immigration Act of May 19, 1921, in 42 *U.S. Statutes at Large* [part 1] 5).

A few days after Harding issued the order to cease the deportations, the Women's Good Citizenship Association of Dallas held a rally to applaud the federal removal project. They organized a parade and ceremony to celebrate the Fourth of July and to honor the government officials who were working to expel all unwanted aliens. During the ceremonies speakers urged the crowd to support the state legislature's referendum to end alien voting and praised the federal government for its deportation initiative. One speaker also encouraged the crowd to lobby for legislation in favor of deporting all immigrants who refused to learn English (*Dallas Morning News*, July 5, 1921, p. 8).

Whereas some Texans hailed the state and federal actions to put Mexicans in their place, people of Mexican descent bemoaned the calamity that had befallen them. The deportations had instilled fear in the Mexican quarters of towns and cities and in general created in the public's mind a very negative image of people of Mexican origin because the government had legitimized its actions by depicting Mexicans as undesirable indigents. Adding insult to injury, Mexican immigrants now faced the embarrassing referendum that marked them as unworthy to vote.

On July 23, 1921, when the day of the referendum to end alien voting finally arrived, newspapers across Texas reported that something had caused voters to stay away from the polls (*Austin American Statesman*, July 24, 1921, p. 1; *Dallas Morning News*, July 24, 1921, p. 1; *Fort Worth Telegraph*, July 24, 1921, p. 1; *San Antonio Express*, July 24, 1921, pp. 1, 8). The newspapers estimated that only a fraction of the people eligible to vote had done so. For example, in Bexar, where on a regular basis more than 10,000 people cast their ballots, only 1,277 had voted (*San Antonio Express*, July 24, 1921, p. 1, 8). A few days after the election the state reported that the referendum had been adopted, with 57,622 in favor to 53,910 votes against (*General and Special Laws of Texas, 75th Legislature, Regular Session, 1997*, p. 2). Alien voting had ended in Texas, and married spouses would have to pay only one poll tax.

My review of Texas state documents verified the newspapers' assessment that few people voted, since 750,000 people had paid their poll taxes and were eligible to vote (*Senate Journal, 36th Legislature, Fourth Called Session 1920*, p. 5), yet only a little over 100,000 voted. I was unable, however, to explore voting patterns and determine if the voter turnout in counties with large immigrant populations was low because the county election records no longer exist (see Election Registrar 1918–1922).[15] It is therefore uncertain if people of Mexican descent came out to vote or if they stayed away for fear of being mistaken for a pauper and deported to Mexico.

Once Texas rescinded the right of aliens to vote, Missouri and Arkansas were the only states still allowing immigrants who had filed naturalization papers to vote (Keyssar 2000: table A 12).

The Cable Act and the Ku Klux Klan in Texas

In the early 1920s a strong anti-immigrant movement spread throughout the United States, largely spearheaded by chapters of the Ku Klux Klan (Hine 2003: 91). The Klan gained respectability in many social circles, including within the Women's Christian Temperance Union, among prohibition enforcement organizations, and many women's voting leagues (McArthur and Smith 2003: 140). One of the main goals of the Klan and its sympathizers was to protect America against the perceived burden immigrants posed on the economy. The Klan also adopted a strong position against American radicals, who they charged were communist and were influenced by alien immigrants. The Klan also espoused keeping African Americans, Jews, and other racial minorities separated from whites because allegedly these peoples were inferior to whites.

When the Ku Klux Klan organized in Texas, leading Texas citizens joined its ranks and thereby increased its respectability at the national level. In 1921 the first Klan chapter in Texas was established in Houston (Cox 2005: 136). It differed from the southern chapters in that its membership was composed largely of prominent businessmen and included many local policemen. The Klan gained credibility in Houston and in surrounding cities when its members launched a campaign to enforce Prohibition and stop bootleggers from manufacturing liquor. Chapters were soon established in Waco, Fort Worth, Beaumont, San Antonio, Galveston, Austin, and Dallas. In Dallas the Klan expanded rapidly and became very popular among all social classes, including the city's elite. The middle class and professional groups found the Klan to be a new haven for building influential contacts with the local elite, and soon Dallas became known in Texas as the Ku Klux Klan capital of the United States. Klan meetings were restricted to members but were not kept secret, a strategy employed to get people used to the idea that the Klan was there to stay (Ibid., 155). On May 21, 1921, the mayor of Dallas made his first appearance at a meeting of the Klan and marched with eight hundred masked members. The Dallas police commissioner as well as the chief of police and the sheriff were members. The public displays by the Klan alarmed the former governors Oscar Colquitt and Ferguson, both of whom opposed the group because of its disrespect for law and order and sought to reduce its expansion to more cities by encouraging people to establish organizations to oppose it. Ferguson became an effective campaigner, visiting towns and farming communities where he spoke out against the Klan. Ferguson was able to rally massive support against the Klan but not end its popularity.

A few months after the Dallas parade the Ku Klux Klan entered the political domain and began to endorse candidates and run Klan members for office. By this time the membership of the group had grown to thirteen thousand in Dallas and eight thousand in Houston (Ibid., 141). In 1922, the Klan gained control of many local offices and celebrated a major victory when their candidate for state district attorney was elected to office

(Cox 2005: 158). Within the legislature few representatives either publicly acknowledged if they were members or openly endorsed the Klan. This changed, however, during the National Democratic Convention of 1922, when half of the delegation, including some legislators, dropped their cloak of secrecy and openly pledged support of the Klan (McArthur and Smith 2003: 115). That same year Earle B. Mayfield, a former Klansman born in Overton, Texas, was elected to the U.S. Senate. His election brought national attention to Texas since he admitted to being a former member of the Klan and was not averse to publicly accepting the Klan's senatorial endorsement and support (Richardson, Anderson, and Wallace 1997: 341). This affirmation brought national attention to Texas, contributed to the Klan's respectability, and demonstrated that Texans were sympathetic to the Klan.

Although most Texas legislators were not Klan members, many shared the Klan's view that African Americans should not have a say in Texas politics and believed that unless immigrants naturalized they should not own land in Texas. For example, in 1921 the Texas legislature revisited its Alien Land Law and debated prohibiting aliens from owning property in Texas (*Journal of the House of Representatives, Texas, 37th Legislature, Regular Session, 1921*, pp. 16–17, 388, 962). After a heated debate the legislature compromised and followed the Senate's more moderate proposals. Both houses of the legislature agreed that the state would identify the percentage of land owned by resident aliens and from then on require immigrants to register their property. If immigrants failed to register by January 1, 1923, all unregistered land would be forfeited to the state (Senate Bill 142, *Senate Journal, Texas, 37th Legislature, Regular Session, 1921*, pp. 464, 870, 1032). Furthermore, after March 28, 1921, only naturalized immigrants would be able to purchase land used for ranching, agriculture, or mining. Aliens who lacked naturalization papers would be able to purchase property only in the city or town where they resided. This provision also applied to foreign corporations.[16] In addition to passing the registration bill, the Texas legislature revisited the primary laws in its regular session of January 1923 and made it more difficult for African Americans to vote by passing legislation prohibiting them from voting in primary elections (*General Laws of the State of Texas, 38th Legislature, Regular Session 1923*, p. 74). The county party's executive committee was no longer empowered to decide whether African Americans were allowed to participate, as there was now a state law prohibiting them from doing so. Perhaps not coincidentally, this law was passed after African American women doubled the size of the black vote in Texas.

By 1924 the popularity of the Klan had grown even more, and the Klansmen, believing they had enough support now to win the gubernatorial race, ran the Klansman Felix D. Robertson, a judge from Dallas. They launched their campaign with the slogan "Texas One Hundred Percent American," words that seemed to stress that America was not for Jews, Catholics, African Americans, and aliens (Winegarten and McArthur 1987: 226). The Klan's attempt to take over the governor's seat alarmed many opponents and unified organizations to defeat Robertson. Opponents of the Klan asked Miriam Ferguson to run for governor. She, like her husband, former governor James Ferguson, was an outspoken critic of the Klan, and anti-Klan factions believed the Fergusons had enough political clout to convince legislators sympathetic to the Klan to abandon it. Ferguson won the election, and within a couple of months she introduced legislation to control the Klan. The legislature approved an anti-Klan bill that made attacks on a person punishable by a minimum prison term of five years (Cox 2005: 166). This legislation effectively reduced the Klans' terrorist activities and served to stigmatize the organization by associating it with ignorance, intolerance, and lawlessness.

At the national level the Klan was not as popular as in Texas, but it had influenced the hearts and minds of the U.S. Congress. Most congressmen did not agree with the Klan's tactics of terrorizing communities at night if they disagreed with its creed. Congress did, however, agree with the Klan's immigration criticism and found it necessary to revise the nation's naturalization and immigration laws. There were three major problems: first, immigrant women who had not naturalized had the right to vote; second, the current immigration laws had not stopped southern and eastern Europeans from entering the country; and third, the passage of goods and people on the U.S.-Mexico border had to be more closely inspected. From 1922 to 1924 Congress revisited immigration and naturalization law.

In 1922 Congress revised its naturalization laws concerning married women and passed the Cable Act. This had become necessary because under current law married women acquired the citizenship status of their husbands, and many immigrant women who had never formally applied for U.S. citizenship were allowed to vote, while American-born women who were married to noncitizens were ineligible. This was a problem that concerned Minnie Fisher Cunningham, who was now the secretary of the League of Women Voters in charge of the Washington, D.C., headquarters of the league and responsible for overseeing congressional legislation affecting women voters. Cunningham became a key player in the reforms and worked closely with Sen. John L. Cable to shape the legislation (McArthur and Smith 2003: 100). Philosophically the federal nationality law stood as a barrier to women's autonomous political identity. On a practical level it was one of the few laws that gave voting rights to immigrants who had not been granted U.S. citizenship.

Congress's passage of the Cable Act changed naturalization law so that women no longer acquired their husband's citizenship status. Alien wives were stripped of their citizenship and were required to apply for it on their own behalf. The Cable Act allowed women born in the United States who were married to noncitizens to regain their citizenship so long as they were not married to a Chinese, Japanese, Filipino, Hindu, East Indian, or any other nationality ineligible for citizenship.

In Texas the Cable Act enforced the goals of those legislators and suffragists who in past years disapproved of extending voting rights to alien women. All alien women who had not formally applied for citizenship lost the right to vote. In the case of Mexican women, it became very difficult for many of them to regain their citizenship since federal naturalization law required applicants to speak English and at that time 50 percent of females of Mexican origin in Texas were non-English speakers (U.S. Census 1925: 84).

The U.S.-Mexico Border and the Johnson-Reed Act

The next federal reform targeting immigrants was passed in 1924, when the Congress revised U.S. immigration law. Under the Johnson-Reed Act, or what is commonly known as the Immigration Act of 1924, immigration to the United States from the Eastern Hemisphere was limited further.[17] The Eastern Hemispheric quota was reduced to an annual number of 165,000, thereby cutting legal entry nearly in half (McLemore and Romo 1998: 120). The bar on Asian immigrants was extended to Japan, which in previous years had been given a small quota. The Japanese were denied legal entry. Overall, the quota system was altered to classify the world's population according to nationality and race, ranking them in a hierarchy of desirability for admission. The number of immigrants allowed entry from the United Kingdom and northern Europe increased, while the quota for the countries from the Eastern Hemisphere was limited to a few thousand.

Although the immigration quota did not affect the Western Hemisphere, Congress passed other reforms affecting Mexico. That year Congress established the Border Patrol along the U.S.-Mexico border. Its principal aim was to stop illegal immigration, which at that time was primarily from Europe, but it was also assigned to control the contraband of goods smuggled from Mexico. Liquor was the main contraband since its manufacture, sale, and transportation had been banned nationwide by the federal government. The establishment of the Border Patrol marked a new era in Mexico-U.S. relations. On the one hand the movement of goods and people was to be more closely controlled, yet on the other hand Mexicans were permitted to continue entering the United States freely, which was highly significant because legal entry allowed them to eventually qualify for U.S. citizenship.

At the time of the reforms U.S.–Mexico relations were tense, yet cordial and stable. The two countries realized that commerce and trade benefited them both and needed to continue. Relations had also improved after the Obregón government agreed to a post-Revolution financial reparation plan, and in return the U.S. government retained its liberal immigration policy toward Mexico. Although U.S. corporations received only around one-third of what they considered was owed to them, the U.S. government regarded the settlement as a fair one and agreed to continue doing business. A few years earlier, on September 1921, Mexico's Supreme Court had rendered its ruling on U.S. reparations and finally closed one of the most bitter chapters in U.S.–Mexico relations (Vázquez and Meyer 1985: 130). The justices upheld Article 27 of the Mexican Constitution but sided with the U.S. government and gave foreign companies the legal right to sue for their confiscated property. The Court ruled that foreigners must be compensated. President Obregón, seeking to strengthen his presidency and to resume international trade and free immigration, endorsed the ruling and agreed to form a binational commission to finalize the negotiations (Meyer, Sherman and Deeds 2007: 507). The payment plan, however, took a couple of years to finalize. The Mexican government agreed to pay U.S. investors $508,830,321 million for some of the confiscated property and corporate losses (Sloan 1978: 296; Vázquez and Meyer 1985: 130). Mexico negotiated an annual payment plan of $30 million, which at that time was one-fourth of the income of the federal government. This was a heavy burden for future generations of Mexicans to repay. Most of the confiscated land was not returned or compensated, as the Mexican government believed it had been improperly appropriated. Most of the oil fields, however, were returned. The Court had ruled that if U.S. companies could prove that they had constructed working wells then they regained their oil rights; otherwise the land was declared undeveloped and part of the land improperly granted to U.S. investors. The ruling represented a compromise: Mexico was not going to repay U.S. corporations for its own land, but it did recognize that U.S. financial investments and losses had to be repaid.

When Congress passed the Immigration Act of 1924 and designed its border policy, its intent was to regulate the movement of people and commerce along the border. However, one of the government's main goals was to apprehend illegal aliens from Europe. As a result of the restrictive immigration quotas passed a few years earlier, thousands of eastern and southern Europeans, according to estimates by the Bureau of Immigration, were entering illegally through Mexico and Canada. This led the bureau to regularly visit European immigrant neighborhoods and increase the number of deportation raids. The bureau estimated that in the mid-1920s approximately 20 percent of Europeans were illegal aliens (Ngai 2004: 61).

Restrictions were placed on the Mexican population, but differed depending on the immigrant's occupation. As a result of the ongoing need for farm labor, the agribusiness industry lobbied Congress to be lenient with agricultural workers. All immigrants were required to enter through custom ports, but only some were required to pay a fee. The fees charged of Mexicans and Canadians were called visa fees rather than head taxes.[18] Any immigrant, including Mexicans, who entered the country illegally after July 1, 1924, could be deported (Ngai 2003: 10). The visa fee, however, was waived or was kept very low for persons who declared they were agricultural workers. If farmworkers planned to work for six months only, they did not have to pay a fee (National Archives 2007a), but if they applied for a longer stay they were required to pay a nominal fee, which would be returned to them on their way out. If agricultural workers decided to reside permanently in the United States they were required to go to a port of entry or visit one of the immigration district offices, register, and pay a fee set by the secretary of labor. If they failed to register, they lost their nonresidential legal status and became illegal aliens. Nonagricultural workers who declared their intention of becoming permanent residents were required to pay a visa fee of $9 plus other processing fees. This fee was imposed on heads of households (spouses) (Immigration and Nationality Act, May 24, 1924, sec. 17, in 43 *U.S. Statutes at Large* [part 1] 153–156, 162) (fig. 5.3).[19]

In retrospect, even though the fees may have caused hardships for some immigrants, the visa entry policy was relatively liberal, since Mexicans could declare agriculture their occupation, gain entry, work, and save money to pay the fee later. Congress likewise authorized the secretary of labor to reduce the fees and allow families to pay their fee after entry. A fee could be set as low as $4 (U.S. Department of Labor 1925: 177; U.S. Department of Labor 1927: 180). In addition, Congress decided to waive the visa fee for Canadian and Mexican immigrants who were agricultural workers and had entered legally prior to 1924[20] (43 *U.S. Statutes at Large* [part 1] 162, 164).

A second area in which Congress was lenient toward Mexicans was in not enforcing the literacy test (39 *U.S. Statutes at Large* [part 1] 877; Reports

Figure 5.3. Crowd at Brownsville depot. Runyon (Robert) Photograph Collection. Center for American History, UT-Austin (RUN 02905).

of the Department of Labor 1920: 168). Since 1917 males (and females if they immigrated alone) sixteen to fifty-four years of age had been required to be literate. Only agricultural workers and immigrants who were to live with family members and whose relatives had naturalized were not required to pass a literacy test. To Mexicans the waiving of the literacy requirement was important, as many would not otherwise have qualified for legal entry. In those days, according to the Mexican government, approximately 70 percent of the population was illiterate (Meyer, Sherman, and Deeds 2007: 587). Furthermore, enforcing of the literacy test would have not been in the best interests of U.S. farmers.

Finally, after much planning by federal agencies, on May 28, 1924, the Border Patrol was established under the umbrella of the Immigration Service (43 *U.S. Statutes at Large* [Part 1] 242; Coerver and Paszton 2004: 225) (fig. 5.4). Congress allocated $1 million for its initial funding. Four hundred and fifty agents, all of whom were Anglo-Americans, were hired to patrol the border. One Mexican American border patrol agent was eventually hired three years later. Since then the U.S.-Mexico border has gradually become increasingly militarized and the number of agents has increased over time. Immigrants nonetheless continued to flow freely even after Mexicans

Figure 5.4. U.S. Immigration Service building (Brownsville, Texas, 1924). Runyon (Robert) Photograph Collection. Center for American History, UT-Austin (RUN 03945).

were required to pay a visa fee. The annual reports of the secretary of labor from 1925 to 1928 indicate that on an annual basis permanent legal residency was given to Mexicans in numbers ranging from a high of 81,722 in 1927 to a low of 32,378 in 1925 (U.S. Department of Labor 1927: 6; U.S. Department of Labor 1928: 75). Most Mexicans entered legally and paid their fees either at the time of entry or later, when they applied for permanent residency. By 1927, the commissioner of immigration, Harry E. Hull, in his annual report to James J. Davis, the secretary of labor, acknowledged that although very few Mexicans entered illegally, many were falsely claiming farmwork as their occupation in order to pay a low entry fee. He also estimated that for the same reason most Mexicans who applied for permanent legal residency falsely reported agriculture as their occupation. Hull noted that this was a financial problem, but since Congress did not require immigration agents to verify an applicant's occupational claim, the Bureau of Immigration was required to allow them entry and process their permanent legal residency when they filed their papers (U.S. Department of Labor 1927: 7).

After the reforms of the 1920s, U.S. immigration policy toward Mexico remained relatively liberal until the mid-1960s, with the exception of the years of the Great Depression, when Mexican immigration was temporarily halted. During these four decades, the reforms allowed Mexicans to gain legal entry and qualify for U.S. citizenship. It might have been difficult for some to meet the income and language requirements set for naturalization, but at least they had an option and a challenge to meet. For those Mexicans who were seeking a better life and who were willing to sell their labor to the highest bidder, legal entry enabled them to follow a path toward U.S. citizenship and change their national allegiance. From the end of the Mexican Revolution to this day, however, despite experiencing several periods of political stability, the Mexican government has not been able to legislate laws giving workers a realistic living wage. This failure has prompted Mexicans to persevere in their search for U.S. labor markets that will pay them the value of their labor, or at least a higher wage than is available in Mexico. Thus the longing and the quest to find labor markets that pay fair wages continue to lead Mexicans to a new land, a land where many choose to live permanently and in doing so abdicate their Mexican citizenship in order to have a better life.

Looking Back at Mexican Naturalization Patterns

The Mexicans' naturalization history in Texas obviously does not end here. My detailed historical narrative, however, stops at this point for three reasons. First, in 1921, when the Texas legislature chose to end alien voting in Texas, a major chapter in the Mexican immigrants' naturalization history ended. Before then, naturalization and voting practices were intertwined in Texas, and it was necessary to follow this relationship until the laws were reformed. Second, I also shift my discussion at this point because the federal government continued to give Mexicans legal entry, and as long as that opportunity was available they were able to pursue a path toward citizenship. Numerical quotas were not set for Mexico, and this allowed the flow of legal immigration to flourish. Third, in my concluding chapter my analysis of Texas naturalization patterns continues to the present, but they are examined as part of a larger national pattern because immigration reforms in the 1940s and 1960s dramatically reshaped Mexican immigration, and the largest immigration flows were to states other than Texas. This pattern, which continues to this day, calls for a broader analysis if one is to understand why immigration laws changed and how the changes affected Mexicans' ability to naturalize, including those from Texas.

Before I move on to the present, however, I want to examine a few important events that shaped the Mexicans' naturalization history in the 1930s. First, I comment on the deportation of Mexican immigrants from the United States during the Great Depression since this event was a turning point for Mexico and shaped its policy toward the United States. During the Great Depression of 1929 to 1933 the U.S. government deported around four hundred thousand Mexicans (Ngai 2004: 135). The Mexican government saw these deportations as signifying a return to U.S. foreign policies mirroring those of the Porfirian period. Deporting Mexicans was a very cruel and unfriendly policy to enact against a neighbor who had a history of passing trade policies that generated huge profits for U.S. corporations, in particular the oil industry. Deportation was considered an unjust action since most Mexicans had entered legally.[21] Moreover, the deportations affected thousands of Mexican Americans who were children of immigrants and were forced to leave when their parents were expelled (Hoffman 1974).

In 1934, as the deportations were coming to an end, a new president, Lázaro Cárdenas, was installed in Mexico. He was critical of the way in which the Mexican Congress had responded to the deportations and disagreed with the oil deal Obregón had negotiated with the U.S. government (Gilly 1994: 362). President Cárdenas believed that if the United States was unwilling to maintain its liberal immigration policy, it was necessary for Mexico to reexamine its foreign policies. As part of Cárdenas's reforms he revisited the Mexican Supreme Court's interpretation of Article 27 and began to reconsider U.S. ownership of the oil wells. In addition, Cárdenas enforced the country's labor laws and required all firms, including U.S. corporations, to recognize labor unions as legal bodies that could negotiate wage and working condition contracts. He also increased the national educational budget in an effort to decrease the country's illiteracy rate, which among the adult population was still 70 percent (Meyer, Sherman, and Deeds 2007: 578). Cárdenas also enacted the largest agrarian reform policy in the history of Mexico, awarding over forty-one million acres to 788,936 landless families (Gilly 1994: 362). Obregón had redistributed land, yet his administration returned less than 5 percent of the land confiscated by President Díaz (Ibid., 260).

When U.S. oil companies refused to comply with Cárdenas's labor reforms, under the pretext that their employees were the best-paid workers in the country, Cárdenas took the companies to court (Pérez 2010). In 1938, after a series of court hearings, the Mexican Supreme Court upheld the lower court's decision in favor of Cárdenas. U.S. executives refused to obey the Supreme Court's order and in retaliation threatened to withdraw their investments, behavior that Cárdenas considered a flagrant disregard of Mexican law. It was also a belligerent act of aggression against the Mexican government and a transparent sign of imperialistic actions to come. U.S. corporations refused to obey Mexican law, and the U.S. government had no regard for the welfare of Mexican immigrants. That is, when Mexican citizens were deported from the United States, Mexico had to accept the U.S. government's decision and comply with its laws. However, if American citizens living on Mexican soil were unwilling to abide by the same international principles, then the international relationship was unbalanced and no longer of benefit to Mexico. Cárdenas was not naive and realized that Mexico could not expect its rich neighbor to treat Mexicans as equals; but it was fundamentally necessary, he believed, for Mexican law to be respected.

On March 18, 1938, President Cárdenas signed a decree nationalizing Mexico's oil industry (Meyer, Sherman, and Deeds 2007: 532). The holdings of all oil companies, including seventeen U.S. oil corporations, were confiscated. Mexico no longer felt obliged to continue allowing oil companies to extract oil under the pretext that Mexico had to pay reparations for the losses U.S. businessmen incurred during the Mexican Revolution. Oil companies had recovered their original investments several times over, and it was now time for oil profits to belong to Mexico.

Mexico received congratulatory support from throughout Latin America. Cárdenas was praised for moving Mexico toward an independent economy. The United States did not retaliate and accepted Mexico's decision. Nationalization of the oil industry marked a new era in U.S.-Mexico relations. Mexico's oil no longer belonged to the United States, and American companies learned that they must obey Mexican law. Likewise, Mexico made it understood that the liberal flow of Mexican immigration to the United States was closely intertwined with its country's U.S. business negotiations. This was a very important political and symbolic act on the part of the Mexican government for it took a stance against the abusive treatment of its people in Mexico and abroad (Pérez 2010). This also placed pressure on the U.S. government to retain its open-door policy, and for Mexicans who chose to leave their country this was a critical stance, for as long as legal entry was made possible they continued to have the right to naturalize.

I end by commenting on one last point: Did European immigrants in Texas have the same rate of naturalization completion as Mexicans before the naturalization law reforms of 1906? As I mentioned in the introduction, I examined the naturalization records of all Texas counties to identify where Mexicans had applied and to determine the total number of applications filed by Mexicans. My aim was to conduct a historical study of Mexican immigrants and not to focus on the entire history of Texas naturalization patterns. The latter approach would have been a different type of study and, owing to the enormous database, was beyond my research interest. Nonetheless, as I inspected all of the county indexes I compared the naturalization rates of Mexicans and Europeans in the eighty-six counties where Mexicans had applied. However, as I conducted my research I found that maintaining a tabulation of the European immigrant population in counties where only one or a few Mexicans applied did not yield significant findings. I concluded that the most relevant manner of answering my question was to compare the rates in counties where Mexicans applied in large numbers. I also chose to look at some counties where a sizable number of Mexicans had filed papers. In this way I could compare rates and determine if there were any significant patterns. To present this data I have prepared two tables. Table 5.4 provides a composite of the applications submitted in South Texas, Bexar, and the southern coastal counties. Most of the Mexicans' applications came from these regions, and over 88 percent came from South Texas and Bexar. A considerably large number of applications also came from the counties adjacent to South Texas and bordering the coast. In table 5.5, I present a separate table of the data I collected from other counties where a large number of Mexicans filed applications, or where there was a significant pattern. I expected table 5.5 to also offer a meaningful overview of the Mexican immigrants' acceptance rates.

In reviewing the naturalization indexes and examining court records, I found that in general the application process was difficult for all immigrants. In most cases, immigrants who applied for naturalization had to visit the courts two or more times, and it took individuals many years to complete the process. However, I also found that without a doubt European immigrants were granted citizenship at a very high rate in comparison to Mexicans. In South Texas a total of 21,044 Mexicans applied from 1848 to 1906, and 305, or 1.4 percent, were granted citizenship. By contrast, 1,970 European immigrants applied in the same period, and a total of 870, or 44 percent, were granted citizenship (table 5.4). These numbers were obtained from the county, district, and federal courts.

Outside of South Texas, several more thousand Mexicans applied. The granting of applications for European and Mexican immigrants, however, remained relatively unchanged. In Bexar County, 38.7 percent of European immigrants received citizenship compared to 1.5 percent of Mexicans. Likewise, in the southern coastal counties the percentage was also lower for Mexicans: 1.2 percent were granted citizenship compared to 47.1 percent of European immigrants. I tried to determine if the acceptance rates for Mexicans and Europeans were possibly different because European immigrants were more determined to complete the process. I found that in most counties around 40 percent of European applicants filed additional documents and returned to the courts more than once in comparison to around 25 percent of the Mexican applicants. However, in the case of Mexicans I found no general pattern among those who returned additional times. For some reason most Mexicans were simply not granted citizenship. As I discussed

Table 5.4. Comparison of Mexican and European Naturalization Acceptance Rates in South Texas, Bexar, and Southern Coastal Counties, 1848–1906

| | Total Mexican Applicants in Texas 28,597[a] | | | | | |
| | Mexican Immigrants | | | European Immigrants | | |
	No. Applied	No. Granted	%	No. Applied	No. Granted	%
South Texas[b]	21,044	305	1.4	1,970	870	44.0
Bexar	4,242	63	1.5[c]	5,414	2,097	38.7[d]
Southern Coastal Counties[e]	653	8	1.2	1,085	512	47.1

[a]This is the total number of Mexican applicants found in district, county, state, and federal courts 28,597. Of these applications, ninety-three had no dates.
[b]South Texas counties included Atascosa, Cameron, Dimmit, Duval, Frio, Hidalgo, Karnes, Kinney, La Salle, Maverick, McMullen, Medina, Nueces, San Patricio/Corpus Christi, Starr, Uvalde, Val Verde, Webb, Zapata, Zavala.
[c]My review of the Index to the Bexar Naturalization Records differs slightly from the tabulation of the District Clerk. I removed from the count duplicate copies of the same index entry. The Bexar County Clerk counted 4,337 applicants.
[d]Two European Americans applied before 1848: William Trapmall in 1840 and Thomas Rocha in 1847.
[e]Southern coastal counties: Aransa, Bee, Goliad, Refugio, and Victoria. The Corpus Christi records were indexed with the San Patricio records.
Sources: Index to Naturalization Records found in Texas State, District, and County Courts, 1846–1939; U.S. District Courts, Southern District of Texas, Galveston Index to Declarations 1871–1905; General Courts Austin, Brownsville, El Paso, Galveston, San Antonio, Jefferson, Texarkana, Tyler, Waco; El Paso Naturalization Records, Declarations of Intention, 1890–1906.

in earlier chapters this fact may have resulted from racial ideologies, bias on the part of the county judge, the mistaken belief by some immigrants that they had been made citizens, or applicants' inability to finance the costs. I offered no conclusive explanation but did argue that the Rodriguez case serves as a template of the obstacles Mexicans underwent in becoming U.S. citizens. Likewise, I discussed that biases on behalf of the judges may have contributed to the low naturalization rates. After all, in 1905 the Commission of Immigration and Naturalization concluded that some county judges were biased and that it was best to remove them from the granting process. Could the judges have been the main problem? Once again I am uncertain. To further explore this issue I examined the applications of Spaniards, who,

Table 5.5. Mexican and European Naturalization Applications in Selected Counties, 1848–1906

| | Total Mexican Applicants in Texas 28,597 | | | | | |
| | Mexican Immigrants[a] | | | European Immigrants[b] | | |
	No. Applied	No. Granted	%	No. Applied	No. Granted	%
Bandera	26	0	0	74	16	22
Caldwell	203	1	.4	315	124	39
Comal	4	0	0	1,520	1,088	72
Comanche	5	0	0	11	9	82
Crockett	196	0	0	7	2	29
Edwards	6	0	0	11	7	64
Gonzales	171	0	0	592	220	37
Guadalupe	135	0	0	2,136	432	20
Menard	46	0	0	22	10	45
Sutton	69	0	0	20	9	45
Travis	324	1	.2	3,227	1,257	39
Tyler	11	0	0	46	8	17
Wilson	3	3	100	32	30	94

[a]In Galveston 72 Mexicans applied and 5 were granted, and in DeWitt 82 and 2 were granted. Both counties had thousands of Anglo American applicants.
[b]Latin Americans, Asians, and Spaniards are not included in this enumeration.
Source: Index to Naturalization Records found in Texas State, District, and County Courts, 1846–1939; U.S. District Courts, Southern District of Texas, Galveston Index to Declarations 1871–1905; General Courts Austin, Brownsville, El Paso, Galveston, San Antonio, Jefferson, Texarkana, Tyler, Waco.

as I mentioned in the introduction, were not counted in the tabulations with Mexicans or European immigrants. I conducted this comparison to determine if race might provide some clue. It did. Spaniards obtained naturalization below the rates of other European nationalities but followed a similar pattern. Overall, very few Spaniards applied for U.S. citizenship in Texas, yet their acceptance rate was much higher than that of Mexicans. In total, 166 Spaniards applied throughout Texas and 40 percent (N = 66) were granted citizenship. The largest number of applications were processed in Cameron County (N = 60). Interestingly, although Spaniards had a much higher acceptance rate than Mexicans, nearly all of the granted applications were issued before the Spanish-American War. After the war very few Spaniards applied for citizenship.

As for other applications from European immigrants in other counties, I found that their acceptance rate ranged from 94 percent to 17 percent (table 5.5). In the sampled counties, with the exception of Wilson County, only a few Mexicans were granted citizenship. In Wilson County three Mexicans applied during the 1880s, and they were all granted citizenship. These men, however, received their final papers at least ten years after they filed for citizenship.

In conclusion, I have attempted here to provide an overview of the Mexican immigrants' naturalization history in Texas. The statistical data I gathered from the naturalization records indicate that thousands of Mexicans applied for citizenship. It is not until after the Rodriguez case that the numbers dwindled. I could not identify with certainty the exact structural conditions that led to this pattern, but I have argued that the Rodriguez ordeal and the bad feelings harbored against Mexicans in Texas during the Spanish-American War led Mexicans to stay away from the courts in order to avoid trouble.

I also demonstrated that the application process picked up in 1906, but because the federal government removed the record keeping from the states and stopped analyzing the data based on national origin, state of residence, and county of residence, it is uncertain when the application process resumed its pre-Rodriguez numbers (see appendix 1).[22] Although the Bureau of Immigration and Naturalization began reporting state data again in 1931, the country of origin of the applicants was not made available, and the number of naturalized Mexican immigrants is uncertain.[23] Not until 1961 were data on the state and national origin of the applicants available again (see appendix 2).

CHAPTER 6

Then and Now: The Path Toward Citizenship

In this chapter I analyze the political process Mexican immigrants currently undergo to become U.S. citizens. I advance a numerical overview of Mexican immigrants' naturalization rates from 1960 to the present and explore the social conditions that over the years have led them to increasingly pursue a path toward citizenship. Unlike other parts of this book, this chapter focuses on Mexican immigrants in general, although I also discuss the particular role of Mexican immigrants in Texas. The macro approach advanced here is employed to highlight major changes in federal legislation and to delineate how, from 1965 to 1976, laws restructured Mexican immigration and in turn impacted naturalization patterns. One of my principal aims is to illustrate that under the reforms of this period the U.S. Congress introduced a system of law that prevented most Mexicans from entering the United States legally and thereby created a statutory structure that reduced the size of the eligible pool of Mexicans qualifying for naturalization. I will illustrate as well that although legal immigration became very difficult, the flow of Mexicans steadily continued. Most newcomers entered as undocumented residents in that for the most part only those who had family in the United States qualified for immigration visas.

In discussing the immigration events of this period, I explore how U.S.-Mexico international politics have shaped U.S. immigration policy toward Mexico. By tradition, as I have argued throughout this book, Mexican immigration to the United States has been stimulated by economic and political problems in Mexico, while on the other hand U.S. corporations have benefited from Mexico's misfortune and profited from the cheap source of labor that enters the country. In 1965, however, this relationship was disrupted when an oversupply of cheap Mexican agricultural labor was viewed by Congress as a liability rather than an asset. To curtail Mexican immigration Congress revised the immigration laws, making it nearly impossible for common laborers and their families to enter legally. Legal entry laws were periodically but only temporarily eased when severe farm labor shortages threatened the interests of agribusiness. For example, in the mid-1980s, when growers reported that they were suffering from a shortage of farmworkers, the federal government responded by allowing thousands of undocumented agricultural workers to adjust their illegal status to permanent legal residency. However, as I illustrate, in meeting the labor needs of the agribusiness industry Congress complicated immigration policy in that a legal procedure that did not discriminate against people who were not engaged in agricultural occupations now had to be instituted.

The chapter concludes with a discussion of current debates on immigration and naturalization reforms and the Mexican government's response. I examine not only congressional resolutions that explore new ways of stopping undocumented Mexican immigration but also resolutions proposing to radically alter U.S. naturalization laws. Specifically, I turn to debates over House Resolution (H.R.) 4437, which aimed to convert many U.S. citizens and undocumented workers into felons if they did not abide by U.S. immigration laws. Under this resolution U.S. citizens and permanent legal residents who knowingly aided undocumented people (for example, gave shelter or health care) or facilitated their entry would be charged with felony crimes. In the case of the apprehended undocumented aliens, H.R. 4437 proposed changing their conviction for illegal entry from a misdemeanor (for first entry) to a felony crime. The intent of this legislation was to create barriers preventing undocumented aliens from adjusting their status to permanent legal residency, as a felony conviction would disqualify them from such an adjustment and ultimately block their path toward citizenship. In the area of naturalization law I examine a series of birthright resolutions introduced from 1993 to 2008 that have attempted to rescind the U.S. citizenship status of children born in the United States of parents who are undocumented. The primary aim of these resolutions, as publicly stated by their congressional sponsors, is to facilitate the deportation of undocumented parents who use their children's U.S. citizenship as a legal basis for remaining in the United States. I argue that although controlling illegal immigration may be the public rationalization of birthright advocates, it is transparently obvious that the reform movement is tied to electoral politics.

Some state legislators in Texas have been active supporters of birthright reform. In the past when several congressional resolutions failed to pass, Texas representatives who supported the reforms turned to the Texas legislature in efforts to pass similar laws at the state level. For example, on

June 29, 2007, ten Texas House members introduced House Bill (H.B.) 28 to revise state law to redefine who is a legal resident in Texas and thus eligible to receive state benefits, including government employment (H.B. 28, Texas Legislature On line www.house.state.tx.us). The legislation sought to classify U.S. citizens whose parents were undocumented as illegal Texas residents. In this way, the representatives attempted to pass birthright legislation without violating federal law since they were not redefining the concept of U.S. citizenship, but only addressing who was a legal resident in Texas. Redefining Texas residency, rather than attempting to determine who is a U.S. citizen, was a clever way of bypassing federal law since only the U.S. Congress is authorized to redefine the citizenship clauses of the U.S. Constitution. Although it is unlikely that any type of birthright legislation will be adopted in Texas because of its potential violation of federal law, the introduction of H.B. 28 was mean-spirited and a direct assault on people of Mexican descent.

Immigration and Nationality Act Amendments of 1965: Mexico's Open-Door Immigration Policy Ends

In 1965, the U.S. Congress passed the Immigration and Nationality Act Amendments of October 3, 1965, and reformed an archaic system that allocated legal entry on the basis of race and ethnicity and awarded both preferential treatment and large quotas to northern and western European countries, and nearly barred Asian peoples from obtaining legal entry (79 *U.S. Statutes at Large* 911). The reforms radically altered immigration law. In a revision hailed by the majority of Congress as a triumph of a modern Republic and an expression of liberal democracy (Ngai 2004), the quota system based on national origin was revoked, and a more democratic policy was instituted for the Eastern Hemisphere. While most scholars have concurred that the new policy regulating immigration from the Eastern Hemisphere marked an ideological break with past racist practices, others have argued that the same sentiments cannot be expressed when one looks at Western Hemispheric reforms, in particular those intended to regulate Mexican immigration (De Genova 2002; cf. Feagin and Booher Feagin 2003).

Under the act a new quota raised the total annual limit from 150,000 to 290,000. A ceiling of 170,000 was set for all countries in the Eastern Hemisphere, each being limited to a quota of 20,000. For the first time in history, however, a numerical quota was assigned to the Western Hemisphere, limiting the total number of annual entrants to 120,000. Mexico was not allotted a specific quota but had to share the general limit with the entire Western Hemisphere. Exacerbating matters, Congress extended occupational restrictions to immigrants from the Western Hemisphere, making it difficult for working-class Mexican laborers to qualify for entrance. Under section 212a of the act, Congress mandated that aliens seeking to enter the United States for the purposes of performing skilled or unskilled labor may obtain a visa only if the secretary of labor has certified a labor scarcity in that specific job category (79 *U.S. Statutes at Large 917*). In 1965 only artists, physicians, surgeons, lawyers, architects, teachers, college professors, and engineers were certified as needed labor (Ibid., 917, sec. 8b32). Immigrants who were unskilled or did not work in the designated professions could enter only via a special order issued by Congress or the attorney general. Legal entry for all poor and working-class people essentially ended, as it was unlikely that they would obtain work permits.

For Mexicans who were planning to immigrate and permanently reside in the United States the revisions were bad news and made legal entry difficult. Most Mexicans who had no relatives in the United States did not qualify for permanent residency unless they were eligible for one of the professional visas. The open-door policy was over, and the era of the undocumented began. Most Mexicans became ineligible to enter legally.

Background to the Reforms of 1965: The Bracero Program

The immigration amendments of 1965 were the final stage in a series of congressional reforms passed to incrementally curtail Mexican immigration. By this time the Mexican immigrant population in the United States in general had grown gradually (1960 N = 575,902), but in California it had increased radically (U.S. Census 1961a: 1–366). In the previous twenty years Mexican immigrants had more than doubled in California, increasing from 134,312 to 277,462 (U.S. Census 1943: 88; U.S. Census 1961b: 6–233). Texas was no longer the state with the largest number of Mexican immigrants.[1] Congressmen attributed this unwelcomed growth in California to the bracero program and to the open-door immigration policy Mexico had enjoyed for over a century. The amendments of 1965 followed the termination of the bracero program a few months earlier.

The bracero program had been established during World War II to replenish the labor shortages caused by the military drafting of young male farmworkers. Public Law 45 established the program, a contract labor agreement under which agricultural workers who resided in the Western

Hemisphere were hired on a six-month contract, which was renewable upon the approval of an agribusiness employer (Durand 2007; McLemore and Romo 1998).[2] Under the program a small number of men were also allowed to work in the railroad industry. Mexico became the main source of labor for the United States owing both to the facility with which labor could be rapidly transported from Mexico to the United States and to the fact that the two countries had established labor networks dating back to the nineteenth century (Rothenberg 2000).

The bracero program benefited Mexico financially in that the remittances sent by the braceros raised the standard of living of many Mexican families. In the more than two decades of the program's existence, nearly five million contracts were certified, and the men worked in twenty-five states from as far north as Minnesota to as far south as the U.S.-Mexico border (Galarza 1964: 53–54; U.S. Department of Labor 1963: 80). Although the bracero program was established as an agribusiness relief project during World War II, and 167,925 men were contracted during this period, the federal government allowed the program to continue after the war ended. During these postwar years, the number of braceros admitted annually ranged from a low of 5,900 to a high of 135,900, and the men were restricted to working in the agribusiness industry (Driscoll 1999).

In the late 1950s American corporations asked Congress to expand the program beyond the agribusiness industry. Angered by this request, American labor union activists launched a counterattack to dismantle the program altogether (Craig 1971). Unions lobbied Congress, arguing that braceros depressed the wages of American farmworkers and that expanding the program to other industries would create similar results. The unions were soon joined by the Catholic Church and by Mexican civil rights organizations, including the National Farm Workers Association led by the labor activist Cesar Chavez, and together the coalition took a more aggressive stance. To gain support, activists in the coalition appealed to the American public, stressing the deplorable conditions in which American farmworkers lived because growers did not have to offer them a competitive wage since there was an abundant amount of cheap bracero labor. Agribusiness lobbyists, headed by the American Farm Bureau, countered by emphasizing that the bracero program benefited the American public by keeping down the cost of food. When growers paid low wages, the lobbyists maintained, the savings were passed on to consumers.

In 1963 the Department of Labor intervened in the debate and refused to support the agribusiness lobbyists. It issued a report concurring with the activists that there was an oversupply of agricultural labor (Cockroft 1986).

According to Secretary of Labor Willard Wirtz, U.S.-born farmworkers and the braceros that remained in the United States after their contracts expired composed an oversupply of labor, and it was not necessary to import new workers (U.S. Department of Labor 1963). Many of the braceros had remained in the United States either as permanent legal residents or undocumented aliens. The department noted that new workers were unnecessary since immigration law allowed braceros to easily adjust their status to permanent legal residency. Compounding the allegedly lax immigration laws, which were identified as having created the oversupply of labor, was the willingness of farmers to sponsor their workers. Many farmers gave braceros an affidavit of support or a letter promising permanent employment. Both types of documents fulfilled the braceros' economic requirement for gaining an immigration visa, or what was called a green card. The department claimed that because thousands of braceros could easily obtain letters of support many were choosing to adjust their status rather than return home.

The Department of Labor was correct in claiming that the adjustment process was very liberal because at that time any bracero who had entered legally, obtained an affidavit of support from an employer or relative, and paid the twenty-five-dollar adjustment fee was free to remain in the United States (66 *U.S. Statutes at Large 182*, 230, 239).[3] The braceros' legalization had also been facilitated by reforms made by the Immigration and Nationality Act of 1952, which eliminated the literacy requirement for immigration (Ibid. 181). The secretary of labor no longer had to waive the literacy requirement for agricultural workers.

In 1963 Congress began hearings to determine if the bracero program should be terminated or expanded to other industries. Once again the Department of Labor was asked by Congress to investigate how current levels of Mexican immigration would affect future U.S. labor patterns. The department reported that Mexican immigration had peaked at over 55,000 in 1962 and accounted for over 40 percent of all immigration from the Western Hemisphere (Grebler, Moore, and Guzman 1970: 76). An immediate drop in immigration was advised to curtail the oversupply of agricultural labor. Agribusiness disagreed, charging that during harvest season there were insufficient numbers of workers. Moreover, corporations in favor of expanding the bracero program to other industries refused to concede. Congress responded to the lobbying efforts of the supporters and opponents of the bracero program by passing legislation to appease both sides. First, to address the problems raised by the Department of Labor, Congress ordered that legal immigration from Mexico be temporarily reduced through administrative orders given to the Immigration and Naturalization Service (INS). At this time immigration law would not be revised. Second, to address the concerns of the agribusiness industry, the bracero program would be allowed to continue, although workers would be limited to agricultural occupations. Finally, serious consideration was given to the proposals presented by American corporations, and a creative labor solution was designed. Though the bracero program would not be expanded to other occupations, a commission would be established to explore whether American companies would benefit from employing inexpensive labor in Mexico. Congress gave the president the power to establish a commission to investigate the pros and cons of export-oriented industries. Specifically, the commission was mandated to determine if establishing American assembly plants in Mexico would benefit the American economy. If the final report of the commission was positive, the commissioners were to prepare a plan to negotiate with Mexico and present it to the president of the United States. Plans for establishing assembly plants in Mexico were not unfamiliar to Congress, but the issuance of a directive to begin negotiations with Mexico and select sites for the assembly plants was unprecedented.

Congress had actually begun to consider establishing assembly plants in Mexico on October 11, 1962, when it passed the Trade Expansion Act of 1962 granting the president the authority to negotiate trade tariff reductions for American corporations (76 *U.S. Statutes at Large* 872–903). Under the act, future U.S. assembly factories established in Mexico would be charged reduced tariffs for manufactured goods entering the United States from Mexico. In this way companies would not be penalized for reducing their manufacturing costs by employing cheap labor outside of the United States. In addition, Mexico had agreed not to impose duties on materials originating in the United States and assembled in Mexico. Thus, when strong opposition to the bracero program reached a peak in 1963, Congress and Mexico were prepared to enact an alternate plan to ensure that American corporations would continue to have access to cheap Mexican labor.

Although the Mexican government enthusiastically supported the plan because it would create thousands of jobs, negotiations temporarily stalled when U.S. corporations disagreed over the location of the plants. They wanted the plants to be located along the border to reduce the costs of transporting materials and assembled goods between the countries, while Mexico preferred that the plants be established in the interior of the country, where unemployment was high (Iglesias-Prieto 2001; Tiano 2006).

While negotiations with Mexico progressed, Congress took further steps to address some of the complaints cited by the Department of Labor. Oddly, it chose to address only immigration while doing nothing to resolve the wage problem identified as the result of the excessive level of incoming bracero labor. Congress instructed the Department of Labor to stem the flow of legal immigration from Mexico by slowing down the application process (U.S. Department of Labor 1963: 81; U.S. Department of Labor 1964: 59). All letters in support of applicants were to be investigated (see *Emmanuel Braude et al., Appellant v. W. Willard Wirtz, Secretary of Labor, U.S. et al., Appellees* 1965).[4] In addition, Congress instructed the department to ask government agencies that provided social services to indigents to identify the immigrants receiving and applying for charity relief or medical services. If the services had been already provided, the agencies were required to bill the immigrant's sponsor (see *County of San Diego v. Anatalio T. Viloria* 1969).[5] In general these two measures were designed to discourage employers and family members from sponsoring braceros and to establish a procedure for identifying deportable immigrants who had fallen on hard times and no longer qualified to live in the United States. Mexican immigration fell from 55,253 in 1963 to 32,962 in 1964 (United States Department of Justice 1971: table 14), but the number of braceros entering the United States was allowed to increase. During the same period 264,601 temporary workers were granted entry (Grebler, Moore, and Guzman 1970: 68).

The net effect of the immigration and trade policies enacted by Congress was mainly to serve the interests of American corporations. The immigration policies allowed agribusiness to continue having a fresh supply of cheap labor, while the Trade Act made the expansion of the bracero program a moot point since arrangements had been made for corporations to hire cheap labor in Mexico.

A New Era: The End of the Bracero Program

In 1964, when the negotiations to establish assembly plants in Mexico were completed, Congress chose to terminate the bracero program, and a year later it ended its open-door policy toward Mexico. Labor unions, the Catholic Church, and Mexican civil rights organizations were in favor of terminating the bracero program but were divided on the immigration reforms that followed. The program was terminated mainly as a result of the coalition movement and of Chavez's inspiring leadership. Chavez launched a national campaign to bring to the public's attention the plight of the American farmworker and to prove that Congress was reluctant to do anything about the situation. Through a media campaign aired on television and radio and published in newspapers and by organizing protest marches, Chavez appealed to the American public's sense of decency, social justice, and Christian values. He illustrated that throughout the United States growers could pay farmworkers whatever wage they wanted because the federal government had created the conditions to exploit this class of workers. Particularly effective in Chavez's campaign was the distribution of a CBS documentary film entitled "Harvest of Shame." First aired in 1960 and later distributed through activist circles in churches and universities and on college campuses, the film exposed the shameful living conditions farmworkers were forced to endure largely because of Congress's reluctance to grant them a minimum wage (Rothenberg 2000; Zeta Acosta 1972). Farmworkers, like maids and home caregivers, were excluded from the Fair Standard Act of 1935, which required workers to be paid a federal minimum wage. The American public learned that Congress had repeatedly refused to set a minimum wage for agricultural workers and, by allowing the bracero program to continue, created an oversupply of agricultural labor. Enjoying an abundant source of cheap bracero labor, the growers had no reason to raise the wages of their employees (Tichenor 2008). Making matters worse, Congress excluded farmworkers from the unemployment insurance program. The rationale for both policies was to protect agribusiness from high labor costs and in turn to pass the savings along to the American consumer. Sadly, no consideration was given to the families who bore the burden of these unjust policies.

Chavez's facts were indisputable. Statistics from the Department of Labor indicated that in the early 1960s most farmworkers were being paid 80 cents an hour and less; only a few farmers in California paid an hourly wage of $2.47 (Galarza 1964: 103, 152; Menchaca 1995: 94, 127). On average a farmworker's family lived on an annual income of $500, which, compared to the median U.S. family household income of $5,600 in 1960 (U.S. Census 1962: 1), placed them in impoverished conditions. With these indisputable facts in hand, Chavez and his main supporters—the American Federation of Labor-CIO and the Catholic Church—were able to convince the White House that it was time to end the bracero program and begin to legislate fair agricultural laws. In 1964, President Lyndon B. Johnson personally asked Congress to terminate the program, and on December 31 of that year it was brought to closure (Menchaca 1995: 94). All braceros present in the United States were ordered to return home.

Because many Americans were concerned that the abrupt termination of the program would bring undue hardship upon the families of braceros, Congress informed the public that Mexico and the United States had enacted the Border Industrialization Program as a repatriation incentive (Cañas and Coronado 2002; Miller 1981). American corporations were to begin build-

ing assembly plants in Mexico and to give employment preference to braceros. As soon as the Mexican government approved the plants' locations, the
corporations were prepared to begin construction. The Mexican government
had conceded to U.S. demands that the plants be built along the border, and
on September 1, 1965, construction began (Twin Plant News, 2008). Over
the course of that year twelve plants were built in locations called twin cities, meaning regions where there were cities on both sides of the border. The
plants, which came to be known as maquiladoras, were first established in
Ciudad Juarez, across from El Paso; in Nogales, across from Nogales, Arizona; in Tijuana, across from San Diego; in Mexicali, across from Calexico,
California; in Reynosa, across from McAllen; and in Matamoros, across
from Brownsville. Overall, three thousand workers were employed at these
plants (Beaumier 1990: 2). Although some braceros were hired to work in
the maquiladoras, the corporations chose to employ a workforce composed
mainly of women (Tiano 2006), in particular young women because they
were viewed to be a cheaper and more pliable source of labor. Braceros were
considered to be high-risk employees because they would command higher
wages and eventually organize into labor unions. At this time the Mexican government agreed to prohibit collective bargaining as part of the trade
agreements, and American corporations were assured that workers would
not organize. In the end, the maquiladora system failed to resolve the unemployment problem of braceros because neither government intervened to
demand that the corporations give them preferential employment.

One month after the Border Industrialization Program began and less
than a year after the bracero program ended, the U.S. Congress put into
action its final policy for reducing Mexican immigration. Under the Immigration and Nationality Act Amendments of October 3, 1965, Congress, as noted earlier, limited the number of immigrants from the Western
Hemisphere and no longer allowed skilled or unskilled workers to qualify
for legal entry unless a labor shortage was certified by the Department of
Labor.[6] Policies aimed at reducing legal immigration were now firmly in
place. Oddly, the INS did not launch a nationwide effort to deport the braceros, conducting an aggressive deportation campaign only in the large cities of the Southwest, where braceros had likely turned to industrial occupations (Samora 1970: 85). Most farm communities were not affected (see
Menchaca 1995).

After the immigration amendments of 1965, the best way for a Mexican
to qualify for legal entry or for an adjustment to permanent legal residency
was through the sponsorship of an immediate family member. However,
only applicants who were sponsored by a U.S. citizen qualified to obtain
their papers with deliberate speed because they were not counted as part of

the numerical quota. Permanent legal residents were authorized to sponsor a relative, but their family members had to wait for a quota slot to become available, which often took ten years or more. By 1976, the INS reported that four hundred thousand Mexicans were on the waiting list and estimated that several hundred thousand more were living illegally in the United States (*Silva v. Bell* 1979: 6).

In spite of the fact that under the reforms of 1965 the best and quickest way to legalize a family member was to naturalize and become a U.S. citizen, Mexicans did not rush to the INS to apply for naturalization. Indeed, the number of applicants actually declined. In 1962, for example, 7,205 Mexicans nationwide became naturalized, but in every year over the next decade and beyond the number fell (Statistical Yearbook of Immigration and Naturalization 1961–2001, tables: Persons Naturalized by Selected Country of Former Allegiance and State; Department of Homeland Security Database N-400). By 1976, when the next immigration reform was implemented, the number had sunk to 5,602.

Factors Affecting Naturalization

It is perplexing why, after the reforms of 1965, the rate of naturalization in the Mexican immigrant population remained low, given the considerable benefits of becoming a citizen. Most likely the English-language requirement of naturalization law continued to be a major impediment. The literacy requirement may also have been an obstacle, but this was less likely since Mexico had waged a war against illiteracy, and at this point only 38 percent of the Mexican population was illiterate (Meyer, Sherman, and Deeds 2007: 577, 578). Another factor that may have played a part in dissuading Mexicans from becoming U.S. citizens was their romantic attachment to Mexico. Because many Mexicans migrate to the United States in hopes of succeeding financially, they may not consider it necessary to naturalize since they view their stay in the United States as temporary. I am persuaded by anthropologists' observations that for generations a constant found among immigrant communities has been their dream of saving money and investing their hard-earned cash in property back home (Royce 1982). In short, most immigrants never relinquish the romantic notion of one day returning home and becoming the owner of a *ranchito*. Only when they realize that their dream is unrealistic because they have become rooted in the United States or because it is financially unattainable do Mexican immigrants consider becoming U.S. citizens.

This observation is substantiated by decennial reports of the Census Bureau, which reveal that very few permanent legal residents apply for naturalization within the first five years of their residency in the United States (Cornwell 2006). Less than 9 percent of all immigrants naturalize when they meet their five-year residency requirement (U.S. Census 2001: 3), although naturalization rates increase as the number of years immigrants remain in the United States increases. For example, the Census Bureau reported that immigrants who entered before 1970 had an 80.4 percent naturalization rate in 2000, and Hispanics had a similar naturalization rate, 74.2 percent. Naturalization records also indicate that immigrants who naturalize, including Mexicans, tend to be very rooted and have established permanent bonds to persons and property in the United States. Over two-thirds are married, they have taken English classes, they have resided a minimum of eight years in the United States, and they indicated that voting and securing their political status were their main reasons for naturalizing (Balistereri and Van Hook 2004; Brettell 2006; Simanski and Rytina 2005). Studies of Mexican and Asian homeownership indicate that the majority of immigrants who naturalize have resided in the United States for over twenty years and own their homes (Jensen 2001; Rodriguez 1999). These people have abandoned the dream of returning to their ancestral land.

What naturalization records and census data do not reveal is that many Mexican immigrants did not naturalize in the early 1970s because they were undocumented. In 1970, the decennial census counted 759,711 foreign-born Mexicans, but what it occluded was the percentage who were undocumented (U.S. Census 1974: 17). For many Mexicans, especially the braceros who did not return home after the immigration reforms of 1965, the reality was that their failure to depart converted them from temporary legal residents into undocumented aliens with no right to apply for naturalization. Likewise, when restrictions were placed on legal entry, many braceros who were permanent legal residents or undocumented and who were unable to wait for quota slots to open up for their families chose to reunite and paid for their families' illegal passage. Not having legal residence, therefore, was the main impediment preventing undocumented people from becoming U.S. citizens.

The Western Hemispheric Reforms of 1976

In 1976 the path to citizenship became more difficult for many Mexicans. That year Congress revised the immigration laws once again, nearly closing the doors to legal immigration and making it very difficult for some U.S. citizens to sponsor their undocumented relatives. On October 20 the Immigration and Nationality Act Amendments of 1976, or what came to be known as the Western Hemispheric Act, were passed (90 *U.S. Statutes at Large* [part 2] 2703). After several years of heated congressional debates over how to decrease legal immigration from the Western Hemisphere and find ways of deporting undocumented braceros without unduly distressing the agribusiness industry, Congress found a solution. Under section 2 of the act, countries in the Western Hemisphere that were not colonies of other nations were given a 20,000 maximum annual ceiling for legal immigration. This was a major reform, as the annual quota of 120,000 was no longer to be allocated on a first-come, first-served basis. For Mexico this meant that fewer people would qualify for legal entry because in past years the annual number of Mexicans given legal entry was larger than the new quota. In 1976, when President Gerald Ford signed the act, Public Law 94–571, into law, he authorized Congress's actions but raised concerns over how the legislation would affect Mexico (Woolley and Peters 2008). According to the president, legal immigration from Mexico would be reduced by half since about 40,000 Mexicans entered annually.

The numerical restriction was a compromise given that in previous years many congressmen had tried to pass harsher restrictions against Mexico. For example, when Congress debated a series of resolutions to regulate Mexican immigration in 1973, some congressmen considered legal and illegal immigration from Mexico to have reached crisis proportions, while others felt it had been severely reduced and policy was adversely affecting the agribusiness industry. Congressional hearings were held that year to discuss amending policy toward Mexico. Allegedly, 1 to 2 million undocumented aliens resided in the United States, of whom most were Mexicans (*Congressional Record, 93rd Congress, First Session,* vol. 119, part 30, 1973, p. 14180). Moreover, those who favored restrictions on Mexican immigration argued that the Western Hemispheric quota set in 1965 had failed to reduce legal immigration from Mexico. Although there was conclusive evidence that at first the quota had reduced all forms of Mexican immigration, they argued that beginning in 1968 Mexican immigration was once again on the rise. They alleged that Mexican immigration would not be sufficiently altered until the sponsorship laws were changed to reduce the number of incoming legal residents. Those who favored restricting Mexican immigration thus supported resolutions to restrict U.S. citizens from sponsoring their relatives. Such constraints were deemed necessary not only because, according to INS records, U.S. citizens of Mexican descent were sponsoring a large number of applicants, but also because Mexican immigration continued to grow since these admittees were not counted against the numerical quota. Indeed, this was the case: federal records indicate that by the early 1970s, owing to the nonquota sponsorship policy, the number of Mexicans entering annually ranged from 50,105 to 71,586 (Statistical Yearbook of the Immigration and Naturalization Service 1980: 36). Moreover, on an annual basis Mexicans accounted for 41 percent to 47 percent of the total Western Hemispheric quota.

To limit legal immigration, Rep. Joshua Eilberg proposed limiting the sponsorship privileges of U.S. citizens. He recommended that sponsored applicants be required to wait at least two years before being granted entry (*Congressional Record, 93rd Congress, First Session,* vol. 119, part 29, 1973, p. 31359). In this way the number of nonquota immigrants would be reduced. Other congressmen fiercely opposed Eilberg's plan and introduced resolutions ranging from not placing any limits on Mexican immigration to including the sponsored relatives of U.S. citizens within a proposed 20,000-quota limit. The State Department disagreed with all of these propositions and recommended giving Canada and Mexico a higher ceiling owing to their history of immigration. It was not advisable to radically limit immigration from these countries, the department noted, since over a century of liberal immigration policies had created family networks across borders, and restrictions on immigration would create a tremendous backlog of people on the waiting list as well as a tremendous illegal entry problem. A quota of 35,000 for Mexico and Canada was recommended.

Rep. Peter Rodino concurred that larger quotas should be given to Canada and Mexico and that no restrictions should be placed on U.S. citizens sponsoring relatives. He also favored a slightly larger quota for Mexico, around 41,707, a number he based upon estimated projections of the need for farm labor. Rodino also proposed that a guest worker agricultural program be established since the numerical limit set for Mexico would not supply the needed agricultural labor. Rodino argued that a guest worker program would resolve many problems for the United States. First, it would give growers their labor, and, second, it would reduce legal immigration from Mexico. According to Rodino, many Mexicans applied for permanent legal residency only because they did not want to enter or live illegally in the United States. If a temporary guest worker program were established, the number of legal applicants would decline and the growers would not be forced to hire undocumented workers. As part of the plan Representative

Rodino supported placing sanctions on employers who knowingly hired undocumented workers. Sanctions, he argued, would stamp out the source of illegal immigration since employers would not hire illegals for fear of being fined. Many congressmen supported Rodino's resolution, while opponents argued against the large quota assigned to Mexico and in addition strongly objected to a guest worker program in the belief that what amounted to a new bracero program would only stimulate illegal immigration, given that in the past braceros did not return home when their contracts expired. These congressmen likewise opposed placing fines on employers. In the end, Congress could not agree on how to regulate Mexican immigration or on how to regulate the illegal hiring practices of the agribusiness industry. It was best to leave things alone.

A few years later, in 1976, however, as legal immigration again was on the rise, the congressmen compromised. Under the Western Hemispheric Act of 1976 a numerical quota of 20,000 was placed on every country in the Western Hemisphere. Congress also passed new laws to prohibit undocumented workers who lived in the United States from adjusting their status to permanent legal residency. First, undocumented aliens would not be allowed to adjust their status if they continued working in the United States; second, after 1976 applicants were required to file their adjustment papers in their home country. Both provisions, passed under section 212, were designed to force undocumented workers to leave if they hoped to become legal residents someday and ultimately citizens (90 *U.S. Statutes at Large* [part 2] 2705). All proposals to impose employer sanctions for illegally hiring undocumented workers failed to pass.

These were not the most onerous restrictions Congress passed. It ordered the Department of Labor and the INS to enforce provision 201b of the Immigration and Nationality Act of 1965, which prohibited minor children of undocumented aliens from sponsoring their parents (79 *U.S. Statutes at Large* 911) but which had been generally ignored (see *Congressional Record, 94th Congress, Second Session*, vol. 122, part 26, 1976, p. 33633). Beginning in 1976 all undocumented parents who sought adjustment could be sponsored only by an adult child twenty-one years of age or older (U.S. Citizenship and Immigration Service, "Interoffice Memorandum, AFM Update: Chapter 22 Employment-Based Petitions (AD03-01)," sec. 22.1d. 1976 Amendments). Before 1976 it was common procedure not to deport alien parents who had a child born in the United States and to allow them to work in the country until their adjustment was finalized. This administrative process, however, was terminated when the Western Hemispheric Act passed. From this point on, if parents planned to adjust their status they were to stop working, leave U.S. soil, and apply for immigration when their child turned twenty-one. The policy was allegedly enacted to discourage undocumented people from having children in the United States as a means of qualifying for legal residency. Congressional critics of this sponsorship policy could not stop it from being enforced or garner support against it, since legal counsel had informed Congress that it violated no constitutional rights.

Enforcement of this immigration policy was sanctioned by the 10th Circuit Court a few months earlier and found not to violate a person's constitutional rights. In 1975 the justices ruled in *Cervantes v. The Immigration and Naturalization Service and the Department of Justice* that undocumented parents of children born in the United States could be deported and did not qualify for adjustment merely for having a U.S.-born child. Only when an undocumented parent of a child who was a U.S. citizen met certain requirements would deportation orders be suspended and that person be allowed to adjust his or her status. The requirements were that a parent must have entered legally, be married to a legal resident or U.S. citizen, and be able to prove that his or her U.S.-born children would suffer undue hardship. In the case of the parents in *Cervantes* the court ruled that since both parents had entered without authorization and their child was an infant they could be deported because the child would not suffer undue hardship.

After the *Cervantes* ruling and the passage of the Western Hemispheric Act, the adjustment process for parents was much more complicated and costly and resulted in only a small percentage of parents being able to adjust their status through their U.S.-born offspring. Only those who had the financial means to hire legal counsel or were fortunate enough to be represented by nonprofit legal aid centers had any prospects of remaining in the United States. For example, in 1980 only 1,639 of the 31,849 Mexicans sponsored by U.S. citizens were parents sponsored by their children (Statistical Yearbook of the Immigration and Naturalization Service 1980: 18, 20).[7]

Furthermore, the passage of the Western Hemispheric Act reduced Mexican immigration to the United States. In 1974 the size of the newly legalized Mexican population totaled 47 percent of the total Western Hemispheric immigration quota, but within three years it had dropped by half to 23.5 percent (Ibid., 36). Interestingly, as the numbers granted legal entry progressively fell, a converse pattern occurred in Mexicans' naturalization rates: Mexicans began to apply for naturalization in large numbers. By the

Table 6.1. Mexicans Naturalized by Decade in Selected States, 1961–2008

Decade	All Mexicans	Texas		California		New Mexico		Arizona		Illinois	
		Total State	Mexico[a]	Total State	Mexico	Total State	Mexico	Total State	Mexico	Total State	Mexico
1960s[b]	54,154	46,066	24,614 (59%)	183,233	18,151 (10%)	3,081	965 (31%)	8,151	2,684 (33%)	74,218	2,136 (3%)
1970s[c]	65,016	48,929	22,166 (51%)	258,795	24,009 (9%)	3,321	1,156 (35%)	10,454	3,413 (33%)	89,074	5,697 (6%)
1980s[d]	170,895	122,022	50,350 (41%)	556,153	77,237 (14%)	6,290	1,627 (26%)	22,680	6,553 (29%)	96,222	14,051 (15%)
1990s	854,792	329,083	157,967 (48%)	1,602,070	477,685 (30%)	6,375	2,947 (46%)	41,227	21,747 (53%)	228,818	69,023 (30%)
2000–2009	1,116,027	470,852	184,343 (39%)	2,029,484	566,938 (28%)	15,183	7,945 (52%)	115,704	47,693 (41%)	351,188	75,991 (22%)

[a]The percentage is for the total number of people from Mexico in comparison to all countries, per state.

[b]Data by state and country of origin begin in 1961, when country of origin was first reported.

[c]The data for the states for the years 1973 to 1979 are only based on persons eighteen years of age and over (Department of Homeland Security, Immigration Statistics Office, N-400 data).

[d]In the 1980s data were not available for two years for New Mexico and one year for Arizona.

Source: Statistical Yearbook of the Immigration and Naturalization Service, 1961 to 2001; Yearbook of Immigration Statistics 2002–2009. Tables: Persons naturalized by State or Territory of Residence and Region and Country of Birth.

early 1980s the number of naturalized Mexicans had increased substantially; whereas in 1976 5,602 Mexicans naturalized, the number had grown to 26,807 ten years later and continued to increase year by year (table 6.1).

The Immigration Reform and Control Act of 1986: A Legal Path Toward Citizenship

Whereas the immigration policies of the 1970s can be distinguished as representing the most illiberal mandates ever taken against Mexican immigration up to that time, a reverse trend occurred in the 1980s. Congress not only reversed its illiberal policies, but also allowed 2.7 million people to adjust their undocumented status. This marked the beginning of an era in which the United States enacted good neighbor policies toward Mexico (Castañeda 2007: 87; Rytina and Caldera 2007: 2). Improved relations, however, were based not on altruistic principles, but on U.S. security interests and a serious labor shortage in the agricultural industry.

In 1979, during President Jimmy Carter's administration, the U.S. government found itself embroiled for the first time in a serious conflict in the Middle East when Arab nations accused the U.S. government of imperialism and of practicing unfair policies against Palestine in favor of protecting Israeli economic interests. The conflict erupted after the shah of Iran was ousted from power following the outbreak of the Iranian Revolution. Because the shah had been a longtime ally of the United States, the U.S. government was accused by the Iranian masses of having supported an unpopular dictator. The Mideast conflict escalated when, on November 4, 1979, Iranian students took American diplomats hostage to show the United States that Iran would no longer tolerate American imperialism (Mobasher 2006: 107). As the hostage standoff continued for 444 days, the world believed the U.S. government was on the brink of declaring war against Iran, since Carter had been unable to negotiate a resolution to the crisis. During the conflict U.S.-Mexico relations improved, and the U.S. government once again found Mexico to be a trusted ally.

At the same time U.S.-Middle East relations were heating up Mexico discovered massive oil deposits in the Gulf of Mexico and in the states of Chiapas and Tabasco (Grayson 1980). By this time Mexico was one of the main oil exporters in the world, but the new discoveries gave Mexico international clout and made the country the fourth largest world exporter of oil (Meyer, Sherman, and Deeds 2007: 594–595). In 1980 the new discoveries were found to amount to sixty billion barrels in proven oil reserves, with two hundred billion in probable oil deposits, meaning a more labor-intensive process was needed to extract oil. The proven oil reserves could easily be tapped and extracted. After the discoveries the Organization of Petroleum Exporter Countries, or OPEC, actively courted Mexico to join the cartel, which at that time was dominated by Middle Eastern countries. Mexico rejected the invitation largely for political and economic reasons. Executives of Petróleos Mexicanos, or PEMEX, the company entrusted by the federal government to administer and oversee the production and distribution of the nation's oil reserves, also advised against joining OPEC. The main reason given was that OPEC was dominated by Saudi Arabia and Iran, and Mexico would have little say in determining policy, particularly in setting oil prices. For Mexico it was best to remain independent in order to retain control of the price of Mexican oil and be able to set the amount of oil that could be released for sale.

The Mexican Congress not only rejected OPEC's invitation, but also openly supported the Carter administration during its crisis with Iran. Mexico demonstrated its solidarity by escalating the production of oil to compensate for oil shortages in the United States caused by the Iranian conflict and the resultant decline in the exportation of OPEC oil (Székely 1992: 260). During the conflict Mexico sold 58.3 percent of its oil and exported 730,000 barrels per day to the United States out of a total daily foreign oil production of 1,252,500 barrels (Grayson 1980: 179, 228). The total amounted to 40 percent of U.S. foreign oil purchases. The Iranian dispute proved to the United States that Mexico was an important ally and that Americans benefited by maintaining cordial relations.

The Iranian hostage crisis finally came to an end when President Ronald Reagan took office in 1981. With the discovery of oil in Mexico and the swearing in of a new U.S. administration that valued Mexico as a trusted ally, trade relations improved for Mexico. The United States and Mexico enacted profitable trade agreements, accords which increased Mexico's gross domestic product by 5 percent (Bean and Lowell 2007: 74). As part of the trade negotiations Mexico also borrowed heavily from the United States to develop its oil industry. The number of working wells increased, and plans to establish new oil refineries were set in motion. In anticipation of reaping large profits from the sale of oil, Mexico also borrowed to improve its national infrastructure by expanding its food banks, increasing the number of schools, constructing and refurbishing the transportation infrastructure, and making expenditures in other social service programs. In total, by 1982 Mexico had borrowed $80 billion from foreign banks (U.S. General Accounting Office 1996: 3). The problem with the development program was that Mexico's federal budget had insufficient funds to cover the annual foreign loan installment payments. The shortage, however, was not considered to be a problem since the expected oil profits would exceed the annual foreign debt payments. Unfortunately for Mexico, in 1982 OPEC began flooding the market with oil, which brought down the price and left Mexico in financial crisis (Grayson 1980: 145; U.S. General Accounting Office 1996: 3). It had massive oil reserves it could not sell and consequently was unable to earn capital and make its foreign debt payments on time. The Mexican government immediately imposed an austerity program and cut domestic spending in order to pay the foreign debt. The austerity measures caused inflation in Mexico to soar to 63.7 percent by 1985, as millions of jobs were lost (Meyer, Sherman, and Deeds 2007: 604).

In response to Mexico's financial crisis the Reagan administration and U.S. banks stepped in to stabilize the economy by instituting a gradual financial bailout plan (Harvey 2006). Together, U.S. banks and the federal government issued Mexico loans to pay its foreign debts while also calling a moratorium on U.S. bank loans, negotiating agreements with Japan and Europe to liquidate Mexican loans, and helping the country establish a secure payment plan to repay the United States. In return, Mexico secured its loans by using its future oil profits as collateral. As part of the deal the U.S. government required Mexico to make an immediate prepayment in oil, $1 billion worth of its oil reserves (U.S. General Accounting Office 1996: 3).

Stabilizing Mexico's economy was financially important to the U.S. government for two main reasons: trade and immigration. Since Mexico was the third largest importer of U.S. goods, the bailout would ensure Mexico's ability to continue trading. Furthermore, the loans were projected to stabilize the economy and save thousands of jobs, an outcome the U.S. government projected would check the flow of immigration by undocumented aliens.[8] The INS estimated that if the U.S. government did nothing to help Mexico the flow of illegal border crossers would be massive and increase by at least 50 percent (Bean and Lowell 2007: 77). A commission Reagan established to address the problem of illegal immigration and advise him on reforms reported that illegal immigration was on the rise, but that deportation of the undocumented population was not recommended (Levine, Hill, and Warren 1985).

Reagan's concern over illegal immigration coincided with forceful demands made by the American Farm Bureau Federation to renew the bracero program (Shulman 1986). The agribusiness industry alleged that farmers were facing a serious agricultural labor shortage, one which was forcing them to hire undocumented workers. The shortage was attributed to impractical immigration policies, one of which was Congress's reduction of legal immigration to such an extent that there were insufficient permanent legal residents to harvest the fields. Exacerbating the problem, most farmworkers who were legal had aged, and the only supply of labor was undocumented (see Levine 2004b; Report of the Commission on Agricultural Workers 1993). The last time farmworkers had been allowed legal entry was at the end of the bracero program twenty years earlier, and most had now retired, left farming, or were not very productive in their old age. Farmers needed relief now, and they demanded access to a labor supply.[9]

In March 1982 Congress began to debate immigration reform and explore ways of addressing the agricultural labor shortage (Menchaca 1995; Mines and Anzaldúa 1982). At first, Congress was concerned only with addressing the problems of the agribusiness industry, but as Mexico's financial crisis worsened and unauthorized immigration began to rise, adjusting the status of undocumented residents became a priority and was heatedly debated. By 1984 a consensus on how to address the agribusiness shortage had nearly been reached. A large majority of congressmen agreed to allow growers to hire undocumented workers for three years and begin an agricultural guest workers' program fashioned on the bracero program (Cockcroft 1986). Mexican civil rights organizations, including the United Farm Workers Union led by Chavez, immediately protested that a guest worker program would drive wages down. The Mexican American Legal Defense and Educational Fund (MALDEF) proposed instead that Congress curtail illegal immigration by raising the immigration ceiling for Mexico to 60,000 and allowing undocumented aliens to adjust their status. MALDEF viewed amnesty, that is, adjusting the status of Mexican undocumented workers already living in the United States, as a more reasonable solution than importing new guest workers. The fund also supported Rodino's resolution to impose employer sanctions, considering it the best way to deter illegal immigration.

After Rodino introduced his employer sanctions resolution, the American Farm Bureau Federation began to seriously consider MALDEF's amnesty proposal. In principle the federation opposed employer sanctions but concurred with MALDEF that an adjustment provision would solve the illegality problem. Agribusiness lobbyists, however, presented their plan and agreed to support amnesty for undocumented farmworkers if the workers who were legalized agreed to remain in farm labor for at least three years after being given a green card. Under this plan, applicants had to prove that they worked in agriculture to receive amnesty.

On November 6, 1986, the houses of Congress reached a consensus and passed the Immigration Reform and Control Act of 1986 (IRCA) (100 *U.S. Statutes at Large* [part 4] 2967). All sides had to compromise. First, under Title 2, "Legalization," Congress agreed to extend amnesty to all people who had entered the United States illegally before January 1, 1982, and had lived continuously in the United States (Ibid., 3384). Lobbyists for MALDEF and other civil rights organizations succeeded in persuading Congress that extending amnesty only to farmworkers and requiring them to remain on the farms was nothing but a modern-day indentured servitude program. If farmworkers were to be given amnesty, so should other people who had been made illegal by immigration laws. Attorneys for the Catholic Church had been important players in passing this reform. Agribusiness lobbyists, however, did obtain a special provision for their labor, one which did not apply to the rest of the undocumented population. It provided that people who had worked in farm labor for three months preceding the passage of the act would qualify for amnesty even if they had entered after 1982. This very liberal policy was clearly included to appease the agribusiness industry.

Second, an agricultural guest worker program was established to fulfill the needs of the agribusiness industry. Under Title 3, "Reform of Legal Immigration," the Department of Labor was authorized to allow temporary agricultural workers to be certified for labor contracts. Their residency in the United States was not to exceed three years. Furthermore, on an annual basis until 1993, the U.S. attorney general was allowed to adjust the status of some temporary agricultural workers to permanent legal residency (Ibid., 3427, 3433). Third, Title 1, "Control of Illegal Immigration," was written to gain the support of those who feared the guest worker program would stimulate unlawful entry. Sanctions were imposed on employers who hired undocumented workers after November 6, 1986 (Ibid., 2968), including a series of escalating fines that rose according to the seriousness of the offense—the highest financial penalty amounted to $10,000 per worker—plus a six-month prison sentence for the employer. Furthermore, a stricter monitoring system was put in place to discourage employers from hiring undocumented workers. The blame for illegality was to be shared by employers and workers. Employers were required to verify whether a person was authorized to work in the United States, and they were given specific instructions to follow. Moreover, Congress increased its funding of the INS specifically to maintain close surveillance of the U.S.-Mexico border.

After IRCA passed, millions of people qualified for amnesty, but applicants who hoped to adjust their status had to meet a series of requirements.

First, they had to submit an application within twelve months of IRCA's passage. This meant they had to come out of the shadows and undergo an administrative adjustment process that did not necessarily guarantee them legal residency. To be approved ultimately for adjustment they were expected to understand ordinary English, pass a medical exam, take classes on American history and U.S. government, have no felony convictions and at most three misdemeanor convictions, and agree not to apply for any social service relief benefit for five years after adjustment. If they fulfilled these requirements their temporary status would be terminated thirty-one months after they submitted an application.

As part of the deal the federal government issued $1 billion in assistance grants to be distributed among the states to aid the applicants in fulfilling their adjustment requirements. The states were authorized to develop programs that went beyond the adjustment process. The IRCA Americanization programs were authorized to teach immigrants how to apply for U.S. citizenship. Furthermore, to facilitate the naturalization process Congress allowed IRCA applicants to fulfill the five-year residency requirement by counting all years in U.S. residence, even the years during which they had been undocumented. In sum, IRCA put thousands of people on the path toward citizenship, and it certainly eased Mexico's financial crisis. Of the 2.7 million applicants who adjusted their status under IRCA 2 million were Mexican (agricultural and nonagricultural applicants) (Simanski 2008; Rytina and Caldera 2007:2).[10] These people could finally join the thousands of immigrants who had entered the United States legally and be eligible for U.S. citizenship.

In retrospect, although the Iranian conflict was a tragedy, it proved to the United States that Mexico was a trusted ally; and the negotiations that followed benefited Mexican immigrants. Mexicans who had become settled in the United States despite their illegal status now had an opportunity to become U.S. citizens and no longer had to worry about being deported. In the 1990s the number of Mexicans who naturalized in the country surged in comparison to the previous decade (see table 6.1; appendix 2). For example, in Texas it increased from 50,350 in the 1980s to 157,967 by the end of the 1990s, in California from 77,237 to 477,685, in Illinois from 14,051 to 69,023, in Arizona from 6,553 to 21,747, and similar increases were recorded in other states (Statistical Yearbook of the Immigration and Naturalization Service 1980 to 1999, see naturalization tables). From 1996 on, Mexico was the leading country of origin for people naturalizing in the United States (Simanski and Rytina 2005; Simanski 2006).

Bad Times: No More IRCA

Throughout the 1990s Congress revisited immigration law but did not pass major amnesty legislation. Most of the liberal changes that affected Mexican people were directed at adjusting the legal status of farmworkers and their families. These were sensible considerations since American citizens by choice did not want to work in farm labor. Allowing a trickle of farm laborers to adjust their status on an annual basis served the interests of the agribusiness industry and the welfare of the nation as a whole (see Levine 2004a).

Under a temporary adjustment program contained within IRCA and designed for agricultural workers, Congress allowed farm laborers to adjust their status to permanent legal residency (sec. 210A, in 100 *U.S. Statutes at Large* [part 4] 3417). The 210A program permitted undocumented farm laborers to apply for legalization as seasonal agricultural workers, or SAW, applicants and also set policy to allow farm laborers who arrived after the passage of IRCA to adjust their status. This program was to be terminated by 1993.[11] The families of the legalized farmworkers were also allowed to apply for legal residency. The initial agreement under IRCA was set at a maximum of 350,000, but a provision was appended allowing the Department of Labor and the attorney general to adjust the number of people who were legalized under this program. Perhaps not surprisingly, the numbers allowed entry under this provision exceeded the original intent. The Department of Homeland Security estimates that from 1987 to 2007, 1.1 million farmworkers and their dependents, 900,000 of whom were of Mexican origin, were legalized under the 210A provision of SAW (Simanski 2008). And of those who were legalized under the 210A program many entered the country after the passage of IRCA. An additional 400,000 agricultural workers were legalized under different programs not related to IRCA (Castañeda 2007: 87; see Statistical Yearbook of Immigration and Naturalization 1994: 19).

Mexican families not engaged in farm labor did not qualify for adjustment under the 210A program (i.e., they arrived after 1986). A few thousand Mexicans who were legalized under IRCA, however, were given the opportunity to adjust their family's status in 1990. Under the Immigration Act of 1990, Congress allowed 55,000 applicants to adjust their status or to apply for entry if they were sponsored by an immigrant who had been legalized under IRCA (104 *U.S. Statutes at Large* [part 6] 4978). Individuals who received legal status under this provision were not to be counted against the global limit for permanent legal resident entries or against the country of origin limits. The problem with this temporary program was that only a small percentage of the applicants related to IRCA immigrants would be fortunate enough to receive an entry visa. To qualify, the competition was fierce, since there were 1.1 million Mexicans who received amnesty through the nonagricultural provision in IRCA (Simanski 2008; Statistical Yearbook of Immigration and Naturalization 1994: 19). Most Mexican immigrants who wished to sponsor family members, therefore, had to follow the traditional process and wait for a visa under Mexico's entry limit.[12] The quickest way to legalize family members was to naturalize and sponsor one's relatives since in 1990 new admission restrictions were enacted, making it more difficult to sponsor relatives. In 1990, as part of the immigration and naturalization reforms of that year, Congress overhauled the admission process for family sponsorship and placed a numerical limit on such visas. A worldwide ceiling of 480,000 (out of 700,000 worldwide) was set for relatives sponsored by permanent legal residents and U.S. citizens. Although it was still relatively easy and quick for U.S. citizens to sponsor their immediate relatives, this was the first time Congress placed a limit on U.S. citizenship sponsorship. That is, even though a limit was placed, the relatives of U.S. citizens were given priority over other applicants, and if the global limit for that year was reached, those sponsored by U.S. citizens could still be given a visa. Their visas would merely be subtracted from the following year's family-sponsored visas (Statistical Yearbook of Immigration and Naturalization 1994: A2-2). The main consequence of this provision was that the waiting time increased for people who were not naturalized and were waiting to receive visas for their relatives. Thus the best approach to reducing the waiting period was for immigrants to naturalize.

The changes in 1990, however, were not as radical as those which followed. In the mid-1990s Congress once again revisited immigration law. The series of reforms that followed were prompted by what Congress perceived to be an immigration crisis caused by yet another economic disaster in Mexico. Once again Congress supported the executive branch's decision to offer Mexico assistance, but this time the congressmen were opposed to any type of amnesty provision as part of the deal. Instead, they favored reforms to stop immigrants at the border. They also supported legislation to make it difficult for anyone to sponsor relatives.

Mexico's financial crisis was caused by several factors, but it was precipitated by the devastating effects of the deregulation of the international markets under the North American Free Trade Agreement (NAFTA). On January 1, 1994, the United States, Canada, and Mexico signed a commerce treaty to end protectionist tariffs and allow goods to travel freely from country to country (Harvey 1998: 170). The agreement benefited many corporations in Mexico, specifically large-scale agricultural producers who were able to sell their crops in U.S. and Canadian markets at much lower prices than the domestic farmers. The agreement also benefited U.S. and Canadian industrialists who were able to flood the Mexican markets with less expensive electronics, cars, and home goods. On the other hand, within a few months of the signing of the agreement, NAFTA had devastated the small farmers of Mexico, specifically coffee producers in the state of Chiapas and small industrialists who could not lower their prices to compete with the international corporations (Stephen 2007). As a result, thousands of Mexican farmers and industrialists went bankrupt, and thousands of people lost their jobs. Making matters worse, Mexican capitalists, disappointed with the financial situation, withdrew their investments from Mexico. This all followed a series of political blunders that ranged from the privatization of federal industries, the mishandling of revolutionary movements in southern Mexico, the assassination of the front-runner in the Mexican presidential campaign, and, worst of all, the *tesobono* debacle. Tesobonos were treasury bonds secured by the federal government and made attractive to investors by guaranteeing their interest rate based on the value of the dollar rather than on the Mexican peso (U.S. General Accounting Office 1996). The federal government, in anticipation of the wealth NAFTA was expected to produce, issued tesobonos to increase the federal budget. As the economy worsened, however, largely as a result of NAFTA, Mexicans began to cash in their tesobonos, and the federal government gradually went bankrupt because it had insufficient funds to pay the interest it had promised investors. Those who cashed in their tesobonos early realized a gain, but the majority of investors were left holding worthless treasury bonds. Unfortunately, NAFTA did not produce the wealth federal officials had projected, and the bankrupted government did not have enough funds to run the country or pay its domestic and foreign debts.

To stabilize the Mexican economy, the U.S. government and U.S. banks issued Mexico a series of loans amounting to $20 billion in direct funds and also became guarantors for $28 billion in loans to be issued by Canada, the International Monetary Fund, and the Bank for International Settlements (Ibid., 2, 6). This package plan came to be known as Peso Shield (see Trouillot 2003). The loans were to be issued on a ten-year installment plan, with the first U.S. loan issued in January 1995. In turn, Mexico was required to make timely annual payments and to pay an annual $700 million in interest. Although the plan was controversial, the U.S. Congress endorsed it since failure to do so would have affected the American economy. If the Mexican economy was not stabilized, trade with Mexico, still the third largest importer of U.S. goods, would decline and 700,000 U.S. jobs would be lost. In total, the United States supplied 69 percent of Mexico's total foreign imports, which amounted to 10 percent of U.S. exports (U.S. General Accounting Office 1996: 3). In addition, the INS had projected that if the Mexican economy was not stabilized a 30 percent increase in undocumented immigration could be expected (Ibid., 113).

Before releasing funds to Mexico, the U.S. government required the Mexican government to agree to a U.S.-designed Recovery Plan. The U.S. government imposed an austerity program on all government domestic spending in Mexico for the next ten years. Mexico not only was to submit to the U.S. Treasury Department an annual budget explaining its federal expenditures, but also was required to guarantee the loans with its oil profits. To ensure that the oil profits were sufficient to cover the annual payments, the United States under the Recovery Plan was allowed by agreement with Mexico to set the amount of oil to be exported for the next ten years. If Mexico refused to follow the export plan and decreased its volume of oil sales by 15 percent to 25 percent, the U.S. Treasury was authorized to require immediate payment of U.S. loans. At this time Mexico was the third largest exporter of foreign oil to the United States, its exports constituting 12 percent of U.S. foreign oil (U.S. General Accounting Office 1992: 2). Moreover, the U.S. government was allowed to set the price of oil for the next ten years and determine which countries could buy Mexican oil. If Mexico did not meet its oil quota or sold oil on the spot to unauthorized buyers, it would default on the loan.

The U.S. government recognized that the Recovery Plan would shock the Mexican economy, lead to high unemployment rates, and stall national financial growth. Nonetheless, reducing domestic spending was indispensable since most of the government's revenues, including the income generated from the oil sales, was needed to pay the interest and installment payments on the foreign debt. The austerity program was viewed by the U.S. Treasury as the best approach to stabilizing the Mexican economy. Mexico's payment of its debts would ensure global investors that credit could be issued to private investors in the country, and in turn this would restore Mexico's financial global standing. By spring 1995 Mexico's economy was stabilized, and international banks began issuing credit to Mexican corporations even as they reinstated Mexico as a stable country in which foreign investments were secure.

In preparation for the flow of Mexican immigrants displaced by the austerity program, the U.S. government revisited immigration law. In late 1994 Congress began not only to study border enforcement policies to lessen the impact of border crossers on the U.S. economy, but also to consider ways of discouraging permanent legal residents from sponsoring relatives. While Congress debated immigration reform, on September 17, 1994, President Bill Clinton enacted Operation Gatekeeper, whose aim was to improve security along the U.S.-Mexico border and reduce the movement of border crossers and contraband (Inda 2007: 145; Stephen 2007: xiv). Clinton increased the funding of the border patrol and established additional checkpoints on interior highways (Nevins 2002). On September 30, 1996, Congress passed the Illegal Immigration Reform and Immigrant Responsibility Act (IIRIRA) (110 U.S. *Statutes at Large* [part 4] 3009) to enforce security along the U.S. borders and overhaul sponsorship requirements. Under Title 1, "Improvement to Border Control," one thousand border patrol agents were added, a border fence was to be constructed along the border in San Diego and other parts of California, more immigration stations were to be built in the interior of the United States to facilitate the detention of undocumented border crossers, and the number of immigration inspectors was to increase to protect legal workers through work site raids (Ibid., 669).

Under Title 5, "Restriction on Benefits to Aliens," permanent legal residents and undocumented aliens were disqualified from receiving social services, including Social Security, unemployment insurance, Medicare, Medicaid, and other types of federal benefits (Ibid., 674). Only permanent legal residents who were senior citizens and had worked ten quarters in the United States were exempt, as well as all types of AIDS patients who required medical treatment. Other permanent legal residents or undocumented aliens could claim federal assistance only during national disasters. Congress's intent in passing the benefit restrictions was to place pressure on immigrants to leave if they had medical problems or if they had fallen on hard times. The restrictions were also designed to discourage people from sponsoring family members unless they were prepared to be financially responsible for their medical and living expenses.

Furthermore, to discourage people from sponsoring relatives, income restrictions were raised and more responsibilities delineated. Under Title C, "Affidavits of Support," Congress required sponsors to reimburse the federal government for all expenses incurred by an immigrant who had relied on federal medical or financial assistance (Ibid., 676). Likewise, Congress raised the sponsor's affidavit of support. An exact financial figure was set to determine if a permanent legal resident earned enough income to sponsor a relative. Under IIRIRA alien sponsors had to have an annual income of

125 percent above the poverty level. Previously the amount had been set by an immigration officer's assessment of the sponsor's financial stability. This new requirement did not apply to U.S. citizen sponsors.

The IIRIRA reforms not only made it difficult to sponsor relatives, but also disqualified legal immigrants from applying for federal benefits. The irony of the reforms is that immigrants and undocumented people were required to pay taxes but were not able to receive services after paying into the system. These were not good times for immigrants, and it became painfully clear that it was to their benefit to naturalize if they were going to enjoy the same legal rights as other taxpaying U.S. citizens. Most important, for immigrants who had relatives in Mexico, U.S. citizenship gave them the advantage to more quickly legalize their relatives, without meeting the 125 percent income requirement.

IIRIRA erased all the gains farmworkers had made under earlier immigration laws. Since 1986 Congress had allowed over a million farmworkers and their families to qualify for legalization, yet in 1996 it cut the federal services they could apply for. It is uncertain why Congress did not exempt farmworkers from IIRIRA since it was a well-known fact that they were the poorest people in the nation, generally earning a household income of less than $7,500 (Rothenberg 2000: 6). It was nonsensical for Congress to allow farmworkers to legalize and send for their families and later be unwilling to financially assist them. It appears, however, that Congress was aware of this inconsistency and beginning in 1994 passed a series of laws to reform the adjustment process.[13] Under the 1994 Immigration and Nationality Technical Corrections Act, sec. 219, the 210A adjustment program was terminated (108 *U.S. Statutes at Large* [part 5] 4305; Rothenberg 2000: 227). In its place a new agricultural labor program was established, one which no longer allowed farmworkers to adjust their status. Under the 1994 reforms, and later under IIRIRA, agricultural workers were still welcomed but only for temporary work (sec. 218 of IIRIRA). From that point on, they entered under a new H2A temporary visa program, and their numbers were allowed to increase annually.[14] For example, in 1994, 7,000 temporary agricultural workers came from Mexico (Castañeda 2007: 86). By the late 1990s the annual number had grown to around 41,000 (Levine 2004b: 5), and in 2005 rose to 75,000 (Castañeda 2007: 86).

A special provision was added in IIRIRA, however, to allow some agricultural workers to adjust their status if they returned home. The attorney general was authorized to annually adjust the status of farmworkers (secs. 214, 245). To qualify they must have worked on U.S. farms and returned home at the end of their contracts (secs. 210, 213). They were then to submit their application to a U.S. consular agent in their country of origin and prove their profession was still agricultural labor. After 1995 fewer than 1,400 agricultural workers were allowed to adjust their status on an annual basis, and after 2003 the number dwindled to between 6 and 22.[15]

In retrospect, during Mexico's troubled economic times it was logical that Mexicans who were permanent legal residents preferred to remain in the United States and seek naturalization. In 1996, the number of Mexicans granted naturalization peaked at 217,418, considerably higher than the 67,238 of the previous year. By naturalizing Mexicans were following a more general pattern seen throughout the United States. In 1996 the overall number of naturalized citizens from all countries doubled in comparison to the previous year and reached a record number, 1,044,689. Never before had so many people naturalized in one year alone (Yearbook of Immigration Statistics 2003: 141,157).

History Repeats Itself: The Birthright Debate

During the 1990s Mexican immigrants applied for U.S. citizenship for various reasons. As I discussed earlier, the great majority were prompted by the immigration reforms passed by Congress. On the one hand liberal reforms such as IRCA allowed millions of Mexicans to qualify for citizenship, while on the other hand IIRIRA penalized Mexicans who failed to naturalize and thus prompted thousands to seek citizenship. Although the federal reforms were a major impetus pushing many Mexicans to naturalize, others chose to become U.S. citizens to protect their civil rights, in particular in California, where a hostile social movement against Mexican and Latino immigrants became widespread.

In the early 1990s an anti-immigrant social movement targeting Mexicans began in California and over the years gained massive popularity. During this period the population of Mexican origin boomed in California. It had doubled in the last ten years (N = 3.6 million, 1980) (U.S. Census 1982: 1). In 1990, of the 13,393,208 people of Mexican descent residing in the United States 6,118,996 lived in California (U.S. Census 1993a: 5; U.S. Census 1992a: 222). Texas continued to be home to the second largest concentration of people of Mexican origin, yet their numerical size was significantly smaller than that of California (tables 6.2, 6.3). Furthermore, the increase in the Mexican population in California was largely attributable to the growth of the foreign-born population. Forty percent of California's Mexican-origin population was foreign-born in 1990 (U.S. Census 1993b:

Table 6.2. Population of Mexican Origin in Texas and California, 1990

	Mexican Origin Total = 13,393,208			
	U.S.-Born		Mexican Foreign-Born	
	No.	%	No.	%
California	3,644,848	60	2,474,148	40
Texas	2,983,388	77	907,432	23
Other States	2,305,135	68	1,078,257	32
Total States	8,933,371	67	4,459,837	33

Sources: U.S. Census 1993a: 5; U.S. Census 1992a: 222; U.S. Census 1993b: 165; U.S. Census 1992b: 29; U.S. Census 1993c: 144.

165; U.S. Census 1993a: 5). Sadly, as the social movement against Mexicans intensified in California, thousands sought naturalization as a form of self-defense, as this would shield them from the full impact of IIRIRA and allow them to vote for elected officials who would represent their views.

Ironically, California's anti-Mexican social movement of the 1990s in many ways paralleled the anti-Mexican movement launched by the Populists in Texas a century earlier. Similar events converged at two points in time, which led to the rise of a similar nativist movement. In both places and historical moments parallel situations were manifest: the Mexican immigrant population increased significantly, nativists charged Mexican immigrants were a burden on the state's economy, particularly on the schools, the U.S.-born children of Mexican immigrants were charged with being illegitimate and undeserving voters, and a social movement gained ground to purify the vote. Although in Texas in 1897 the U.S. Western District Court *In re Rodriguez* brought closure to most of these nativist charges and ruled that people of Mexican origin could not be denied citizenship on the basis of race or parental origin, in the 1990s the same legal charges were resuscitated in California, albeit veiled in new legal cloaks. This time anti-immigrant activists in California proposed that Mexican Americans born in the United States should be denied U.S. citizenship if their mothers were undocumented aliens. Allegedly this was the best way to curb illegal immigration into California and cleanse the electoral process of millions of voters who were un-American and undeserving to be U.S. citizens (see Schuck and Smith 1985). How did the birthright debate and the anti-Mexican immigrant social movement in California flourish and influence thousands of Mexican immigrants to seek naturalization for purposes of self-defense?

In 1993 Gov. Pete Wilson called on American citizens to help him end the economic crisis undocumented aliens were creating in California (*Harvard Law Review* 1994: 1026).[16] He charged that illegals were a financial drain on the state's social service budgets, specifically on the schools and county hospitals. He alleged that the thousands of undocumented women who were giving birth were the main problem. These mothers were characterized as immoral and economic parasites because they could not afford to pay for their hospital stay, and, worst of all, they were having babies for the sole purpose of adjusting their illegal status (Inda 2002). Allegedly undocumented mothers and their children posed a financial burden because their children must be schooled and given free health care. This financial assessment was based on studies commissioned by the state government. Researchers had been asked to survey county hospitals that catered to indigent and Mexican populations. On the basis of these surveys, the researchers concluded that approximately 40 to 50 percent of the total births in California were attributable to undocumented alien mothers (Wood 1999: 494; *Congressional Record, Proceedings and Debates, 103rd Congress, First Session*, vol. 139, 1993, p. H1006). These studies also projected that

Table 6.3. Mexican Foreign-Born, 1930–2000

Decade	Mexican Foreign-Born	Total Mexican Ancestry
1930	641,462	1,422,533
1940	377,433	—
1950	451,490	891,980[a]
1960	575,902	1,735,592
1970	759,711	2,339,151
1980	2,199,221	8,740,439
1990	4,459,837	13,393,208
2000	9,177,487	20,640,711

[a]For 1950 and 1960 in the total Mexican ancestry category the enumerations include only the foreign-born and those of mixed foreign-stock families with at least one foreign-born parent.
Sources: U.S. Census 2003: 5; U.S. Census 2001: 4; U.S. Census 1993a: 5, U.S. Census 1992a: 222; U.S. Census 1982: 1; U.S. Census 1983: 1–17; U.S. Census: 1974: 17; U.S. Census 1961a: 366, 1–254; U.S Census 1954: 75, 130; U.S. Census 1953a: 82, 84; U.S. Census 1953b: 6; U.S. Census 1943: 88; U.S. Census 1933: 84, 90, 129.

about 50 percent of the so-called citizen children would eventually apply for food stamps. Governor Wilson urged his supporters to take action and end the illegal invasion of California by ending the practice of birthright citizenship. This was the only way to discourage illegal aliens from coming to California for the sole purpose of having so-called anchor babies. If the U.S.-born children of undocumented mothers were denied citizenship, Wilson projected, undocumented migration would decrease, the costs incurred because of welfare dependents would decline, and the children and their mothers would be deported, thus freeing California of future expenses. In general, the birthright legislation would lead to state financial relief. In 1993 Governor Wilson, working together with California Rep. Elton Gallegly, authored legislation to reduce illegal immigration to California by rescinding the citizenship status of people born to undocumented alien mothers (Eisgruber 1997: 56; *Harvard Law Review* 1994: 1026). On March 3, 1993, when Representative Gallegly introduced H.R. 129, "The Citizenship Reform Act of 1993," he did not find it necessary to occlude his position that Mexicans were the prime target of the legislation. Gallegly openly professed his war against illegal Mexican immigration:

> Mr. Speaker, as indispensable parts of my package of proposals for curbing illegal immigration, I introduce today, two bills dealing with the issue of automatic birthright citizenship. Both are aimed at ending the practice prevalent along the border for pregnant alien women to cross illegally into the United States for the purpose of obtaining, at taxpayers' expense, free medical care during their pregnancy, and free delivery of their babies in public hospitals, and then enabling those children to be declared American citizens at birth, with all the rights, privileges, and benefits available to citizens of the United States. (*Congressional Record, Proceedings and Debates, 103rd Congress, First Session,* vol. 139, 1993, p. H 1005)

Gallegly then argued that revising the citizenship clause of the Fourteenth Amendment of the U.S. Constitution was necessary because persons who did not respect American law were invading the country. He stated,

> We must recognize, however, that the United States is also a nation of finite resources and opportunities which must be available to, and shared by, all its citizens. Today, in many parts of this country, especially California, our cities and towns are being overrun with immigrants, both legal and undocumented, who pose major economic and law enforcement problems for local governments, and place an added burden on their already strained budgets.

I need not recite the economic, social and political problems that this
crisis of illegal immigration poses to Federal, State, and local governments,
to communities and neighborhoods, and to families, small businesses, law
enforcement, medical facilities, health providers, schools, social welfare
agencies, transportation systems, and to other legal immigrants seeking jobs
and assistance. (Ibid., H 1006)

Gallegly then argued that determining citizenship on the basis of parental
origin did not violate the Constitution because the Founding Fathers never
imagined the present reality, and they surely never intended to give citizenship to the floods of illegals entering the country. He believed that in
modern times citizenship must be determined by congressional legislation,
based on the beliefs of the citizenry, not by constitutional case law. Under
current citizenship law, the U.S. Constitution delineates who is a citizen,
and the courts interpret the citizenship clause of the Constitution. Under
section 1 of the Fourteenth Amendment the U.S. Constitution delineates
that "All persons born or naturalized in the U.S., and subject to the jurisdiction thereof, are citizens of the U.S. and of the state wherein, they reside"
(Ibid., H1005).

Representative Gallegly proceeded to explain that the citizenship clause
of the Fourteenth Amendment is based on the principle of *ju solis,* a legal
philosophy adopted from English common law and practiced in the United
States since its inception as an English colony. Although determining
citizenship is a domain of the courts protected by constitutional law, Gallegly proposed that it was time to take this power away from the courts
by amending the U.S. Constitution and give it to the citizenry. Two revisions were needed to fulfill his mandate. First, section 1 of the Fourteenth
Amendment would be revised to rescind the legal principle of ju solis. New
language would be inserted declaring that the U.S.-born children of undocumented alien mothers were not citizens. Gallegly offered the following
revision: "Section 1: All persons born in the United States and subject to
the jurisdiction thereof, of mothers who are citizens or legal residents of the
United States, and all persons naturalized in the United States are citizens
of the United States and of the State where they reside" (Ibid., H 1006).

He then advanced a second proposal giving Congress, rather than the judicial courts, the power to interpret the meaning of the Fourteenth Amendment. Section 2 of the 14th Amendment would be revised to read, "The
Congress shall have power to enforce this article by appropriate legislation"
(Ibid., H 1007).

To Gallegly's disappointment, few of his colleagues in Congress supported his resolution. Most concurred that regulating unauthorized immi-

gration was imperative, but that changing the U.S. Constitution to do so was unnecessary. Congressmen suggested that other policies be designed without forcing Congress and the country to embark upon a divisive debate over a constitutional amendment that most likely would not be ratified because birthright citizenship was an American philosophical principle. Furthermore, debating the resolution would be a waste of time, as a supermajority of Congress was needed to pass it as well as ratification by three-fourths of the state legislatures (Houston 2000). Both measures were deemed unlikely to succeed.

Following the failed initiative, Governor Wilson continued to move forward against undocumented immigration, and in 1994 his agenda gained momentum when a grassroots organization named Save Our State (SOS) placed Proposition 187 before the voters (Rodriguez 2007: 244). The referendum was creative, as its aim was to make California a hostile place for undocumented immigrants, and through this strategy reduce unauthorized immigration. If Proposition 187 passed, undocumented aliens would be disqualified from receiving any type of state-funded social service, including schooling and medical care. Proposition 187 also required police officers, teachers, and health care workers to turn in any person whom they suspected of being undocumented.

When the SOS movement began, some Mexican Americans supported the social service exclusionary provision of Proposition 187, as it appeared to be a strategy to regulate unauthorized immigration and was not directed at the legal or native-born populations. On the day of the election the proposition passed by a margin of three to two. Approximately 23 percent of people of Mexican origin voted for the proposition (Rodriguez 2007: 243).[17] However, after its passage it became clear that the proposition merely masked general bad feelings about the perceived "browning" of California. Many California residents resented the growing numbers of people of Mexican descent regardless of whether they were U.S.-born, legal, or illegal. In fact, people of Mexican descent were a very large and growing population, one that lived everywhere, came in different colors, and belonged to all social classes. Likewise, the anti-Mexican feelings were projected onto other Latino groups, as many white Americans could not distinguish ethnic differences and in general perceived Latinos to be immigrant and undocumented. Latinos who had permanent legal residence were specifically susceptible to the anti-Mexican propaganda because many were monolingual Spanish speakers or spoke with Spanish accents and were often mistaken for undocumented Mexicans (Ochoa 2004). Furthermore, though undocumented immigrants had been the named subjects of the proposition, in general people of Mexican descent and other Latinos felt the impact of the propaganda, as many white residents of California held the misconception that most Latinos were either undocumented or were the children of undocumented parents (Chavez 2008). Mexican Americans and native-born Latinos were also perceived by many white Americans to have unfairly acquired the right to vote because they were the children of undocumented aliens, and they were misusing the ballot box to support causes that true Americans were against (Wood 1999).

Although the U.S. 9th District Court ultimately ruled that most measures of Proposition 187 were unconstitutional and would not be implemented, for people of Mexican origin and other Latinos the damage was done: the resolution's passage had created a hostile ambiance for them. In response to the hostile environment, people of Mexican origin and other Latino groups sought relief through the ballot box. Mexican American political activists launched several campaigns to register voters and elect candidates who would put an end to the anti-Mexican immigrant hysteria. Between 1994 and the late 1990s Latinos became the fastest growing ethnic groups to register to vote, with an annual net increase of around 347.6 thousand new voters (William C. Velasquez Institute 2008: 5). In the case of voters of Mexican origin the number of registered voters increased by 44 percent. The growth was nationwide but largely attributable to voters of Mexican origin in California. A similar pattern occurred among Salvadoran and Guatemalan immigrants in California.[18]

For the anti-immigrant political activists who had worked so diligently to pass Proposition 187, the naturalization surge was unexpected and unwelcomed. They reacted to this miscalculation by regrouping to seek a solution to the electoral nightmare they had created. They decided to resuscitate the birthright debate. SOS activists and other California citizens took up Representative Gallegly's earlier cause. Their principal aim was to purify the vote by preventing the U.S.-born children of undocumented mothers from becoming citizens. People who were living in the United States illegally and were opposed to the goals of SOS would thus not be able to vote in the future. This was an opportune time to introduce birthright legislation, as congressmen throughout the country were in the midst of considering illegal immigration reform, which, as discussed earlier, eventually was codified under IIRIRA. This turn of events also coincided with Mexico's economic turmoil following Peso Shield and President Clinton's Operation Gatekeeper in California.

On January 4, 1995, U.S. Rep. Brian Bilbray of California introduced legislation to deny U.S. citizenship to children born in the United States of parents who were not permanent legal residents or citizens.[19] Gallegly's earlier legislation was reintroduced but expanded to include groups who were on temporary visas. New procedural methods to convert the bill into law were also introduced. Under H.R. 1363, or the "Citizenship Reform Act of 1995," Bilbray and his twenty-nine cosponsors tried to bypass the traditional procedures required of Congress to amend the U.S. Constitution (*Congressional Record, Proceedings and Debates, 104th Congress, First Session,* vol. 147, part 27, 1995, p. 2522). H.R. 1363 proposed that the Fourteenth Amendment could be revised by an administrative order of Congress without ratification by the states. Congress could do this by amending the Immigration and Nationality Act (INA), a power given to Congress by the U.S. Constitution. Since naturalization law delineates who qualifies for U.S. citizenship, the law could be revised and a new one written to define who is a U.S. citizen. In this way birthright citizenship could be nullified and a new definition prescribed by Congress. According to Bilbray and his supporters, once the INA act was revised, the Fourteenth Amendment of the U.S. Constitution would automatically have to be amended to create a uniform citizenship law (Houston 2000). Amending the INA would bypass the ratification procedure required to amend the U.S. Constitution. On March 30, 1995, Congress debated H.R. 1363. They discussed amending the citizenship clause of the INA and denying citizenship to children whose parents were undocumented or on temporary visas. H.R. 1363 read, "A bill to amend the Immigration and Naturalization Act to deny citizenship at birth to children born in the U.S. of parents who are not citizens or permanent resident aliens" (*Congressional Record, Proceedings and Debates, 104th Congress, First Session,* vol. 141, 1995, p. H4031). At the close of the debate, matters were unresolved, and the resolution was left for future consideration. More support would have to be generated for it to pass.

In the meantime the Justice Department issued the opinion that H.R. 1363 was unconstitutional. Once again the Justice Department opposed the resolution, as it had in 1993 when Gallegly introduced the first version. Walter Dellinger, the assistant attorney general, wrote the opinion advising the House Judiciary Committee that the resolution violated the U.S. Constitution on several grounds (Dellinger 1995). Dellinger concurred with the resolution's sponsors that Congress had the power to amend the Fourteenth Amendment and pass legislation to change the nation's citizenship policies. But Congress, he stated, must follow the legal procedure outlined in the Constitution and could not revise the amendment through de facto means.

Dellinger then addressed a second argument presented by the birthright reformers, namely, that the children of the undocumented came under the jurisdiction of U.S. immigration laws rather than the protection of the Fourteenth Amendment because their parents had entered illegally. According to the supporters of H.R. 1363, the Constitution gave Congress the power to exclude certain groups from U.S. citizenship. This was constitutional as over the years the judicial courts had upheld this right. If Congress, therefore, chose to use illegal entry as the motive to deny a group U.S. citizenship, it could do so without violating the Constitution. Many legal precedents indicated that this was the case. In 1857 the U.S. Supreme Court ruled in *Dred Scott v. Sandford* that the Constitution allowed Congress to exclude free blacks from U.S. citizenship, and in 1884 the Supreme Court again upheld this right in *Elk. v. Wilkens* when it ruled that only Congress had the power to decide when detribalized Native Americans could be treated as citizens (Carens 1987; Houston 2000; Schuck and Smith 1985). Disregarding the fact that these rulings had eventually been nullified by congressional legislation, the supporters of H.R. 1363 argued that the courts upheld the right of Congress to exclude certain groups from citizenship. These legal precedents therefore allowed Congress to deny citizenship to the U.S.-born children of undocumented aliens.

Dellinger responded that these cases did not pertain to the legal issue under consideration because in 1898, in *U.S. v. Wong Kim Ark,* the U.S. Supreme Court had ruled that the "subject to jurisdiction" clause of the Fourteenth Amendment applied to the U.S.-born children of alien parents. Under this legal principle a person born in the United States is considered part of the classes subject to the jurisdiction of the state and is considered a U.S. citizen. In *Wong Kim Ark* the justices ruled that only alien enemies, children born in foreign ships, and diplomats and their children were not subject to the jurisdiction of the state. These exemptions neither applied to the U.S.-born children of the undocumented, nor in any way implied that they acquired the alien status of their parents. For over a century the courts and attorney generals had consistently applied this meaning to the "subject to jurisdiction" clause, and its meaning could not be arbitrarily changed by Congress. Furthermore, Dellinger added that under *Wong Kim Ark* the Supreme Court had affirmed the principle of ju solis when it ruled that U.S.-born persons did not acquire the citizenship status of their alien parents. The only exceptions to the ju solis rule were the same as those applied to the "subject to jurisdiction" clause. Therefore, because the children of undocumented parents were not enemies of the state and did not conform to the other excluded categories, they were part of the classes of people included within the meaning of the citizenship clause of the Fourteenth Amendment.

Following the Department of Justice's report, Congress failed to pass H.R. 1363 and instead chose to regulate immigration through other means. As discussed earlier, Congress decided to discourage both legal and unauthorized immigration from Mexico by passing the Illegal Immigration Reform and Immigrant Responsibility Act of 1996. Unfazed by the failure of H.R. 1363, the supporters of birthright legislation continued forward. From 1997 to 2007, seven more resolutions were introduced, largely spearheaded by Republican congressmen. The wording of the resolutions went back and forth from trying to amend the immigration and naturalization laws to pushing forward a resolution to amend the U.S. Constitution. All of the resolutions failed to pass, and the U.S.-born children of undocumented parents retained their citizenship and the right to vote when they came of age.

While these resolutions were being advanced, people of Mexican origin and other Latinos maintained the momentum to stop the anti-immigrant hysteria by exercising their right to vote. At the national level Latinos continued to register to vote in overwhelming numbers. On an annual basis the number of Latino registered voters continued to triple in size. In California, by the year 2000 the voter registration drives had brought about a change in the ethnic makeup of the California legislature. That year twenty of the eighty seats in the state assembly and seven of the forty seats in the state senate were held by Latinos, most of them of Mexican descent (Rodriguez 2007: 251). At the national level in the period 1992–2004 the number of Latino elected officials had grown tremendously. In 1992 there were 3,500 Latino elected officials, and by 2004 the number had increased to 5,000 (William C. Velasquez Institute 2008: 5–6).

House Resolution 4437

In 2005 Congress again chose to revise the INA to resolve what it perceived to be the problem of the rising level of unauthorized Mexican immigration. Many resolutions were introduced, including birthright legislation. The difference this time, in comparison to previous sessions, was the mean nature of the debates. A new strategy advanced to control unauthorized immigration was to penalize the families, friends, and citizens who shielded undocumented people from detection. In 2005 the U.S. House of Representatives passed H.R. 4437, entitled "Border Protection, Antiterrorism, and Illegal Immigration Control Act of 2005" (H.R. 4437, in www.govtrack .us/congress). Republicans overwhelmingly supported the bill, while most Democrats rejected it. Of the 239 legislators who voted in favor of the resolution, 203 were Republicans and 36 were Democrats.[20] The aim of the bill was to reduce unauthorized immigration by increasing border security and by criminalizing the behavior of individuals who knowingly gave aide to undocumented aliens. Next, the bill was to be voted on by the Senate. If the bill passed the Senate, the reforms would be of historic proportions, since people who were found to have offered shelter, transportation, and medical assistance to undocumented aliens could now be arrested and converted into aggravated felons (Title 2). The rationalization for criminalizing such behavior was to deter family members, church congregations, and city governments from shielding undocumented people from detection. The prison sentence was set at one year. Furthermore, illegal entry was raised from a civil crime carrying a maximum fine of $250 to an aggravated felony mandating a similar prison sentence.

In March 2006, as the Senate was set to begin debate, Cardinal Roger M. Mahoney of the Los Angeles Archdiocese (California) spoke out against H.R. 4437, announcing that if the bill passed his priests would be instructed to defy the legislation (Watanabe 2006). Other controversial measures contained in the bill included the installation of seven hundred miles of border fencing along the U.S.-Mexico border (Title 10), mandating city councils and county boards to cooperate with the federal government in arresting and detaining aliens (Title 2,6), mandating local law enforcement officers to arrest any drunk person who appeared to be an alien and investigate their residential status (Title 6), and prohibiting state, county, and local governments from receiving federal funds if sanctuary policies for undocumented aliens were adopted (Title 2).

The proposed legislation did not have a guest worker program or amnesty provision. Congress, however, did oppose including a birthright provision in H.R. 4437 and did not adopt any other birthright bill. For example, Senate Bill 2117, presented by Sen. James Inhofe, a Republican from Oklahoma, was not supported. His bill proposed to clarify the circumstances under which a person born in the United States was a U.S. citizen. The bill died upon introduction (S. 2117, in www.govtrack.us/congress). Likewise H.R. 698, a birthright resolution introduced by Nathan Deal of Georgia, failed. The bill was supported by 86 Republicans and 1 Democrat from Minnesota. In principle, passing birthright legislation was probably unnecessary since H.R. 4437 already contained provisions that would lead to similar ends. Given that under H.R. 4437 the U.S.-born children of undocumented families could be arrested for aiding their undocumented parents and siblings, this provision made life a living terror and eventually could lead to the exodus of such types of people.

While the American public awaited the Senate's action, opponents of the anti-immigrant legislation organized and began to publicly protest against what they perceived to be a social injustice. The first protest, organized on March 10, 2006, in Los Angeles, was attended by over one hundred thousand people.[21] Soon marches and rallies were being held throughout the country, the largest in Los Angeles, Dallas, Chicago, Philadelphia, Monterey, Santa Cruz, Seattle, Milwaukee, Phoenix, Denver, Riverside, Atlanta, Kansas, Charlotte, Sacramento, Austin, San Diego, and El Paso. A few days later, on March 24 and 25, nationwide marches were organized to take place simultaneously throughout U.S. cities. Millions of people attended; the crowd in Los Angeles alone was estimated to be between half a million and one million protesters. Speakers at the rallies demanded that the Senate defeat the ideals set forth in H.R. 4437 and instead pass a comprehensive immigration reform bill that included amnesty for the estimated eleven million undocumented people residing in the United States. Instrumental in the organization of the nationwide marches was the radio personality Piolín Sotelo, whose early morning nationally syndicated show "Piolín por la mañana" encouraged people to protest and informed listeners across the country when and where the rallies were to be held. Other local Spanish-language newscasters also informed listeners of local events. The rallies continued throughout the country until mid-June 2007.

During the Senate debates most representatives overwhelmingly disagreed with the aggravated felony charge provisions of H.R. 4437, while favoring increased funding for border security. As the deliberations proceeded for months, most senators chose not to support the House's immigration reforms and instead developed their own modified resolutions. Of various Senate bills introduced, Senate Bill 2166, the "Comprehensive Immigration Reform Act," received the most support. The debate continued until June 18, 2007, when negotiations broke down and it became obvious that no bill would obtain a majority consensus. The main issues dividing the senators were amnesty for undocumented residents and resuming a large-scale agricultural guest worker program. Unlike the past, when negotiations for IRCA were finalized between opposing sides, this time there was no middle ground for opponents of amnesty (Associated Press, May 18, 2007; MALDEFian, June 18, 2007; William C. Velasquez Institute, May 18, 2007). Under IRCA, amnesty for undocumented workers was negotiated after its advocates compromised and agreed to support an agricultural guest worker program if amnesty was included in the immigration reforms. Advocates for amnesty, who opposed a guest worker program, compromised because the benefits of doing so far outweighed the costs. This time, however, there was no middle ground. Those who supported amnesty were willing to compromise, but those who opposed it were not. The popular slogan of the anti-amnesty proponents became, "No Amnesty. No How. No Way."

The only provision that members of both houses of Congress had earlier agreed on was improving border security. The Secure Fence Act of October 26, 2006, was passed to reinforce and construct new fences along the U.S.–Mexico border (120 *U.S. Statutes at Large* [part 3] 2638). The existing fences along the California border were to be reinforced and extended, while new ones were to be constructed along Arizona, New Mexico, and Texas. Budgetary appropriations were also made for the Department of Homeland Security.

While the debates were taking place, Mexican immigrants once again began to apply for naturalization in large numbers, and beginning in 2007 the Department of Homeland Security reported a surge in the number of granted applications. In 2007, the number of Mexican immigrants naturalizing peaked at 18.5 percent of the total foreign-born naturalizing that year, and the following year it increased to 22.2 percent (N = 122,258 out of 660,477) (Rytina and Caldera 2007: 2, 3; Lee and Rytina 2008: 2). Mexico also continued to be the leading country of birth of those naturalizing. Overall this surge replicated the radical increase that had occurred among Mexicans following the passage of IIRIRA. A similar pattern was found among Cubans, Dominicans, Salvadorans, and Guatemalans.[22]

Mexico's Reaction to the Immigration Debates: The Politics of Oil

The immigration debates shocked the Mexican government. President Vicente Fox of Mexico had not anticipated the passage of the harsh legislation in the House. On the contrary, he expected to negotiate a guest worker program. President George W. Bush had assured Fox that he supported comprehensive immigration reform, including a guest worker program (The White House, Press briefing, Scott McClellan, January 10, 2004). The Fox administration readily understood the current reality and expected large-scale deportations to begin in the near future.

During the debates Mexico adopted a wait-and-see attitude. In the meantime relations between the two countries ran smoothly in terms of trade and finances. Mexico remained the third largest supplier of oil to the United States, while U.S. corporations continued to be Mexico's largest foreign investors (U.S. Department of State, April 2008). U.S. corporations made up approximately 47 percent of all foreign investments in Mexico. Furthermore, the maquiladora program continued to run smoothly, with nearly three thousand plants in operation, of which 90 percent were partially or fully owned by U.S. corporations (Cañas and Gilmer 2007; Legislative Finance Committee, 2008). Mexico found the passage of H.R. 4437 and the Senate's refusal to support a guest worker program perplexing since U.S. farmers were annually increasing their demand for H2-A agricultural workers (Castañeda 2007: 86). Approximately 75,000 entered annually in 2005 and 2006 (Ibid.; Barr, Jefferys, and Monger 2008: 4).

The U.S. Congress's mean-spirited stance was considered a reversal in attitude following the good relations that had transpired after the attack of 9/11 and Hurricane Katrina. Both times Mexico had proven it was a trusted ally of the United States, and in turn the U.S. government graciously accepted Mexico's support. After 9/11, Mexico agreed to finance a costly security program to protect the United States against terrorists planning an attack from Mexico. A "22-Point Smart Border Agreement" was endorsed by both countries, and in Mexico the accord led to the reorganization of the nation's law enforcement agencies (Shirk 2003). Implementation of the agreement was costly for Mexico since dealing with terrorist threats was not one of its federal funding priorities; previously the responsibility had been mainly entrusted to local police. The reorganization required all levels of law enforcement to coordinate their activities and to train personnel to be alert and prepared to deal with terrorist attacks. Thus when Congress debated establishing a fence along the border and converting unauthorized border crossers into felons—rather than guest workers—this was a shock to the Mexican government. The congressional actions were also a direct reversal of the good-natured actions Congress had taken toward Mexico in the aftermath of 9/11. For example, on July 2, 2002, President Bush granted posthumous citizenship to undocumented aliens who had died in combat during the Iraq and Afghanistan wars when he signed the "Expedited Naturalization Executive Order" (The White House, July 3, 2002). And less than two years later several congressmen gained enough support to change U.S. law and grant the families of these fallen heroes the same benefits given to American citizens (Martinez 2003: 76).[23] Previously posthumous citizenship was a symbolic gesture of gratitude because dependents of undocumented heroes were not eligible to receive military benefits.

More recently, and during the House debates over H.R. 4437, Bush showed his high regard for Mexico when he allowed Mexican troops to enter U.S. soil following Hurricane Katrina. On September 1, 2005, he accepted Mexico's offer of food and medical aid for the victims of the hurricane. He approved the entry of 196 Mexican troops, rescue experts from the Mexican Red Cross, and a team of medical doctors (Alvarez 2005; Michael 2005a, 2005b). This was the first time since the Mexican-American War of 1846 to 1848 that Mexican troops entered U.S. territory. Four rescue teams of the Mexican Red Cross assisted in finding and rescuing survivors, while the Mexican ship *Papaloapan* brought two mi-17 helicopters, eight all-terrain vehicles, seven amphibious vehicles, two tankers, and radio communication equipment to help in the rescue of victims. The Mexican Air Force and Mexican Army delivered food and clothing to the victims sheltered in Houston and San Antonio.

International relations in general were good, or at least Mexico thought so. Mexico acknowledged that undocumented immigration was a problem but believed the maquiladora program and U.S. investments in Mexico outweighed the problems border crossers produced. These people, after all, worked for less than the value of their labor was worth. From Mexico's point of view, the only area of contention was that the Mexican Congress had recently regained its power to terminate the oil agreements made under Peso Shield and favored policies not necessarily beneficial to the United States. In 2004, when Mexico completed its debt payment to the United States for the loans received under the Peso Shield agreements, U.S. regulation over Mexican oil ended, and Mexico regained the right to set the amount of oil production and to determine whom to sell its oil to. Although many Mexican congressmen favored reducing the amount of oil production in order to reserve deposits for future use and sale, President Fox repeatedly assured President Bush that this would not happen (Cruz 2007; see U.S. Government Accountability Office 2007).

In February 2006, two months after H.R. 4437 passed the House, the Mexican Senate and President Fox held a series of meetings with academics, former policy makers, journalists, and social activists to explore the change of mood within the U.S. Congress. Their task was to develop a plan to convince the U.S. Senate not to pass H.R. 4437 (Castañeda 2007: 150). The Mexican Congress and the executive branch concluded their mission by devising a proposal to pass comprehensive immigration reform in Mexico. Their aim was to convince the U.S. Congress not to penalize Mexican nationals residing in the United States, as Mexico was willing and able to regulate illegal immigration. The plan to be instituted promised to deter, dissuade, and discourage persistent and permanent illegal immigration from Mexico to the United States. Mexico's new immigration policy would go beyond its present commitment to stop illegal immigration on the southern border along Guatemala and Belize. In addition, Mexico would pursue a comprehensive immigration reform plan affecting both its northern and southern borders. To reduce unauthorized border crossings the federal government was prepared to prohibit any person from exiting Mexico if they did not have the correct permits and financial proof that they could fund their stay in the United States. Some congressmen had suggested stricter legislation, such as fining deported aliens. This provision was defeated since it would have caused severe hardship among people already in distress. Furthermore, an incentive reentry program would be established to encourage Mexican guest workers to return home. Returning guest workers would be given tax-deductible benefits, including tax deductions for building homes in their communities.

The Fox administration had high hopes that the White House would accept Mexico's comprehensive immigration reform plan and in turn lobby the U.S. Congress to drop its legislation. On March 29 to 31, 2006, Fox presented the plan to Bush during the presidential Cancun Summit meetings. Acquiring Bush's support was essential.

During the talks President Fox was optimistic that Mexico's plan was sufficiently strong to gain President Bush's endorsement. He also pursued amnesty for undocumented people at the meetings, but realistically it was public knowledge that this was a lost cause since Bush had never expressed support for general amnesty (The White House, Press briefing, Scott McClellan, January 10, 2004). Fox was confident that the reentry plan for guest workers would convince Bush to support an agricultural guest worker program. As part of the negotiations, Fox presented a favorable oil agreement by promising to increase the sale of oil to the United States, regardless of the growing national opposition to increasing production (Cruz 2007; Pérez 2010). Fox also anticipated that Bush would be pleased to learn that Mexico was prepared to purchase from U.S. corporations over $50 million of oil drilling technology to explore new oil deposits recently discovered in the gulf coast area (Embassy of the U.S. 2007; newmax.com 2006; U.S. Government Accountability Office 2007).

Fox was disappointed to hear that Bush was not impressed with the plan and did not consider making immigration concessions as a means of negotiating a favorable oil agreement. The oil deposits had been confirmed, but because the feasibility of extracting the oil had not yet been determined, the U.S. government was not convinced that the deposits merited consideration in the negotiation talks. Bush asked Mexico not to intervene in U.S. affairs and informed Fox that he would support the legislation passed by Congress (Associated Press, March 31, 2006; The White House, March 30, 2006). Bush disappointed Fox further when he requested that security over Mexico's southern border be improved by building a fence along the Mexico–Guatemala border to reduce illegal immigration from Central America into the United States.

Following the talks, President Fox and the Mexican Congress resigned themselves to the reality that the U.S. Congress was in support of neither amnesty nor a guest worker program. Needless to say, after the failed talks Mexico did not implement any of its reforms or agree to build a fence along the Mexico-Guatemala border. On the contrary, Fox publicly admonished the U.S. government for passing the Security Fence Act and depicted this as a hateful act against Mexico and not the best way to secure a neighbor's border (Castañeda 2007). Furthermore, in late 2006 he announced that Mexico would reduce its production of oil. The 2 million barrels a day currently sold to the United States would immediately decline to 1.4 million barrels a day (Energy Information Administration, August 26, 2008; Energy Information Administration, September 9, 2008; PEMEX, September 9, 2008).[24] By 2008, Mexico would reduce its U.S. sales by 50 percent and reduce the amount of oil to 1 million barrels per day. The official rationale given for the cutbacks was the need to conserve oil for future generations. Whether this was true or a transparent rationalization to mask nationalistic sentiments is uncertain, as oil historically has been big business in Mexico (Brown and Knight 1992). Currently, Mexico depends heavily on its foreign oil exports since 30 percent of the federal budget is based on its oil revenues (U.S. Department of State 2008). Mexico is also highly dependent on the United States and cannot afford to annoy the U.S. government. In 2007 U.S. corporations exported over $136 billion in goods to Mexico, while Mexico exported $223 billion to the United States (U.S. Census 2008; U.S. Department of State, 2008).

The Birthright Debate in Texas

Unlike California, Texas did not experience a hostile statewide referendum against Mexican immigration in the 1990s. Likewise, although Mexican immigrants in Texas replicated the naturalization surges of the 1990s, largely in response to IIRIRA, naturalization patterns have differed in Texas because Mexicans have a long history of consistently applying for naturalization in large numbers (Freeman, Plascencia, Gonzales Baker, M. Orozco 2002). For example, since the 1960s Mexico has been the leading country of birth of the newly naturalized citizens of Texas, ranging from 59 percent to 39 percent of the total (see appendix 2, table 6.1). And in 2008

Mexican Tejanos comprised 49 percent of the total number of naturalized citizens for that year (N = 40,068 out of 82,129) (Yearbook of Immigration Statistics 2008, table: Persons naturalized by State or Territory of Residence and Region and Country of Birth, 2008). Nonetheless, although a social movement against Mexican immigration like the one in California was not carried out in Texas, this does not mean that the birthright debate is dead in the state or that congressional representatives from Texas do not consider undocumented migration a problem. On the contrary, most representatives from Texas supported H.R. 4437 and opposed amnesty. Twenty-one of the 32 representatives from Texas in the House supported passage, 10 opposed it, and 1 person failed to vote (govtrack.us). In the Senate, although H.R. 4437 failed to pass and only the border fence and enforcement policies were adopted, the Texas senators, John Cornyn and Kay Bailey Hutchison, heatedly opposed amnesty. Both senators supported a guest worker program but considered amnesty a mistake that should not be repeated (Cornyn 2005; Cornyn 2007; Hutchison and Cornyn 2007; McKenzie 2007).

Although at this time it is uncertain what legislation will be supported in the U.S. Congress by the congressional representatives from Texas, and whether they will reject or support the two extremes of immigration reform, to either criminalize illegal entry or to give amnesty to the undocumented, it is unlikely that they will support federal birthright legislation. In the senate, Texans have never supported revoking the U.S. citizenship of Mexican Americans when their parents are undocumented aliens, while in the House Democrats are opposed to birthright legislation and Republicans are divided. From 2005 to 2009 four birthright resolutions have been introduced in Congress, receiving minimal to moderate support from the Republican Texas House members (H.R. 698, H.R. 133, at www.govtrack.us/congress; H.R. 126, H.R. 1868 in www.thomas.gov).[25] However, the fact that the Texas representatives are divided and the majority did not support birthright legislation does not mean the issue can be dismissed as a thing of the past. Not at all, because when the last resolution was introduced on April 2, 2009, fourteen of the twenty Republican representatives supported passage of a moderate version. They supported H.R. 1868, which denied citizenship only to children both of whose parents were undocumented and rejected Representative Gallegly's resolution (H. R. 126) to deny citizenship to all children whose mothers were undocumented, regardless of the legal status of the father.

Currently, although at the national level the birthright legislation does not have much congressional backing, in Texas there is growing support for it, and several dedicated advocates and organizations have developed a clever argument. Some Texas legislators have introduced the idea that some of the political rights U.S. citizens enjoy can be determined by state legislatures when a citizen's parents are undocumented. This is a unique idea that explores the division of power between the states and the federal government.

On April 21, 2008, I observed the following scenario unfold when I attended a public hearing at the Texas State Capitol to hear public testimony on the question of whether the state legislature should pass a uniform law mandating all counties to give office space to Immigration Custom Enforcement (ICE) agents (Texas House of Representatives, Committee on State Affairs, Agenda, April 21, 2008). Currently, in most counties this decision is left to the county sheriff and the county commissioners. The hearing also explored whether the state legislature should remove the county commissioners from the decision-making process. Many county sheriffs throughout Texas support the coordinaton of enforcement efforts, and the office space issue is not a problem. However, in Travis County, the home of the state legislature, citizens who opposed giving ICE office space raised a valid point that needed to be addressed by the state legislature. Opponents of the ICE-sheriff initiative had charged that the Travis County Board of Commissioners, not the sheriff, had the legal right to determine if office space could be given to ICE agents. After county hearings were held on this issue, legal counsel for the county concluded that the sheriff had the sole right to make the agreement with ICE agents. Yet giving ICE permanent office space was a different matter since the county owned the sheriff's building. Administratively, to allocate space the sheriff needed approval from the county. After a series of town hall meetings the county commissioners chose not to intervene and left matters to the Travis County Sheriff's Office (Guttin 2010).

Within the state legislature, the Travis County case came to the attention of many legislators because a valid legal point about the division of power between the county commissioners and the county sheriff had been raised. Some members of the legislature who favored increasing the presence of immigration agents at the county jail determined that this issue had to be resolved and a uniform state law passed to remove the county commissioners from the decision-making process. Supporters of the coordinating efforts therefore asked the House Committee on Legislative Affairs to hold a hearing and listen to public testimony on the ICE-sheriff debate. When I attended the hearing on April 21 I was surprised to discover that the county jail issue was closely tied to the birthright debate.

At the hearing the witnesses were divided. Most of the opposition came from civil rights organizations such as the Mexican American Legal Defense and Educational Fund (MALDEF) and the Texas Council on Family Violence. The advocates for the proposition ranged from private citizens unaffiliated with organizations to members of national organizations such as the Heritage Foundation, U.S. Border Watch, and local immigration reform groups such as Texans for Immigration Reform and Citizens for Immigration Reform. In total, seventeen groups and private citizens testified.

After listening to the testimony for six hours I was struck by one element common to every testimony. The witnesses briefly stated their position but then took a longer time to either advocate for or argue against the reintroduction of bills in the state legislature to instate birthright legislation. This perplexed me because the witnesses were providing testimony on a federal matter. In sum, the advocates of the ICE coordinating efforts favored revoking the citizenship of children born to undocumented parents and in their testimony expressed a monolithic iteration of popular slogans. Their testimonies appeared to be coordinated, practiced, and dramatically staged. Rep. Leo Berman, representing District 6 (Tyler), was the first to testify. He began by stating that he supported the presence of ICE in the county jails because it was Texas's legal right to defend its borders against illegal aliens. He got right to the point. After making a brief statement on ICE, he dedicated the remainder of his time to arguing why Texas needs to pass birthright legislation. Representative Berman argued that since the U.S. Congress refused to amend the Fourteenth Amendment and deny birthright citizenship to the children of undocumented aliens, the state legislature had the legal right and obligation to control its borders.

Berman then continued to educate the public on the virtues of passing birthright legislation. As I looked around at the audience I observed that half were laughing, while the other half were cheering. A few elderly ladies even appeared to be praying in support of Berman. According to Berman, in Texas illegal immigrants introduce infectious diseases such as polio, malaria, tuberculosis, and shags. The illegal aliens' anchor babies were a worse problem, as in their teenage years they were prone to violence and most of them joined gangs. Allegedly illegal aliens and their babies each cost the state $150,000. In a public statement Berman had released the previous day he stated the same points but added that Texas had to act now. Allegedly the illegal alien problem was growing worse because Arizona and Oklahoma recently passed laws to reduce illegal immigration, and illegals from those states were now moving to Texas (Maynard 2008). He estimated that the illegal population in Texas had grown to two million.

Berman proudly concluded his testimony by announcing that he was working with several congressmen to reintroduce federal birthright legislation. He informed the audience that birthright reform advocates in Congress were prepared to amend the U.S. Constitution, rather than once again try to revise the INA, as the latter efforts had proven futile. All legal interpretations indicated that to end automatic birthright citizenship the U.S. Constitution had to be amended. No one had tried to amend the U.S. Constitution since 1999. Berman professed that the political atmosphere to reform the Constitution was prime, as Americans were tired of spending millions of dollars on illegals. He also announced that he planned to reintroduce birthright reform through the state legislature, despite his opponents having killed his last bill. Berman was referring to the previous legislative session. On January 29, 2007, at the same time the birthright legislation was being considered in Congress, in Texas Berman sponsored House Bill 28, entitled "An act relating to the eligibility of an individual born in this state whose parents are illegal aliens to receive state benefits" (H.B. 28, Texas Legislature online www.house.state.tx.us). His aim was to rescind most of the political rights and privileges U.S. citizens held in Texas, if at the time of their birth their parents were undocumented residents. Berman proposed that through state administrative action it was legal to deny certain U.S. citizens most state rights. H.B. 28 read as follows: "This chapter applies only to an individual: (1) who is born in this state on or after the effective date of this chapter; and (2) whose parents are illegal aliens at the time the individual is born. Sec. 2352.003. ELIGIBILITY. An individual to whom this chapter applies is not entitled to and may not receive any benefit provided by this state or a political subdivision of this state including . . . (Ibid.)" The political rights and social benefits to be denied included prohibiting such people from receiving professional licenses, such as practicing law and medicine, making them ineligible for state employment, denying them Texas pensions for city, county, or state government employment, and making them ineligible for state benefits such as public housing, medical care, and schooling. The bill was cosponsored by 10 House representatives. Essentially the bill redefined the rights U.S. citizens were allowed to enjoy on account of their birth and parental origin. Their status would have been below even that of a second-class citizen since in Texas they would be treated as undocumented aliens. Texas would have redefined who is an illegal alien in the state and created a new legal category which I call illegal alien citizen.

During the same legislative session that H.B. 28 was introduced Representative Berman and other House members sponsored companion legislation targeting Latino immigrants, regardless of their legal status.[26] H.B. 29 proposed taxing money grams sent from Texas to Mexico and to Central and South America. Similar fees would not be placed on money grams sent to other destinations. The tax revenue generated from the money grams would be used to fund indigent health care for U.S. citizens. A series of bills were also sponsored to identify and detain people suspected of being illegal aliens. One bill was designed to prohibit U.S. citizens and residents from protecting undocumented aliens from detection. Oddly, all of these bills paralleled the provisions found in the failed congressional H.R. 4437. H.B. 1012 would prohibit local governments from passing laws that failed to fully enforce federal and state immigration policies. The bill's intent was to prohibit city and county governments from passing sanctuary laws allowing churches to protect undocumented aliens. In some cities in Texas sanctuary laws prohibit immigration agents from entering church property to remove aliens under deportation orders. H.B. 2180 would have allowed police officers to arrest a person suspected of being a criminal illegal alien. H.B. 2998 was similar and would have mandated police officers to verify the immigrant status of any person detained or under arrest, including those stopped for minor traffic violations. To the disappointment of the sponsors the bills were rejected in committee. David Swinford (R-Dumas), chair of the State Affairs Committee, reported that all the bills violated federal immigration law and would not be allowed to continue for a legislative vote because immigration was a federal matter (Castillo and Selby 2007). The only bill affecting foreign-born residents that passed the legislature and became law was Senate Bill 1260, which required a noncitizen applying for a driver's license to have proof of legal entry if unable to present a Social Security card (S.B. 1260, Texas Legislature online www.house.state.tx.us).[27]

Despite the outcome of Representative Berman's failed legislation, he announced he would not give up. Berman kept his promise, and at the ICE-sheriff hearing on April 21, 2008, he once again began to lobby for the passage of birthright legislation in Texas (Maynard 2008). Furthermore, on February 2, 2009, Berman introduced H.B. 256 resolving that a child born in the United States of undocumented parents is not a U.S. citizen and cannot be issued a Texas birth certificate (H.B. 256, Texas Legislature online www.house.state.tx.us). Once again he tried to use state law to amend federal law. The bill died in committee.

I hope that Representative Berman's social movement will not grow in Texas. Only in Farmer's Branch, Texas, a suburb of Dallas, has a city council approved similar mean-spirited policies. In 2006 the city council passed a law banning apartment rentals to undocumented immigrants (Valencia 2008). The ordinance was ruled unconstitutional by a federal judge since its enforcement required landlords to verify a tenant's legal status and this violated federal immigration law. Following the judgment, the Farmer's Branch

City Council, like Representative Berman, refused to give up. To bypass the federal order, the city council passed a ruling requiring all prospective tenants to get a rental license from the city. Farmer's Branch would then ask the federal government for an applicant's legal status before approving the rental license. Currently, opponents are challenging the ruling.

What is more worrisome than the isolated Farmer's Branch case, however, is the 2010 party platform of the Texas Republican Party. This is an indicator "of bad times to come." Besides endorsing a plank to end automatic birthright citizenship, the delegates adopted an immigration plank similar to Arizona's strict law that requires law enforcement officers to ask people when arrested to prove their legal residency (Republican Party of Texas 2010: 20; S.B. 1070, revision H.B. 2162 in Arizona State Legislature, www.azleg.gov). Critics of Arizona's S.B. 1070 have argued that this law is not just about immigration (Baugh 2010). It is a law that targets Latinos and Native Americans and places them under a police state solely based on the color of their skin. It will lead to racial profiling of citizens and permanent residents who are Latino and Native American because only groups who physically resemble undocumented aliens will be asked to prove their legal status. Opponents have also argued that it not only violates federal law, but is also a public testimonial of the resentments held by many white citizens against Latinos and can lead to civil rights violations (Archibold 2010). At the convention some delegates opposed its adoption, including Gov. Rick Perry, who argued that it was a divisive plank and was not right for Texas if it eventually became law (Fox News, June 13, 2010, www.foxnews.com).

The aim of my brief detour to Texas legislative politics was to offer final scenarios of citizenship issues affecting people of Mexican origin. I certainly hope that the birthright legislation does not move forward, either at the national or state level, as this would be a sad moment in U.S. civil rights history. In my view, it would also be a social injustice for any American to lose his or her birthright citizenship and be transformed into an illegal alien citizen who in the future would have to go through the naturalization process in order to vote in the United States. If this happened, it would truly be a new chapter in the Mexicans' naturalization history, one which I hope I will never write.

Nonetheless, I concede that unauthorized Mexican immigration is a dilemma that most likely will continue to exist as long as the economies of Mexico and the United States are so vastly different and as long as American capitalists are willing to increase their profits by paying low wages to unauthorized workers. This is an ugly part of American capitalism, but it is also part of an economic tradition that dates back to the aftermath of the

U.S. Civil War. On the other hand, it is also a fact that most Mexicans do not want to live here, including the majority of the poor. I believe this is an area of research that needs to be better understood. We need to investigate further what conditions dissuade Mexicans from embarking on a journey to the United States. Is it perhaps their nationalism, the regional economies, the militarization of the border, the horror stories they hear from returning border crossers, the inability to raise enough money to cross the border, or the lack of desire due to one's elite economic position in comparison to the rest of the nation? In addition to studying why people stay home, it is also important to research why the Mexican government has failed to legislate a realistic living wage in Mexico. Mexicans no longer live during the Porfirian regime, yet it is difficult to understand how a federal government can legislate laws that guarantee only its poorest citizens a minimum daily wage that ranges from $52.30 pesos to $49.50 pesos, depending on the zone (U.S. Department of State 2009). In U.S. currency, these daily wages are equal to $5.15 and $4.80, respectively. The question is, who profits from this economic wage legislation? Is it only Mexican employers who profit?

Texas Naturalization Records
and Archives, Pre-1906

An explanatory note is needed concerning the content, location, and limitations of Texas naturalization records prior to 1906. These records are significant, as they provide statistical data on Mexican immigrants' naturalization proceedings from the mid-nineteenth century to 1906. Texas naturalization records are found in the Lorenzo de Zavala State Library and Archives in Austin and at the National Archives Southwest Region at Fort Worth. Records are also located in various courts of the counties and in some Texas state universities.

The records in the Lorenzo de Zavala State Library and Archives include microfilms of most of the county and district naturalization records found in Texas (i.e., indexes, declarations/applications, petitions of intention, granted certificates, and court records of litigation). The original naturalization records, however, are located in the archives of the courts which processed the applications (National Archives 2005).

The National Archives Southwest Region at Fort Worth has custody of the original indexes of all naturalizations granted or denied in Texas from 1840 to 1906. These indexes are separated in ten volumes and are titled "Index to Naturalization Records Found in Texas State, District and County Courts, 1846–1939." Microfilms of these records are also found in the Lorenzo de Zavala State Library and Archives. The Work Projects Administration compiled these indexes in 1941. The National Archives at Fort Worth also has custody of the naturalization records of the federal courts in Texas, which date from 1840 to 1990, as well as of the records of the Texas Immigration and Naturalization Bureau district offices. The federal court records, however, are incomplete for the years after 1906. Some of the federal court records have been microfilmed; copies of these have been given to the county courts or state universities.

In conducting my research, I examined the naturalization indexes at Fort Worth and used the indexes to identify the counties where Mexican immigrants had applied for citizenship in Texas. This allowed me to construct a timeline of Mexicans' naturalization patterns. I also examined the immigration and naturalization records and the federal court records from the nineteenth century to 1940. I found that after 1939 the records were fragmented, and thus I turned to statistical data prepared by the U.S. Census Bureau, the Bureau of Immigration and Naturalization, the

Department of Homeland Security, and the State Department of Labor. Finally, to explore particular cases I examined the naturalization files at the Lorenzo de Zavala State Library and Archives.

Texas naturalization records begin in 1840, a few years after the independence of Texas from Mexico. Records of applications filed by Mexicans, however, did not begin until 1848. In 1845, when Texas was annexed to the United States, U.S. naturalization law governed all proceedings, including the manner of compiling records. Throughout the nineteenth century federal law allowed all courts of record to process naturalization applications. A court of record consisted of a court that practiced common law, had a sitting judge, a seal, and a clerk or notary public who could record all proceedings (2 *U.S. Statutes at Large* 153). In Texas the courts of record were the county, district, state, and federal courts. The county courts, however, received the majority of the applications. Because precinct courts were not allowed to naturalize, most Mexican justices of the peace were ineligible to process naturalization applications. As I discuss in this book, during the nineteenth and early twentieth centuries a person of Mexican descent was not appointed or elected to a judgeship position above the county level. Moreover, throughout the nineteenth century a person of Mexican descent acted as a county judge in only three counties. Their appointments, however, were infrequent.

Until 1906 all courts were required to maintain an index with information that included who had applied, the applicant's country of origin, place of entry, disposition of the application, and final decision (denial or granting). No information on race or religion was gathered. Most courts also kept a duplicate of the naturalization declaration (the application) and the certificate of granted naturalization. Because the federal government did not issue standard guidelines for the printing of applications or certificates, each court designed its own forms and gathered different information. These records were not centralized, as the federal government allowed the originating courts to keep their records.

In 1906 the U.S. Congress deemed it necessary to centralize the record keeping of the naturalization records throughout the United States. This was done to create a national database and to reduce fraud; the federal government suspected that county judges were manipulating the naturalization process (U.S. Commission on Naturalization 1905). In states where county judges were elected, the federal government suspected that judges issued naturalization certificates when it was convenient for their election. Under the Naturalization Act of 1906 the U.S. Congress established procedural safeguards to uniformly gather information on the applicants and create a standard granting procedure (34 *U.S. Statutes at Large* [part 1] 596). The Bureau of Immigration and Naturalization was also established at this time for the specific purpose of centralizing all naturalization and immigration records, producing standard application forms, and enforcing the state's compliance with federal law.

Standardizing of the application process was deemed necessary by Congress after a report submitted in 1905 by the United States Commission on Naturalization indicated that various courts committed serious errors when processing applications. The commission found that some states collected detailed data on the applicants, while others noted only the name of the applicants (U.S. Commission on Naturalization 1905). A few states were so lax in their processing that naturalization logs were either lost or not stored. The commission found that, as a result of such bookkeeping, individuals who lost their certificates had no way of proving they had naturalized, and the only way of obtaining a new certificate was to convince a judge to issue one. This administrative structure easily opened the process to fraud. A second major problem cited by the commission was the unreasonable fees assessed of the applicants in some states, especially the fee for the final papers (Ibid., 12, 25, 91). For example, in some states the final fee was as low as two dollars while in other states it was as high as seven dollars. The commission concluded that both types of fees were unreasonable. Low fees were insufficient to cover the costs of the court proceedings, including the clerk's salary and the forms, while high fees were a burden to the applicants. To address this problem, the commission advised that a standard fee for filing final papers be set at five dollars. This fee, however, did not include charges for extra copies of the certificates or special fees associated with litigation.

Concerning Texas, the Commission on Naturalization commended the courts for their careful and detailed record keeping. Texas was one of the states that maintained and preserved its indexes, logs, and court proceedings. One problem with Texas was cited, however. It was determined that an excessive number of courts were processing applications, and it was necessary to streamline the process (Ibid., 22). This was not unique to Texas. It was a common problem found in the larger states. The commission recommended that throughout the nation the number of courts be reduced by preventing county courts and all other lower courts from handling naturalization proceedings. Under the Naturalization Act of 1906 the county courts and other lower courts were removed from processing naturalization applications. Naturalization proceedings were henceforth limited to federal courts and to state courts of record with unlimited jurisdiction over monetary litigation. In cities with over one hundred thousand residents only the federal courts were to process applications. In Texas this meant that the county courts would no longer be able to process applications because they were limited to hearing cases dealing with disputes not to exceed one hundred dollars.

Furthermore, from 1906 on all naturalization records were to be stored by the Bureau of Immigration and Naturalization for the purpose of creating a national database. The centralization mandate produced a uniform process as well as causing the number of courts processing applications to fall throughout the country (Meyerink and Szucs 1997: 450). In Texas the county courts no longer received new applications after the restructuring, their only duty being to update their files with the data provided by the bureau. State, district, and federal courts continued to process applications and update their records. The state and federal courts in Texas, however, left most of the work to the district judges (General Courts Austin, Brownsville, El Paso, Galveston, San Antonio, Jefferson, Texarkana, Tyler, Waco). By 1910 most applications were processed in eighty-nine district courts (*Texas Almanac* 1912: 78–81).

Implications of the Centralization of Records and Limitations of Naturalization Data to this Study

In theory the centralization of data in Texas may have been a good idea to reduce electoral fraud, as 232 county judges were debarred from their naturalization jurisdiction (*Texas Almanac* 1912: 63–70). The restructuring also created a national database of all immigrants naturalized after 1906. In practice, however, the restructuring also destroyed an important local source of American history because the county courts had been one of the main governmental institutions that indexed applications, recorded oaths, heard litigation, identified immigrants' place of origin, identified ports and places of entry (i.e., ranchos), and stored records. By 1906, at least half of the applications had been processed by county courts and the records stored locally.

The centralization of the records also led to another significant change in the reporting of data. When the federal government took over the record keeping, the bureau was not required to report data by county or state. Between 1906 and 1931, the federal government reported national statistical data of petitions filed, granted, or denied and did not provide state or county data. It also did not provide statistical data on the applicants' country of origin. This accounting method therefore destroyed an important source of state- and county-level data for Texas. It was not until 1931 that the federal government instructed the Naturalization Bureau to provide statistical data by state (Scott 2007). By this time, the Bureau of Immigration and Naturalization had been separated into the Bureau of Immigration and the Bureau of Naturalization (8 USC 1440). These data, however, did not report county information or information on the applicants' place of origin. It was not until 1962 that the federal government instructed the reconsolidated Bureau of Immigration and Naturalization to begin reporting statistical data on nativity and state of residence. The consequence of these data collection mandates after 1906 for me was that I had to turn to U.S. Census documents and other federal statistical data to determine the number of Mexicans who were obtaining citizenship in Texas. The federal data, however, did not provide the same detailed information as those found in the pre-1906 county and district naturalization records. Moreover, I found that the federal data often failed to report information on Mexicans.

The Work Projects Administration and the Recovery of Texas Naturalization Records

In 1941, under a federal emergency program, the War Department and the Justice Department hired thousands of workers for six months to index all U.S. naturalization applications filed before September 27, 1906, as there was no central record of who had been granted or denied citizenship prior to 1906 (see Guadalupe County, Naturalization Index, p. 30, reel 1993311; Schaefer 1997). The program was called the Work Projects Administration (WPA). In Texas four hundred workers were hired to complete this mandate. The WPA workers in Texas were able to review most of the records. Unfortunately, some of the county records had been lost or were unavailable at the time the WPA began their index. For the Mexican immigrant population, the bulk of missing data is for Presidio County, whose records from the 1890s to 1906 have been lost. Likewise, the county records for El Paso were unavailable and not included in the index. Since then, the El Paso records have been recovered and are in the custody of the National Archives at Fort Worth. Some of the El Paso records, however, are incomplete. The indexes for the 1890s provide information only on who applied, not on who was granted naturalization. Likewise, the El Paso files for the late 1880s are unavailable.

I found the WPA indexes to be very useful. They not only provided an overview of the number of applicants who applied for citizenship and were denied or granted papers, but also identified where an applicant filed his or her application, how many times a person appeared in front of a judge or clerk to review their case, and sometimes the problems with a file. Furthermore, the indexes contained information on the courts that processed the applications, which allowed me to track down records on particular applicants.

Biographical Research

When I began my data collection and found that the naturalization indexes identified the original location of the court proceedings I chose to conduct biographical research on some of the applicants. In particular I became very excited when I discovered that some of the applicants' files contained information about court proceedings dealing with other matters. Sometimes the naturalization files cross-referenced court proceedings dealing with civil disputes or government inquiries. Soon, however, I discovered that tracking down the records was an exhaustive process: locating the files took weeks and in some cases months. I also found that in some cases the files no longer existed, or if they did the material was too fragmented to be useful. For example, in the case of Ricardo Rodriguez, about whom I write extensively in this study, the naturalization indexes contain references to several of his court appearances. Most of the original records, however, have been lost. His declaration of intention to become a citizen, the judge's order granting him naturalization, and other court records pertaining to *In re Rodriguez* (1897) are available. The deposition of witnesses, the court trial transcripts, as well as a copy of Rodriguez's certificate of naturalization, on the other hand, are not available.

After doing nearly a year of biographical research, I concluded that at this time this approach was inappropriate for my project. Locating records for individual applicants was time consuming and did not provide sufficient information about the naturalization process. I also learned that the biographical approach did not allow me to gain an overview of Mexicans' naturalization history because I needed first to identify statistical patterns in their naturalization application flows. Once I had reconstituted the statistical flow of applications, I was able to place these patterns within a historical timeline and understand more thoroughly what was happening to Mexicans as an ethnic group.

Although doing biographical research was time consuming, it is important to note the type of information that is available. To illustrate this I will provide case studies from my research. One of the first persons I began to do biographical research on was a man named Epitacio Mondragon. I became interested in his case because his place of birth was missing in his naturalization application; I knew he was married to one of the descendants of the Seguin family (Chabot 1937: 197; Inclan, n.d.). The Seguins were among the original Mexican settlers of Texas and members of the Mexican American elite (Montejano 1987). I was intrigued as to why Mondragon had applied for naturalization. To investigate his case I searched for the files cited in the naturalization index. Once I located these files, I found that they provided additional information on other court proceedings. After reviewing

Mondragon's records I was able to capture a glimpse of both his life and a moment in San Antonio history.

The Bexar County Court naturalization records indicate that Mondragon was twenty-seven years old when he was granted citizenship on January 14, 1860 (Index to Naturalization Records Found in Texas State, District and County Courts, 1846–1939 roll 1; Bexar County Court, vol. K–Q, R–Z 1836–1963, Naturalization Papers, box A, doc. 60). He had applied for citizenship because he was uncertain if he was a Mexican or a U.S. citizen. Based on Mondragon's age at the time of his application, he was born in Texas prior to independence (Church of Jesus Christ of Latter-day Saints 2008). I then proceeded to examine other records, including those identified in his naturalization file, and I found information that allowed me to piece together a larger narrative. It was necessary for Mondragon to verify his U.S. citizenship because on December 27, 1859, he was appointed Bexar County collector of taxes and soon became embroiled in serious legal troubles (Bexar County Court, vol. 2A, 1859–1860, pp. 295–299). Not only had he competed for a very sought after and prestigious position, but within days of his appointment he was robbed by armed men while working in his office at San Antonio (no date noted) (Bexar County Court, vol. 2, 1860, pp. 365–367). Because a large sum of money was stolen the county conducted an investigation and held a hearing to discuss the matter. During the hearing Mondragon requested that he be absolved of all financial responsibility. When the hearing concluded, the judge found Mondragon innocent and ordered him to purchase an iron safe to protect the county from further robberies. He was not required to replace the stolen money, which amounted to $243.50. Interestingly, on the basis of all of the records about Mondragon that I reviewed, I found that the county investigation occurred during the same month that he filed for U.S. citizenship. It is very likely, therefore, that Mondragon applied for citizenship to secure his position as collector of taxes. Perhaps when the county investigated the robbery Mondragon's date of birth cast some shadow on his citizenship status, and he was asked to clear all doubt by applying for citizenship. In the nineteenth century a person was required to be a U.S. citizen in order to hold a government job (*Laws of Texas*, 1:1403; *Laws of Texas*, 8:781).

In my review of naturalization records, case files like Mondragon's are rare. His case is exceptional because he held an important county position. Unlike the case of Mondragon, however, where I had to follow a paper trail and spend a great deal of time locating records, in other cases records about an applicant are found in the same file. I found that the naturalization papers of Luis Antonio Zuloaga were easy to locate. Like Mondragon, he was a person of Mexican descent who held high status. Zuloaga's naturalization papers were filed together with the transcript of his state bar exam results. In 1897 the Webb County Courthouse expedited Zuloaga's naturalization file. This occurred when Texans were waiting for the Western District Court of San Antonio to announce whether federal law prohibited Mexicans of Indian descent from naturalizing (i.e., *In re Rodriguez* 1897). A federal suit had been filed by the leadership of the People's Party to stop Mexican immigrants from voting in Texas. The party was also in the midst of a lobbying campaign to pressure the Texas legislature to pass state immigration reforms. Papers in Zuloaga's naturalization file reveal that he obtained citizenship the same day he applied. They also show that a few months later, on March 2, 1898, he passed the Texas State bar exam and that three prominent attorneys formed his examination committee (Webb County Civil Minutes 1897–1900 vol. 9). State Senator E. A. Atlee of Webb, Capt. Theo W. Dodd, and Juan A. Valle concurred in the opinion that Zuloaga was prepared to practice law. Senator Atlee represented several counties in South Texas, and he had a long history of opposing state legislation that adversely affected immigrants. Interestingly, Zuloaga's examination papers certify that he was a naturalized citizen. Reading his case files, I found it difficult to understand why his exam records noted that he was a naturalized citizen since at that time lawyers in Texas did not need to be citizens to practice law (*Laws of Texas* 8:781–834; Leibowitz 1983). Only when an attorney was an employee of the state, city, or county government did he need to be a citizen. An attorney also had to be a U.S. citizen when appointed or elected to a judicial position. Since the clerk did not note why Zuloaga applied for citizenship we do not know if he was trying to secure a judicial appointment or if he applied for other reasons.

Other files, however, offer limited information. Most likely this is owing to the fact that the cases were about common people. One such case is that of Juan Antonio Flores from Webb County (Webb County Civil Minutes 1897–1900 Vol. 9). I became interested in his file because problems were noted with his application. I was also interested because he received U.S. citizenship around the same time as Zuloaga, when federal law was still unclear whether Mexican immigrants of Indian descent could naturalize. I thought perhaps I could discover some information about his race. I did not. In 1897 Flores was asked to appear in front of a judge because he had filed his application two years earlier in Zapata County, and when he returned to complete the process the clerk was uncertain if his application was active. After meeting with Flores, Judge A. L. McLowe decided that he was a good man of high moral character and would be granted U.S. citizenship. The judge's notes, besides saying something about Flores's character, disclose that the petitioner was a farmer. No other note was included in his file concerning other court appearances. I tried to search for additional information, for example, in land records, but was unsuccessful.

Although the biographical approach proved to be limiting for this study it was nonetheless very useful. For example, in my efforts to corroborate or expand upon information I found in the applicant's files I turned to nineteenth-century Spanish-language newspapers. In my review of these newspapers I discovered that the editor of *El Regidor*, Pablo Cruz, was a naturalized Mexican immigrant. As I examined documents about his life I found substantial information about his accomplishments because he had been a respected person in San Antonio and was identified by local historians and journalists as a civic leader and successful businessman (Batts 1907). Most important of all, through his editorials, Cruz left firsthand, eyewitness accounts of Texas politics and the Mexican immigrant's struggle to obtain U.S. citizenship. I am thus greatly indebted to Cruz's editorials, for they allowed me to understand more deeply the naturalization statistical data I was analyzing. In sum, the biographical approach was fruitful, yet it was also time consuming and at times offered only fragmented, limited information.

Limited Findings on Afromexicano Immigrants

Throughout my study I tried to search for information on Mexican women and to examine the naturalization records of 1840–1906 to determine if Mexicans were treated differently on account of their race. I had previously written a book on Mexican Americans' racial history and wanted to pursue this line of thought in a study of Mexican immigrants (Menchaca 2001). My endeavor to identify women was successful, and I wrote a chapter on this subject with explanations of the problems and limitations I encountered. Especially useful in this task were the state legislative debates over suffrage and the Jane Y. McCallum archives. On immigrants' racial background, however, the naturalization records provided limited information. The indexes and declarations provided information only on place of origin, not on a person's race. Therefore, I was not able to determine if Mexicans who were considered white were granted U.S. citizenship more often than Mexicans who were Indian, mestizo, or black. The only physical information noted in the naturalization records referred to physical deformities, such as major facial scars. Therefore, because the naturalization data did not offer information on race I turned to census, treaty, and court records. I found that treaty and court records provided valuable information on how Mexican immigrants' indigenous ancestry affected their legal status in Texas. However, little information on afromexicano (Mexicans of black descent) immigrants was available.

Nonetheless, throughout my research I proceeded to search for any information I could find on afromexicano immigrants. I did my best and followed Michel-Rolph Trouillot's (1995) advice to inspect the archive for any information about minority groups that might have been noted by chance because of the archive maker's superfluous curiosity about low-status people. Unfortunately, the naturalization records did not provide information on race, and the census provided fragmented information. The census bureau only reported data on afromexicano immigrants for a few years, and when it did so, only statewide enumerations were given. County data were not available. Although I could not provide an extensive analysis, I nevertheless chose to pay close attention to how people of Mexican origin were affected by events and laws used to discriminate against black people. Specifically, I found that Texas voting history provided rich material on the common experiences Mexican immigrants and African Americans encountered (i.e., poll taxes, white primaries, suffragists' positions).

Persons Naturalized in Texas and by Mexican Origin, 1907–2009

Date	All States	All Persons Texas	Texas Mexican	All States Mexican
1907–1909	72,290			
1910–1919	990,737			
1920–1929	1,781,491			
1930–1939	1,507,932	7,640[a]		
1940–1949	2,148,021	26,396		
1950–1959[b]	1,136,850	30,875		
1960–1969	1,129,306	46,066	24,614	54,154
1970–1979[c]	1,412,266	48,929	22,166	65,016
1980–1989	2,054,924	122,022	50,350	170,895
1990–1999	4,978,665	329,083	157,967	854,792
2000–2009	6,822,117	470,852	184,343	1,116,027

[a]Data are for the total number of persons granted naturalization that decade. In 1907 the Bureau of Immigration and Naturalization began reporting cumulative national data, state data were first reported in 1931, and country of origin in 1961.

[b]In 1950 the U.S. Census reported the national origin of the naturalized citizens. For Mexico, out of a total of 451,490 foreign-born immigrants 118,950 were naturalized (U.S. Census 1954:3A-130; U.S. Census 1953a: 3B-82). The estimate for Texas was 43,179 Mexican immigrants naturalized out of a total of 188,547 (U.S. Census 1953b: 3C-15).

[c]Data on the Mexican population for 1973–1979 are only for ages eighteen and over (Department of Homeland Security, Immigration Statistics Office, N-400 data).

Source: Statistical Yearbook of the Immigration and Naturalization Service, 1961–2001; Yearbook of Immigration Statistics, 2002–2009 (Tables: Persons Naturalized by State and Territory of Residence and Region and Country of Birth; Petitions for Naturalized Filed, Persons Naturalized, and Petitions Naturalized Denied: Fiscal Years 1907-2009)

Abbreviations

TNR   Index to Naturalization Records Found in Texas State,
                         District and County Courts, 1846–1939
General Courts   General Courts Austin, Brownsville, El Paso, Galveston,
                         San Antonio, Jefferson, Texarkana, Tyler, Waco
Naturalization Tables   Statistical Yearbook of the Immigration and Naturaliza-
                         tion Service: Persons Naturalized by Selected Country of
                         Former Allegiance and State of Residence
NAWSA   National American Woman Suffrage Association

Notes

Chapter One

1. The U.S. Congress, after purchasing southern Arizona from Mexico, enacted the Gadsen Treaty in 1854. The citizenship articles of the Treaty of Guadalupe Hidalgo were adopted in the Gadsen Treaty (see Menchaca 2001: 226–228).

2. Full title of decree: Decreto: expedido con el objeto de facilitar recursos para la traslación de las familias mexicanas que se hallen en el territorio cedido á los Estados-Unidos del Norte.

3. For a review of the citizenship rights Mexicans exercised after Mexican independence, see Guillermo de la Peña 1993: 243–261; Hutchinson 1969: 166–171, 239–244, 255–259.

4. See *Boyd v. Nebraska* (1891:135) for a comprehensive history of the political rights state and territorial legislatures held in determining citizenship legislation. In 1787, Congress gave the state and territorial legislatures the right to establish citizenship eligibility requirements as long as there were five thousand residents (137, 159, 166, 169). Congress, however, retained the right to amend or rescind those requirements in territories (168,170). This political right was not removed until the passage of the Fourteenth Amendment in 1868.

5. Aguirre Beltrán used *afromestizo* as a general term to include all people of African descent. For a historical discussion of terms used to characterize Spaniards and Mexicans of African descent, see Aguirre Beltrán, 1991a: 153–179, 218–219; *Residents of Texas 1782–1836:* 3.

6. It was not until 1930 that the U.S. Census Bureau tried to enumerate the total number of people of Mexican origin under one category. That year all people of Mexican origin were categorized by their ancestry, including the foreign-born. Their race was also noted, and nearly all were counted as nonwhite (see President's Research Committee 1935). This enumeration model, however, was used only in the decennial census of 1930 and used to recalculate the previous decennial census.

7. See de León 1987 for an extended discussion of the racial comments U.S. newspapers made of Mexicans during the nineteenth century.

8. *Sam Smith Appellant v. Maria de Jesusa Smith Appelle, 1845–1846.* State of Texas Archives, doc. no. M-119. Appeal from the District Court Bexar County Fall

Term 1846 to the Supreme Court. This archive contains the court transcripts and depositions for the trials of 1845 and 1846.

9. See Menchaca (2008) for a detailed discussion of international and Mexican law pertaining to the marriage laws adopted by the U.S. government.

10. The Extradition Treaty was concluded on December 11, 1861, but was not ratified until June 20, 1862.

11. After Mexican independence the Mexican Congress passed a series of property laws privatizing tribal properties in 1824. Tribal land was to be distributed among members. Tribal councils, which constituted the highest authority within the tribal government, no longer held corporate control of the land. However, in 1829 the Mexican Supreme Court ruled that tribes could retain authority over the tribal lands if the tribe voted in favor of such action. This allowed tribal councils to continue administering the land for all tribal members. The court, however, did reduce the authority of the tribal councils by ruling that members who wanted to privatize their holdings could do so (see Hall and Weber 1984:20; Menchaca 2001: 188–191). Under the Reform Laws this practice ended.

12. See the newspaper *La Bandera* for an overview of the assistance Governor Vidaurri rendered the Confederacy along the Texas border (*La Bandera,* September 25, 1863: 1).

13. The full text of the Fourteenth Amendment was received by the Department of State on June 16, 1866, and thus the U.S. Statutes at Large report this as the date of passage.

14. Translated title of convention. In Spanish it read "Convención entre los Estados-Unidos Mexicanos y los Estados-Unidos de America, para determinar la Ciudadanía de las personas que emigran del uno al otro pais."

Chapter Two

1. "Index to Naturalization Records Found in Texas State, District, and County Courts, CA. 1846–1939" hereafter is abbreviated as TNR, followed by the relevant microfilm roll. When the National Archives, Southwest Region, Fort Worth microfilmed the records there were ten rolls. The Lorenzo de Zavala Library and Archives, however, divided the rolls into seventeen. The numbers cited in the text are based on the legend provided by the National Archives.

2. During the Civil War, in addition to the naturalization certificates issued in Starr County, one other Mexican applied for citizenship in Bexar County.

3. The U.S. Congress on July 19, 1867, decreed that soldiers or sailors who had deserted their units in 1865 had not lost their U.S. citizenship (15 *U.S. Statutes at Large* 14). In 1906, Congress reiterated this sentiment when it passed the Nationality Act of 1906 and declared that enlisted men who had served faithfully in the Civil War had not lost their citizenship (34 *U.S. Statutes at Large* [part 1] 596).

4. Baggett (1974:442) argues that only eleven delegates were African Americans; Winkler (1916:107) gives the number as ten.

5. For Cameron County the Texas naturalization index does not provide the country of origin for some of the Spanish surname applicants. They were counted here as Mexican since the U.S. Census of 1870 did not identify any foreign-born

Spaniards living in Cameron County nor were any identified in the naturalization indexes and declarations for 1869 (Cameron County Civil Minutes, roll 1016181; TNR 2). In 1860 there were 59 Spaniard residents in the state of Texas, and by 1870 the number had grown to 150 (U.S. Census 1864: 490; U.S. Census 1872: 392). A few Spaniards, however, began to apply for naturalization in the mid-1870s.

6. The first applications filed by Mexican women in Texas were also filed at this time in Cameron County. The first female applicants were Adelida Cantu and Luz Espinoza.

7. District 24 included Frio, Uvalde, Kinney, Medina, Maverick, Bandera, Kerr, and Kendall.

8. District 23 consisted of Karnes, Live Oak, San Patricio, McMullen, Bee, Victoria, Aransas, Calhoun, DeWitt, Goliad, and Refugio.

9. District 22 was composed of Atascosa, Comal, and Bexar.

10. In the 1870s, 37 petitions were granted to Mexicans (out of 4,952). They were issued in the counties of Robertson 8, Aransa 7, Bexar 3, Cameron 3, Hidalgo 2, Nueces 3, Starr 1, and San Patricio 1 (TNR: rolls 1,3,7,8). The federal courts also granted applicants papers: 4 by the Austin Federal Court and 5 by the Brownsville Federal Court (General Courts Austin, Brownsville, El Paso, Galveston, San Antonio, Jefferson, Texarkana, Tyler, Waco; hereafter cited as General Courts).

11. In 1874 Judge Norton of Robertson County conferred citizenship on 37 of 38 Chinese applicants (TNR, roll 8). At this time in Texas the courts did not bar Chinese people from naturalizing since the federal courts had not yet issued an opinion on this subject (Haney López 1996).

12. Two divisions of the Texas Rangers were established. One division patrolled the border, and the second supervised the surviving Indians of West Texas (Levario 2007).

13. The escapades of McNelly and his Rangers are based on the oral history memoirs of Clyde Wantland (Durham 1962). Wantland, a Texas Ranger in McNelly's company, rode with McNelly and witnessed the events narrated in this section. Upon retiring from the Texas Rangers, Wantland was employed by the King Ranch.

14. In 1877 the *New York Times* reported the lynching of one hundred Mexican Tejanos, who, after being accused of cattle rustling, were hung by vigilantes (de León 1987: 98). The Rangers did nothing to stop the attacks.

15. After the Mexican-American War of 1846–48, the U.S. government validated 89.2 percent of the Mexican land grants in South Texas. Nearly all the land was owned by Mexicans (Texas General Land Office 1988; see Menchaca 2001).

16. In 1877 the U.S. extraction of Mexican silver is estimated to have been 25 million pesos, and of gold 1.5 million pesos (Lorey 1999: 39). The value of the peso and the dollar were approximately the same until the end of the 1890s (Pletcher 1958).

17. The county of Val Verde was organized in 1885. It was cut out of the South Texas county of Kinney and the West Texas counties of Pecos and Crockett. Owing to its shape, Val Verde lies in both South and West Texas. Because most of the county was carved out of West Texas counties, the 922 Mexican immigrants living in Val Verde in 1890 are included here as part of West Texas (U.S. Census 1894: 672).

18. From 1880 to 1890 the growth of the Mexican immigrant population in Bexar County was minimal. It grew from 3,408 to 3,561 (U.S. Census 1882: 528; U.S. Census 1894: 669).

19. According to the U.S. Census of 1890, 52 percent of workers were engaged in agricultural occupations either as laborers, farmers, or cotton mill workers (U.S. Census 1897a: 612). The occupations of farming and ranching (i.e., stock raising, stables) accounted for 55 percent of the total workforce.

20. The U.S. Census of 1890 does not provide a separate ethnic breakdown for Mexican immigrants engaged in farm labor.

21. The first Alien Land Law was passed in 1848. Since that time the Texas legislature had required aliens who inherited land to become U.S. citizens or relinquish their inheritance (*Laws of Texas*, 3:131). This inheritance statute was maintained in the revisions of 1854 and 1891.

22. The Alien Land Law of 1891 was ruled unconstitutional in *Gunter v. Texas Land and Mortgage Company* (1891). Six months after the law passed Jot Gunter tried to use it to challenge a lien that had been placed on his property by the Texas Land and Mortgage Company for failure to pay a loan. Gunter's attorneys had argued that since this British corporation could not comply with the Alien Land Law all mortgage liens held by the corporation were void. The justices disagreed, ruling that such an argument had merit but violated property law.

23. During the debates over the Alien Land Act reforms Mexicans filed naturalization petitions in greater numbers. In 1892, the petitions climbed significantly in El Paso and in the South Texas counties of Atascosa, Frio, Hidalgo, Karnes, Kinney, McMullen, Medina, Nueces, and Starr as well as in the recently organized county of Val Verde (located in South and West Texas). In these counties the applications doubled or tripled in number from previous years and increased to at least 100 petitions per county (TNR, rolls 1–2, 7–10). The most dramatic increase in petitions is found in Starr County, where they climbed to 512 in 1892 in comparison to 1889, when only 2 petitions were filed (TNR, roll 8). Outside of South Texas there was an increase in Bexar, where the petitions climbed to 286 from 63 the previous year. And in the central counties of Bell, Caldwell, Kimble, Kerr, Gonzales, and McLennen, where historically only a handful of applications were filed, they increased in the range of 10 to 40. In West Texas there was no surge, yet the first applications were submitted in Crockett, Sutton, and Menard. Mexicans also began to apply in the northern counties of Grayson, Shackelford, Tarrant, Hamilton, and Limestone, where the number of applications were modest at first but by 1894 had increased. For example, in Crockett only 3 applications were submitted in 1892, and by 1894 the number had increased to 123.

Chapter Three

1. From 1892 to 1896, Congressional District 11 contained the counties of Aransas, Atascosa, Bee, Cameron, Calhoun, DeWitt, Dimmit, Duval, Encinal, Frio, Goliad, Guadalupe, Hidalgo, Jackson, Karnes, La Salle, Live Oak, McMullen, Nueces, Refugio, San Patricio, Starr, Uvalde, Victoria, Webb, Wharton, Wilson, Zapata, and Zavala (Michael 1892: 184; Pulsifer 1896: 128).

2. Martin (1970: 210) and Abramowitz (1953: 268) concur that in 1894, twenty-

two People's Party members were elected to the House of Representatives. The *Rules of Order of the House of Representatives of the 24th Legislature* (1895: 34–37), however, classified only seventeen members of the House of Representatives as members of the People's Party. The other five members whom the *Southern Mercury* identified as having run on the People's ticket were classified as Democrats.

3. Contrary to the expectations of the party, African Americans in Wharton, Jackson, and Calhoun counties did not vote for the People's ticket. Most voted for the Democratic Party (Martin 1970: 61, 95, 97).

4. The immigrant population in McBride's district ranged from 29 percent in Comal County to 7 percent in Blanco; 85 percent of the total immigrant population were German (U.S. Census 1894: 669–670; U.S. Census 1892: 41).

5. A microfilm copy of Ricardo Rodriguez's naturalization application and some court records can be found in the Lorenzo de Zavala State Library and Archives, reel 1019305, titled "Bexar County Probate Minutes, Vol. V-1892–1893." The original filing papers, however, have been misplaced. According to the records of the U.S. District Court, Western District of Texas at San Antonio, all federal records pertaining to Rodriguez's application and court documents were transferred to the National Archives, Southwest Region, at Forth Worth. The locator number is A 010831, archives 7NC2180001 FE 48W205. The original container storing the records in the federal courthouse was agency container 155, per container 118482, date 1887–1910. Although the federal court has records of the transfer, the center at Fort Worth does not have the entire file. The available records include only the granting of Rodriguez's naturalization petition.

6. Naturalization applicants were required to have resided in the county where they had filed their papers for at least five years, and one year in the state (Naturalization, Revised Statutes 1870, Section 2165, in 16 *U.S. Statutes at Large* 254).

7. Pablo Cruz editorial: "Como habrán observado nuestros lectores del REGIDOR, desde hace algunos días hemos dado preferente lugar á las traducciones de artículos políticos publicados por periódicos afiliados en el partido del pueblo, por considerar que estos estaban inspirados en verdadero patriotismo y que las doctrinas practicadas por los partidarios del tercer partido, son las que tienden á favorecer las aspiraciones de la clase más numerosa de las sociedad, ó sea el pueblo.

. . . ha venido á poner de manifiesto el egoismo y escaso patriotismo de los magnates que ocupan el poder, pues estos, olvidando que deben al pueblo el ocupar esos puestos, solo trabajan en beneficio de unos cuantos capitalistas . . . obedecen ciegamente á unos cuantos capitalistas corruptos, y destruyen el bienestar del pueblo para aumentar la riqueza de esos vampiros insaciables.

El Partido del Pueblo es destinado á dar un golpe de muerte á los hombres que lo explotan y lo escarnecen; por consiguiente, creemos que todos los honrados labradores de raza mexicana residentes de Texas, deben imitar a sus compañeros alemanes, suesos é friandeses, y trabajar para que el partido popular eche para siempre á sus enemigos, asegurándose de esta manera su bienestar y su dignidad" (*El Regidor*, October 14, 1893, 1).

8. Floyd McGown ran for Austin city council for Ward 10 on December 1889. He lost the election (Office of the City Clerk, Election History, Austin City Connection). I was unable to find any information on Thomas Franklin.

9. A ranchería is composed of approximately a couple of hundred people and is surrounded by family ranches (Carroll and Haggard 1942; Ebright 1991; Mar-

gadant 1991). Indians founded most rancherías in Mexico. As time passed and Indians married Spaniards and other peoples, many rancherías became inhabited by the mestizo descendants of these Indian communities (see Bonfil Batalla 1998).

10. The letter written by Mr. Valle in Spanish: "May 23, 1896, Señor Don Matías Romero, Ministro de Mexico, Washington, Muy Señor Mío, Sírvase U. perdonarme el que me tomo la libertad de suplicarle me informe si existe en vigor el tratado de naturalizacion entre México y los Estado Unidos, concluido en 1868, ó alguno otro, se ese no lo esta. Quisieramos tratar con inteligencia el asunto de la naturalizacion de Mexicanos. En este país ahora que en el juzgado del distrito federal está para resolverse la cuestión, pero se alega que el tratado de 68 no está en vigor, si ha habido otra convención al efecto, y que los Mexicanos 'no son Blancos' en el sentido legal. De U. afino. S.S. Fidel Valle."

11. Pablo Cruz's editorial: "Las Causas que los impresan á la matanza de los gringos y sour Krouts son las que siguen: Protegidos por la ley los gringos y alemanes en todo Texas, roban al obrero su salario; esto es cuando no los asesinan y los hacen salir del país. Debería Vd. nivelar las balanzas que sobre su corte tiene la estátua de la justicia: entonces el italiano, el negro, el infortunado mexicano, el español, el francés, el cubano, y no solo los alemanes y gringos serían tratados con equidad, y entonces sí que la estátua representaría la justicia, no la infamia! . . . No perderemos trabajo al mayor Elmendorf, pero confiamos en la justicia de Dios . . .
McMinn y la policía se encuentran alarmados, muchos de ellos no comen ni duermen desde que oyeron leer la carta anterior" (*El Regidor*, July 2, 1896, 1).

12. For party affiliation, see Texas Legislative Manual for 1897 (1897) and the *Houston Post* (1897).

13. The vote in the House of Representatives is missing in the congressional record. In the Senate forty-seven voted in favor, six opposed, and thirty-six abstained. The senators from Texas, both Democrats, were divided: Senator Horace Chilton voted in favor and Roger Q. Mills against the resolution (*Congressional Record, Proceedings and Debates, 54th Congress, Second Session,* Vol. 29, Part 2, 1897, p. 1520).

14. On reconsideration, eight Texas Democrats and one Republican voted against reconsideration. Three Texas Democrats voted for passage. Within months of the veto Senator Lodge wrote similar legislation and introduced the bill through the Senate. It received an unfavorable review by the Committee on Immigration and Naturalization and failed to gain enough support to pass when voted on by the Senate (*Congressional Record, 55th Congress, Proceedings and Debates, 55th Congress, Third Session,* Vol. 31, Part 2, 1898, p. 92).

15. See the statement made by Representative Andrew R. Kiefer, representing the members of Congress opposing amendment of the immigration laws of the United States (H.R. 7864). His powerful statement concluded that the proposed statutes were hateful, cruel, and immoral (*Congressional Record and Appendix, 54th Congress, Second Session,* Vol. 29, Part 3, 1897, pp. 18–19).

Chapter Four

1. Thirty-six Mexican applicants were granted U.S. citizenship in the 1890s. Four were granted after 1897.

2. In San Antonio, Mexicans lost majority control of city alderman positions by 1842, and thereafter Spanish-surnamed aldermen were infrequently elected (Calderón 2002). In 1842 Juan Seguin was the last Mexican American mayor of San Antonio until Henry Cisneros was elected in the 1980s.

3. See chapter 5. Although most states recognized that the Nationality Act of 1790 naturalized the family of a male declarant, some states disagreed with the interpretation of the act.

4. The case that finally forced the U.S. Supreme Court to offer a uniform resolution on these issues was sparked by a young Chinese American man whose name was Wong Kim Ark. Wong Kim Ark was born in California and after returning from a vacation in China was detained and denied entry into the Port of San Francisco (Chang 2003; Menchaca 2008). In 1895, he appealed his case and won. The U.S. District Court of Northern California ordered his release on the basis that he was a U.S. citizen and was allowed to live in the United States. The U.S. Customs Office appealed and with support from the district attorney of the United States took the case to the Supreme Court. Their intent was to obtain a national ruling that Asian Americans, by law, could be treated as immigrants and could be deported under the Chinese Exclusion Acts.

5. "Correspondiendo a la convocazion que varios ciudadanos de esta población hicieron circular el Sábado último, se tuvo una junta de Mexico-Texanos el domingo á las 8 de la noche, en el salón de la 'Sociedad Benevolencia Mexicana,' de esta ciudad, con el unico objecto de protestar contra todas aquellas personas que de modo alguno hayan provocado odios altamente perjudiciales á todos los residentes en los Estados Unidos, de raza Mexicana" (*El Regidor,* May 26, 1898, 2).

6. "Trató en él con verdadera sensates un punto muy importante, siendo este el derecho que todo hombre mayor de edad tiene de escoger la nacionalidad que mas le plazca, siempre que al adoptarla lo guie un fin noble. Llamar renegado al que por causas legítimas ha aceptado como suya la ciudadanía de este ó cualquier otro país, teniendo conciencia de las leyes y constitución que lo rigen y deseando de buena fé respetarlas y defenderlas, no es porcierto el calificativo que se le debe aplicar. Así lo juzgan las personas sensatas de todas nacionalidades y muy justo es que así sea; mas el que de una manera pérdida abdique de los derechos de ciudadanía que le dieran el suelo a donde nació, sin la conciencia plena de los solemnes lazos que contrae con el país de su adopción, comete una falta gravísima que no solo es censurable si no hasta punible" (*El Regidor,* May 26, 1898, 2).

7. "Pues he ahí lo que proclama la doctrina Monroe, que se reconozcan los propios derechos que cada ciudadano tiene en su propio suelo: que los nacionales ejerzan la autoridad, el gobierno del propio país, que ellos solos intervengan en sus asuntos públicos sin intervención extraña sin influencia de afuera, porque nuestra América debe ser madre para los que somos sus hijos verdaderos.

Hemos dicho que no hay fundamento legítimo—y razonado para suponer que los Estados Unidos pretendan la anexión de la Perla de las Antillas, y menos aún la de nuestro propio territorio, porque tenemos la persuación de que nuestros vecinos buscan en nosotros todos los medios razonables para estrechar una sincera confraternidad y comunidad de ideas y de intereses.

Quieren para nosotros los de la raza latina, no una conquista bruta de la barbarie, que por razón natural les atraería el odio, el rencor y la animadversión de nuestros pueblos, sino la conquista pacífica de la civilización, del progreso, de la industria, del trabajo, de la ciencia y del comercio" (*El Regidor,* June 16, 1898, 1).

8. The granting of citizenship to Mexican immigrants remained low, following the pattern of previous decades. Between 1900 and 1906, seventy-four Mexicans were naturalized (TNR), of whom forty-six were from Bexar County (TNR, roll 1).

9. The executive committee of the Populist Party supported the poll tax legislation, but the majority of the rank and file did not (Cantrell and Barton 1989: 691; see Miller 1986).

10. Alexander W. Terrell served in the House and Senate of Texas. When he introduced the election reforms he was a member of the House (Texas Legislature 1962).

11. For an example of the constitution of a White Man's Association in 1889, see article 15 of the Jay Bird Democratic Association in Fort Bend, Texas: "The object of this association is to combine and unite the White people for the advancement and prosperity of the county; for the purpose of securing a faithful and honest discharge of official duty by all public servants. . . . We therefore declare that any white man now residing in this county, or who shall hereafter acquire citizenship in this county, who shall undertake to lead against this association any political faction or voting population to the principles and objects of this association, shall be considered and treated as a social and political outcast" (Jay Bird Association, 1889).

12. White primary vote result in 1903: Senate votes 26 yes and 0 no; House votes 103 yes, and 0 no (*Laws of Texas,* 12:159).

13. The Election Reforms of 1905 were introduced in the House. House Resolution no. 8 passed the House with 60 votes, 29 opposed, 2 no vote, and 39 absent (*House Journal, Texas 29th Legislature, Regular and First Called Session 1905,* p. 305). All of the representatives from South Texas and Presidio opposed passage. The 2 representatives from El Paso were divided, and the 2 representatives from Bexar supported the legislation. In the Senate the vote was 18 for, 5 opposed, and 9 absent. The representatives of South Texas, El Paso, and Presidio supported passage (*Senate Journal, Texas, 29th Legislature, Regular and First Session Called 1905,* p. 274).

14. In 1907, 1 out of 5 county commissioner seats in Kinney was held by a Mexican American, and in Webb 2 out of 5 (Election Registers 1907–1912).

15. The black male population in three South Texas counties was larger than 2 percent. In 1900 black males in Kinney twenty-one years of age and older constituted 19 percent of the voters, in Nueces 5 percent, and in Starr 4 percent (U.S. Census 1901: 999–1002).

16. The U.S. Census of 1900 and 1910 did not provide either an ethnic breakdown for the native born or a county analysis of the number of people born outside of the state.

17. Francis W. Seabury was well liked by the Mexican community throughout his career. He first came to South Texas as a young man and obtained a position as city attorney of Brownsville. He later established a legal practice in which he litigated many cases involving Mexicans.

18. In the Francis W. Seabury Papers there are over one hundred letters from Mexicans expressing gratitude for Seabury's assistance in legal matters.

19. "Abril 28, 1908, Mr. Jesus Ramirez, San Pedro del Medanito, Texas. Muy Señor mío y Amigo,

Hay una elección primaria del partido democrático el sábado, 2 de Mayo, 1908, para elegir representantes del partido para la convención nacional. El Lic. Wells está muy interesado en esta elección y nos ha pedido, como favor especial para el, que saquemos todos los votos posibles para la boleta encabezada por el Senador Joseph W. Bailey. En los demás precinctos vamos a hacer todo lo posible para esta boleta, pero en el suyo confiamos enteramente en Ud. En Falfurrias, mucha gente va a votar encontra la boleta favorecida por Mr. Wells, yo por esto es mas importante sacar una mayoría buena en el resto del condado. Manuel Guerra está haciendo todo lo que pueda en Roma y San Antonio Viego, yo, Monroe, Jacob Guerra y los demás amigos en este precincto, otros están trabajando en le Gruella y en el Salineño. Este asunto es mas importante que parece, porque una mayoría encontra Bailey, o una mayoría pequeña a su favor, sería como un triunfo para nuestros adversarios. Ellos lo consideran como una prueba de la poca influencia que tiene Mr. Wells con su mismo partido . . . y debemos ayudarlo como él nos ha ayudado en otras ocasiones. No es cuestión de hacer muchos gastos, sino de conseguir todos los votos de nuestros amigos y dependientes" (Francis W. Seabury Papers, Center for American History, 2G/53).

20. Willacy was carved out of Cameron and Hidalgo counties (Gournay 1995: 118).

21. After Brooks County was carved out of Starr, the participation of the voters in the primary election of 1912 fell by 50 percent (see table 4.5).

22. On February 12, 1914, the Democratic county central committee of Dimmit County established a white primary system to exclude Mexicans and blacks. The county commissioners did not intervene on behalf of those excluded. The *Javeline,* a newspaper in Carrizo Springs in Dimmit County, described the meeting: "White Man's Primary Sentiment Unanimous: The White Man's Primary mass meeting was held as scheduled Thursday afternoon at one o'clock and the reign of the Mexican vote in Dimmit is doomed. . . .

The meeting was emphatic in its desire that the vote in this primary be limited to white voters and by that meant that all Mexicans and negroes be excluded" (*Javeline,* February 13, 1914).

23. The states with the largest number of haciendas were Oaxaca, Sonora, Veracruz, Chihuahua, Tabasco, and Chiapas (Callahan 1932; Spicer 1981).

Chapter Five

1. For a review of state cases, see *American Digest* 1898: no. 157.

2. The full title of the Naturalization Act of 1906 is "Act to establish a Bureau of Immigration and Naturalization, and to provide for the naturalization of aliens throughout the United States."

3. Information provided by Department of Homeland Security in a letter sent March 15, 2007, by Jean R. Scott, Immigration Statistics, concerning the storage of naturalization records after 1906.

4. The U.S. Census of 1900 did not identify the foreign languages spoken by immigrants. In 1906 a person must have lived in the United States for five years before acquiring citizenship, and a declaration could be filed two years after settling in the United States.

5. The Immigration Act of February 5, 1917, placed an entry fee on Mexicans, but it differed from the head tax placed on other immigrants in that the secretary of labor would set the fee. The act also placed an immigration bar on Asians and raised the head tax to eight dollars.

6. Jane Y. McCallum Papers:: box 5, file 11–15 "Correspondence E. League to NAWSA, n.d. 1914–1919"; box 6, file 10 "A.R.E. 004, 1916–1918 Correspondence"; box 33, file 9 "Poll Taxes."

7. See Ayala (2005: 108) for a summary of news articles describing the social activities of Cruz Azul. Fundraisers were often held in expensive hotels, events which only the Mexican American middle and upper classes could afford to attend.

8. Legislative vote for House Joint Resolution 3: 122 yes, absent 18 (*Journal of the House of Representatives, Texas 36th Legislature, Regular Session, 1919*, p. 141).

9. See Keyssar (2000: table A12) for a list of states passing English-only assistance laws during elections. In Texas interpreters were prohibited in 1918, and a person could not receive assistance from an election judge unless he or she had been a citizen for twenty-one years.

10. The U.S. Census did not have information on an additional 7,794 immigrant women (U.S. Census 1922c: 986).

11. The U.S. Census of 1920 does not break down the gender of the groups who had filed first papers. There were 1,323 Mexicans, including men and women, who were classified as foreign-born with first papers of naturalization (U.S. Census 1925: 84).

12. Each county was also permitted to levy an additional sum, not to exceed twenty-five cents.

13. Representative Canales lost support within the Democratic Party when, in 1920, he filed charges against the Texas Rangers for harassing Mexicans in South Texas (Anders 1996b: 953–954). He did not seek reelection.

14. During the next ten years the size of the black population of Harris County fell. In 1910, African Americans made up 37.5 percent of the county's residents, and by 1920 the number had fallen to 23 percent (U.S. Census 1913d: 659; cf. U.S. Census 1922b: 1000).

15. When the Lorenzo de Zavala State Library and Archives duplicated the election registrars, the election of 1921 was not microfilmed, and the location of the original documents is unknown.

16. After the Alien Land Act of 1921 passed it was unclear if it applied to Mexicans and Canadian immigrants. In 1946 the attorney general of Texas clarified the law and issued the opinion that immigrants from Mexico and Canada were exempt (Title 5, Article 166, Alien Ownership of Land Prohibited, in Vernon's Annotated Revised Civil Statutes, Vol. 1, 1959: 482). The confusion had resulted from the conflicting language found in articles 15 and 16. Under article 15 all aliens without U.S. citizenship were prohibited from purchasing certain property in Texas, whereas article 16 exempted Canadians and Mexicans.

17. In 1921 under the Emergency Quota Act (the Johnson Act), the U.S. Con-

gress for the first time limited the total number of immigrants who could be admitted in a single year. This limit did not apply to the Western Hemisphere as long as a country was not a possession of another nation (Waters and Ueda 2007: 695).

18. The name of the entry fees was provided by Marian Smith, Department of Homeland Security, Historical Office Division, e-mail June 16, 2009. Also see U.S. Department of Labor 1927 (p. 6) for the types of fees charged of immigrants.

19. Statistical records of the visa fees paid at the Mexican border were first collected in 1925. These data, however, were not reported by country of origin until 1930, and the earlier figures were aggregated with the general data on head taxes (U.S. Department of Labor 1925; National Archives 2007a; National Archives 2007b). Likewise, statistical data on the fees paid by Mexican agricultural workers who applied for permanent legal residency was first recorded in 1945.

20. In 1940 some immigrants who had entered after 1924 and did not have proof of legal entry were allowed to register for permanent legal residency and pay a fee (National Archives 2007b).

21. For the size of the Mexican permanent legal resident population, see U.S. Department of Labor, Annual Reports of the Secretary of Labor for 1925 to 1932.

22. Information provided by the U.S. Department of Homeland Security, letter from Jean R. Scott, Immigration Statistics, March 15, 2007.

23. After 1906 the Bureau of Immigration and Naturalization underwent reorganization and was separated into two bureaus. The bureaus were once again consolidated in 1933 (U.S.C., Title 8, Aliens and Nationality, 1440 to end, pp. 495–497).

Chapter Six

1. In 1950 the Mexican immigrant population in the United States numbered 451,490, the majority of whom, 196,077, resided in Texas. (U.S. Census 1954: 71–74, 130). California's Mexican immigrant population was the next largest in size, and it numbered 162,309.

2. Public Law 45 was enacted into law on August 4, 1942, but was revised two times subsequently (see Menchaca 1995: 90).

3. Family members of braceros had to pay a ten-dollar fee to apply for legal entry (66 *United States Statutes* 230).

4. On July 1, 1963, the Department of Labor began implementing Congress's directive to disqualify eligible immigration applicants, if their entry would adversely affect the labor market (U.S. Department of Labor 1964: 59). The AFL-CIO was not satisfied with the restrictions, and five months later brought suit against the federal government to terminate the permanent legal status of Mexican immigrants who worked in the United States but returned to Mexico at the end of the day. The AFL-CIO charged that this was a serious labor problem along the Texas-Mexico border. Robert Kennedy, the U.S. attorney general, disagreed and did not support changing the permanent legal status of Mexican migrant workers. The case was finally resolved by the U.S. Court of Appeals District of Columbia Circuit and a decision rendered on behalf of the federal government (*Texas State AFL-CIO, et al., Appellants v. Robert F. Kennedy, U.S. Attorney General and Raymond F. Farrell, Commissioner of the U.S.INS, Appellees* 1964).

5. In 1969, the California Court of Appeals, Fourth Appellate District, ruled in *County of San Diego v. Anatolio T. Viloria* that sponsors were not required to reimburse the government for services that were provided to indigent populations. An immigrant who had become indigent had to be treated in the same way as other indigents.

6. Immediately after the amendments of 1965 became law, six agricultural corporations initiated litigation to stop the federal government from applying the occupational restrictions upon Mexican agricultural workers. *Emmanuel Braude et al., Appellant v. W. Willard Wirtz, Secretary of Labor, U.S., et al., Appellees* 1965. The corporations lost.

7. Department of Homeland Security annual data from 1980 to 2004 indicate that Mexican parents gaining permanent legal residency through sponsorship by a U.S. son or daughter varied, ranging from a low of 1,581 in 1982 to a high of 31,874 in 2000. And since 2000 the numbers have remained at least in the low 20,000 range. From 2004 to 2007 the DHS does not offer a breakdown by country of birth. See Statistical Yearbook of Immigration and Naturalization for specific years cited from 1980 to 2002, and Yearbook of Immigration Statistics for 2002 to the present at www.dhs.gov.

8. David Harvey (2006) argues that for U.S. investors the Mexican bailout was a profitable venture. The Mexican government agreed to pay high interest rates on the loans.

9. In 1984 the U.S. Congress extended the federal minimum wage to farmworkers, which in turn raised the farmers' labor costs (Shulman 1986: 155).

10. John Simanski provided these statistics on December 10, 2008, based on his review of the immigration data of the Department of Homeland Security, Office of Immigration Statistics, Policy Directorate.

11. Agricultural workers who were living in the United States before the passage of IRCA were to submit their applications no later than 1988. However, those who arrived after IRCA were allowed to adjust their status under the 210A program (Section 219, Immigration and Nationality Technical Corrections Act of 1994, PL 103-416, in U.S. Citizenship and Immigration Service, Department of Homeland Security, Public Laws Amending the INA, www.uscis.gov, 2008).

12. After 1990 the INS continued to allow the family of IRCA and other applicants to enter legally but preference was given to individuals from countries with a low application ratio (see sec. 201c, 110 *U.S. Statutes at Large* (part 4) 3009).

13. In 1993, 39,243 dependents of agricultural workers were legalized through SAW and other family sponsorship programs. After that year the number of dependents sponsored annually by agricultural workers dwindled to under 1,400 (Statistical Yearbook of the Immigration and Naturalization Service 1993: 45; see yearbooks for preceding years).

14. The H2 program was established under the Immigration and Nationality Act of 1952 and retained thereafter. Since then, however, it has been revised and separated into H2A and H2B programs.

15. Data for material cited: Statistical Yearbook of the Immigration and Naturalization Service 1996: 20, Statistical Yearbook of the Immigration and Naturalization Service 1997: 19; Yearbook of Immigration Statistics 2003: 26; for 2004

data suppressed; Yearbook of Immigration Statistics 2005: 24; Yearbook of Immigration Statistics 2006: 29; Yearbook of Immigration Statistics 2007: 19.

16. Latino Civil Rights activists charged that Pete Wilson largely prompted the anti-immigrant initiative to refuel his struggling reelection campaign for governor (Torres 1996).

17. The ethnic breakdown of Proposition 187 indicates that 63 percent of whites voted in favor of it, 47 percent of Asians, 47 percent of African Americans, and 23 percent of Latinos (Rodriguez 2007: 244; Saito 1998: 102).

18. Prior to 1994 the annual number of naturalized people from El Salvador and Guatemala was low nationwide. El Salvador's numbers generally ranged from a little over 2,000 to under 1,000, and Guatemala's was usually under 1,000 (See the Statistical Yearbook of the Immigration and Naturalization Service 1994 to 2001). Neither group began to migrate in large numbers until the early 1980s.

19. On January 4, 1995, twenty-one congressmen sponsored the birthright legislation, and eight more followed later (*Congressional Record, Proceedings and Debates, 104th Congress, First Session,* vol. 141, 1995, pp. H4031, H4512, H4874, H630, H13870).

20. House vote for HR 4337: Ayes 239, Nays 182, 13 no vote (govtrack.us(a)).

21. Information obtained from CBS, ABC, NBC news for the dates cited. Also, see www.LISTSERV.CYERLATINA.NET/ARCHIVES/LARED-L.HTML for marches in March 2006; see www.univision.com for Piolín Sotelo.

22. Besides Mexico, the countries with large naturalized Latino populations are the Dominican Republic, El Salvador, Cuba, Colombia, Guatemala, Nicaragua, and Peru (Yearbook of Immigration Statistics 2007, Table 1, www.dhs.gov.). Their numbers, however, are considerably lower than Mexico's. For example, in 2007, 122,258 Mexicans naturalized, in comparison to the Dominican Republic, the second-highest country, with 20,645.

23. On July 3, 2002, President Bush signed the Expedited Naturalization Executive Order granting U.S. citizenship to deceased soldiers who had been undocumented U.S. residents (The White House, Expedited Naturalization Executive Order, July 3, 2002). However, at that time benefits were not extended to their families. In 2003 Sen. Barbara Boxer (D-CA) and Rep. Martin Frost (D-TX) introduced the Posthumous Citizenship Act of 2003 (Martinez 2003: 76). On November 24, 2004, Congress amended section 329A of the Immigration and Nationality Act and the National Defense Authorization Act, giving benefits to the families of soldiers who had been granted posthumous citizenship (8 USC 1440-1).

24. In 2005, Mexico produced a total of 3.375 million barrels a day, of which 2 million were sold to the United States. (PEMEX, September 9, 2008, www.pemex.com).

25. The web addresses differ slightly in these two citations: House Resolution 1868 "Birthright Citizenship Act of 2009." Copy of resolution www.thomas.gov/cgi-bin/bdquery. House Resolution 126. "To Amend the Immigration and Nationality Act to Limit Citizenship at Birth, Merely by Virtue of Birth in the U.S., to Persons with Citizen or Legal Resident Mothers." Copy of resolution. www.thomas.gov/cgi-bin/query.

26. The history of Texas bills can be found online: www.house.texas.state.us.

27. Governor Rick Perry signed Senate Bill 1260 on June 15, 2007. It became effective on September 1, 2007 (S.B. 1260, Texas Legislature online www.house. state.tx.us). Opponents of the legislation, including attorneys for the Texas Civil Rights Project, argued against passage because the bill would make the roads unsafe since many undocumented workers and temporary residents with expired visas would not be tested by the Department of Motor Vehicles (Rice 2008).

Bibliography

Abramowitz, Jack. 1953. "The Negro in the Populist Movement." *Journal of Negro History* 38(3): 257–289.

Agamben, Giorgio. 2000. *Means Without End: Notes and Politics.* Minnesota: University of Minnesota Press.

Aguirre Beltrán, Gonzalo. 1991a. *La Población Negra de Mexico 1519–1810.* 1946; reprint, Mexico City: Edición Fuente Cultural.

———. 1991b. *Formas de Gobierno Indigena.* Obra Antropológica 4. 3d ed. Veracruz, Mexico: Instituto Nacional Indigenista, Universidad Veracruzana.

———. 1944. "The Slave Trade in Mexico, 1519–1810." *Hispanic American Historical Review* 24(3): 412–431.

Alonso, Ana Maria. 1995. *Thread of Blood: Colonialism, Revolution, and Gender on Mexico's Northern Frontier.* Tucson: University of Arizona Press.

Alonzo, Armando. 1998. *Tejano Legacy: Rancheros and Settlers in South Texas, 1734–1900.* Albuquerque: University of New Mexico Press.

American Digest. 1898. *Century Edition of the American Digest,* Vol. 2. St. Paul: West Publishing.

Anders, Even. 1996a. "James Babbage Wells Jr." In *New Handbook of Texas,* comp. Ronnie Tyler, 3:877. Austin: Texas State Historical Association.

———. 1996b. "José Tomás Canales." In *New Handbook of Texas,* comp. Ronnie Tyler, 1:953–954. Austin: Texas State Historical Association.

Appiah, Kwame Anthony, and Henry Louis Gates Jr. 1999. *Africana: The Encyclopedia of the African and African American Experience.* New York: Basic Civitas Books.

Archibold, Randal. 2010. "Arizona Enacts Stringent Law on Immigration." *New York Times,* April 21, 2010, www.nytimes.com.

Arreola, David. 2002. *Tejano South Texas: A Mexican American Cultural Province.* Austin: University of Texas Press.

Ashton, John. 1996. "Mifflin Kenedy." In *New Handbook of Texas,* comp. Ronnie Tyler, 3:1064–1065. Austin: Texas State Historical Association.

Associated Press. 2007. "Senators Strike Deal on Immigration Reform Bill, May 18, 2007." www.MSNBC.com.

————. 2006. "Despite Smiles, Divisions Linger after U.S.-Mexico-Canada Summit." *USA Today.* www.usatoday.com.

Austin Papers. Center for American History. University of Texas at Austin.

Ayala, Adriana. 2005. "Negotiating Race Relations Through Activism: Women Activists and Women's Organizations in San Antonio, Texas during the 1920s." Ph.D. diss., University of Texas at Austin.

Baggett, James A. 1974. "Origins of Early Texas Republican Party Leadership." *Journal of Southwestern History* 40(3): 441–454.

Baker, Lee D. 1998. *From Savage to Negro: Anthropology and the Construction of Race, 1896–1954.* Berkeley: University of California Press.

Balistereri, Kelly, and Jennifer Van Hook. 2004. "The More Things Change the More They Stay the Same: Mexican Naturalization Before and after Welfare Reform." *International Migration Review* 38(1): 113–130.

Barksdale, Mary Louise Wimberley. 1932. "The Gubernatorial Administration of James Stephen Hogg." M.A. thesis, University of Texas at Austin.

Barnes, Donna A. 1984. *Farmers in Rebellion: The Rise and Fall of the Southern Farmers Alliance and People's Party in Texas.* Austin: University of Texas Press.

Barr, Alwyn. 2005. "The Impact of Race in Shaping Judicial Districts, 1876–1907." *Southwestern Historical Quarterly* 108(4): 423–439.

————. 2000. *Reconstruction to Reform: Texas Politics, 1876–1906.* Dallas: Southern Methodist University.

Batts, Robert L., publisher. 1907. *A Twentieth Century History of Southwest Texas.* Vol. 1. New York: Lewis Publishing.

Baugh, Josh. 2010. "Split Decision: Council Criticizes Arizona Law." *San Antonio Express,* June 25, 2010, www.mysanantonio.com.

Bean, Frank, and Benjamin Bradshaw. 1970. "Intermarriage Between Persons of Spanish and Non-Spanish Surname: Changes from the Mid-Nineteenth to the Mid-Twentieth Century." *Social Science Quarterly* 51(2): 389–395.

Bean, Frank, and Lindsay Lowell. 2007. "Unauthorized Migration." In *The New Americans: A Guide to Immigration Since 1965,* ed. Mary C. Waters and Reed Ueda, with Helen Marrow, 70–82. Cambridge: Harvard University Press.

Beaumier, Guy. 1990. *Free Trade in North America: The Maquiladora Factor.* Ottawa, Ont.: Research Branch, Canada Library of Parliament, Depository Services Program, BP-247E Report.

Biesele, Rudolph Leopold. 1987. *The History of the German Settlements in Texas 1831–1861.* 1930; reprint, Austin: Eakin Press.

Binkley, William. 1936. *Official Correspondence of the Texas Revolution.* Vol. 3. New York: Appleton-Century.

Bonfil Batalla, Guillermo. 1998. *Mexico Profundo: Reclaiming a Civilization.* Austin: University of Texas Press, Institute of Latin American Studies.

Boom, Aaron. 1966. "Texas in the 1850s, as Viewed by a Recent Arrival." *Southwestern Historical Quarterly* 70(2): 281–288.

Bourdieu, Pierre. 1992. *Outline of a Theory of Practice.* Cambridge: Cambridge University Press.

Brettell, Caroline. 2006. "Political Belonging and Cultural Belonging: Immigration Status, Citizenship, and Identity Among Four Immigrant Populations in a Southwestern City." *American Behavioral Scientist* 50(1): 70–99.

Brown, Jonathan, and Alan Knight, eds. 1992. *The Mexican Petroleum Industry in the Twentieth Century.* Austin: University of Texas Press.

Bryan, William J. 1896. *The First Battle: A Story of the Campaign of 1896.* Chicago: W. B. Conkey.

Bulletin of the University of Texas. 1915. *Studies in Farm Tenancy in Texas.* Bulletin of the University of Texas, no. 21, April 10, 1915.

Burke, J. Jr., comp. 1879. *Burke's Texas Almanac and Immigrant's Handbook for 1879.* Houston: J. Burke Jr.

Cabrera, Luis. 1914. "The Mexican Situation from a Mexican Point of View." *Journal of Race Development* 4(3): 245–261.

Calderón, Esteban B. 1975. *Juicio Sobre la Guerra del Yaqui y Génesis de la Huelga de Cananea.* Mexico: Centro de Estudios Históricos del Movimiento Obrero Mexicano (CEHSMO).

Calderon, Roberto. 2002. "Tejano Politics." In *Handbook of Texas Online.* Austin: Texas State Historical Association. www.tshonline.org.

Callahan, James M. 1932. *American Foreign Policy in Mexican Relations.* New York: Macmillan.

Campbell, Randolph. 1992. "Scalawag District Judges: The E. J. Davis Appointees, 1870–1873." *Houston Review* 14: 75–88.

———. 1996. "Wesley B. Ogden." In *New Handbook of Texas,* comp. Ronnie Tyler, 4:115. Austin: Texas State Historical Association.

Cantrell, Gregg, and D. Scott Barton. 1989. "Texas Populists and the Failure of Biracial Politics." *Journal of Southern History* 55(4): 659–692.

Cañas, Jesus, and Robert W. Gilmer. 2007. "Economic Trends in the Desert Southwest: Mexico Regulatory Change Redefines Maquiladora." *Crossroads,* no. 1. Federal Reserve Bank of Dallas. www.dallasfed.org.

Cañas, Jesus, and Roberto Coronado. 2002. "Maquiladora Industry: Past, Present and Future." *Business Frontier,* no. 2. Federal Reserve Bank of Dallas. www.dallasfed.org.

Carens, Joseph H. 1987. "Who Belongs? Theoretical and Legal Questions About Birthright Citizenship in the United States." *University of Toronto Law Journal* 37: 413–443.

Carroll, H. Bailey, and J. Villasana Haggard. 1942. *The New Mexico Chronicles.* Albuquerque: Quivira Society.

Castañeda, Jorge G. 2007. *ExMex: From Migrants to Immigrants.* New York: New Press.

Castillo, Juan, and W. Gardner Selby. 2007. "Immigration Proposals Falter." *Austin American-Statesman,* March 27, 2007, A-1.

Chabot, Fredrick. 1937. *With the Makers of San Antonio: Genealogies of the Latin, Anglo-American, and German Families with Occassional Biographies.* San Antonio: Graphic Arts.

Chang, Iris. 2003. *The Chinese in America: A Narrative History.* New York: Penguin Books.

Chavez, Leo. 2008. *The Latino Threat: Constructing Immigrants, Citizens, and the Nation.* Stanford: Stanford University Press.

Cheeseman, Bruce S. 1996. "Richard King." In *New Handbook of Texas,* comp. Ronnie Tyler, 3:1107–1108. Austin: Texas State Historical Association.

Church of Jesus Christ of Latter-Day Saints, The. 2008. "Family Group Record: Epitacio Mondragon." www.familysearch.org.

Clements, Roger. 1955. "British Investment and American Legislative Restrictions in the Trans-Mississippi West, 1880–1900." *Mississippi Valley Historical Review* 42(2): 207–228.

Coatsworth, John. 1978. "Obstacles to Economic Growth in Nineteenth-Century Mexico." *American Historical Review* 83(1): 80–100.

Cockcroft, James D. 1986. *Outlaws in the Promised Land: Mexican Immigrant Workers and America's Future.* New York: Grove Press.

Coerver, Don, and Linda Hall. 1984. *Texas and the Mexican Revolution: A Study in State and National Border Policy 1910–1920.* San Antonio: Trinity University Press.

Coerver, Don, and Suzanne Paszton. 2004. *Mexico: An Encyclopedia of Contemporary Culture and History.* 4th ed. Santa Barbara: ABC-CLIO. Edición Fuente Cultural, 1989.

Cook, Sherburne, and Woodrow Borah. 1974. *Essays in Population History: Mexico and the Caribbean.* Vol. 2. Berkeley: University of California Press.

Corry, John. 1998. *Prelude to a Century.* New York: Fordham University Press.

Costello, J. G., and D. Hornbeck. 1989. "Alta California: An Overview." In *Columbian Consequences.* Vol. 1: *Archaeological and Historical Perspectives on the Spanish Borderlands West,* ed. D. H. Thomas, 303–331. Washington, D.C.: Smithsonian Institution Press.

Coursey, Clark. 1962. *Courthouses of Texas.* Brownwood, Tex.: Banner Printing.

Cox, Patrick. 2005. *The First Texas News Barons.* Austin: University of Texas Press.

Craig, Richard. 1971. *The Bracero Program: Interest Groups and Foreign Policy.* Austin: University of Texas Press.

Cruz Serrano, Noé. 2007. "Reducera-Pemex su nivel de exportación." *El Universal* January 2007. El Universal.com.mx.

Dale, Edward E. 1951. *The Indians of the Southwest: A Century of Development under the United States.* Norman: University of Oklahoma Press.

Davids, Jules. 1976. *American Political and Economic Penetration of Mexico, 1877–1920.* New York: Arno Press.

Davis, Ellen A., and Edwin H. Grope. 1929. *The New Encyclopedia of Texas.* Vol. 3. Dallas: Texas Development Bureau.

De Genova, Nicholas. 2002. "Migrant 'Illegality' and Deportability in Every Day Life." *Annual Review of Anthropology* 31: 419–447.

de la Peña, Guillermo. 1993. "Individuo, Etnia, Nación: Paradojas y Antinomias de la Identitidad Colectiva." In *Epistemología y Cultura: En Torno a la Obra de Luis Villoro,* ed. E. Garzón Valdín and F. Salmerón, 243–261. Universidad Nacional Autónoma de México, Instituto de Investigaciones Filosóficas.

de León, Arnoldo. 1987. *They Call Them Greasers: Anglo Attitudes toward Mexicans in Texas, 1821–1900.* Austin: University of Texas Press.

de León, Arnoldo, and Kenneth L. Stewart. 1997. *Tejanos and the Numbers Game: A Socio-Historical Interpretation from the Federal Censuses, 1850–1900.* Albuquerque: University of New Mexico Press.

Derecho Internacional Mexicano, Vol. 1. 1877. *Tratados y Convenciones Celebrados y Ratificados por la Republica Mexicana.* Jose Fernandez, compiler. Mexico: Imprenta de Gonzalo A. Esteva.

Derecho Internacional Mexicano, Vol. 3. 1880. *Leyes, Decretos Y Ordenes Que Forman Derecho Internacional Mexicano o Que Se Relacionan con el Mismo.* Mexico: Tipografía Literaria de Filomeno Mata.

Drimmer, Jonathan C. 1995. "The Nephews of Uncle Sam: The History, Evolution, and Application of Birthright Citizenship in the United States." *Georgetown Immigration Law Journal* 9: 667–717.

Driscoll, Barbara. 1999. *The Tracks North: The Railroad Bracero Program of World War II.* Austin: University of Texas Press.

Duncan, Robert. 1996. "Political Legitimation and Maximilian's Second Empire in Mexico, 1864–1867." *Mexican Studies/Estudios Mexicanos* 12(1): 27–66.

Durand, Jorge. 2007. "The Bracero Program (1942–1964): A Critical Appraisal." *Migración y Desarollo,* Second semester, 25–40.

Durham, George. 1962. *Taming the Nueces Strip: The Story of McNelly's Rangers.* Austin: University of Texas Press.

Dysart, Jane. 1976. "Mexican Women in San Antonio, 1830–1860: The Assimilation Process." *Western Historical Quarterly* 7(4): 365–375.

Ebright, Malcolm. 1991. "Introduction: Spanish and Mexican Land Grants and the Law." In *Spanish and Mexican Land Grants and the Law,* ed. Malcolm Ebright, 3–11. Manhattan, Kan.: Sunflower University Press.

Eisgruber, Christopher. 1997. "Birthright Citizenship and the Constitution." *New York University Law Review* 72: 54–96.

Engstrand, Iris. 1992. *Arizona Hispánica.* Madrid: Editorial Mapre.

Feagin, Joe, and Clairece Booher Feagin. 2003. *Racial and Ethnic Relations.* Englewood Cliffs: Prentice-Hall.

Foley, Neil. 1997. *The White Scourge: Mexicans, Blacks, and Poor Whites in Texas Cotton Culture.* Berkeley: University of California Press.

Folkenflik, David. 2009. "What's Behind Lou Dobb's Leaving CNN?" *National Public Radio,* Nov. 12, 2009. www.NPR.org.

Fox News. 2010. "At Convention, Texas GOP Passes Immigration Plank Similar to Arizona Law," June 13, 2010, *FoxNews,* www.foxnews.com.

Forbes, Jack. 1966. "Black Pioneers: The Spanish-Speaking Afro-Americans of the Southwest." *Phylon* 27: 233–246.

Freeman, Gary, Luis Plascencia, Susan Gonzales Baker, and Manuel Orozco. 2002. "Explaining the Surge in Citizenship Applications in the 1990s: Lawful Permanent Residents in Texas." *Social Science Quarterly* 83(4): 1013–1025.

Galarza, Ernesto. 1964. *Merchants of Labor: The Mexican Bracero Story.* Santa Barbara: McNally and Loftin.

Garcia, Maria Christina. 1996. "Mexican Women's League." In *New Handbook of Texas,* comp. Ronnie Tyler, 4:194. Austin: Texas State Historical Association.

Garcia, Mario T. 1998. *The Making of a Mexican American Mayor: Raymond L. Telles of El Paso.* El Paso: Texas Western Press.

Gillette, William. 1969. *The Right to Vote: Politics and the Passage of the Fifteenth Amendment.* Baltimore: Johns Hopkins University Press.

Gilly, Adolfo. 1994. *La Revolución Interrumpida* (Edición Corregida y Aumentada). Mexico D.F.: Edicion, Era, Coleción Problemas de Mexico.

Gilmore, N. Ray, IV. 1963. "Mexico and the Spanish-American War." *Hispanic American Historical Review* 43(4): 511–525.

González Ramirez, Manuel. 1974. *La Huelga de Cananea*. Mexico, D.F.: Fondo de Cultura Económica.

Gould, Lewis L. 1973. *Progressives and Prohibitionists: Texas Democrats in the Wilson Era*. Austin: University of Texas Press.

Gournay, Luke. 1995. *Texas Boundaries: Evolution of the State's Counties*. College Station: Texas A&M University Press.

GovTrack.us. House vote on Passage: H.R. 4437 [109th]: Border Protection/Anti-terrorism and Illegal. www.gov.track.us/congress (2005).

Gray, William. 1965. *From Virginia to Texas, 1835: Diary of Colonel William F. Gray*. Houston: Fletcher Young.

Grayson, George W. 1980. *The Politics of Mexican Oil*. Pittsburgh: University of Pittsburgh Press.

Grebler, Leo, Joan Moore, and Ralph Guzman. 1970. *The Mexican American People: The Nation's Second Largest Minority*. New York: Free Press.

Grodin, Joseph, Calvin Massey, and Richard Cunningham. 1993. *The California State Constitution: A Reference Guide*. Westport, Conn.: Greenwood Press.

Gutiérrez, David. 1995. *Walls and Mirrors: Mexican Americans, Mexican Immigrants, and the Politics of Ethnicity*. Berkeley: University of California Berkeley.

Guttin, Andrea. 2010. *The Criminal Alien Program: Immigration Enforcement in Travis County, Texas*. Washington, D.C.: Immigration Policy Center, American Immigration Council.

Haas, Lisabeth. 1995. *Conquests and Historical Identities in California 1769–1936*. Berkeley: University of California Press.

Hackney, Sheldon. 1971. "Contemporary Views of Populism: The Omaha Platform of the People's Party." In *Populism: The Critical Issues*, ed. Sheldon Hackney, 1–10. Boston: Little, Brown.

Hall, Thomas, and David Weber. 1984. "Mexican Liberals and the Pueblo Indians, 1821–1829." *New Mexico Historical Review* 59(1): 5–31.

Hamilton, Richard. 2006. *President McKinley, War and Empire*. Vol. 1. New Brunswick: Transaction.

Hammond, George, and Agapito Rey, eds. 1953. *Don Juan de Oñate: Colonizer of New Mexico, 1595–1628*. Volume 5. Albuquerque: University of New Mexico Press.

Harris, Charles H., III, and Louis R. Sandler. 1980. "The 1911 Reyes Conspiracy: The Texas Side." *Southwestern Historical Quarterly* 83 (April): 325–348.

Harvard Law Review. 1994. "Notes: The Birthright Citizenship Amendment: A Threat to Equality." *Harvard Law Review* 107 (5): 1026–1043.

Harvey, David. 2006. "Neo-Liberalism and the Restoration of Class Power." In *Spaces of Global Capitalism: Towards a Theory of Uneven Geographical Development*, 69–116. New York: Verso.

Harvey, Neil. 1998. *The Chiapas Rebellion: The Struggle for Land and Democracy*. Durham: Duke University Press.

Heizer, Robert, and Alan Almquist. 1977. *The Other Californians: Prejudice and Discrimination under Spain, Mexico, and the United States to 1920*. Berkeley: University of California Press.

Hibbard, Benjamin H. 1965. *A History of the Public Land Policies.* Milwaukee: University of Wisconsin Press.

Hicks, John D. 1964. *The Populist Revolt: A History of the Farmers' Alliance and the People's Party.* 1931; reprint, Lincoln: University of Nebraska Press.

Hine, Darlene Clark. 2003. *Black Victory: The Rise and Fall of the White Primary in Texas.* Columbia: University of Missouri Press.

Hinojosa, Gilbert. 1983. *A Borderlands Town in Transition: Laredo 1755–1870.* College Station: Texas A&M University Press.

Hoffman, Abraham. 1974. *Unwanted Mexican Americans in the Great Depression: Repatriation Pressures, 1929–1939.* Tucson: University of Arizona Press.

Hogg, James Stephen. 1951. *Address and State Papers of James Stephen Hogg.* Robert Cotoner, compiler. Austin: University of Texas Press.

Houston, Michael. 2000. "Birthright Citizenship in the United Kingdom and the United States: A Comparative Analysis of the Common Law Basis for Granting Citizenship to Children Born of Illegal Immigrants." *Vanderbilt Journal of Transnational Law* 33: 693–738.

Houston Post. 1897. *Houston Post Almanac.* Houston: Houston Printing.

Hull, Elizabeth. 1985. *Without Justice for All: The Constitutional Rights of Aliens.* Westport, Conn.: Greenwood Press.

Hutchinson, Bill. 2009. "Lou Dobbs quits CNN: Looks to 'engage in constructive problem solving.'" *New York Daily News,* Nov. 12, 2009. www.nydailynews.com.

Hutchinson, Cecil Alan. 1969. *Frontier Settlement in Mexican California: The Hijar-Padres Colony and Its Origins, 1769–1835.* New Haven: Yale University Press.

Hutchison, Kay Bailey, and John Cornyn. 2007. "We must not repeat the mistakes of 1986." *Dallas Morning News,* May 22, 2007. dallasnews.com.

Hyman, Harold, and William Wiecek. 1982. *Equal Justice Under Law: Constitutional Development, 1835–1875.* New York: Harper and Row.

Iglesias-Prieto, Norma. 2001. *Beautiful Flowers of the Maquiladora: Life Histories of Women Workers in Tijuana.* Austin: University of Texas Press.

Inclan, John. n.d. "Joseph Antonio Seguin and Don Geronimo Ximenex Flores Abregon." *Somos Primos.* www.somosprimos.com.

Inda, Jonathan Xavier. 2007. "The Value of Immigrant Life." In *Women and Migration in the U.S.-Mexico Borderlands: A Reader,* ed. Denise A. Segura and Patricia Zavella, 134–157. Durham: Duke University Press.

———. 2002. "Biopower, Reproduction, and the Migrant Woman's Body." In *Decolonial Voices: Chicana and Chicano Cultural Studies in the 21st Century,* ed. Arturo J. Aldama and Naomi H. Quiñonez, 98–112. Bloomington: Indiana University Press.

Jensen, Leif. 2001. "The Demographic Diversity of Immigrants and Their Children." *In Ethnicities: Children of Immigrants in America,* ed. Ruben Rumbaut and Alejandro Portes, 21–56. Berkeley: University of California Press.

Jones, Richard, and Albert Kauffman. 1994. "Accessibility to Comprehensive Higher Education in Texas." *Social Science Journal* 31: 263–283.

Jordan, Terry G. 1982. *German Seed in Texas Soil: Immigrant Farmers in Nineteenth-Century Texas.* Austin: University of Texas Press.

Keyssar, Alexander. 2000. *The Right to Vote: The Contested History of Democracy in the United States.* New York: Basic Books.

Kingston, Mike, Sam Attlesey, and Mary G. Crawford. 1992. *The Texas Almanac's Political History of Texas*. Austin: Eakin Press.

Kingston, Mike. 1988. *A Concise History of Texas: From the Texas Almanac*. Austin: Texas Monthly Press, Dallas Morning News.

Knight, Alan. 1986. *The Mexican Revolution*. Vol. 1: *Porfirian Liberals and Peasants*. New York: Cambridge Press.

Konvitz, Milton. 1946. *The Alien and the Asiatic in American Law*. Ithaca: Cornell University Press.

Lamar, Howard R. 1970. *The Far Southwest 1846–1912: A Territorial History*. New York: W. W. Norton.

Lansky, Bruce. 2007. *100,000 Baby Names*. Minetonka, Minn.: Meadowbrook Press.

Larson, Robert W. 1968. *New Mexico's Quest for Statehood, 1846–1912*. Albuquerque: University of New Mexico Press.

Lee, Erika. 2004. "American Gate Keeping: Race and Immigration Law in the Twentieth Century." In *Not Just Black and White: Historical and Contemporary Perspectives on Immigration, Race, and Ethnicity in the U.S.*, ed. Nancy Foner and George Fredrickson, 119–144. New York: Russell Sage Foundation.

Leibowitz, Arnold H. 1983. *Immigration Law and Refugee Policy*. New York: Matthew Bender.

Levario, Miguel Antonio. 2007. "Cuando Vino la Mexicanidad: Authority, Race, and Conflict in West Texas, 1895–1924." Ph.D. diss., University of Texas at Austin.

Levine, Daniel B., Kenneth Hill, and Robert Warren. 1985. *Immigration Statistics: A Story of Neglect*. Washington: National Academy Press.

Limón, José. 1974. "El Primero Congreso Mexicanista, 1911." *Aztlan* 5 (Fall): 85–117.

Lorey, David. 1999. *The U.S.-Mexican Border in the Twentieth Century: A History of Economic and Social Transformation*. Wilmington, Del.: SR Books.

Luckingham, Bradford. 1994. *Minorities in Phoenix: A Profile of Mexican American, Chinese American, and African American Communities, 1860–1992*. Tucson: University of Arizona Press.

Ludlow, Leonor, and Carlos Marichal, eds. 1998. *Un Siglo de Deuda Pública en México*. Instituto de Investigaciones Históricas-UNAM. Mexico, D.F.: UNAM.

Mack, William, and Donald Kiser. 1926. *Corpus Juris: Being a Complete and Systemic Statement of the Whole Body of the Law As Embodied in and Developed by All Reported Decisions*. Vol. 39. New York: American Law Book.

Mahoney, Harry, and Marjorie Mahoney. 1998. *Mexico and the Confederacy 1860–1867*. San Francisco: Austin and Winfield.

MALDEFian, June 18, 2007. "MALDEF Welcomes Continued Debate on Comprehensive Immigration Reform: Senate to Resume Immigration Debate This Week." MALDEF National Headquarters, Los Angeles, Regional Office. 634 S. Spring Road St., Los Angeles, CA. 90014. www.maldef.org.

Margadant S., Guillermo. 1991. "Mexican Colonial Law." In *Spanish and Mexican Land Grants and the Law*, ed. Malcolm Ebright, 85–99. Manhattan, Kan.: Sunflower University Press.

Marten, James. 1990. *Texas Divided: Loyalty and Dissent in the Lone Star State 1856–1874*. Lexington: University Press of Kentucky.

Martin, Roscoe C. 1970. *The People's Party in Texas: A Study in Third-Party Politics*. 1933; reprint, Austin: University of Texas Press.

Martinez, Ana Luisa. 2003. "The Voice of the People: Pablo Cruz, El Regidor and Mexican American Identity in San Antonio, Texas 1888–1910." Ph.D. diss., Texas Tech University.

Martinez, Elizabeth. 1993. *Henry Cisneros: Mexican-American Leader*. Brookfield, Conn.: Milbrook Press.

Martinez, Guillermo. 2003. "Equal Rights for Latino Heroes: U.S. Citizenship Benefits Should Extend to Families." *Hispanic* (May): 76.

Mattison, Ray. 1967. "The Tangled Web: The Controversy over the Tumacácori and Baca Land Grants." *Journal of American History* 8(2): 71–90.

Maynard, Roy. 2008. "Leo Berman Re-Entering Immigration Battle in Texas." *Tyler Morning Telegraph*, April 20, 2008. tylerpaper.com.

McArthur, Judith, and Harold Smith. 2003. *Minnie Fisher Cunningham: A Suffragist's Life in Politics*. New York: Oxford University Press.

McCornack, Richard. 1955. "Los Estados Confederados y Mexico." *Historia Mexicana* 15(3): 537–352.

McKenzie, William. 2007. "How to break stalemate over illegal immigration." *Dallas Morning News*, October 31, 2007. dallasnews.com.

McLemore, Dale, and Harriet Romo. 1998. *Racial and Ethnic Relations in America*. Boston: Allyn and Bacon.

Menchaca, Martha. 2008. "The Anti-miscegenation History of the American Southwest." *Cultural Dynamics* 20: 279–311.

———. 2001. *Recovering History, Constructing Race: The Indian, Black, and White Roots of Mexican Americans*. Austin: University of Texas Press.

———. 1995. *Mexican Outsiders: A Community History of Marginalization and Discrimination in California*. Austin: University of Texas Press.

Metz, Leon. 1994. *El Paso Chronicles: A Record of Historical Events in El Paso, Texas*. El Paso: Mangan Books.

Meyer, C. Michael, William L. Sherman, and Susan M. Deeds. 2007. *The Course of Mexican History*. 8th ed. Oxford: Oxford University Press.

Meyerink, Kay, and Loretto Dennis Szucs. 1997. "Immigration Finding, Immigration Origins." In *The Source: A Guide Book of American Genealogy*, ed. L. D. Szucs and Sandra Hargreaves Luebking, 441–479. Salt Lake City: Ancestry Publication.

Michael, Victor Hugo. 2005a. "Hacia el norte viaja el Ejército Mexicano." *Mileno*, Mexico, D.F. August 31, 2005. wwww.presidencia.gov.mx.

———. 2005b. "El Ejército regresa a Texas 162 años después." *Mileno*. Mexico, D.F. September 1, 2005. wwww.presidencia.gov.mx.

Miller, Robert R. 1985. *Mexico: A History*. Norman: University of Oklahoma Press.

———. 1965. "Matias Romero: Mexican Minister to the United States during the Juarez-Maximilian Era." *Hispanic American Historical Review* 45(2): 228–245.

———. 1958. "Californians Against the Emperor." *California Historical Society Quarterly* 37(3), 193–214.

Miller, Worth Robert. 1986. "Building a Progressive Coalition in Texas: The

Populist-Reform Democrat Rapprochement 1900–1907." *Journal of Southern History* 52 (May): 163–182.

Miller, Tom. 1981. *On the Border: Portraits of America's Southwestern Frontier.* New York: Harper and Row.

Mines, Richard, and Ricardo Anzaldúa. 1982. *New Migrants vs. Old Migrants: Alternative Labor Market Structures in the California Citrus Industry.* Monograph 9. San Diego: University of California, San Diego, Program in United States Mexican Studies.

Mintz, Sidney. 1985. *Sweetness and Power: The Place of Sugar in Modern History.* New York: Penguin Books.

Mobasher, Mohsen. 2006. "Cultural Trauma and Ethnic Identity Formation Among Iranian Immigrants in the United States." *American Behavioral Scientist* 50(1): 100–117.

Montejano, David. 1987. *Anglos and Mexicans in the Making of Texas, 1836–1986.* Austin: University of Texas Press.

Morales, Donna S., and John P. Schmal. 2004. *The Dominguez Family: A Mexican-American Journey.* Berwyn Heights, Maryland: Heritage Books.

Murillo, Oscar Cuevas. 2008. "La Reforma Liberales, Materia de Propiedad Según Wistano Luis Orozco y Andrés Molina Enriquéz." *Investigaciones Jurídicas de UNAM,* 97–128. Mexico: Universidad Autónoma de Zacatecas. www.jurdicas.unam.mex.

Murphy, James. 1970. *Laws, Courts, and Lawyers: Through the Years in Arizona.* Tucson: University of Arizona Press.

———. 1966. *The Spanish Legal Heritage in Arizona.* Tucson: Arizona Pioneers' Historical Society.

Nevins, Joseph. 2002. *Operation Gatekeeper: The Rise of the "Illegal Alien" and the Making of the U.S.-Mexico Boundary.* New York: Routledge.

Newcomb, William. 1986. *The Indians of Texas: From Prehistoric to Modern Times.* Austin: University of Texas Press.

Newsmax.com. 2006. "Vicente Fox Announces Huge Oil Find." March 14, 2006, newsmax.com.

Ngai, Mae M. 2004. *Impossible Subjects: Illegal Aliens and the Making of Modern America.* Princeton: Princeton University Press.

———. 2003. "The Strange Career of the Illegal Alien: Immigration Restriction and Deportation Policy in the United States, 1921–1965." *Law and History Review* 21(1): 1–29.

Niemeyer, Vic. 1963. "Frustrated Invasion: The Revolutionary Attempt of General Bernardo Reyes from San Antonio in 1911." *Southwestern Historical Quarterly* 67: 213–225.

Norton, Charles. 1912. *Men of Affairs of San Antonio.* San Antonio: Newspaper Artist Association.

Nunn, W. C. 1962. *Texas Under the Carpetbaggers.* Austin: University of Texas Press.

Ochoa, Gilda. 2004. *Becoming Neighbors in a Mexican American Community: Power, Conflict, and Solidarity.* Austin: University of Texas Press.

Official Correspondence of the Texas Revolution, 2:561. American History Center, University of Texas at Austin.

Olmstead, Virginia Langham, comp. 1981. *Spanish and Mexican Censuses of New Mexico 1750–1830.* Albuquerque: New Mexico Genealogical Society.

Omi, Michael, and Howard Winant. 1994. *Racial Formation in the United States: The 1960s to the 1990s.* 2d ed. New York: Routledge.

Ong, Aihwa. 2007. "Introduction: Neoliberalism as Exception, Exception to Neoliberalism." In *Neoliberalism as Exception: Mutations in Citizenship and Sovereignty,* 1–27. Durham: Duke University Press.

Orozco, Wistano Luis. 1895. *Legislación y Jurisprudencia Sobre Terrenos Baldíos.* Mexico, Impresa de el Tiempo.

Paredes, Américo. 1957. *"With His Pistol in His Hand": A Border Ballad and Its Hero.* Austin: University of Texas Press.

Paschal, George. 1874. *A Digest of the Laws of Texas.* 4th ed. Vol. 2. Houston: E. H. Cushing.

PEMEX. September 9, 2008. *Monthly Petroleum Statistics: Volume of Crude Oil Exports.* www.pemex.com.

Pérez, Ana Lilia. 2010. *Camisas Azules, Manos Negras: El Saqueo de Pemex desde Los Pinos.* Mexico, D.F.: Grijalbo Mondadori.

Pitre, Merline. 1985. "Robert Lloyd Smith: A Black Lawmaker in the Shadow of Booker T. Washington." *Phylon* 46(3): 262–268.

Pletcher, David. 1958. "The Fall of Silver in Mexico, 1870–1910 and Its Effect on American Investments." *Journal of Economic History* 18(1): 33–55.

Pollack, Norman. 1967a. *The Populist Mind.* New York: Bobbs-Merrill.

———. 1967b. "Introduction." In *The Populist Mind,* ed. N. Pollack, xix–xlviii. New York: Bobbs-Merrill.

Ramsdell, Charles W. 1970. *Reconstruction in Texas.* Austin: University of Texas Press.

Republican National Committee. 2008. *2008 Republican Platform.* Committee on Arguments for the 2008 Republican National Committee. www.gop.com.

Republican Party of Texas. 2010. *2010 State Republican Platform.* Page 20. State Republican Party. *Texas Tribune,* June 24, 2010. Copy of platform www.static .texastribune.org/media/documents

Residents of Texas 1782–1836. Reprint of the Spanish and Mexican Censuses made in 1984. University of Texas, Institute of Texan Cultures. St. Louis: Ingmire Publications.

Rhodes, James Ford. 1922. *The McKinley and Roosevelt Administration 1897–1909.* New York: Macmillan.

Rice, Rod. 2008. "Critics: Security Trumps Safety for New Driver License Rules." www.TXLawHelp.org.

Richardson, Rupert, Adrian Anderson, and Ernest Wallace. 1997. *Texas: The Lone Star State.* 7th ed. Englewood Cliffs: Prentice-Hall.

Robinson, William W. 1948. *Land in California.* Berkeley: University of California Press.

Rodriguez, Gregory. 2007. *Mongrels, Bastards, Orphans, and Vagabonds: Mexican Immigration and the Future of Race in America.* New York: Pantheon Books.

———. 1999. *From Newcomers to New Americans: The Successful Integration of Immigrants into American Society.* Washington, D.C.: New American Foundation. National Immigration Forum.

Rodriguez, Ricardo, comp. 1903. *Código de Extranjería*. Mexico: Herrero Hermanos, Editores.

Romero, Matías. 1897. "The United States and the Liberation of the Spanish-American Colonies." *North American Review* 165(488): 70–86.

———. 1896. "The Philosophy of the Mexican Revolutions." *North American Review* 162(270): 1–17.

———. 1889. "The Annexation of Mexico." *North American Review* 148(390): 525–537.

Romo, Ricardo. 1975. "Responses to Mexican Immigration, 1910–1930." *Aztlan* 6(2): 173–194.

Rothenberg, Daniel. 2000. *With These Hands: The Hidden World of Migrant Farmworkers Today*. Berkeley: University of California Press.

Royce, Anya Peterson. 1982. *Ethnic Identity: Strategies of Diversity*. Bloomington: Indiana University Press.

Saito, Leland. 1998. *Race and Politics: Asian Americans, Latinos, and Whites in a Los Angeles Suburb*. Urbana: University of Illinois Press.

Samora, Julian. 1970. *Los Mojados: The Wetback Story*. Notre Dame: University of Notre Dame Press.

San Antonio City Directory 1885. Lorenzo de Zavala State Library and Archives. Genealogy Division. Austin, Texas.

Saunders, Robert. 1971. "Southern Populists and the Negro." In *Populism: The Critical Issues*, ed. Sheldon Hackney, 51–66. Boston: Little, Brown.

Scarborough, Jane Lynn. 1972. "George W. Paschal, Texas Unionist and Scalawag Jurisprudent." Ph.D. diss., Rice University.

Schaefer, Christina. 1997. *Guide to Naturalization Records of the United States*. Baltimore: Genealogical Publishing Co.

Schea, Danny. 2009. "Lou Dobbs Tells O'Reilly: I'm Staying 'In Public Arena,'" CNN Didn't Want Me in Obama Era (video). *Huffington Post*, November 23, 2009. www.huffingtonpost.com.

Schiesei, Martin. 2003. "Pat Brown: The Making of a Reformer." In *Responsible Liberalism: Edmund G. Brown and Reform Government in California, 1958–1967*, ed. Martin Schiesei, 1–21. Los Angeles: Edmund G. 'Pat' Brown Institute of Public Affairs.

Schoen, Harold. 1937. "The Free Negro in the Republic of Texas: The Law in Practice." *Southwestern Historical Quarterly* 40(4): 267–289.

Scholes, Walter. 1957. *Mexican Politics During the Juárez Regime, 1855–1872*. Columbia: University of Missouri Press.

Schoonover, Thomas, ed. and trans. 1991. *A Mexican View of America in the 1860s: A Foreign Diplomat Describes the Civil War and Reconstruction*. Cranbury, N.J.: Associated University Press.

Schuck, Peter, and Rogers M. Smith. 1985. *Citizenship Without Consent: Illegal Aliens in the American Polity*. New Haven: Yale University Press.

Schwartz, Rosalie. 1975. *Across the Rio to Freedom: United States Negroes in Mexico*. El Paso: University of Texas El Paso.

Scott, Florence Johnson. 1935. *Old Rough and Ready on the Rio Grande*. San Antonio: Naylor.

Scupin, Raymond. 2003. "U.S. Ethnic Relations: Anglos and the 'White Ethnics.'"

In *Race and Ethnicity: An Anthropological Focus on the U.S. and the World*, ed. Raymond Scupin, 102–124. Upper Saddle River, N.J.: Prentice-Hall.

Shirk, David. 2003. "Law Enforcement and Security Challenges in the U.S.-Mexican Border Region." *Journal of Borderlands Studies* 18(2): 1–24.

S.H.S. 1924. "The Constitutionality and Scope of the Alien Land Laws." *University of Pennsylvania Law Review and American Law Register* 72(2): 148–158.

Shulman, Robert, comp. 1986. *Laws Affecting Farm Employment in California*. North Highland, Calif.: Cooperative Extension, University of California Division of Agricultural Resources.

Sitton, Thad, and James H. Conrad. 1998. *Nameless Towns: Texas Sawmill Communities, 1880–1942*. Austin: University of Texas Press.

Slayden, Ellen Maury. 1963. *Washington Wife: Journal of Ellen Maury Slayden from 1897–1919*. New York: Harper and Row.

Sloan, John W. 1978. "United States Policy Responses to the Mexican Revolution: A Partial Application of the Bureaucratic Model." *Journal of Latin American Studies* 10(2): 283–308.

Smith, Marian. 1998. "Woman and Naturalization, ca. 1802–1940." *Prologue Quarterly of the National Archives* 30(2): 146–153.

Soza, Edward, comp. 1998. "Affidavits of Contest vis-à-vis Arizona Hispanic Homesteaders, 1880–1908." Arizona General Land Commission Publication. Archives and Correspondence. Altadena, California.

———. 1994. "Hispanic Homesteading in Arizona 1870–1908, under the Homestead Act of May 20, 1862, and Other Public Land Laws." Arizona General Land Commission Publication. Archives and Correspondence. Altadena, California.

Spicer, Edward. 1981. *Cycles of Conquest: The Impact of Spain, Mexico, and the United States on the Indians of the Southwest 1533–1960*. Tucson: University of Arizona Press.

Stelter, Brian, and Bill Carter. 2009. "Lou Dobbs Abruptly Quits CNN." *New York Times*, November 11, 2009. www.NYTimes.com.

Stephen, Lynn. 2007. *Transborder Lives: Indigenous Oaxacans in Mexico, California, and Oregon*. Durham: Duke University Press.

———. 2002. *Zapata Lives! Histories and Cultural Politics in Southern Mexico*. Berkeley: University of California Press.

Strong, Donald S. 1944. "American Government and Politics: The Poll Tax: The Case of Texas." *American Political Science Review* 382 (Aug.–Dec.): 693–709.

Székely, Gabriel. 1992. "The Oil Industry and Mexico's Relations with the Industrial Powers." In *The Mexican Petroleum Industry in the Twentieth Century*, ed. Jonathan Brown and Alan Knight, 256–279. Austin: University of Texas Press.

Takaki, Ronald. 2000. *Iron Cages: Race and Culture in Nineteenth-Century America*. 1979; reprint, New York: Alfred A. Knopf.

Taylor, Elizabeth A. 1987. "The Woman Suffrage Movement in Texas." In *Citizens at Last: The Women Suffrage Movement in Texas*, ed. Ruthe Winegarten and Judith N. McArthur, 13–48. Austin: Ellen C. Temple.

Taylor, Paul. 1970. *Mexican Labor in the United States*. Vol. 1. 1928; reprint, New York: Arno Press.

Texas Almanac. 1914. *The Texas Almanac and State Industrial Guide.* Dallas: Galveston-Dallas News.

——. 1912. *Texas Almanac and State Industrial Guide for 1912.* Dallas: Galveston-Dallas News.

——. 1910. *Texas Almanac and State Industrial Guide 1910.* Dallas: A. H. Belo and Galveston-Dallas News.

Texas Archives Resources. Santa Rosa Ranch, Inventory of the Santa Rosa Ranch Papers, 1890–1910. Texas Archives Resources online. Lorenzo de Zavala State Library and Archives. www.tsl.state.tx.us.

Texas General Land Office. 1988. *Guide to Spanish and Mexican Land Grants in South Texas.* Austin: General Land Office, Gary Mauro, Land Commissioner.

Texas League of Women Voters. 1922. *"Know Your County": A Handbook on County Government and a digest of Election Laws of Texas.* Georgetown, Tex.: Texas League of Women Voters.

Texas Legal Directory for 1876–77. Compiler Henry Lewis Bentley. Austin: Texas Democratic Statesman.

Texas State Register, for the Year of the Lord 1860. Galveston, Tex.: A. Hanford.

The Handbook of Texas Online. Austin: Texas State Historical Association. www.tshaonline.org.

The New Handbook of Texas. 1996. "Alien Land Law," comp. Ronnie Tyler, 1:106. Austin: Texas State Historical Association.

Thompson, Jerry. 2000. *Vaqueros in Blue and Gray.* Austin: State House Press.

——. 1996. "Juan Nepomuceno Cortina." In *New Handbook of Texas,* comp. Ronnie Tyler, 2:343–344. Austin: Texas State Historical Association.

Thompson, Seymour. 1878. *A Treatise on Homestead and Exemption Laws.* St. Louis: F. H. Thomas.

Tiano, Susan. 2006. "The Changing Gender Composition of the Maquiladora Workforce along the U.S.-Mexico Border." In *Women and Change at the U.S.-Mexico Border: Mobility, Labor and Activism,* ed. Doreen J. Mattingly and Ellen R. Hansen, 73–90. Tucson: University of Arizona Press.

Tichenor, Daniel J. 2008. "Strange Bedfellows: The Politics and Pathologies of Immigration Reform." *Labor Studies in Working-Class History of the Americas* 5(2): 39–60.

Timmons, W. H. 2004. *El Paso: A Borderlands History.* El Paso: University of El Paso Press.

Tjarks, Alicia. 1974. "Comparative Demographic Analysis of Texas, 1777–1793." *Southwestern Historical Quarterly* 77 (Jan.): 291–338.

Torres, Joseph. 1996. "Latinos Speak Out." *Hispanic* (Dec.): 18–24.

Trouillot, Michel-Rolph. 2003. *Global Transformations: Anthropology and the Modern World.* New York: Palgrave/Macmillan.

——. 1995. *Silencing the Past: Power and the Production of History.* New York: Beacon Press.

Truett, Samuel, and Elliott Young, eds. 2004. *Continental Crossroads: Remapping U.S.-Mexico Borderlands History.* Durham: Duke University Press.

Twin Plant News. 2008. "What is a Maquila?" *Mexico's Industrial Magazine Since 1985.* www.twinplantnews.org.

Tyler, Ronnie. 1973. *Santiago Vidaurri and the Southern Confederacy.* Austin: Texas State Historical Association.

———. 1972. "Fugitive Slaves in Mexico." *Journal of Negro History* 57(1): 1–12.

Valenica, Richard. 2008. *Chicano Students and the Courts: The Mexican American Legal Struggle for Educational Equality.* New York: New York University Press.

Vásquez, Josephina Zoraida, and Lorenzo Meyer. 1985. *The United States and Mexico.* Chicago: University of Chicago Press.

Ward, Roger. n.d. *Texas Naturalizations to 1906: Cameron County.* Athens, Ga.: Popyrus Publishing.

Wagoner, Jay J. 1970. *Arizona Territory 1863–1912.* Tucson: University of Arizona Press.

Walter, Tamra Lynn. 2007. *Espíritu Santo de Zúñiga: A Frontier Mission in South Texas.* Austin: University of Texas Press.

Watanabe, Teresa. 2006. "Justice for Immigrants." *Times,* March 1, 2006. www.times.com.

Waters, Mary, and Reed Ueda. 2007. "Immigration and Naturalization Legislation." In *The New Americans: A Guide to Immigration Since 1965,* ed. Mary Waters and Reed Ueda, with Helen Marrow, 687–700. Cambridge: Harvard University Press.

Weber, David. 1992. *The Spanish Frontier in North America.* New Haven: Yale University Press.

———. 1982. *The Mexican Frontier, 1821–1846: The American Southwest under Mexico.* Albuquerque: University of New Mexico Press.

Weeks, O. Douglas. 1930. "The Texas-Mexican and the Politics of South Texas." *American Political Science Review* 24(3): 606–627.

Westphall, Victor. 1965. *The Public Domain in New Mexico 1854–1891.* Albuquerque: University of New Mexico Press.

White, Owen. 1923. *Out of the Desert: The Historical Romance of El Paso.* El Paso: McMath.

William C. Velasquez Institute. 2008. *SVREP President's Report #1 (2008): The Latino Voter Registration Surge in 2008.* www.wcvi.org.

———. 2007. "Senator Robert Menendez's remarks as prepared for delivery," May 18, 2007. Senator's Menendez's speech. Forwarded by William C. Velasquez Institute, National Office.

Winegarten, Ruthe. 1996. "Texas Association of Women's Clubs." *New Handbook of Texas,* comp. Ronnie Tyler, 6:292–293. Austin: Texas State Historical Association.

———. 1995. *Black Texan Women: 150 Years of Trial and Triumph.* Austin: University of Texas Press.

Winegarten, Ruthe, and Judith N. McArthur, eds. 1987. *The Woman Suffrage Movement in Texas.* Austin: Ellen C. Temple.

Winkler, Ernest William. 1916. *Platforms of Political Parties in Texas.* Austin: Bulletin of the University of Texas, no. 53.

Wolf, Eric. 1982. *Europe and the People Without History.* Berkeley: University of California Press.

———. 1969. *Peasant Wars of the Twentieth-Century.* New York: Harper and Row.

Wood, Charles. 1999. "Losing Control of America's Future—The Census, Birthright Citizenship, and Illegal Aliens." *Harvard Journal of Law and Public Policy* 22(22): 465–522.

Woods, Richard. 1984. *Hispanic First Names: A Comparative Dictionary of 250 Years of Mexican-American Usage.* New York: Greenwood Press.

Woolley, John T., and Gerhard Peters. 2008. "927—Statement on Signing the Immigration and Nationality Act Amendments of 1976." Gerald Ford, 38th President of the United States: 1974–1977. The American Presidency Project Online. Pages 1–3. Santa Barbara: University of California. wwww.presidency.ucsb.edu/ws/?pid=6495.

Yale Law Journal. 1971. "Notes: Constitutional Limitations on the Naturalization Power." *Yale Law Journal* 80(4): 769–810.

Zabludovsky, Jaime Enrique. 1998. "La Deuda Externa Pública." In *Un Siglo de Deuda Pública en México,* ed. Leonor Ludlow and Carlos Marichal, 152–189. Instituto de Investigaciones Históricas-UNAM. Mexico, D.F.: UNAM.

Zelden, Charles L. 1993. *Justice Lies in the District: The U.S. District Court, Southern District of Texas, 1902–1960.* College Station: Texas A&M University Press.

Zeta Acosta, Oscar. 1972. *The Autobiography of a Brown Buffalo.* New York: Random House.

Cases

Boyd v. Nebraska, 143 U.S. 135 (1891)

Cervantes v. The Immigration and Naturalization Service and the Department of Justice, 5 Federal Reporter, 2d 89 (1975)

Cook v. De La Garza, 5 Texas Reports 358 (1853)

County of San Diego v. Anatalio T. Viloria, 80 California Reporter 89 (1969)

Dred Scott v. Sandford, 60 U.S. 393 (1857)

Elk v. Wilkens, 112 U.S. 94 (1884)

Emanuel Braude et al., Appellant v. W. Willard Wirtz, Secretary of Labor, U.S., et al., Appellees, 350 Federal Reporter, 2d 702 (1965)

Ex parte Rodriguez, 39 Texas 705 (1874)

Ex parte Sauer, 81 Federal Reporter 355 (1891)

Guess v. Lubbock, 5 Texas Reports 535 (1851)

Gunter v. Texas Land and Mortgage Company, 82 Texas Reports 496 (1891)

In re Ah Yup, 5 Sawy 155 (District Court, California 1878)

In re Camille, 6 Federal Reporter 256 (1880)

In re Kanaka Nian, 21 Pacific Reporter 993 (1889)

In re Look Tin Sing, 10 Sawy 353 (Circuit Court, D. California 1884)

In re Rodriguez, 81 Federal Reporter 337 (District Court, W. D. Texas, 1897)

McMullen v. Hodge and Others, 9 Texas Reports 34 (1849)

Nevada v. Ah Chew, 16 Nevada 50 (1881)

People v. Juan Antonio, 27 California 404 (1865)

People v. Hall, 4 California 399 (1854)

People v. Pablo De La Guerra, 40 California 311 (1870)

Silva v. Bell, 65 Federal Reporter, 2d 978 (1979)

Simms v. Simms, 175 U.S. 162 (1899)

Smith v. Smith, 127 Texas Reports 621 (1846)

Smith v. Smith, 1845–1846. Appeal from the District Court Bexar County Fall Term 1846 to the Supreme Court. *Sam Smith Appellant v. Maria de Jesusa Smith Appelle.* Doc. No. M-119. Lorenzo de Zavala State Archives and Library, State Archive division, Austin, Texas

Suñol v. Hepburn, 1 California 254 (1850)

Texas State AFL-CIO, et al., Appellants v. Robert F. Kennedy, U.S. Attorney General and Raymond F. Farrell, Commissoner of the U.S. INS et al., Appellees, 330 Federal Reporter, 2d 217 (1964)

United States v. Wong Kim Ark, 169 U.S. 649 (1898)

Statutes

California Constitution 1849. Reprinted in original form: San Marino, California. Friends of the Huntington Library, 1949.

California Statutes 1851. The Statutes of California, 2nd Session of the Legislature, 6 January 1851 to 1 May 1851 at the City of San Jose.

Compiled Laws of Arizona 1864–1877 (1877).

General and Special Laws of Texas, 75th Legislature, Regular Session 1997.

General Laws of Texas, 37th Legislature, Regular Session 1921.

General Laws of Texas, Regular Session, 22nd Legislature, 1891.

General Laws of the State of Texas, 38th Legislature, Regular Session 1923.

Laws of Texas, Supplement, 1822–1897.

Laws of Texas, Vol. 20, 1920–1921.

Laws of Texas, Vol. 12, 1903–1905.

Laws of Texas, Vol. 11, 1897–1902.

Laws of Texas, Vol. 10, 1891–1897.

Laws of Texas, Vol. 8, 1878–1879.

Laws of Texas, Vol. 7, 1871–1873.

Laws of Texas, Vol. 6, 1867–1871.

Laws of Texas, Vol. 4, 1854–1861.

Laws of Texas, Vol. 3, 1847–1854.

Laws of Texas, Vol. 2, 1838–1846.

Laws of Texas, Vol. 1, 1837.

Texas Revised Civil Statutes 1911 (1921).

8 USC 1440–1(2004).

120 U.S. Statutes at Large, Part 3 (2006).

116 U.S. Statutes at Large, Part 3 (2002).

110 U.S. Statutes at Large, Part 4 (1996).

108 U.S. Statutes at Large, Part 5 (1994).

104 U.S. Statutes at Large, Part 6 (1990).

100 U.S. Statutes at Large, Part 4 (1986).

90 U.S. Statutes at Large, Part 1 (1976).

90 U.S. Statutes at Large, Part 2 (1976).

79 U.S. Statutes at Large (1965).
76 U.S. Statutes at Large (1962).
66 U.S. Statutes at Large (1952).
43 U.S. Statutes at Large, Part 1 (1923–1925).
43 U.S. Statutes at Large, Part 2 (1923–1925).
42 U.S. Statutes at Large, Part 1 (1921–1923).
42 U.S. Statutes at Large, Part 2 (1921–1923).
39 U.S. Statutes at Large, Part 1 (1915–1917).
39 U.S. Statutes at Large, Part 2 (1915–1917).
34 U.S. Statutes at Large, Part 1 (1905–1907).
34 U.S. Statutes at Large, Part 2 (1905–1907).
33 U.S. Statutes at Large, Part 1 (1901–1903).
16 U.S. Statutes at Large (1869–1871).
15 U.S. Statutes at Large (1867–1869).
14 U.S. Statutes at Large (1865–1867).
12 U.S. Statutes at Large (1859–1863).
10 U.S. Statutes at Large (1851–1855).
2 U.S. Statutes at Large (1799–1845).
1 U.S. Statutes at Large (1789–1799).
Vernon's Texas Statutes 1970 Supplement (1970).

U.S. Government Documents, Reports, Journals, Manuscripts

Alvarez, Capt. Steve. 2005. "Mexican Forces Wind Up Humanitarian Mission." *American Forces Press Service News Articles.* U.S. Department of Defense. www .defense.gov.

Barr, Macreadie, Kelly Jefferys, and Randall Monger. 2008. *Nonimmigrant Admissions to the United States: 2007.* Office of Immigration Statistics: Policy Directorate Department of Homeland Security.

Center for Military History. 1993. *Correspondence Relating to the War with Spain: Including the Insurrection in the Philippine Islands and the China Relief Expedition, April 15, 1898 to July 30, 1902.* Vol. 1. Washington, D.C.: Center for Military History, United States Army.

Commission on Naturalization. 1905. *Report to the President of the Commission on Naturalization, Executive Order March 1, 1905.* Washington, D.C.: GPO.

Congressional Record and Appendix, 54th Congress, Second Session, Vol. 29, Part 3, 1897. Washington, D.C.: GPO.

Congressional Record, Proceedings and Debate, 52nd Congress, First Session, Vol. 23, Part I, 1892. Washington, D.C.: GPO.

Congressional Record, Proceedings and Debate, 55th Congress, Second Session, Vol. 31, Part 1, 1898. Washington, D.C.: GPO.

Congressional Record, Proceedings and Debate, 55th Congress, Special Session, Vol. 30, Part 2, 1897. Washington, D.C.: GPO.

Congressional Record, Proceedings and Debate, 55th Congress, Third Session, Vol. 31. Part 2, 1898. Washington, D.C.: GPO.

Congressional Record, Proceedings and Debates, 110th Congress, First Session, Vol. 153, 2007. Washington, D.C.: GPO.

Congressional Record, Proceedings and Debates, 104th Congress, First Session, Vol. 147, Part 27, 1995. Washington, D.C.: GPO.

Congressional Record, Proceedings and Debates, 104th Congress, First Session, Vol. 141, 1995. Washington, D.C.: GPO.

Congressional Record, Proceedings and Debates, 103rd Congress, First Session, Vol. 139, 1993. Washington, D.C.: GPO.

Congressional Record, Proceedings and Debates, 54th Congress, Second Session, Vol. 29, Part 2, 1897. Washington, D.C.: GPO.

Congressional Record, Proceedings and Debates, 51st Congress, First Session, Vol. 21, Part 1, 1889. Washington, D.C.: GPO.

Congressional Record, 94th Congress, Second Session, Vol. 122, Part 26, 1976. Washington, D.C.: GPO.

Congressional Record, 93rd Congress, First Session, Vol. 119, Part 30, 1973. Washington, D.C.: GPO.

Congressional Record, 93rd Congress, First Session, Vol. 119, Part 29, 1973. Washington, D.C.: GPO.

Congressional Record, 57th Congress, Second Session, Vol. 36, Part 3, 1903. Washington, D.C.: GPO.

Congressional Record, 57th Congress, Second Session, Vol. 36, Part 1, 1902–1903. Washington, D.C.: GPO.

Coolidge, L. A., comp. 1897. *Official Congressional Directory, 55th Congress, Second Session*. Washington, D.C.: GPO.

Cornwell, Derekh. 2006. *Naturalization Rate Estimates: Stock vs. Flow.* Department of Homeland Security, Office of Immigration Statistics, Policy Directorate.

Cornyn, John. 2007. "Cornyn: Comprehensive Immigration Reform Must Remain Top Priority." cornynsenate.gov.

———. 2005. "The Comprehensive Enforcement and Immigration Reform Act of 2005." cornynsenate.gov.

Crain, William Henry. 1894. *Speeches of Hon. W. H. Crain of Texas in the House of Representatives January 17 and 20, 1894, and October 31, 1893.* Washington, D.C.: Press of Hartman and Cadick.

Dellinger, Walter. 1995. *Legislation Denying Citizenship at Birth to Certain Children Born in the United States.* United States Department of Justice, Office of Legal Counsel. www.usdoj.gov.

Department of Homeland Security. *Aliens Expelled, Fiscal Years 1892–2000.* www.dhs.gov.

Embassy of the U.S. 2007. *Mexico: Trade and Commerce.* September 18, 2007. www.usembassy-mexico.gov.

Energy Information Administration. September 9, 2008. *Table 4a. U.S. Petroleum Supply, Consumption, and Inventories.* Official Energy Statistics from the U.S. Government. www.eia.gov.

Energy Information Administration. August 26, 2008. *Crude Oil and Total Petroleum Imports Top 15 Countries.* Official Energy Statistics from the U.S. Government. www.eia.gov.

First Legislative Assembly. 1851. New Mexico Organic Law [Act] of 1850. In *Laws of the Territory of New Mexico.* Santa Fe, N.M.: James L. Collins.

Halford, A. J., comp. 1902. *Official Congressional Directory, 57th Congress, Second Session*. Washington, D.C.: GPO.

House Bill 28. "An Act relating to the eligibility of an individual born in this state whose parents are illegal aliens to receive state benefits." Texas Legislature Online. www.house.state.tx.us.

House Bill 256. "An Act relating to birth records of children born in the State; creating an offense." Texas Legislature Online. www.house.state.tx.us.

House Bill 2162. "NOW: immigration border security." Arizona House of Representatives, Forty-ninth Legislature, 2nd Regular Session. Signed by Governor May 4, 2010. www.azleg.gov.

House Journal, Texas, 36th Legislature, Fourth Called Session, 1920. Austin: A. C. Baldwin and Sons, State Printers.

House Journal, Texas, 24th Legislature, Regular and Called Sessions, 1895. Austin: Ben C. Jones, State Printers.

House Journal, Texas, 29th Legislature, Regular and First Called Session, 1905. Austin: State Printers.

House Journal, Texas, 25th Legislature, Regular and First Called Session, 1897. Austin: State Printers.

House Journal, Texas, 24th Legislature, Regular Session, 1895. Austin: Ben C. Jones, State Printers.

House Journal, Texas, 35th Legislature, 1918, Fourth Called Session. Austin: Von Boeckmann-Jones.

House Journal, Texas, 27th Legislature, 1901, Regular Session. Austin: State Printers.

House Resolution 1868. "Birthright Citizenship Act of 2009." Copy of resolution. www.thomasgov/cgi-bin/bdquery.

House Resolution 4437. "Border Protection, Antiterrorism, and Illegal Immigration Control Act of 2005." 109th Congress, 2D Session, December 17, 2005. Copy of resolution. www.govtrack.us/congress.

House Resolution 133. "Citizenship Reform Act of 2007." Copy of resolution. www.gov.track.us/congress.

House Resolution 698. "Citizenship Reform Act of 2005." Copy of resolution. Library of Congress, Thomas. www.thomas.loc.gov/cgi-bin/bdquery.

House Resolution 126. "To Amend the Immigration and Nationality Act to Limit Citizenship at Birth, Merely by Virtue of Birth in the U.S., to Persons with Citizen or Legal Resident Mothers." Copy of resolution. www.thomas .gov/cgi-bin/query.

Hoyt, John, comp. 1877. *The Compiled Laws of the Territory of Arizona.* Detroit: Richmond, Backus.

Jennett, Elizabeth LeNoir. 1941. *Biographical Directory of the Texas Conventions and Congresses.* Austin: Forty-Seventh Texas Legislature, State Archives.

Journal of the House of Representatives, Texas, 22nd Legislature, Extra Session, 1892. Austin: Henry Hutchings, State Printer.

Journal of the House of Representatives, Texas, 37th Legislature, Regular Session 1921. Austin: Von Boeckmann-Jones.

Journal of the House of Representatives, Texas, 36th Legislature, Regular Session, 1919. Austin: Von Boeckmann-Jones.

Journal of the House of Representatives, Texas, 24th Legislature, 1895, First Called Session. Austin: Ben C. Jones, State Printers.

Journal of the Senate of Texas, 22nd Legislature, Extra Session, March 14, 1892. Austin: Henry Hutchings, State Printer.

Journal of the Senate of Texas, 24th Legislature, First Called Session October 1 to October 7, 1895. Austin: Ben C. Jones, State Printers.

Journal of the Senate of Texas, 35th Legislature, Fourth Called Session, 1918. Austin: A.C. Baldwin and Sons, State Printers.

Journal of the Senate of Texas, 37th Legislature, Regular Session, 1921. Austin: A. C. Baldwin and Sons, State Printers.

Journal of the Senate of Texas, 27th Legislature, 1901. Austin: State Printers.

Lee, James, and Nancy Rytina. 2008. "Naturalization in the U.S.: 2008." Department of Homeland Security, Office of Immigration Statistics, Policy Directorate. www.dhs.gov.immigrationstatistics.

Legislative Finance Committee. 2008. *Maquiladoras.* State of New Mexico, Legislative Finance Committee, Finance Facts Understanding State Financial Policy, nmlegis.gov

Legislative Manual for the State of Texas. 1879. Austin: E. W. Swindells.

Levine, Linda. 2004a. *Farm Labor Shortages and Immigration Policy.* Congressional Research Service Reports. Washington, D.C.: National Council for Science and the Environment. CRS Report 30395.

———. 2004b. *Immigration: The Labor Market Effects of a Guest Worker Program for U.S. Farmers.* Congressional Research Service Reports. Washington, D.C.: U.S. Commission on Agricultural Workers. CRS Report 97–712E.

Michael, W. H. 1892. *Fifty-Second Congress [First Session] Congressional Directory for the Use of the United States Congress.* Washington, D.C.: GPO.

National Archives. 2007a. Mexican Border Crossing Records. College Park, Md.: National Archives and Records Administration. www.archives.gov.

———. 2007b. Permanent and Statistical Manifests on Alien Arrivals at Eagle Pass, Texas, June 1905–1953. College Park, Md: National Archives and Records Administration. www.archives.gov.

———. 2005. "Genealogists/Family Historians-Naturalization Records." College Park, Md.: National Archives and Records Administration. www.archives.gov.

Office of the City Clerk, Election History, Austin City Connection. malford.ci.austin .tx.us.

President's Research Committee. 1935. *Recent Social Trends in the United States.* New York: McGraw-Hill.

Pulsifer, Pitman. 1896. *Fifty-Fourth Congress [Second Session] Official Congressional Directory, for the use of the United States Congress.* Washington, D.C.: GPO.

Report of the Commission on Agricultural Workers. 1993. *The Winter Vegetable Industry in South Texas.* Executive Summary, prepared for the Commission on Agricultural Workers 1989–1993. Texas State Government. Austin: State Printers.

Reports of the Department of Labor. 1920. *Report of Department of Labor, Part 1.* U.S. Department of Labor, Wirtz Labor Library, Digital Archives. www.dol .gov.

Rules of Order of the House of Representatives of the 24th Legislature, 1895. Austin: Ben C. Jones, State Printers.

Rytina, Nancy, and Selena Caldera. 2007. *Naturalizations in the United States: 2007.* Department of Homeland Security, Office of Immigration Statistics, Policy Directorate. www.dhs.gov.immigrationstatistics.

Scott, Jean R. Letter to author, March 15, 2007. Department of Homeland Security, Immigration Statistics.

Senate Bill 1260. "An Act relating to the issuance of a nonresident/commercial driver's license." Governor signed bill June 15, 2007. Texas Legislature Online. www.house.state.ts.us.

Senate Bill 2117, "Enforce Act." 109th Congress, 2D Session, December 15, 2005. Copy of resolution. www.govtrack.us/congress.

Senate Bill 1070. "An Act Amending Titles 11, 13, and 41 of Arizona Revised Statutes; Relating to Unlawfully Present Aliens." State of Arizona, Senate, Forty-ninth Legislature, 2nd Regular Session, 2010. Signed by Governor April 23, 2010. www.azleg.gov.

Senate Journal, Texas, 36th Legislature, Fourth Called Session, 1920. Austin: A. C. Baldwin and Sons.

Senate Journal, Texas, 24th Legislature, Regular and Called Sessions, 1895. Austin: Ben C. Jones.

Senate Journal, Texas 29th Legislature, Regular and First Called Sessions, 1905. Austin: State Printers.

Senate Journal, Texas, 37th Legislature, Regular Session, 1921. Austin: Von Boeckmann-Jones.

Senate Journal, Texas, 36th Legislature, Regular Session, 1919. Austin: A. C. Baldwin and Sons.

Simanski, John. SAW data. E-mail to author on December 12, 2008. Department of Homeland Security, Office of Immigration Statistics, Policy Directorate.

———. 2006. *Mapping Trends in Naturalization: 1980–2003.* Department of Homeland Security, Office of Immigration Statistics, Policy Directorate. www.dhs.gov.immigrationstatistics.

Simanski, John, and Nancy Rytina. 2005. *Naturalizations in the United States: 2005.* Department of Homeland Security, Office of Immigration Statistics, Policy Directorate. www.dhs.gov.immigrationstatistics.

Statistical Yearbook of the Immigration and Naturalization Service (1961–2001). Immigration and Naturalization Service. U.S. Department of Justice. Washington, D.C.: GPO.

Texas General Land Office. 1988. *Guide to Spanish and Mexican Land Grants in South Texas.* Austin: General Land Office, Gary Mauro, Land Commissioner.

Texas House of Representatives, Committee on State Affairs, Agenda, April 21, 2008, Room E2.010, Texas State Capital. Allison Scott, Clerk.

Texas Legislative Manual. 1897. *Texas Legislative Manual for 1897.* Austin: Ben C. Jones, State Printers.

Texas Legislature. 1962. *Members of the Texas Legislature, 1846–1962.* Austin: Fifty-Seventh Texas Legislature.

The White House. 2006. *President Bush Meets with President Fox in Cancún, Mexico.* Office of the Press Secretary, March 30, 2006.

———. 2004. The White House. *Press Briefing by Scott McClellan,* in the James S. Brady Briefing Room, 12:44pm, January 10, 2004, www.ilw.com/lawywer .immigdaily/exec_branch.

———. 2002. *Expedited Naturalization Executive Order.* The White House. Office of the Press Secretary, July 3, 2002.

U.S. Census. 2008. *U.S Exports to Mexico from 2003–2007.* www.census.gov.

———. 2003. *The Foreign Born Population: 2000.* U.S. Dept. of Commerce: Economics and Statistics Administration. December 2003. Washington, D.C.: GPO.

———. 2001. *The Hispanic Population in the United States: Population Characteristics*. U.S. Dept. of Commerce: Economics and Statistics Administration. March 2001. Washington, D.C.: GPO.

———. 1993a. *1990 Census of Population: Persons of Hispanic Origin in the United States*. Washington, D.C.: GPO.

———. 1993b. *1990 Census of Population: General Population Characteristics California, Sec. 1 of 4*. Washington, D.C.: GPO.

———. 1993c. *1990 Census of Population: General Population Characteristics Texas, Sec. 1 of 3*. Washington, D.C.: GPO.

———. 1992a. *1990 Census of Population: General Population Characteristics California, Sec. 1 of 3*. Washington, D.C.: GPO.

———. 1992b. *1990 Census of Population: General Population Characteristics Texas, Sec. 2 of 2*. Washington, D.C.: GPO.

———. 1982. *1980 Census of Population: Persons of Spanish Origin by State: 1980*. Washington, D.C.: GPO.

———. 1983. *1980 Census of Population: General Social and Economic Characteristics, California*. Sec. 1 of 2. Washington, D.C.: GPO.

———. 1974. *1970 Census Population: Supplementary Report Distribution of Foreign Stock Population*. Washington, D.C.: GPO.

———. 1962. *Current Population Reports Consumer Income*. Series P-60, No. 37. Washington, D.C.: GPO.

———. 1961a. *Census of Population: 1960 Volume 1, Characteristics of the Population, Part I, U.S. Summary*. Washington, D.C.: GPO.

———. 1961b. *Census of Population: 1960 Volume 1, Characteristics of the Population, Part 6, California*. Washington, D.C.: GPO.

———. 1954. *U.S. Census Population 1950: Special Reports, Nativity and Parentage*. No. P.E. No 3-A. Washington, D.C.: GPO.

———. 1953a. *U.S. Census Population 1950: Special Reports, NonWhite Population by Race*. No. P.E. No 3-B. Washington, D.C.: GPO.

———. 1953b. *U.S. Census of Population 1950: Special Reports, Persons of Spanish Origin*. No. P.E. 3-C. Washington, D.C.: GPO.

———. 1943. *Sixteenth Census of the U.S.: 1940 Population, Vol. II, Characteristics of the Population, Part I*. Washington, D.C.: GPO.

———.1933. *Abstract of the Fifteenth Census of the United States*. Washington, D.C.: GPO.

———. 1932. *Fifteenth Census of the United States: 1930, Population, Volume 3, Part 2*. Washington, D.C.: GPO.

———. 1925. *Fourteenth Census of the United States: State Compendium*. Washington, D.C.: GPO.

———. 1922a. *United States Bureau of the Census Abstract*. Washington, D.C.: GPO.

———. 1922b. *Fourteenth Census of the United States 1920, Vol. 2*. Washington, D.C.: GPO.

———. 1922c. *Fourteenth Census of the United States Taken in 1920, Vol. 3*. Washington, D.C.: GPO.

————. 1913a. *Thirteenth Census of the United States Taken in the Year 1910*. Vol. 1: *Population, 1910*. Washington, D.C.: GPO.

————. 1913b. *Thirteenth Census of the United States Taken in the Year 1910*. Vol. 3: *Population, 1910*. Washington, D.C.: GPO.

————. 1913c. *Thirteenth Census of the United States Taken in the Year 1910*. Vol. 7: *Agriculture*. Washington, D.C.: GPO.

————. 1913d. *Thirteenth Census of the United States Taken in the Year 1910, Abstract of the Census with Supplement for Texas*. Washington, D.C.: GPO.

————. 1902. *Abstract of the Twelfth Census of the United States 1900*. Washington, D.C.: GPO.

————. 1901. *Twelfth Census of the United States, Taken in the Year 1900, Population, Part 1*. Washington, D.C.: GPO.

————. 1897a. *Report of the Population of the United States at the Eleventh Census, 1890, Part II*. Washington, D.C.: GPO.

————. 1897b. *Compendium of the Eleventh Census of the United States: 1890, Part III*. Washington, D.C.: GPO.

————. 1895. *Report of the Population of the United States at the Eleventh Census, 1890, Part 1*. Washington, D.C.: GPO.

————. 1894. *Compendium of the Eleventh Census: 1890, Part II*. Washington, D.C.: GPO.

————. 1892. *Statistical Abstract of the United States, 1891, Fourteenth Number*. Washington, D.C.: GPO.

————. 1885. *Compendium of the Tenth Census (June 1, 1880), Part I*. Washington, D.C.: GPO.

————. 1882. *Statistics of the Population of the United States at the Tenth Census*. Washington, D.C.: GPO.

————. 1872. *The Statistics of the Population of the United States, Ninth Census–Volume 1*. Washington, D.C. : GPO.

————. 1864. *Population of the United States in 1860, The Eight Census*. Washington, D.C.: GPO.

————. 1862. *Preliminary Report on the Eight U.S. Census, 1860*. Washington, D.C.: Government Printing Office.

————. 1854. *Statistical View of the United States Census; Being a Compendium of the Seventh Census*. Washington, D.C.: GPO.

————. 1853. *The Seventh Census of the United States: 1850*. Washington, D.C.: GPO.

U.S. Citizenship and Immigration Service. "Interoffice Memorandum, AFM Update: Chapter 22 Employment-Based Petitions (AD03–01)." Department of Homeland Security. HQPRD70/23.12. www.dhs.gov.

U.S. Citizenship and Immigration Service. 2008. Section 219, Immigration and Nationality Technical Corrections Act of 1994, PL 103–416. Public Laws Amending the INA. Department of Homeland Security, www.dhs.gov.

U.S. Commission on Naturalization. 1905. *Report to the President on the Commission on Naturalization, Appointed by Executive Order March 1, 1905*. Washington, D.C.: GPO.

U.S. Department of Justice. 1971. Immigrants Admitted, By Country of Origin of Birth, Years Ended June 30, 1962–1971. (Table 14) Immigration and Naturalization Service. Department of Homeland Security. Office of Immigration Statistics.

U.S. Department of Labor. 1964. *Fifty-Second Annual Report, U.S. Department of Labor.* Washington, D.C.: GPO. Wirtz Labor Library, Digital Archives, www .dol.gov.

———. 1963. *United States Department of Labor Annual Report, 1963.* Washington, D.C.: GPO. Wirtz Labor Library, Digital Archives, www.dol.gov.

———. 1928 (Part 2). *Report of the Commissioner General of Immigration.* Washington, D.C.: GPO. Wirtz Labor Library, Digital Archives. www.dol.gov.

———. 1927. *Annual Report of the Commissioner General of Immigration, 1927.* Washington, D.C.: GPO. Wirtz Labor Library, Digital Archives, www.dol .gov.

———. 1925. *Annual Report of the Commissioner General of Immigration 1925 (Part 2).* Washington, D.C.: GPO. Wirtz Labor Library, Digital Archives, www.dol.gov.

U.S. Department of State. 2009. *2008 Human Rights Report: Mexico.* Bureau of Democracy, Human Rights, and Labor (February 25, 2009). www.state.gov.

———. 2008. *Background Note: Mexico Profile.* Bureau of Western Hemisphere Affairs, April 2008. www.state.gov.

U.S. General Accounting Office (GAO). 1996. *Mexico's Financial Crisis: Origins, Awareness, Assistance, and Initial Efforts to Recover.* Report to the Chairman, Committee on Banking and Financial Services, House of Representatives. Prepared by the U.S. General Government Office. Washington, D.C.: General Government Division.

———. 1992. *Issues Affecting Potential U.S. Trade and Investment.* Report to the Chairman, Committee on Banking and Financial Services, House of Representatives. Prepared by the National Security and International Affairs Division. Washington, D.C.: United States General Accounting Office.

U.S. Government Accountability Office (GAO). 2007. *Crude Oil: Uncertainty about Future Oil Supply Makes It Important to Develop a Strategy for Addressing a Peak and Decline in Oil Production.* Report to Congressional Requesters. Washington, D.C.: United States Government Accountability Office.

Vernon's Annotated Revised Civil Statutes of the State of Texas. Vol. 1. 1959. Kansas City, MO: Vernon Law Book Company.

Yearbook of Immigration Statistics 2007–2009. Department of Homeland Security. Office of Immigration Statistics. www.dhs.gov.

Yearbook of Immigration Statistics (2002 to 2006). Department of Homeland Security. Office of Immigration Statistics. Washington, D.C.: GPO.

Archives

Bexar County Court. *Bexar County Court Journal, Vol. 2A, 1855–1868.* Bexar County Records. Roll 1019358. Austin: Lorenzo de Zavala State Library and Archives, Genealogy Division.

———. *Bexar County Court Journal, Vol. 2,* 1860. Bexar County Records, 2R 351. Center for American History, University of Texas at Austin.

———. 4th Civil Minute Book A-B. Roll 1019350. Austin: Lorenzo de Zavala State Library and Archives, Genealogy Division.

———. Vol. K–Q, R–Z, 1836–1963. Roll 1019350. Austin: Lorenzo de Zavala State Library and Archives, Genealogy Division.

Bexar County Declarations of Intentions 1852–1906 Cantu to Garnica. Roll 1020148. Austin: Lorenzo de Zavala State Library and Archives, Genealogy Division.

Bexar County Naturalization Papers, 1851–1859, Book A. Roll 1019979. Austin: Lorenzo de Zavala State Library and Archives, Genealogy Division.

Bexar County Probate Minutes, Vol. 5, 1892–1893. Roll 1019305. Austin: Lorenzo de Zavala State Library and Archives, Genealogy Division.

Cameron County. Declarations to become a citizen of U.S. 1876–1904, Vol. 3. Roll 1016182. Edinburg, Tex.: University of Texas-Pan American.

Cameron County Civil Minutes. County Court 1867–1899 Vol. A, 1899–1910 Vol. B. Roll 1016181. Edinburg, Tex.: University of Texas-Pan American.

El Paso Naturalization Records (El Paso), Declarations of Intention, 1890–1906. Record Group 21, E48W087A, (ARC ID 584737, A-21-2-6), Folder No. 1 to 160: (Federal Court) Western District of Texas, at El Paso. George Baylor, Clerk of the U.S. District Court. National Archives, Southwest Region, Fort Worth.

Election Registers, 1918–1922. *Election Registrar 1918–1922*. Reel 19. Austin: Lorenzo de Zavala State Library and Archives, State Archive Division.

Election Registers, 1907–1912. *Elected, Appointed Officials: 1907–1912*. Reel 17. Austin: Lorenzo de Zavala State Library and Archives, State Archive Division.

Election Registers, 1888–1889. *Election Returns, November 6, 1888*. Reel 12. Austin: Lorenzo de Zavala State Library and Archives, State Archive Division.

Election Registers, 1860–1865. *Register of Elected and Appointed State and County Officials, 1860–1865*. Reel 3,4. Austin: Lorenzo de Zavala State Library and Archives, State Archive Division.

Election Registers, 1838–1972a. *Registers of Elected and Appointed State and County Officials, 1889–1891*. Reel 13. Austin: Lorenzo de Zavala State Library and Archives, State Archive Division.

Election Registers, 1838–1972b. *Registers of Elected and Appointed State Officials, 1894–1896*. Reel 14. Austin: Lorenzo de Zavala State Library and Archives, State Archive Division.

Election Registrar, 1838–1861. *Register of Elected and Appointed National and County Officials, 1838–1861*. Reel 1, 2. Austin: Lorenzo de Zavala State Library and Archives, State Archive Division.

Election Registrar, 1870–1883. *Local, State, and County Officials, 1870–1883*. Reel 5–7. Austin: Lorenzo de Zavala State Library and Archives, State Archive Division.

Francis W. Seabury Papers, Box 2G/53, Austin: Center for American History, University of Texas at Austin.

General Courts Austin, Brownsville, El Paso, Galveston, San Antonio, Jefferson, Texarkana, Tyler, Waco. Record Group 85, WPA Index Texas Naturalization, 7RA-211. National Archives, Southwest Region, Fort Worth.

Guadalupe County, Naturalization Index. Records of the Immigration and Naturalization Service, San Antonio District Office, Texas. Microfilm Roll 5, 7RA-211. Austin: Lorenzo de Zavala State Library and Archives, Genealogy Division.

House Bill No. 105. "An Act to provide that women may vote in all primary elections and nominating conventions, Texas prescribing qualifications for such voters, providing for registration of 10,000 and over, and declaring an emergency." Executive Office, Austin: Lorenzo de Zavala State Archives and Library, State Archive Division, AT 328.1 TL, 1918.

House Bill No. 107. "An Act amending Article 3093 of Chapter 10 of Title 49 of the 1911 Revised Statutes of Texas so as to provide that no one shall vote in primary elections or conventions unless he is a citizen of the United States." Executive Office, Austin: Lorenzo de Zavala State Archives and Library, State Archive Division, AT 328.1 TL, 1918.

Index to Naturalization Records Found in Texas State, District and County Courts, 1846–1939. Records of the Immigration and Naturalization Service, San Antonio District Office, Texas. Microfilm Rolls 1–10, 7RA-211. Lorenzo de Zavala State Library and Archives, Genealogy Division, Austin (TNR).

Jane Y. McCallum Papers, Austin History Center, Austin Public Library, Austin.

Jay Bird Association. 1889. "Constitution of White Men's Unions in Southeast Texas." In White Man's Union, Box 2H428. Austin: Center for American History, University of Texas at Austin.

List of Aliens Arriving at Brownsville, Del Rio, Eagle Pass, El Paso, Presidio, Rio Grande City, and Roma, Texas, May 1903–June 1909. Publication Number: AA3365. National Archives, Southwest Region, Fort Worth.

Matías Romero Papers. 74 Microfilm reels (Banco de Mexico, April 1, 1959, microfilmed). University of Texas at Austin, Benson Latin American Collection.

Nueces County Declarations, 1852–1906. A–D/F–H, Roll 1012902. Austin: Lorenzo de Zavala State Library and Archives, Genealogy Division.

Southern District, a. Brownsville: Orders Granting Citizenship 1875–95. Record Group 21, Volume E, No. 485019c, No. E48-5-019C. National Archives, Southwest Region, Fort Worth.

———. b. Brownsville: Declarations of Intention, 1874–1884. Record Group 21, Volume E, No. 485019B, 7RA-392. National Archives, Southwest Region, Fort Worth.

Texas State Library and Archives Commission, "Primary Suffrage." Archives and manuscripts, online. Women's Suffrage Movement. www.TexasStateLibrary.gov. November, 2, 2005.

U.S. District Court, San Antonio, Minute Book D. Ricardo Rodriguez Oath and Certificate Record. No. 48W099. National Archives, Southwest Region, Fort Worth.

U.S. District Courts, Southern District of Texas Galveston, Index to Declarations 1871–1905, Record Group 21, E. 48-S-05, Declarations of Intention 18711905 E. 48-S-050D. National Archives, Southwest Region, Fort Worth.

U.S. Immigration and Naturalization Service, San Antonio District, General Letters Received, 1898–1899, 1905–1907, E. TX 16, Letters Received from the Bureau 1906, E. TX 17. Box 1,1995. Record Group 85. National Archives, Southwest Region, Fort Worth.

Webb County Civil Minutes 1897–1900, Vol. 9, Reel 1017263. Edinburg, Tex.: University of Texas-Pan American.
Webb County Declarations. Vol. 1, 1883–1884, Vol. 2, 1884, Vol. 3, 1884–1886. Reel 1017219. Edinburg, Tex.: University of Texas-Pan American.
Webb County Declarations, Vol. 4,1886–1892, Vol. 5, 1892–1895, Vol. 6, 1895–1900. Reel 1017220. Edinburg, Tex.: University of Texas-Pan American.
White Man's Union Associations, box 2H428. Austin: Center for American History, University of Texas at Austin.

Newspapers

Austin American-Statesman, 1921, 2007
Austin Daily American-Statesman, 1897
Arizona Republic, 1959
Centinela del Rio Grande, 1861
Church News, 1892
Dallas Morning News, 1895, 1897, 1921, 2005, 2007
El Cronista, 1898
El Regidor, 1893, 1896, 1897, 1898
Evolución, 1919
Fort Worth Telegraph, 1921
Houston Daily, 1897
Javeline, 1914
La Bandera, 1863
La Prensa, 1921
National Economists, 1892, 1893
New York Times, 2010
San Antonio Daily Express, 1896, 1897, 1898
San Antonio Express, 1921, 2010
Southern Mercury, 1895, 1896
Texas State Times, 1854
Tyler Morning Telegraph, 2008
Washington Post, 1892

Index

Paschal, Thomas, 129–130, 156–157.
See also *In re Rodriguez*
People's Party: Alien Land Law, 102–
105; demise of party, 141–143; elec-
toral politics, 105–108, 110–113;
founded, 101; fusion politics, 121,
126–129; Populist philosophy, 119–
120; Prohibition Party, 110–111. *See
also* Crain, William Henry; Farmer's
Alliance; German immigrants; *In re
Rodriguez*
People v. Pablo De La Guerra (1870),
67–70
Pickett, John T. (Col.), 35–36. *See also*
U.S. Civil War
Proposition 187, 294–295, 337n.17

Racialization: afromestizos, 21–22, 25–
30; aftermath of Mexican American War, 19; Indians, 20–21; state
laws, 23–24
railways: in Mexico, 80, 88–89, 91, 177;
in Texas, 82–83, 85–89, 93–94, 101–
105. *See also* Hogg, James
Reconstruction: closure, 60–67; Fourteenth Amendment, 46–47; Military Reconstruction Acts, 46; naturalization applications, 57; Texas
Reconstruction Convention, 58–59
Regeneración, See Magón, Ricardo
Flores
Rodino, Peter, 273–274, 280
Rodriguez, Ricardo. See *In re
Rodriguez*
Romero, Matías: archives, 13; commerce agreements, 50; French invasion, 40–44; *In re Rodriguez*, 133–
134; Naturalization Treaty of 1868,
47–49; opposition to U.S. annexing
Mexican territory, 148–150. *See also*
Juárez, Benito

Salt War Riots, 77–79
Seabury, Francis (Rep.): McBride debate, 117; Mexican community,
332nn.17–18; Wells Election,
192–194

Secure Fence Act 2006, 301
Seward, William H., 37, 40, 43–44,
47–49
Slavery, 18–19, 21–22, 25–32. *See also*
afromexicanos; U.S. Civil War
Smith, Maria de Jesusa, 30–31, 325n.8
Sociedad Honorífica Mexicana, 241
Southern Mercury, 138–139
Spanish-American War: conflict, 164;
Mexican Americans during, 169–
176; overview, 11, 160; Spanish sur-
render, 166–167; U.S. declaration of
war, 165

Teller Amendment, 166
Terrell, Alexander W., 182–184, 186
Texas Bureau of Immigration, 74,
97
Texas Equal Suffrage Association
(women's), 13, 214, 218–220, 223–
228, 231. *See also* women's suffrage
Texas House Bill 28, 309
Texas Naturalization Index: explanation of contents, 12, 313–320,
326n.1; U.S. Civil War, 56
Texas poll taxes: effects on elections,
183–187; election of 1921, 244; extended to women, 235–240; introduced, 179–182; South Texas,
188–194. *See also* White primaries;
women's suffrage
Texas Rangers, 74–79, 148, 327nn.12–
14
Thirty-Fifth Texas Legislature. *See*
exclusion of aliens from Texas
primaries
Thirty-Seventh Texas Legislature:
Alien Land Law, 246; referendum
to end alien voting, 235–240
Treaty of Guadalupe Hidalgo: De La
Guerra, 68–70; Gadsden Treaty,
154, 325n.1; *In re Rodriguez*, 124,
131–132, 153–154; numerical size of
conquered population, 24–25; overview, 17–19; U.S.-Mexico reclamation agreements, 47–48. *See also*
racialization